TUDOR AND STUART SUFFOLK

Tudor and Stuart Suffolk

B. Gordon Blackwood

Carnegie Publishing

First published in 2001 by
Carnegie Publishing Ltd
Carnegie House, Chatsworth Road,
Lancaster LA1 4SL
publishing: www.carnegiepub.co.uk
book production: www.wooof.net

Copyright © B. Gordon Blackwood 2001

ISBN 1-85936-078-5

British Library Cataloguing-in-Publication data
A catalogue record for this book is available from the British Library

Typeset and designed by Carnegie Publishing Ltd
Printed and bound in the UK by The Cromwell Press, Trowbridge

Contents

List of Maps

Preface and Acknowledgements

This book aims to be comprehensible, but not comprehensive. Thus no attempt has been made to give a full account of Suffolk during the Tudor and Stuart periods, and for reasons of space much has had to be left out. Instead, the book concentrates mainly on the impact on Suffolk of three major events: the Reformation, the Great Rebellion and the 'Glorious Revolution'. To maintain a sense of perspective, events and personalities are placed in a national context and, where appropriate, comparisons are made with other counties.

I would like to thank various public bodies which helped me to find and to use manuscripts in their care. I am thinking particularly of the staffs of the Public Record Office, the British Library, House of Lords Record Office, Dr Williams's Library, Bodleian Library, Cambridge University Library, and both the Ipswich and Bury branches of the Suffolk Record Office.

Extracts from Crown-copyright records in the Public Record Office appear by permission of the Controller of H.M. Stationery Office.

I am grateful to the Suffolk Local History Council for permission to include much of my article – 'Parties and Issues in the Civil War in Suffolk', *Suffolk Review*, NS 18 (Spring 1992) – as part of the fifth chapter of this book.

I am indebted to a number of historians in the preparation of this work. Valuable information and stimulating comments were provided by Mrs Audrey Butler on Suffolk choir nuns abroad; by Dr J. T. Cliffe on the landed incomes of some Suffolk gentry after the Restoration; by the late Gwyneth Dyke on several Suffolk Royalists; by Frank Grace of University College, Suffolk, on the economy and Puritans of seventeenth-century Ipswich; by Professor John Morrill of Cambridge University on William Dowsing; by Dr Pat Murrell on Suffolk voters and elections in the late 17th and early 18th centuries; by Mrs Valerie Norrington on early Suffolk Quakers; by Peter Northeast on religious guilds and the dispersal of Suffolk monastic lands; by John Sutton of Anglia Polytechnic University on William Dowsing, Bury riots in 1648 and 1688, the Ipswich Mutiny of 1689, the Association Oath Roll of 1696, and Archbishop William Sancroft; by Michael Tupling on the fate of the Bury monks after the Dissolution; and by Dr David Dymond, the doyen of Suffolk historians, on several topics, especially religious guilds, farming and the woollen cloth industries. Needless to say, none of these persons is responsible for any errors or deficiencies which appear in the book.

The following illustrations have been reproduced by kind permission of The British Museum, p. 180; G. F. Cordy, pp. 35, 39, 44, 46–7, 49, 61–2, 64, 68, 75–8, 98, 125, 133, 135, 145–6, 149, 154–6, 168, 172, 174–5, 214, 227, 234, 252; John Grigg/Private Collection, p. 148; A. Hodge, pp. 17–19, 39–40, 63, 65, 208; Ipswich Borough Museums, pp. 128, 184; National Portrait Gallery, London, pp. 13, 67, 87, 108, 248; Patrick Phillips, p. 50 and jacket illustration; Private Collection/Photographic Survey Department, Courtauld Institute of Art, p. 181; Sotheby's London, p. 220; Suffolk Record Office, Bury St Edmunds branch, pp. 78, 86, 187, 209, 212; Suffolk Record Office, Ipswich branch, pp. 24–5, 47, 49, 66, 88, 116, 127, 173, 185, 201; The Syndics of Cambridge University Library, pp. 100, 105, 211; Witt Library, Courtauld Institute of Art, pp. 129, 158.

For permission to reproduce Maps 1, 5–7, 10, 12, 15 and cover map, I must thank Cambridge University Press, D. N. J. MacCulloch, Royal Historical Society, Suffolk County Council and Suffolk Institute of Archaeology and History, and Suffolk Record Office (Ipswich branch).

Finally, I would like to record my immense debt to my wife for all her moral and practical support throughout the preparation of this work.

Felixstowe, 2001   B. G. B.

Abbreviations

Al. Cant.	J. and J. A. Venn (eds), *Alumni Cantabrigienses to 1751,* 4 vols (CUP, 1922–27)
Al. Oxon.	J. Foster (ed.), *Alumni Oxonienses: the Members of the University of Oxford, 1500–1714,* 4 vols (Parker & Co., Oxford, 1891–92)
Besse, vol. I	Joseph Besse, *The Sufferings of the People called Quakers … 1650 to 1689,* vol. 1 (London, 1753)
BIHR	*Bulletin of the Institute of Historical Research*
BL	British Library, London
Add. MS.	Additional Manuscript
Blackwood, *Lancs. Gentry*	B. G. Blackwood, *The Lancashire Gentry and the Great Rebellion 1640–60* (Chetham Society, 3rd series, XXV, 1978)
Blome, *Britannia*	Richard Blome, *Britannia* (London, 1673)
Bod. Lib.	Bodleian Library, Oxford
Calamy Revised	A. G. Matthews (ed.), *A Revision of Edmund Calamy's Account of the Ministers and others Ejected and silenced in 1660–62* (OUP, 1934)
CCAM	M. A. E. Green (ed.), *Calendar of the Proceedings of the Committee for Advance of Money, 1642–1656,* 3 vols (HMSO, 1888)
CCC	M. A. E. Green (ed.), *Calendar of the Proceedings of the Committee for Compounding with Delinquents, 1643–60,* 5 vols (HMSO, 1889–92)
Chambers, *Register*	D. S. Chambers (ed.), *Register of the Archbishop of Canterbury's Faculty Office* (OUP, 1966)
Chorography	D. N. J. MacCulloch (ed.), *The Chorography of Suffolk* (Suffolk Records Society, XIX 1976)
Clarendon, *Rebellion*	Edward Hyde, earl of Clarendon, *History of the Rebellion* (ed.) W. D. Macray, 6 vols (OUP, 1888)
CJ	*Journals of the House of Commons,* from 1542

Concise DNB	*The Concise Dictionary of National Biography*, 3 vols (OUP, 1992)
Copinger, *Manors*	W. A. Copinger, *The Manors of Suffolk*, 7 vols (T. Fisher Unwin, London, 1905–11)
Craig, thesis	See chapter 3, p. 275 n. 63
CRS	Catholic Record Society publications
CSPD	*Calendar of State Papers Domestic*
CUL	Cambridge University Library
CUP	Cambridge University Press
Davis, *Heresy and Reformation*	See chapter 3, p. 275 n. 60
Defoe, *Tour*, vol. 1	Daniel Defoe, *A Tour Through the Whole Island of Great Britain*, vol. I (London, 1724)
DKR	*Ninth & Tenth Reports of the Deputy Keeper of the Public Records* (HMSO, 1848–49)
DNB	L. Stephen and Sidney Lee (eds), *Dictionary of National Biography*, vols I–XXI (OUP, 1921–22)
Dugdale	W. Dugdale, *Monasticon Anglicanum* (eds) J. Caley, H. Ellis, and B. Bandinel, 6 vols in 8 (London, 1817–30)
Dymond & Martin	David Dymond and Edward Martin (eds), *An Historical Atlas of Suffolk* (3rd & enlarged edn, Suffolk County Council & Suffolk Institute of Archaeology and History, 1999)
Dymond & Northeast	David Dymond and Peter Northeast, *A History of Suffolk* (Revised edn, Phillimore, 1995)
Econ. HR	*Economic History Review*
Everitt, *Suffolk*	A. M. Everitt (ed.), *Suffolk and the Great Rebellion, 1640–1660* (Suffolk Records Society, III, 1960)
Fines *Register*	See chapter 3, p. 96, p. 280 n. 212
Firth & Rait	C. H. Firth and R. S. Rait (eds), *Acts and Ordinances of the Interregnum, 1642–60*, 3 vols (HMSO, 1911)
Foxe, *A&M*	See chapter 3, p. 280 n. 213
GI Adm. Reg.	J. Foster (ed.), *Register of Admissions to Gray's Inn, 1521–1889* (Hansard Publishing Union Ltd, 1889)
Gilchrist & Oliva	See chapter 3, p. 277 n. 110
HJ	*Historical Journal*

HLRO	House of Lords Record Office, Houses of Parliament
HMSO	Her Majesty's Stationery Office
Holmes	Clive Holmes (ed.), *The Suffolk Committees for Scandalous Ministers 1644–1646* (Suffolk Records Society, XIII, 1970)
Ive, thesis	I. G. A. Ive, 'The Local Dimensions of Defence: The Standing Army and Militia in Norfolk, Suffolk and Essex 1649–1660' (unpublished PhD thesis, University of Cambridge, 1987)
JBS	*Journal of British Studies*
JFHS	*Journal of the Friends Historical Society*
JSAHR	*Journal of the Society for Army Historical Research*
Kingston	Alfred Kingston, *East Anglia and the Great Civil War* (Elliot Stock, London, 1897)
Kirby, *Suffolk Traveller*	John Kirby, *The Suffolk Traveller: or A Journey through Suffolk* (Ipswich, 1735)
Knowles & Hadcock	D. Knowles & R. N. Hadcock, *Medieval Religious Houses in England and Wales* (Longman, 1971)
LJ	*Journals of the House of Lords*, from 1509
LP	J. Gairdner and R. H. Brodie (eds), *Letters and Papers, Foreign and Domestic, of the reign of Henry VIII*, vols X-XXI (HMSO, 1887–1932; Kraus Reprint, 1965)
MacCulloch, 'Catholic and Puritan'	Diarmaid MacCulloch, 'Catholic and Puritan in Elizabethan Suffolk', *Archive for Reformation History*, LXXII (1981)
MacCulloch, 'Consolidation'	Diarmaid MacCulloch, 'The Consolidation of England, 1485–1603', in John Morrill (ed.), *The Oxford Illustrated History of Tudor and Stuart Britain* (OUP, 1996)
MacCulloch, *Suffolk*	Diarmaid MacCulloch, *Suffolk and the Tudors: Politics and Religion in an English county 1500–1600* (OUP, 1986)
MacCulloch, *Suffolk Review*	Diarmaid MacCulloch, 'The Impact of the Reformation on Suffolk Parish Life', *Suffolk Review*, NS 15 (Autumn, 1990)
MacCulloch, thesis	D. N. J. MacCulloch, 'Power, Privilege and the County Community: County Politics in Elizabethan Suffolk' (unpublished PhD thesis, University of Cambridge, 1977)
NH	*Northern History*
NS	New Series
OS	Old Series
OUP	Oxford University Press

P&P	*Past and Present*
PRO	Public Record Office, London
C	Chancery
C54	Close Rolls
C203	Petty Bag Office, Various Certificates
E	Exchequer
E101	King's Remembrancer, Various Accounts
E113	Bills and Answers against defaulting accountants
E164	K.R., Miscellaneous Books
E178	Special Commissions of inquiry
E179	K.R., Lay Subsidy rolls, Schedule of Contributors to the 'Free and Voluntary Gift', Hearth Tax Assessments
E377	Lord Treasurer's Remembrancer, Recusant Rolls, Pipe Office Series
E379	L.T.R., Sheriffs' Accounts of Seizures
LR	Land Revenue Office
LR2	Miscellaneous Books
SP	State Papers Domestic
SP16	Charles I
SP23	Committee for Compounding
SP25	Council of State
SP28	Commonwealth Exchequer Papers
SP29	Charles II
SP44	Entry Books
Wards	Court of Wards and Liveries
Wards 5	Feodaries' Surveys
Wards 9	Miscellaneous Books
PSIA (H)	*Proceedings of the Suffolk Institute of Archaeology (and History)* (1848 – date)
Reyce, *Breviary*	*Suffolk in the XVIIth Century: The Breviary of Suffolk by Robert Reyce* (ed.), Lord Francis Hervey (John Murray, London, 1902)
RH	*Recusant History*
RHS	Royal Historical Society publications
SRO (B)	Suffolk Record Office, Bury St Edmunds branch
SRO (I)	Suffolk Record Office, Ipswich branch
B105	Quarter Sessions Order Books
EE1	Aldeburgh borough records
FB19	Mickfield parish records
FB130	Gislingham parish records
HD36	Letters sent to Ipswich Corporation
HD224	Miscellaneous collections

TRHS	*Transactions of the Royal Historical Society*
UP	University Press
Valor	J. Caley and J. Hunter (eds), *Valor Ecclesiasticus*, 6 vols (Record Commission, 1810–34)
VCH Suffolk	Wm. Page (ed.), *The Victoria History of the Counties of England, Suffolk*, 2 vols (Archibald Constable & Co. Ltd, 1907, 1911)
Walker Revised	A. G. Matthews (ed.), *Walker Revised: Being a Revision of John Walker's Sufferings of the Clergy during the Grand Rebellion 1642–60* (OUP, 1948)
Walker, Sufferings	John Walker, *An Attempt towards an Account of the Numbers and Sufferings of the clergy of the Church of England, Heads of Colleges, Fellows, Scholars, etc. who were sequestered, Harassed, etc. in the late Times of the Grand Rebellion* (London, 1714)

Notes

In quotations from contemporary sources the original spelling has been generally retained.

The year is taken to begin on 1 January and not 25 March, which was still the practice during our period.

Full references to books, articles and theses are given in the List of Abbreviations above or in the first citation in the Notes below; elsewhere abbreviated references are generally used.

Map I: Highland and Lowland Zones

Land over 800 feet (244 m)

0   100 km
0   100 miles

R. Tyne

CUMBRIA

PENNINES

R. Tees

North Yorkshire Moors

YORKSHIRE WOLDS

R. Humber

The Peak

LINCOLNSHIRE WOLDS

R. Trent

MIDLAND PLAIN

THE FENS

WALES

R. Severn

R. Ouse

SUFFOLK

COTSWOLD HILLS

MENDIP HILLS

SALISBURY PLAIN

R. Thames

LONDON

NORTH DOWNS

THE WEALD

SOUTH DOWNS

Exmoor

R. Exe

Bodmin Moor

DARTMOOR

CORNWALL

Tudor and Stuart Suffolk: topography, population and economy

Topography

Suffolk has a number of distinctive topographical features. First, it is clearly part of the lowland zone of Britain, unlike, say, Cumbria, which forms part of the highland zone (see Map 1). Robert Reyce, Gentleman, that verbose but perceptive writer, seemed pleased that Suffolk lacked the mountainous landscape of north-west England. Writing in 1603, he remarked that 'This country [county] delighting in a continuall evenes and plainnes is void of any great hills, high mountaines, or steep rocks'.[1] He did, however, add that Suffolk 'is nott always so low, or flatt, but that in every place, it is severed and devided with little hills easy for ascent'.[2] Map 2 shows that some parts of Suffolk were over 200 feet above sea level.

Second, Suffolk was, and is, a maritime county facing the North Sea. In 1735 John Kirby of Woodbridge explained that Suffolk 'is a maritime county, being bounded on the East with the Ocean [North Sea], on the West with Cambridgeshire, and on the South with the River Stour dividing it from Essex; on the North with the Little-Ouse and Waveney dividing it from Norfolk'.[3] Sixty-two years earlier Richard Blome had described Suffolk in almost identical terms. 'This County', he wrote, 'is of a large extent, and hath for its Eastern bounds the German Ocean [North Sea]; for its Southern the River Stower which disjoyneth it from Essex; for its Western, Cambridgeshire; and for its Northern, the Waveney, and the little Owse which severeth it from Norfolk'.[4] Earlier still, the anonymous writer of the *Chorography of Suffolk* (*c.* 1600–05) almost anticipated Kirby and Blome when he described 'The limits & principall boundes of Suff.' in the following passage:

> Suff. is situated in the east parts of this Islande borduring on the north upon Norff. divided from it by 2 rivers Ouse the lesser and Waveney. It hath on the west Cambridgeshire separated from it by the Dike commonly called the Devills Dike etc. It hath on the east the german sea [North Sea], on the south Essex parted from the same by the river Stour.[5]

It will be noticed that the Chorographer, Blome and Kirby emphasised the importance of the major rivers when defining the external boundaries of Suffolk. This seems geographically sensible. However, a sense of proportion is necessary. The Rivers Waveney and Stour do not separate Suffolk from its northern and southern neighbours to the extent that the Mersey separates Lancashire from Cheshire. Similarly, the 'Devills Dike' can hardly be said to separate Suffolk from Cambridgeshire in the way that the Pennines separate Lancashire from Yorkshire. In short, Suffolk was not a self-contained unit during our period. As we shall see, its broadcloth and linen industries belonged as much to the surrounding counties of Essex and Norfolk respectively.

A third topographical feature that should be mentioned is the Suffolk coastline. A glance at Map 2 shows that Robert Reyce was right to be worried about the county's safety:

> I must confess … [Suffolk] lyeth open and is ready for forreigne invasion, there bee so many havens, harbours, creekes, and other places of ready discent, that the enemy is soon entered, and this is more confirmed by the frequent proofe of the silly Dunkirkes [pirates] who before the peace concluded between Spaine and England, robbed our shores, came into our havens and carried away our loden vessels, rifling often times whole townes.[6]

Piracy and wars against foreign powers were to have adverse effects on the maritime trade of Suffolk during the seventeenth century.

Another characteristic of Suffolk, so emphasised by contemporary writers, is its healthy climate. Reyce boasted that 'the aire is as sweet and healthfull generally, as in any other country [county] whatsoever'. He admitted that the north winds were 'somewhat peircing', yet they were 'deemed very apt and fitt for recovery of health in decayed bodies, for which cause it is well observed that the physitians from the universitie have prescribed unto their sick patients to live in this aire'.[7] Later Richard Blome echoed the sentiments of Reyce. He too thought that Suffolk was 'blest with an Air so sweet and wholesome, that London Physicians oft times prescribe it for the cure of their consumptive Patients'.[8]

Finally, it must be emphasised that Suffolk is not topographically uniform. It has long been recognised that the county contains several distinct regions and landscapes, which are largely the product of different soils (see Map 2). The Chorographer identified three regions: 'The Woodlande[9] and High Suffolck'[10] in the centre of the county; 'that p't of the contrye that is nere unto the sea'; and the heathlands of the north-west.[11] A century later John Kirby noted the same three divisions. 'This County is naturally divided into the Sandlands, the Woodlands, and the Fielding'.[12] The former 'extend itself by the Sea Coast from Languard-Fort [near Felixstowe] to Yarmouth'; the Woodlands stretched from 'the North-East Corner of

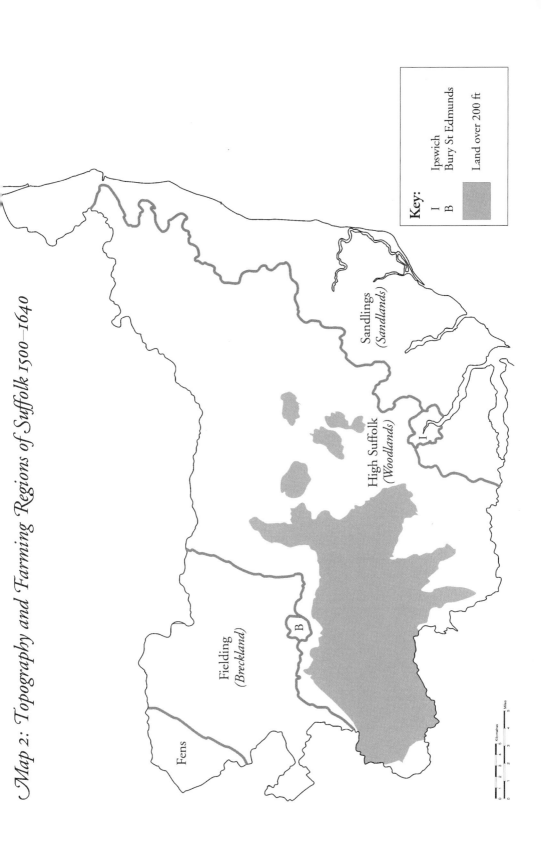

Map 2: Topography and Farming Regions of Suffolk 1500–1640

Fens

Fielding
(*Breckland*)

B

High Suffolk
(*Woodlands*)

Sandlings
(*Sandlands*)

I

Key:

I   Ipswich
B   Bury St Edmunds

Land over 200 ft

Kilometres 0 1 2 3 4 5

Miles 0 1 2 3 4 5

the Hundred of Blything, to the South-West Corner of the County at Haverill', while the Fielding comprised 'all the Hundred of Lackford, and the remaining parts of the Hundreds of Blackbourne, Thedwestry and Thingoe'.[13] These three different landscapes [14] produced different kinds of farming. But more about that later. Meantime we must ask how Suffolk was peopled during the Tudor and Stuart period.

Population

The national background

During the Tudor and much of the Stuart period the population of England, like that of Europe, greatly expanded. The population of England was approximately 2.7 millions in 1541, 4.1 millions in 1601, 5.0 millions in 1641 and roughly the same in 1701. In short, the national population almost doubled between the Reformation and the Great Rebellion.[15] London's growth was even more spectacular. In the 1520s, with a population of only 55,000, London was smaller than Paris, Venice, Naples and Constantinople, but by 1750 it had surpassed them all, having 675,000 inhabitants.[16] London was, of course, unique. Between 1500 and 1700 its population increased tenfold, from 55,000 to 575,000. No other English town experienced such a high rate of growth. Norwich and Bristol 'only' doubled their populations between the reign of Henry VIII and the reign of William III. Moreover, London dwarfed all other English towns. In 1700 London had approximately 575,000 inhabitants, but the *second* largest town, Norwich, had only 30,000.[17] Nevertheless, most large provincial towns, except perhaps Coventry and Salisbury, experienced population growth, especially during the sixteenth century.[18] Moreover, the *proportion* of the English population resident in towns rose considerably: in 1500 perhaps rather more than 10 per cent lived in towns of more than 1,000 inhabitants; by 1700 the figure was about 20 per cent.[19] Clearly the Tudor and Stuart period was one of increasing urbanisation.

The situation in Suffolk

The 1991 Census gives the population of Suffolk as 638,340.[20] During our period the population was considerably less. It has been estimated as about 90,000 in the 1520s, 108,000 in 1603 and 125,000 in the 1670s. The total population increase between the 1520s and the 1670s was 38 per cent.[21] This was below the national average.[22]

Was Suffolk's town growth also below average? Before answering this question we must define the term 'town'. What did it mean during the Tudor and Stuart period? It is hard to say. 'We know what it was not', says Dr John Patten.[23] 'Corporate status and market rights do not define it'.[24] This seems to be true. Certainly legal status 'does not necessarily confer urbanity on a place: for example, the legal Borough of Dunwich was mostly under the sea by the seventeenth century'.[25] Nor does the possession of a market always guarantee urban status. Many smaller market centres failed altogether, like Brandon and Wickham Market. Brandon, 'once a Market-town, hath lost its trade', said Blome in 1673. Wickham Market, despite its name, had 'lost its Market'.[26]

Since corporate status and market rights are inadequate criteria, we are forced to adopt another definition of a pre-industrial town which does at least seem plausible. Professor Jack considers that 'a town, basically, is a node of population concentration and identity'.[27] Clark and Slack have argued that a pre-industrial town had 'an unusual concentration of population'.[28] Size, of course, is not the sole criterion of a town, but it is perhaps the main characteristic. So I shall follow Clark and Slack, plus Lawrence Stone, in defining a Tudor or Stuart town as any place with 1,000 or more inhabitants.[29] Table 1.1 lists those Suffolk towns which had 1,000 or more people at one or more of the dates mentioned, while Map 3 locates those places.

Table 1.1 Population of Suffolk towns 1520s–1670s (rounded figures)

	1524/5	1603	1670s
Bury St Edmunds	3,550 [30]	4,500	6,200 [31]
Ipswich	3,100	5,000	7,900 [32]
Hadleigh	1,500	1,500	2,100
Beccles	1,200	1,100	1,750
Sudbury	1,200	1,350	2,000
Dunwich	1,150	850	300
Lavenham	1,050	1,200	1,500
Long Melford	1,000	1,150	1,750
Woodbridge	950	1,100	1,450
Lowestoft	750	1,000	1,000
Mildenhall	700	1,000	1,900
Aldeburgh	700	1,300	650
Bungay	650	1,050	1,200
Southwold	650	900	1,350
Framlingham	550	750	1,000
Stowmarket	500	800	1,400
Halesworth	250	600	1,000
Total	13,750	21,500	33,500

Source: Patten, *Pre-industrial England,* p.75.

Table 1.1 prompts four comments. First, the urban population of Suffolk more than doubled between the 1520s and 1670s. Second, this urban growth was above the national average.[33] Town dwellers in Suffolk formed 15 per cent of the county population in 1524, 20 per cent in 1603 and 27 per cent in the 1670s.[34] Third, of the seventeen towns listed in Table 1.1, only two

– Dunwich and Aldeburgh – had fewer inhabitants in the 1670s than in the 1520s. The other fifteen grew considerably between the reign of Henry VIII and that of Charles II. Fourth, Bury St Edmunds and Ipswich dwarfed the other towns in Suffolk throughout the sixteenth and seventeenth centuries. Bury was the largest town in Suffolk in 1524. It was also the 'capital' of West Suffolk and one of the major pilgrimage centres in eastern England.[35] Ipswich, the county town, was, however, more thickly populated than Bury by the death of Elizabeth I. In 1610 John Speed opined that Ipswich 'might worthily have borne the title of a Citie',[36] so impressed was he by its population and wealth. By the 1670s Ipswich was not only the largest town in Suffolk but perhaps the eighth largest in England.[37]

We have discussed population growth at some length because it explains so much else about the Tudor and Stuart period, including the economy.

Wealth

Suffolk was noted for its wealth as well as for its population increase during our period. In 1522 Suffolk was the seventh wealthiest county in England, according to the Military Survey (or Loan) of that year.[38] Only London, Kent, Norfolk, Essex, Wiltshire and Devon were richer. Twenty-seven shires lagged well behind Suffolk and six northern counties were not assessed.[39] In Charles II's reign Suffolk was still one of the most prosperous counties in England. According to the Hearth Tax Assessments of 1662,[40] only London (including Westminster and Southwark), Middlesex, Kent, Devon and Norfolk were wealthier.[41]

So much for the county of Suffolk. What about its towns? In 1524 Ipswich was the seventh wealthiest provincial town in England, Bury St Edmunds the twelfth, Lavenham the thirteenth and Hadleigh the twenty-third, according to the Lay Subsidy Assessment. In 1662 Ipswich was still prosperous, being the sixth wealthiest provincial town in the nation, according to the Hearth Tax Assessment. Bury St Edmunds only ranked twenty-sixth in the hierarchy of English towns,[42] while Lavenham and Hadleigh were also less wealthy than formerly. Bury did, however, continue to be an important town in Suffolk. It was 'an industrial town of the first rank until the end of the 17th century',[43] although by then it had also acquired a reputation as a gentry leisure centre.[44] Ipswich, of course, remained the economic giant among Suffolk towns. John Speed only slightly exaggerated when, in 1610, he said that Ipswich was 'blessed with Commerce and buildings' and that its 'trade … doth equall most places of the Land besides'.[45] In 1662 William Schellinks, a Dutch traveller, thought that Ipswich was 'the hub of the county' of Suffolk, having 'a reasonably good harbour' and 'much trade, mostly in drapery'.[46] Cloth, overseas trade and shipbuilding were in fact the town's main economic activities throughout most, though not all, of our period.

Map 3: The Most Populous Towns and Main Industries of Suffolk during the Sixteenth and Seventeenth Centuries

MARITIME TRADE

LINEN

LINEN

SPINNING

SAILCLOTH & SACKCLOTH

BROADCLOTH

Lowestoft

Beccles

Bungay

Southwold

Dunwich

Aldeburgh

Halesworth

Framlingham

Woodbridge

Ipswich

Stowmarket

Hadleigh

Mildenhall

Bury St Edmunds

Lavenham

Sudbury (nd)

Long Melford

Key:

nd   New Draperies
Underlined places denote Broadcloth Manufacturing Centres

Kilometres

Miles

Frank Grace has said that 'in the late medieval period through to the mid-17th century Suffolk's importance in the economic life of the country can arguably be said to have reached its height'.[47] It is hard to disagree with this statement. The wealth of Suffolk manifested itself in many ways, but most noticeably in extensive building operations. Many churches were built, or re-built, in the fifty years or so before the Reformation. Guildhalls appeared in many towns and market centres in the same period. Manor houses were also built or extended by the gentry, especially during the sixteenth century. However, churches, guildhalls and manor houses are best discussed later. Meanwhile we must ask what made Suffolk one of the wealthiest counties in England. It would appear to have been developments in agriculture, industry and coastal and overseas trade.

Agriculture

Today most British people live in urban or suburban areas and are engaged in commerce, manufacturing and service industries. It is therefore difficult to imagine a time when most men and women lived in villages or hamlets and worked on the land. Around 1520 'roughly three quarters of the population was engaged in farming'.[48] Farmers faced greater demands for basic foodstuffs as the population of England almost doubled between 1541 and 1641.[49] More grain – essential for bread, gruel and drink – and more animals – necessary to provide meat, milk and other dairy produce – were urgently needed. If there was not to be a Malthusian crisis, those needs had to be met.

How well did landowners and farmers cope with increased demand? On this question historians are divided. A. R. Bridbury believed that little agricultural progress was made during the sixteenth century. 'Historians of arable farming have made us very familiar with the deplorably meagre productivity of land devoted to corn'. Animal productivity was also 'extremely low'.[50] By contrast, Professor D. M. Palliser believes that population growth had a generally stimulating effect on the economy, including agriculture. 'Yields of crops, meat and dairy products were all somewhat higher around 1600 than they had been a century or even half a century before'.[51] Certainly William Harrison, a well informed contemporary, was optimistic. In his *Description of England* (1577) he said that total agricultural production was increasing.[52]

It is, of course, extremely difficult to generalise about agriculture as a whole. Dr Joan Thirsk has drawn attention to the great variety of farming regions in England. Map 4 shows these regions, which consisted of areas of mixed farming, open pasture and wood pasture.[53]

What about farming regions in Suffolk? Dr Thirsk has argued that, except for the small fenland corner of north-west Suffolk, there were two main farming regions in the county: an area of mixed farming and an area of

wood-pasture. In the mixed farming region a sheep-corn husbandry prevailed on the loams and sands which extended in a broad arc from West
Suffolk round the northern rim of Norfolk and along the eastern coast of
Suffolk (see Map 4). The sheep-corn region was first and foremost an arable
area and corn was the main interest of both large and small farmers. On
the light soils of Suffolk sheep were the main fertilising agent. The wood-
pasture region covered most of High Suffolk, an area that contained not
only a large portion of that county but also the south-eastern margin of
Norfolk and a small part of Essex (see Map 4). Farms in this region consisted
mostly of pasture and meadow, with a very small proportion of arable land.
The region relied on corn supplies from the light lands because the heavy
clay soils were not, during our period, conducive to arable farming. Most
farmers were engaged in cattle rearing and dairying, though pig-keeping
and horse breeding – the Suffolk Punches, in fact – were not without
importance.[54] 'The encroachment of the plough after 1600'[55] meant that
High Suffolk became slightly less pastoral, though it was not until during
the French Revolutionary and Napoleonic wars that this part of the county
became a mainly arable farming region.

In 1622 some local Justices of the Peace, in anticipation of Dr Thirsk,
said that Suffolk consisted

> of two several conditions of soil, the one champion, which yields for
> the most part sheep and some corn; the other enclosed pasture grounds
> employed most to grazing and dairy, so as the champion doth not
> only serve itself with corn but is forced continually to supply the
> woodland especially in wet cold years.[56]

These magistrates were undoubtedly correct. However, confusion is
caused by the fact that most contemporaries have identified three, not two,
farming areas (see Map 2). The Chorographer, Richard Blome and John
Kirby divided Suffolk into three different landscapes and commented on
the different kinds of farming to be found in each. The Chorographer said
that 'The Woodland & High Suffolck is exceeding fruitfull comparable to
any p't of England for pasture for oxen & kine'. But he considered that
'That p't of the contrye [county] that is nere unto the sea [Sandlings] is
nothing so fruitful neyther so commodious for cattell as the other, but
more fitt for sheep and corne'. As for the 'country' [county] to the
north-west of Bury St Edmunds it was 'fit only for sheepe and conyes,
although in some places of the same there be some places of good and
fertile grounds'. Richard Blome, writing about seventy years later, stated
that the 'Eastern parts all along the coasts for five or six miles Inland, are
generally heathy, sandy' and that 'the husbanding of the ground is for Rye,
Peas ... and sheep-walks, etc.' But the 'more inland part ... called High-
Suffolk, or the Wood-lands ... being clay ground ... is husbanded chiefly
for the Dairy'. He went on to say that 'the parts about Bury, and from

thence North-westerly, are champaign or fielding, abounding with excellent corn of all sorts ...' John Kirby, over sixty years later, gave a detailed account of the agriculture of Suffolk, not only dividing the county into 'the Woodlands, the Fielding and the Sandlands', but sub-dividing the latter 'into the Marsh, Arable, and Heathlands'. He considered that 'The Marsh-land is naturally fruitful, fattening great Numbers of Oxen and Sheep, and sometimes when ploughed affords the greatest Crops of Corne ... That part which is Arable, is naturally good for Tillage, and produces excellent Crops of all sorts of Corn ... The Heathy Part may contain about one-third of the Sandlands, and is used for sheep-walks'. His accounts of farming in High Suffolk and the Fielding were much briefer. The Woodlands or High Suffolk produced 'Suffolk Butter ... and cheese', while the Fielding consisted mostly of 'Sheep Walks, yet affords good Corn in divers Parts'.[57]

If we closely study the remarks of the Chorographer, Richard Blome and John Kirby we can see that High Suffolk was mainly a wood-pasture region and that the Fielding and the Sandlings were sheep-corn areas. Yet it is significant that Kirby comments in some detail about the marshlands of the Sandlings, and this is perhaps what makes the region slightly different from the Fielding. Maybe Dr Joan Thirsk was right to argue that there were three main farming systems, at least in the period 1640–1750: arable, pastoral and intermediate.[58] It is indeed almost an open question whether the farming of the Sandlings should be categorised as arable or as intermediate.

But whether we divide Suffolk into two or three farming regions, the utmost caution is necessary. Professor Overton has rightly warned against oversimplification. 'Empirical investigation', he says, 'reveals that farming regions were not always homogeneous within a *pays* or farming region'.[59] There was certainly no homogeneity about the farming areas of Suffolk. The Fielding was *not entirely* a sheep-corn region; it included some wood-pasture parishes, like Culford, Gazeley and Westley. Likewise High Suffolk was *not entirely* a wood-pasture region; it contained some sheep-corn parishes, like Palgrave, Redgrave and Shelley.[60] Indeed, the importance of *arable* farming in High Suffolk was noticed some 400 years ago by Robert Reyce. He said that 'in the middle parts' [of High Suffolk] lay a district 'enjoying much meddow and pasture, yett far more tillage'.[61]

Farming in Suffolk seems to have flourished, especially in the seventeenth and early eighteenth centuries. This is not surprising. The phenomenal growth of London and the need for increased food supply gave a powerful impetus to agriculture. According to Reyce, grain output in Suffolk kept pace with population growth. Reyce mentioned the 'rich increase of graine; by reason whereof this country [county] so abounding hath evermore had sufficient to feed the populous number of their owne inhabitants'.[62]

New methods were adopted by many Suffolk farmers, thereby raising agricultural productivity. David Dymond and Peter Northeast have said

Map 4: Farming Regions in England, 1500–1640

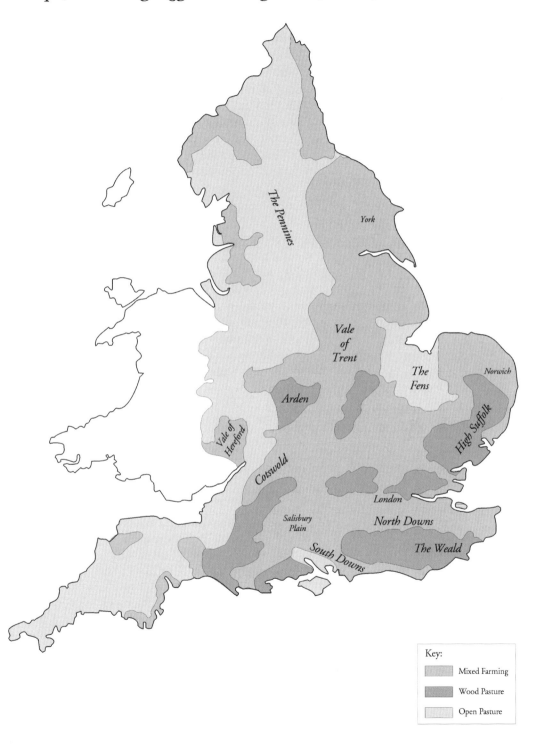

The Pennines

York

Vale
of
Trent

The
Fens

Norwich

Arden

High Suffolk

Vale of
Hereford

Cotswold

London

Salisbury
Plain

North Downs

South Downs

The Weald

Key:

Mixed Farming

Wood Pasture

Open Pasture

that 'well before 1700 the agriculture of Suffolk was experimental, inno-
vating and increasingly specialised'.[63] They were referring mainly to crops.
'Central Suffolk', they say, 'was the first area in England to grow turnips
as a field crop. The practice was established by the mid-17th century and
provided a means of feeding cattle during winter and spring'. They also
say that 'clover was another popular crop from the mid-17th century
onwards'.[64] Unfortunately they, like many other historians, have exaggerated
the importance of turnips and clover. Turnips were certainly known as a
fodder crop from at least the 1630s, while clover appeared in the 1650s.
But, as Professor Overton has argued, these two crops did not make much
impact on farming until after 1750.[65] However, three crops undoubtedly
became important during the seventeenth and early eighteenth centuries;
carrots, barley and hops. Carrots were grown in the Sandlings soon after
1600 as an agricultural crop, being used in part as forage for horses. Carrots
were also grown around Woodbridge as a vegetable crop for export to
London in the later years of the century.[66] Barley has been described as
'the main cash crop' in the light lands of East Anglia. It was a very
marketable crop and in Suffolk and Norfolk between 1660 and 1730 the
average barley acreage per farm increased 3.8% times.[67] Hops seem to have
appeared early in Suffolk. Robert Reyce described the craze for growing
hops in 1603. He conceded that some people were planting hops 'in the
best meadow ground', but he also mentioned other men who were 'draining
unprofitable marshes and moores ... to plant there, which likewise brought
great profit and aboundance'.[68]

More important than the introduction of new crops in the seventeenth
century was the increasing prosperity and productivity of dairy farming.
This was to be found mainly in High Suffolk, a predominantly wood-
pasture region covering at least two-thirds of the county (By contrast, about
two-thirds of Norfolk consisted of sheep-corn husbandry[69]). Contemporaries made some interesting comments on Suffolk pastoral farming,
drawing particular attention to its dairy products. The Chorographer said
that in High Suffolk butter and cheese were made in 'exceeding great
quantitie'. Robert Reyce noted in 1603 'what great profit doth arise from
these dairies, both for butter and cheese'. Daniel Defoe said, a century
later, that High Suffolk was 'famous for the best Butter, and perhaps the
worst Cheese, in England'.[70]

Contemporaries also noticed the national and even international importance of Suffolk's dairy products, which were sent both to London and
abroad. Richard Blome said that the 'great trade is for butter and cheese'
and that 'it was managed by Factors employed by the London cheese-
mongers ... who ship it at the coast for London, and from thence it is
dispersed to forraign parts'. Defoe remarked that Suffolk butter was
'sold, not in London only, but ... sent to the West Indies'. Modern historians have endorsed the remarks of Blome and Defoe. Dr Holderness has

Daniel Defoe (1661?–1731) by Michiel Van der Gucht in 1706.
Best known as a novelist and author of _Robinson Crusoe_, Defoe was also a Dissenter and traveller. His _Tour_ (1724–26) is an invaluable source of social and economic history.

said that 'butter and cheese were among the most important agricultural products from East Anglia from 1600 to 1800'. In 1730 London apparently consumed 56,703 firkins of Suffolk butter and 985 tons of Suffolk cheese.[71]

Contemporaries and historians have also emphasised the importance of cows to the Suffolk dairy farmers. Nesta Evans found that of the 103 wills made by South Elmham residents between 1550 and 1640, 91 per cent mentioned dairy cattle but only 9 per cent named sheep.[72] This conclusion would not have surprised the Chorographer. 'High Suffolk', he said, was 'exceeding fruitful comparable to any p't of England for pasture for oxen and kine', but it was 'not so good for sheepe'. Reyce believed that some Suffolk farmers kept a large number of cows. 'I have seen divers dairies of 40, some 50, some 60 cows'. Defoe saw a connection between cows and wealth. 'The Farmers [of High Suffolk] are so very considerable and their Farms and Dayries so large, that 'tis very frequent for a Farmer to have a Thousand Pounds Stock upon his Farm in Cows only'.[73]

The flourishing state of Suffolk dairying is not surprising. As Joan Thirsk has observed, pasture farming was more profitable than corn growing in seventeenth-century England.[74] In several European countries, too, livestock farming was more rewarding than arable farming in the years 1650–1750.[75] Suffolk pasture farming was clearly not unique in its prosperity.

Industry

England made great industrial progress during the Tudor period. Professor Palliser has stated that the industrial sector expanded and diversified considerably in the late sixteenth century. New industries were established like the weaving of silk, cotton and linen, and the New Draperies were created to rival the traditional woollen industries. The second half of the century also saw a growth in most mining industries: coal, lead, copper and iron.[76] Clearly Suffolk had no mining industries. But it did have traditional woollen industries, New Draperies and a linen industry during our period. Let us deal with each in turn.

Woollen industries (Old Draperies) [77]

Historians have emphasised the importance of woollen cloth manufacture during our period. Dr Tom Webster has said that this manufacture was carried on almost everywhere in Britain as a by-employment.[78] Professor Palliser has argued that textiles were probably the biggest employer of labour outside agriculture, giving much employment in half the counties in the kingdom.[79] However, the chief textile producing areas were the West Country (from Devon to Gloucestershire); the North of England (south-east Lancashire and the West Riding of Yorkshire); the Kentish Weald; and eastern England. The latter included Norwich and parts of north-east Norfolk,[80] north Essex,[81] and above all Suffolk. Norfolk specialised in worsted weaving,[82] but Essex and Suffolk produced coloured broadcloth.[83] In East Suffolk kerseys [84] were manufactured, especially in the villages around Eye, Debenham, Wickham Market and Woodbridge. 'But this industry never assumed the proportions of the broadcloth industry'.[85]

Broadcloth, kerseys and worsted manufactures were collectively known as the Old Draperies. Broadcloth was easily the most important of the three and was mainly located in south-west Suffolk. Cloth was manufactured in market towns such as Hadleigh, Long Melford, Sudbury and, above all, Lavenham, the jewel of Suffolk textile towns. It was also produced in several villages of the south-west: Bildeston, Boxford, Bures St Mary, Clare, East Bergholt, Edwardstone, Glemsford, Great Waldingfield, Little Waldingfield, Nayland, Stoke-by-Clare, Stoke-by-Nayland and Stratford St Mary (see Map 5). The former prosperity of these old cloth towns and villages is proclaimed in their magnificent churches, their guildhalls and their timber-framed buildings.[86] South-west Suffolk was specialising in the manufacture of woollen cloth before the end of the thirteenth century, while in the 1470s the county produced more cloth than any other English shire. The peak of production for woollen cloth came probably in the early sixteenth century.[87] Indeed, Suffolk was the industrial heartland of England from the 1470s until the 1520s. Betterton and Dymond are probably correct in saying that 'Far from being a rural Arcadia, Lavenham in its heyday had more in common with Victorian Leeds and Bradford because from at least the fourteenth to the eighteenth centuries the manufacture of cloth was a major source of employment and wealth'.[88]

There are nine main points to note about the Suffolk broadcloth industry during its golden age.

  1 It produced great wealth. This is suggested by the fact that the hundred
    in which the industry was mainly located – Babergh – was more highly

Map 5: The Cloth-Producing Areas of Suffolk

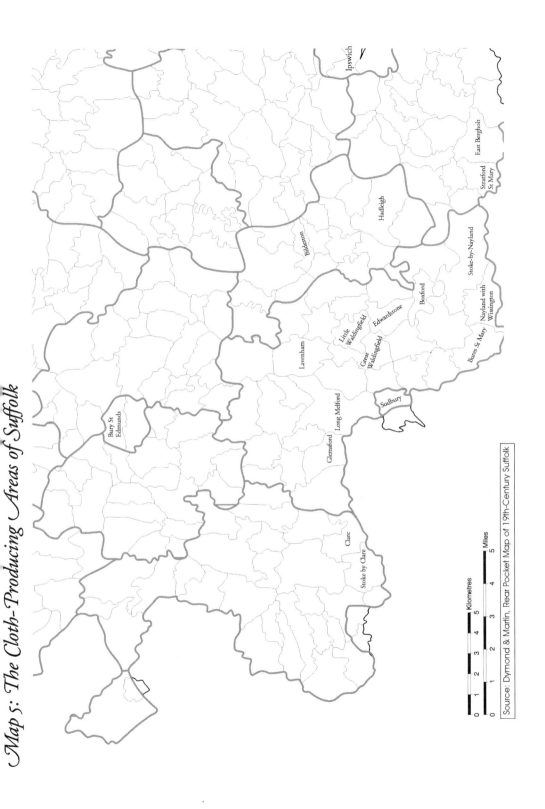

Ipswich

East Bergholt

Stratford St Mary

Hadleigh

Bildeston

Stoke-by-Nayland

Boxford

Edwardstone

Little Waldingfield

Nayland with Wissington

Great Waldingfield

Lavenham

Bures St Mary

Long Melford

Sudbury

Bury St Edmunds

Glemsford

Clare

Stoke by Clare

Kilometres
0 1 2 3 4 5

Miles
0 1 2 3 4 5

Source: Dymond & Martin, Rear Pocket Map of 19th-Century Suffolk

assessed for tax purposes than any other hundred in Suffolk. In the lay subsidy return of 1524 Babergh was assessed at £615 18s. 8d. The second richest hundred – Blything – came far behind, its assessment being only £248 2s. 1d.[89]

2 It was located in a thickly populated region. In 1524 Babergh and Cosford – the main clothing areas – were respectively the second and fourth most densely populated hundreds in Suffolk. The broadcloth industry could not have taken root in Lackford, the most thinly populated hundred in the county.[90] A large labour supply was vital because the broadcloth industry was labour intensive.

3 It was located in a wood-pasture region – High Suffolk – where pastoral farmers had time on their hands, time to engage in industrial pursuits. The broadcloth industry could hardly have succeeded in Lackford hundred because its predominantly arable farming was labour intensive and left little or no time for industrial activities.[91]

4 It was not spread over the entire High Suffolk region because the fast flowing River Stour and its tributaries – The Box, the Brett and the Glem – produced more water power than the slow-moving Waveney in the north.

5 It was largely domestic and rural based, not factory and urban based, though some cloth was manufactured in the larger towns like Ipswich and Bury St Edmunds. Industry was mostly carried on in the home by part-time village farmers or agricultural workers, employing their wives, sisters and children.

6 It took second place to agriculture even in south-west Suffolk. This region was not saturated with industry in the way south Lancashire was during the late Victorian period, and in 1522 farming provided the main employment in two-thirds of townships in Babergh hundred.[92] It is true that in 1522 more than half of the total working population of Lavenham were in various ways connected with clothmaking.[93] By sixteenth-century standards Lavenham was a highly industrialised town. But it may not have been typical.

7 It was 'the most highly capitalistic industry in early Tudor England',[94] dominated by rich merchant clothiers. These clothiers (or 'cloth makers', as they were often called) bought the raw wool mostly from the Midlands, organised its processing (the putting-out system), and marketed the finished product. The richest capitalist in Tudor England (richer even than Thomas Paycock of Coggeshall or the almost legendary Jack Winchcombe of Newbury) was Thomas Spring III of Lavenham. The subsidy return of 1524 shows that he died worth £1,800 in goods, the second highest in Suffolk to the Duke of Norfolk. He left to his widow twenty-six manors and property in seventy-six other places. Spring was

Lavenham, timbered houses, Lady Street
(Photograph: A. Hodge)

Suffolk, and especially Lavenham, is famous for its timber-framed houses such as those in the photograph. Indeed, Lavenham has over 300 listed buildings. The sheer quantity of timber shows the wealth of Lavenham's cloth merchants in the fifteenth century, for mature timber was then already scarce and expensive.

The Crooked House, High Street, Lavenham
(Photograph: A. Hodge)
The distorted and leaning frame of this house shows the strength and adaptability of the medieval oak timbers.

Little Hall Lavenham
(Photograph: A. Hodge)
Little Hall is a timber-framed building in characteristic Suffolk style, dating mainly from
the fourteenth and fifteenth centuries. At the rear of the main house a long two-storeyed
range was built during the seventeenth century, mainly to provide workshops, wool
chambers and other working areas. Various sources indicate that the owners of Little
Hall in the fifteenth century were the Causton family, wealthy clothiers and benefactors
of Lavenham Church.

the wealthiest man in England outside London and the nobility. However, Spring was fairly exceptional and it is important to realise that clothiers ranged from very large employers to others who were barely distinguishable from ordinary craftsmen such as master-weavers.[95]

8 It was a highly specialised industry. Apart from the clothiers, the industry gave employment to large numbers of men, women and children in the different processes of spinning, weaving, dyeing, fulling and shearing. The spinners spun the yarn for the weavers. The latter were originally independent craftsmen, but most were becoming wage earners. Dyers, who coloured the cloth, included some who were independent craftsmen and others who were merely employees of the capitalist – clothiers. Fullers bleached or cleansed the cloth; many lived along the River Stour where a good supply of water was available. Shearmen were engaged in cloth finishing. The towns and villages of the Stour Valley had their own specialisms.[96] Two examples will suffice. In Lavenham in 1522

60 per cent of those involved in the broadcloth industry were clothiers. In Boxford in that year 62 per cent of those involved were weavers.[97]

9 It was geared to the demands of both the home *and* foreign markets. Broadcloth was exported through Ipswich to London, Antwerp, the Baltic, Muscovy, Iberia and North Africa.

From the late sixteenth century, if not earlier, the Suffolk broadcloth industry faced long term decline. Why was this? There were perhaps five main reasons. First, the failure of the Cockayne 'project' of 1614–16 bankrupted many clothiers. Second, foreign competition increased. The cloth manufacturers of France and Holland, now recovering from the Wars of Religion, were expanding. Third, the overseas market, on which Suffolk cloth largely depended, seriously declined. War with Spain (1587–1604) and the Thirty Years War (1618–48) disrupted the industry. Fourth, the English Civil Wars (1642–46, 1648) damaged internal trade. Fifth, changes in consumer preference did great harm. Fabrics known as the New Draperies became more popular than the traditional woollens.

Before discussing the New Draperies, we must emphasise the *gradual* decline of the broadcloth industry. At the beginning of the seventeenth century 'wolling cloth' was made at Hadleigh 'in great abundance', according to the Chorographer.[98] But about seventy years later Blome said that 'in the Southern Track [tract, of Suffolk] the great, but decaying trade, in broadcloth for beyond Sea', was 'out-stript' by the cloths of the West

The Old Wool Hall, Lavenham
(Photograph: A. Hodge)
The Old Wool Hall was originally the hall of the Guild of Our Lady Mary, built in the fifteenth century with an open-hall in the centre and two jettied wings. Its religious function ceased with the Reformation and in the seventeenth century the building was used as a Cloth Hall or Exchange by the merchants. The Hall is now incorporated into the Swan Hotel.

Country. Yet he was not entirely pessimistic and referred to Lavenham as 'a large Clothing-town enjoying a pretty good trade'.[99] Still, its days as a great textile town were numbered, and in the period 1684 to 1780 only 20 per cent of Lavenham people were engaged in textiles.[100]

The New Draperies

Professor Palliser has stated that 'The most important technical innovation (in Elizabeth I's reign) was the diversification of the textile industry by the development of the New Draperies'.[101] These fabrics were lighter, more colourful and cheaper than traditional woollens and worsteds. They were introduced by Protestant refugees from the Spanish Netherlands. Called 'Strangers' in contemporary documents, they first settled in Norwich in 1566 and in Colchester in 1568, and within a remarkably short time they established the New Draperies on a considerable scale. In Suffolk these draperies apparently reached their peak after the Restoration.[102]

The Thirty Years War caused Suffolk and other English merchants to lose their main export, cloth, in north Germany and the Baltic lands, cold countries needing heavy cloth. The way forward for the clothing industry was by developing the New Draperies, lighter fabrics which could be sold to warm Mediterranean countries. Despite these new market opportunities, the Suffolk cloth industry failed to adapt to the new fashion, and this sealed its fate. As a result, towns and villages which had been famed for broadcloth production, such as Bury St Edmunds, Lavenham, Long Melford and East Bergholt, ended up merely supplying yarn to the weavers of Norwich and Essex.[103] According to Richard Blome in 1673, only a few places – Clare, Haverhill, Nayland and Sudbury – took up the new fabrics,[104] mostly bays and says.[105] The New Draperies in Suffolk were clearly less widespread than the Old Draperies had been. Moreover, the New Draperies of the county were overshadowed by those of Norwich and Colchester.[106] These towns were more thickly populated than Suffolk villages, like Clare and Nayland, and could draw on a large supply of labour. This was essential for 'the new draperies appear to have been more labour-intensive than the old'.[107]

We hear less about the New Draperies in Suffolk during the eighteenth century and it would seem that they 'slowly followed the Old Draperies to the West Country and to the North'.[108] In short, they declined.[109] But one branch of the textile industry did flourish in Suffolk during both the seventeenth and eighteenth centuries: linen.

The Linen Industry [110]

At the beginning of our period the most important industrial area of Suffolk was the south-west, where woollen cloth was made. By the end of our period it was the north-east, where linen was produced. In 1673 Richard Blome noted that 'In the Woodlands and North-east part of the County, a considerable trade is driven in linnen made into Huswives-cloth, or sale-cloth'.[111] The Suffolk linen industry grew in the seventeenth and eighteenth centuries and was mainly concentrated in the valleys of the Waveney and Little Ouse. In the hundreds of Blackbourn, Hartismere and Hoxne small villages, such as Fressingfield, Hinderclay, Hopton, Hoxne, Metfield, Palgrave, Stradbroke, Thelnetham and Wortham, were important centres of linen weaving. South Norfolk as well as north Suffolk formed part of the same linen manufacturing area, and many weavers can be found in villages just north of the River Waveney, such as Bressingham, Ditchingham, North Lopham, South Lopham and Pulham Market.[112]

So much for the main centres of the linen industry. Why was it important? It was because linen was widely used for aprons, shirts, sheets, pillow cases, napkins, canvas and sailcloth. Indeed, the making of sailcloth for the navy flourished in and around Ipswich and Woodbridge from about 1575 until the late seventeenth century, when local shipbuilding declined.[113] Bungay, near the Norfolk border, was also known for the production of sailcloth.[114]

The raw materials of linen – hemp and flax – were spun into yarn, bleached and woven on looms. It is widely believed that the linen industry originally grew up in the Waveney valley because more hemp and flax were grown there than elsewhere. But this is unlikely. As Nesta Evans says, 'many parishes, later the homes of linen-weavers, did not apparently grow hemp and flax'.[115] Some of these raw materials were imported from abroad, but how many is impossible to say. It is, however, interesting that 'at the time of the East Anglian linen industry's fastest growth the amounts of hemp and flax arriving in the region's ports were declining sharply'.[116]

Unlike the broadcloth industry of the early sixteenth century, the Suffolk linen industry does not seem to have been organised on a capitalist basis.[117] But in at least five respects it resembled the earlier Suffolk broadcloth industry.

1 It was located mainly in a wood-pasture region (High Suffolk),[118] an area of many small farms and weak manorial organisation.

2 It was combined with farming, in this case dairy farming. Over three-quarters of the inventories of linen weavers show that they were also farmers or smallholders.[119]

3 It was labour intensive and thus took root in a thickly populated area, where there was much immigration from outside.

4 It was organised on a domestic basis. Industry was carried on in the home, the master-weavers employing their wives, sisters and children.

5 It was largely a rural industry. Not until the eighteenth century, when linen weaving was showing signs of decay, did it become mainly urban based, in Beccles, Bungay and Halesworth.

Suffolk linen making flourished as a major regional industry until the late eighteenth century, for two main reasons. First, it concentrated on cheaper, coarser linens and was thus not in competition with fine imported cloth. Second, it catered for a growing, reliable local market in preference to an uncertain foreign market. In short, the linen industry responded to what Joan Thirsk has called 'the development of a consumer society'.[120]

But this prosperity was not to last. By 1820 linen weaving was 'effectively dead in East Anglia'.[121] What caused the decline of the linen industry in Suffolk (and Norfolk) during the last quarter of the eighteenth century? It would appear to have been lack of capital investment and mechanisation. Yet, as Nesta Evans says, even if the East Anglian linen industry had become mechanised and more capital intensive, it would still have been destroyed by its cheaper rival, Lancashire cotton.[122] The Industrial Revolution in the North gradually killed the Suffolk linen industry.

Coastal and overseas trade

English overseas trade had mixed fortunes during the Tudor and Stuart period. Ralph Davis saw English overseas trade in the fifteenth to seventeenth centuries undergoing two waves of expansion (1475–1550, 1630–89), separated by a period of near stagnation.[123]

Suffolk coastal and overseas trade also had mixed fortunes during our period. It flourished in the late Middle Ages. For example, in the fifteenth century Suffolk ships fished in the North Sea and off Iceland and exported broadcloth to many countries. The wealth of those involved is reflected in fine churches, or their remains, all along the east coast of Suffolk. Prosperity continued into the sixteenth century when Suffolk, as a maritime county, was involved with colonisation and voyages of discovery. Thomas Cavendish of Trimley St Martin, Esquire, in 1586–88 was the second Englishman to circumnavigate the globe, while Bartholemew Gosnold discovered and named Cape Cod, Massachusetts, in 1602 and helped to found the first permanent settlement in North America at Jamestown in 1607. Early in the seventeenth century Ipswich ships were sailing to Greenland, France, Spain, the Low Countries and the Baltic, and in the 1630s were taking emigrants to New England.[124]

The rise of the Suffolk coastal port towns was based on a number of factors: the export of broadcloth; the export of agricultural products (especially cheese and butter) to London and abroad; the development of the herring fisheries; and shipbuilding.

The seventeenth century, however, saw a gradual decline of several major Suffolk ports, some earlier than others. There were perhaps four main reasons. First, the Reformation decreased the demand for fish, so the Suffolk herring industry declined.[125] Second, the decay of the Suffolk broadcloth industry from the late sixteenth century meant fewer exports for ships to carry. Third, piracy in the North Sea and the Dutch wars (1652–54, 1664–67, 1672–74) interrupted trade. Last, but not least, coastal erosion ruined some east coast ports.

Let us look at the main ports named in Map 3, starting with Ipswich. This borough was easily the most important port in Suffolk. In its heyday between about 1550 and 1670 it was noted particularly for its manufacture of cloth and canvas, its coal trade and its shipbuilding. Cloth was very important to the prosperity of Ipswich. But when the woollen industry of Suffolk declined, the port's overseas trade inevitably suffered. In 1735 John Kirby lamented 'the loss of the Cloth Trade, of which vast quantities were [formerly] shipped off here for Foreign Parts'.[126] Ten years earlier Richard Gouldsmith commented that 'about eighty years ago Ipswich ... had a noble Manufactory of Cloth, which ... was dressed and dyed in the Town, and exported by your own merchants to the East Country [Baltic]'. He blamed the decline of the cloth trade on the gentrification of the town's upper middle class. 'The Merchants and Manufacturers of the greatest Substance having got large Sums of Money, purchas'd Estates and left off the Trades'. Thus 'the Town' was 'greatly decay'd since the loss of their Manufactory'.[127]

As regards the coal trade between Newcastle and London, Ipswich ships played an important part up to the outbreak of the Civil Wars.[128] But after the Restoration they were, as Dr Reed says, 'steadily and inexorably replaced by ships from Whitby, Scarborough and Newcastle'.[129] Defoe commented that 'just before the late Dutch Wars, Ipswich was ... the greatest Town in England for large Colliers or Coal-ships, employed between New Castle and London'. He believed that 'the loss or decay of this Trade, accounts for the pretended decay of the Town of Ipswich'.[130] As well as the coal trade, shipbuilding greatly declined.[131] In the early seventeenth century Ipswich seems to have been the leading shipbuilding port in England after London.[132] But in the early part of the next century Defoe said that 'since the Revolution [1688], some very good Ships have not been built at this Town' In 1698 Celia Fiennes also noted the decline of the Ipswich shipbuilding industry. 'They have a little dock where formerly they built ships of 2 or 300 tun but now little or nothing is minded save a little fishing for the supply of the town'.[133]

We must not, of course, exaggerate the economic decline of Ipswich after the Restoration. To be sure, the port's coal trade and long distance seaborne commerce almost disappeared in the last decades of the seventeenth century. But, as Dr Reed reminds us, the town's 'coastal trade in agricultural produce, grain, butter, cheese and malt continued to be of the first importance, and was stimulated by the ever-rising demands of the population of London for foodstuffs'.[134]

Like Ipswich, Woodbridge had a prosperous shipbuilding industry for most of the seventeenth century and did well exporting the produce of its

The Moot Hall, Aldeburgh
(Photograph: S.R.O. (I),
SPS 1338)
The Moot Hall has
been the meeting-place
of the town Corporation
since the building was
constructed between
c. 1520–40. It is a
timber-framed edifice,
with brick nogging on
the upper floor inserted
in 1654. In the sixteenth
century the Moot Hall
stood in the town
centre; now it is close to
the encroaching sea – a
clear example of coastal
erosion.

hinterland. In 1673 Blome said Woodbridge had 'a passage trade to London with butter, cheese and sackcloth. Next is the trade of ship-building, for which they had four or five commodious building-Docks, most of them well employed and of a good fame amongst Marines for Workman-ship'.[135] But twelve years later Woodbridge, along with Ipswich, was named as a town where there 'hath been observed more than ordinary decay in building shipps'.[136]

Aldeburgh, too, saw its shipbuilding industry decline in the late seventeenth century.[137] The port also suffered from coastal erosion, though it had prospered temporarily in the sixteenth century. Its population rose from about 700 in 1524 to 1,300 in 1603. But by the 1670s its inhabitants numbered only 650.[138] It is not surprising therefore that in 1673 Blome said that Aldeburgh had 'a decaying trade to the North-Sea'.[139]

Dunwich is the most famous example of a declining east coast town. Before the Norman Conquest it had been the principal fishing port in Suffolk.[140] By the late twelfth century it reached its peak of greatness, having daily markets and eight or nine churches.[141] But Dunwich gradually became a victim of sea erosion. In 1673 Blome said that 'the Sea [had] swallowed up all but two Parishes'. When Defoe visited Dunwich in the early eighteenth century he too considered that the town was 'in Danger of being swallowed up'.[142] By the time Defoe's *Tour* was published the greatest part of Dunwich was indeed beneath the waves.[143] So it is hardly surprising that Dunwich has been called the 'English Atlantis'.

Not all east coast towns lost their battles with the encroaching sea. Southwold, despite its silting haven, managed to thrive. In 1673 Blome said that 'the chief business of the Town is for Sea affairs ... the chief trade is to Iceland, and the North-Sea for Codd; they have also a Coal-trade, and a great passage trade to London with cheese and butter'.[144]

Finally, what about Lowestoft? The scale and prosperity of its fishing industry fluctuated. In the later sixteenth century red herrings were exported in large quantities to Leghorn in Italy, but during the earlier part of the next century the Lowestoft fishing industry 'suffered a reversal of its fortunes'. Dutch competition was primarily responsible for this. Fortunately 'around 1670 ... the North Sea herring fishery experienced a recovery'.[145] In 1673 Blome regarded Lowestoft as 'a thriving town' whose 'chief trade is fishing in the North-Sea for Codd, and at home for Herrings'. He also remarked that Lowestoft had 'a trade to New-castle for coal'.[146] Lowestoft's maritime prosperity continued, and indeed slightly expanded, during the period 1700–1730, to judge by the number of people connected with seafaring pursuits.[147]

Dunwich Beach
(Photograph: S.R.O. (I), K 478/11)
The above picture shows coastal erosion, which has ruined Dunwich. It was once one of England's greatest ports, with a Saxon cathedral, monastic houses, hospitals and many churches. But the entire city is now beneath the waves. The present village and a few ruins are all that remain after 700 years of sea erosion.

Conclusion

From about the 1470s to the 1670s Suffolk was one of the wealthiest, most densely peopled and economically advanced parts of England. The broadcloth industry of the south-west reached the peak of its prosperity between the 1470s and the 1520s. But this affluence did not last. By the end of the seventeenth century the industry had virtually collapsed. Indeed, south-west Suffolk was the first rural manufacturing region in England to *de*-industrialize, apart from the Kentish Weald.[148]

From the late Middle Ages until the Restoration most of Suffolk's leading coastal towns enjoyed great wealth, Iceland and the North Sea being highly profitable areas for both fishing and trading. During the late seventeenth century, however, the east coast ports experienced mixed fortunes. Some, like Dunwich, literally sank into insignificance, while others, like Southwold and Lowestoft, forged ahead.

So much for the debit side of the Suffolk economy. On the credit side the seventeenth century saw the development and progress of dairy farming. Indeed, it has been said that 'the export of cloth to the foreign market gradually yielded in importance to the export of dairy produce for consumption in London'.[149] Apart from agriculture two new industries developed: the New Draperies and linen. The former took root in a few places that had previously manufactured broadcloth. However, the New Draperies were far less extensive than the Old Draperies had been. As for linen, this industry greatly flourished during the seventeenth century and most of the eighteenth, mainly in north-east Suffolk. Unfortunately the hand operated linen industry could not withstand the mechanised factory competition of the industrial North and by the 1820s linen weaving was virtually dead.

It was in fact mostly changes in the eighteenth century which sealed the fate of Suffolk. It was then that developments in the economy of the country as a whole – the growth of an Atlantic trade with North America and the West Indies, the onset of the Industrial Revolution in the North and Midlands – transformed Suffolk from one of the wealthiest regions in England into an area of abject rural poverty.

CHAPTER TWO

Tudor and Stuart Suffolk: government and society

Government

The national background

In most of Europe during the sixteenth and seventeenth centuries the main trend was towards absolute monarchy. By this is meant a form of government in which the prince's authority is unrestricted by any higher authority (like an international church) or by any organ of popular representation (like Parliament). Absolute monarchs tried to impose religious uniformity and, in an inflationary age, to increase taxes. To achieve these aims they increased their armies and bureaucracies, used arbitrary powers, restricted the liberty of the subject, and tried to obliterate or weaken parliamentary institutions, representing nobles, clergy and commoners.

In England the Tudors and early Stuarts were certainly not absolute monarchs. Parliament did not disappear, though Charles I (1625–49) was to rule without it for eleven years (1629–40). Parliament was not a regular part of the constitution – it seldom met – until after the Glorious Revolution of 1688–89, but it played an important role in Tudor times. No English monarch, not even Henry VIII, could legislate or tax without the consent of Parliament. In fact an Act of 1483 declared that non-parliamentary taxation was illegal. Thus it is not surprising that Henry VIII had to withdraw the Amicable Grant in 1525 since it had no parliamentary approval and caused considerable resistance, especially in Suffolk.[1] Another sign of Parliament's strength was that 'by 1500 it was far and away the largest representative body in existence in Europe'.[2] The number of Members of Parliament increased from 296 in 1485 to 547 in 1640.[3] Clearly the Tudors and early Stuarts were not anti-Parliament.

At the local level the Tudors had no professional civil service, and had to rely on unpaid local amateurs (e.g., Justices of the Peace) to enforce their commands. Nor did they have a standing army (except the Yeomen of the Guard). Instead each county had its militia (home guard) under the control of local, unpaid amateurs (e.g. Deputy Lieutenants). In short, the central government's success depended on the willingness of local governors to obey its commands. This situation has been called 'self-government at the King's command', though there was often more emphasis on 'self-government' than on 'the King's command'. Recalcitrant local officials could of course be dismissed by the crown, but such dismissals were only on a moderate scale before the late seventeenth century.[4]

It was not until the period 1681–88 that a real trend towards absolutism could be observed. Charles II after 1681 and James II from 1685 to 1688 tried to manipulate Parliament, to purge drastically the local commissions of the peace, to weaken the privileges of chartered boroughs, and to build up a standing army. Fortunately the Glorious Revolution of 1688–89 prevented the triumph of a continental-style absolutism.[5]

In two important respects, however, the Tudors *did* increase their powers. With the help of the so-called Reformation Parliament the Catholic Church was brought under royal control by the Act of Supremacy, 1534, while during the course of the sixteenth century the powerful nobleman, 'the overmighty subject', was tamed. This last remark may seem controversial. Yet the facts speak for themselves. By the time of the First Civil War (1642–46) only three counties – Essex, Lancashire and Leicestershire – can be confidently regarded as noble dominated.[6] In the following counties, however, it was the gentry, not the nobility,[7] who ruled: Cheshire, Cumberland and Westmorland, Durham, Kent, Northumberland, Somerset, Sussex, Warwickshire and Yorkshire.[8] To these ten counties we might add Norfolk and Suffolk, but more about them later.

Despite the monarch's triumph over the Church and nobility, absolutism was not established. As Professor John Guy has said, 'Thomas Cromwell strengthened royal institutions at the expense of the church and the old "feudal" nobility. But the balance of power at county level remained with the landowners who served as Sheriffs and JPs'.[9] It is this local government that we need to study. Professor Alan Smith has rightly said that 'for the vast majority of Elizabethans of all classes, government was essentially local government'.[10]

The governance of Suffolk[11]

In his brilliant *Suffolk and the Tudors* Professor Diarmaid MacCulloch states that there were four different patterns of administration in Suffolk during the Tudor period: the Anglo-Saxon county divisions, the feudal liberties, the chartered boroughs, and the structures of the diocese of Norwich.[12] This diocese will be dealt with in Chapter 3, but the other administrative units can be examined in the present chapter.

The Anglo-Saxon county divisions

Map 6 shows the parishes, hundreds and liberties of Suffolk during the early Tudor period. Excluding the liberties, Suffolk was, administratively,

Map 6: Parishes, Hundreds and Liberties of Suffolk

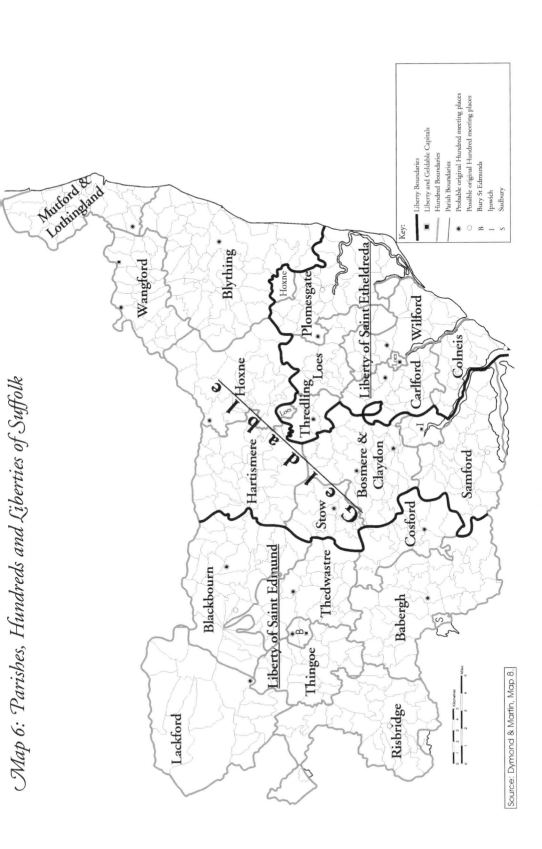

Mutford & Lothingland

Wangford

Blything

Hoxne

Plomesgate

Loes

Liberty of Saint Etheldreda

Wilford

Carlford

Colneis

Hoxne

Thredling

Bosmere & Claydon

Samford

Hartismere

Stow

Cosford

Blackbourn

Liberty of Saint Edmund

Thedwastre

Babergh

Thingoe

B

Risbridge

Lackford

S

Geldable

Loes

Loes

I

Key:

- Liberty Boundaries
- Liberty and Geldable Capitals
- Hundred Boundaries
- Parish Boundaries
- Probable original Hundred meeting places
- Possible original Hundred meeting places
- B Bury St Edmunds
- I Ipswich
- S Sudbury

Kilometres

Miles

Source: Dymond & Martin, Map 8.

a microcosm of England. Let us start at the bottom with the parish and work upwards.

Parishes

The parish was the local unit of ecclesiastical organisation before the nineteenth century. The parish of south-eastern England, unlike that of northern England, was usually coterminous with the township, the lowest level of the local government hierarchy.[13] During the Tudor and Stuart period there were 517 parishes in Suffolk.[14] Parishes became an important part of *secular* as well as ecclesiastical government after the Reformation. By the end of the sixteenth century the parish was a more important unit of administration than the hundred. Parishes were responsible for poor relief from Henry VIII's reign onwards and under Elizabeth I a new official was appointed, the overseer of the poor. Other officials – the parish constable and the churchwarden – can be traced back to medieval times. All parochial officials had to obey the commands of their superiors, the High Constables of the hundreds and the county officials. Above the parish was the hundred.

The hundreds

There were twenty-two hundreds in Suffolk during the Tudor and Stuart periods.[15] The hundred can be traced back to at least the tenth century. Originally the hundred may have represented 100 hides or family holdings. Above the level of each parish the hundred was the basis of all public administration in medieval England, judicial, fiscal and military. Two High Constables were responsible for a variety of financial, military and police duties. Each hundred had its own court, second only to the county court, presided over by a hundred bailiff. From the thirteenth century onwards the rise of royal justice undermined hundred and county courts, and both were largely superseded by the establishment of Quarter Sessions in Tudor times. However, Petty Sessions continued to be held within hundreds until the nineteenth century. Though losing its judicial authority, the hundred was still important for tax and militia purposes in Tudor and Stuart times. Nevertheless, it was clearly losing power to the parish below and the county above.[16]

The county

This was 'the fundamental unit of local government', at least in lowland England.[17] County officials were appointed by the king, but in practice they could flout his commands if they wished, or at least drag their feet. The three main officials were the Sheriff, the Lord Lieutenant and his deputies, and the Justices of the Peace. The former was paid (usually small) fees, but the deputy lieutenants and the JPs received no financial rewards, although expenses would normally be paid. The office of sheriff can be traced back to Anglo-Saxon times. He was originally called the 'shire-reeve'. 'The sheriff enjoyed primacy until the fourteenth century',[18] but from the fifteenth century his power declined. Yet during the early modern period he was responsible for collecting taxes (e.g. Ship Money under Charles I), and recusancy fines (from 1591 to 1691), and for supervising parliamentary elections. In 1485 there were twenty-eight shrievalties covering thirty-eight English counties. But Suffolk had no separate sheriff until 1576. Until then it shared a sheriff with Norfolk.

The Lord Lieutenant replaced the sheriff at the head of the county hierarchy by 1600. He became the King's main representative in the localities. 'Lord Lieutenancies were first set up for groups of counties in 1550, to deal with widespread popular unrest which had boiled over in 1549'.[19] The Lord Lieutenant was often a courtier nobleman, trusted by the Privy Council, who could not be in two places at once, so he appointed two or more deputies. By 1585 the lieutenancy system had become a permanent nationwide network, 'a vital link between central and local government'.[20] The Lords Lieutenant and their deputies were mainly responsible for the training and equipment of the local militia. As Penry Williams says, this 'rendered the Crown less dependent upon noble retainers and the state came nearer to effective control of physical force'.[21] In addition to their important military duties the Lords Lieutenant and their deputies had important civilian tasks, such as enforcing economic regulations, collecting forced loans and supervising recusants.[22]

Beneath the Lords Lieutenant and their deputies came the Justices of the Peace. These were the key figures in local government. The office of JP can be traced back to at least 1361, if not earlier.[23] The JPs of Tudor and Stuart times resembled modern magistrates since they were responsible for enforcing the law. At Quarter and Petty Sessions they were minor judges.[24] But unlike modern magistrates the JPs during our period were also busy administrators.[25] They were responsible for enforcing royal commands in the counties. They administered the poor law, regulated alehouses, fixed wages and prices, and enforced the recusancy laws. These were just some of their duties. Historians clearly recognise the importance of the JPs. Penry Williams says that they 'exercised the most continuous and detailed control over the shires' during the Tudor period, while Professor MacCulloch argues that in the same period real administrative power passed to the JPs and assize judges.[26]

There are four main points to note about the JPs in Tudor Suffolk.

1 Their numbers in the commission of the peace increased. In 1500 the total in the Suffolk commission was thirty but in 1579 it was fifty-six.[27] Generalising about England, Professor Alan Smith says that in 1500 there were on average fewer than ten JPs per shire, but that by the middle of Elizabeth's reign the average was forty or fifty.[28] The number of JPs in Suffolk was clearly above the national average, especially in early Tudor times.

2 Their powers increased. For example, they appointed the High Constables of hundreds. This happened piecemeal during Elizabeth's reign, but it was made official in a county meeting in 1615.[29]

3 They were not parochial in outlook. There was much intercommissioning. Thirty-eight Suffolk men served on the Norfolk Bench and sixteen on the Essex Bench between 1500 and 1603.[30] A good example of a broad-minded Suffolk JP is Sir Nicholas Bacon. Although his main residence was Redgrave in Suffolk, he served on the Norfolk Bench of magistrates in 1584.[31] As MacCulloch says, 'county boundaries were not exclusive frontiers'.[32]

4 They belonged overwhelmingly to the armigerous gentry. 'Probably only two non-armigerous men were named to the Suffolk commission of the peace during the entire [sixteenth] century': Walter Clerke of Hadleigh, clothier, and Robert Wrott, son of a husbandman.[33] Thus the upper classes ruled Suffolk on behalf of the Crown – and themselves?

Professor MacCulloch has argued that 'there was a sense of county identity already perceptible in the fifteenth century'.[34] Yet Suffolk seems a rather divided county, despite increased magisterial control over the hundreds and parishes. Apart from the Anglo-Saxon county divisions, there were three other ancient divisions of the shire: the Geldable and two ecclesiastical liberties: St Etheldreda (sometimes called St Audrey) and St Edmund.

The Geldable included the hundreds of Blything, Bosmere and Claydon, Hartismere, Hoxne, Lothingland, Mutford, Samford, Stow and Wangford, and had two 'capitals', one at Ipswich and the other at Beccles (see Map 6). The Geldable was the only part of Suffolk from which the Crown had been able to extract geld or taxes and in which the sheriff had been able to exercise his full royal authority before the Dissolution of the Monasteries. The Geldable paid half the royal taxes, while the two liberties combined to pay the other half. Because of its small size the Geldable shared a sheriff with Norfolk until 1576.

If the Geldable was firmly under royal jurisdiction, the ecclesiastical liberties were not. But what do we mean by liberties? The term has little or nothing to do with the modern idea of the liberty of the individual citizen. Liberties or franchises meant areas possessing a measure of freedom from royal officials and royal laws. A liberty or franchise depended on a royal grant and meant that the king delegated his power to an important individual or institution. This had happened in the Middle Ages in Suffolk and elsewhere. Perhaps the best known example of a medieval franchise was the Palatinate of Durham whose bishop was given full responsibility for guarding the Scottish border.

The two major Liberties or Franchises in Suffolk were areas where royal jurisdiction was delegated to two Benedictine monasteries. These were the

Liberty of St Etheldreda and the Liberty of St Edmund. The former included the hundreds of Carlford, Colneis, Loes, Plomesgate, Thredling and Wilford. The 'capital' of the Liberty was Woodbridge (see Map 6). The Liberty of St Etheldreda was granted in 970 by King Edgar to St Etheldreda's abbey at Ely. When in 1109 the bishopric of Ely was founded, the Liberty was transferred to the Prior and monks. The monks of Ely lived far away and seem to have been absentee landlords during the Middle Ages.[35] After the dissolution of the abbey in 1539, the Liberty was granted to the Dean and Chapter of the cathedral and thus came indirectly under royal control.[36]

The Liberty of St Edmund comprised the hundreds of Babergh, Blackbourne, Cosford, Lackford, Thedwastre, Thingoe and Risbridge. Its 'capital' was at Bury St Edmunds (see Map 6). The Liberty of St Edmund had formed the dowry of Emma, wife of King Canute, and was granted by her son, Edward the Confessor, to St Edmund's abbey at Bury in the early eleventh century. Far more powerful than the monks of Ely, the Abbot of Bury excluded the Assizes and forced the judges to meet on heathland a mile outside the town.[37] Bury was also exempt from the jurisdiction of the Bishop of Norwich. At the dissolution in 1539, the Liberty reverted to the Crown.[38] This strengthened royal power, yet Suffolk was still a divided county.[39] The Liberty of St Edmund later became the county of West Suffolk, and survived as a distinct administrative unit until 1974. Unlike the Liberty of St Etheldreda, that of St Edmund retained a separate grand jury at the Assizes into the nineteenth century. Thus 'the most potent line of demarcation within Suffolk was the boundary of the ancient ecclesiastical Liberty of St Edmund'.[40] This East-West division was to be very important, not least during the First Civil War in Suffolk (1642–46).

The feudal liberties

Within the three major units – the Geldable and the ecclesiastical liberties – were several small, often fragmented, feudal liberties: the Bishop of Norwich's Liberty of Elmham; the Honour of Clare; the Honour of Eye; the Liberty of the Duke of Norfolk (see Map 7). The last three were sustained by great noblemen or the Crown into the Tudor period.[41] Let us deal briefly with each liberty in turn.

The Bishop of Norwich's Liberty
There is little to say about this Liberty except that it was based on the episcopal estates in South Elmham. It lasted until 1536 and then reverted to the crown.

The Honour of Clare
This was built up by the Clare family in the thirteenth century. The Honour was centred on Clare Castle with extensive estates in Essex and significant

Map 7: Ecclesiastical and Feudal Liberties of Suffolk

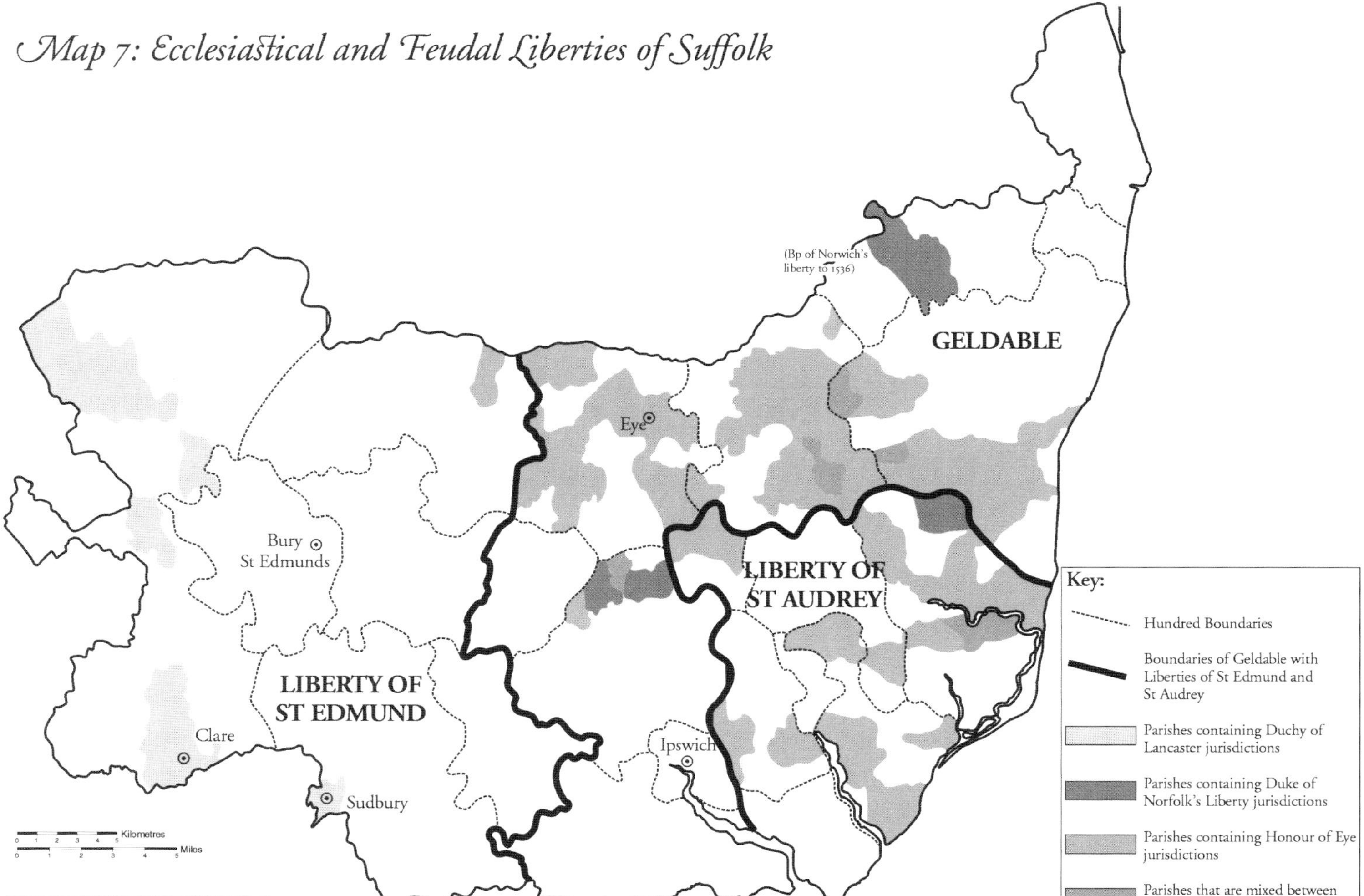

GELDABLE

(Bp of Norwich's liberty to 1536)

Eye⊙

LIBERTY OF ST AUDREY

Ipswich⊙

LIBERTY OF ST EDMUND

Bury ⊙ St Edmunds

Clare⊙

Sudbury⊙

Key:

- ∙∙∙∙∙ Hundred Boundaries
- ▬▬▬ Boundaries of Geldable with Liberties of St Edmund and St Audrey
- Parishes containing Duchy of Lancaster jurisdictions
- Parishes containing Duke of Norfolk's Liberty jurisdictions
- Parishes containing Honour of Eye jurisdictions
- Parishes that are mixed between Norfolk and Eye jurisdictions [?]

Kilometres

Miles

Map based on Professor D.N.J. MacCulloch, Suffolk, Map IV, p.21

property in the south of the Liberty of St Edmund. In 1460 the Honour came to Edward IV through the female line and successive kings made life grants to various female members of the royal family (e.g. Catherine of Aragon and her daughter Mary, Anne Boleyn and Catherine Parr). Mary Tudor later annexed the Honour, including the borough of Sudbury and the manor of Mildenhall, to the Duchy of Lancaster. It then came directly under royal control.[42]

The Honour of Eye

This was held by the Earls and Dukes of Suffolk during the later Middle Ages. The Honour had jurisdiction over seventy-two townships, nearly all in the Geldable and St Etheldreda's Liberty. In 1515 the Honour was granted to Charles Brandon after Henry VIII created him Duke of Suffolk. But in 1537–38 Charles Brandon lost power and Eye reverted to the Crown.[43]

The Liberty of the Duke of Norfolk

This was created by Edward IV in 1468. The Dukes of Norfolk had 139 parishes under their control, but only fifteen were in Suffolk. Their Suffolk section of their Liberty included the ancient castle of the Earls of Norfolk at Bungay, but excluded their important castle at Framlingham and their property around Stoke-by-Nayland in the Stour valley. Yet the Duke of

Framlingham Castle
(Drawn and engraved by T. Higham in [T. K. Cromwell], *Excursions in the County of Suffolk*, 2 vols. (1818–19), II, p. 119 (hereafter *Excursions*))
This castle symbolised the enormous power wielded between 1483 and 1572 by the Howards, Dukes of Norfolk. Yet the family adapted Framlingham as a residence rather than a fortress, and added chimneys without fireplaces beneath! At Framlingham Castle Mary Tudor's supporters rallied to her in 1553 after an attempt to set Lady Jane Grey on the throne. After 1555 Arundel Castle, Sussex, became the Howards' main family seat.

Norfolk was extremely powerful and his immediate authority was more impressive than that of an absentee Dean and Chapter (of Ely) in St Etheldreda's Liberty.[44] After the 4th Duke's execution in 1572 the Norfolk Liberty came into the hands of the Exchequer or family trustees (some being tenants of the Crown).[45]

By obtaining the four feudal and two ecclesiastical liberties, the Tudors increased royal authority in Suffolk at the expense of the nobility and the Church.

The chartered boroughs and parliamentary representation

What is meant by a chartered borough during the Tudor and Stuart period? It was a borough with a royal charter usually, but not always, granting it the right to return Members of Parliament. Those who elected the MPs, municipal officials and councillors were called 'burgesses'. These were a restricted proportion of the urban population. Burgesses included the wealthier traders, residents or property owners of the borough, and generally excluded those of humbler status.

The non-parliamentary boroughs of Tudor Suffolk may be quickly dismissed. They included some important places like Beccles, Hadleigh, Southwold and, before 1621, Bury St Edmunds. They enjoyed certain juridical and economic privileges, but had no parliamentary representation.[46]

Far more important politically were the parliamentary boroughs. From the reign of Edward I (1272–1307) most English cities and many (but not all) boroughs sent representatives to the House of Commons, generally in pairs; these were known as 'burgesses of Parliament' and were reckoned as secondary in status to the county representatives ('The Knights of the Shire'). The increase in the number of Parliamentary seats in Suffolk and elsewhere under the Tudors and early Stuarts shows that these monarchs had no wish to abolish or weaken Parliament. Before the Great Reform Act of 1832 Suffolk returned sixteen MPs. These had included two knights of the shire since 1290, who represented the county constituency of Suffolk. The other fourteen MPs represented seven boroughs, which are located on Map 8. Since 1298 Dunwich and Ipswich had returned two MPs continuously. Orford had returned two MPs since 1298, but did so regularly only from 1529. Under Elizabeth I three boroughs were allowed to return two MPs each: Sudbury from 1558, and Aldeburgh and Eye from 1571. Under James I Bury St Edmunds at last became a parliamentary borough, returning two MPs from 1621.[47]

Who voted in Parliamentary elections? Many did in the county constituencies but far fewer did in borough seats. An Act of 1430 stipulated that all Englishmen who held freehold land to the value of forty shillings or more could vote in the county elections. Derek Hirst has emphasised that inflation increased the number of forty shilling freeholders in Tudor and early Stuart times, so that by 1640 between 27 per cent and 40 per cent

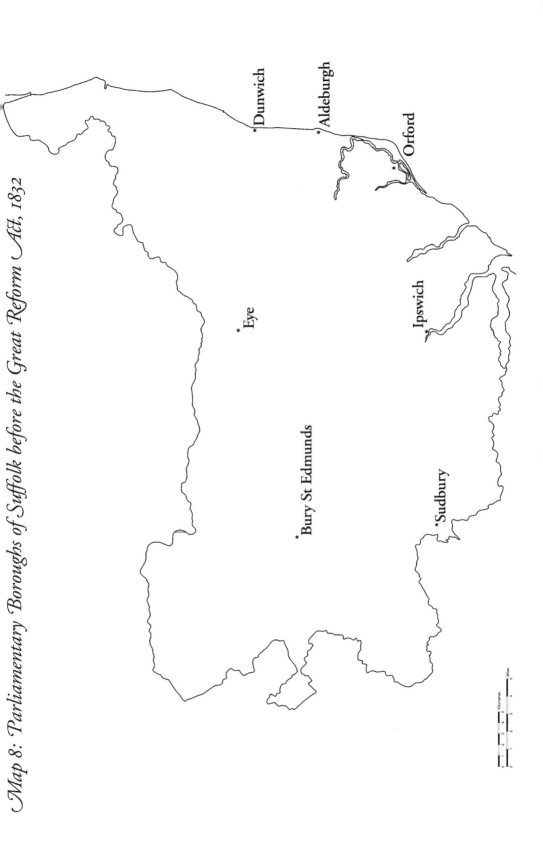

Map 8: Parliamentary Boroughs of Suffolk before the Great Reform Act, 1832

*Dunwich

*Aldeburgh

Orford

*Eye

Ipswich

Bury St Edmunds

*Sudbury

of adult males in England had the vote.[48] Certainly the electorate in the county of Suffolk was expanding, for whatever reasons, from the beginning of Elizabeth I's reign until the election of the Long Parliament in 1640.

The Protectorate (1653–59) saw even greater increases in the size of the electorate. In December 1653 the framers of the Instrument of Government – Britain's first and only written constitution – abolished the forty-shilling freehold vote, and enfranchised those who had a real or personal estate of £200. This had important results for Suffolk. According to Paul Pinckney, the size of the county electorate increased by over 50 per cent between 1640 and 1654. There was yet another large increase in 1656. 'Prosperity', says Pinckney, 'added to the £200 ranks, while newly enfranchised men from the towns appeared in large numbers' at the Suffolk county elections of 1654 and 1656.[49]

The January 1659 election reverted to the old forty shilling freehold franchise,[50] which was not to be abolished again until the Great Reform Act of 1832. This would partly explain why the size of the county electorate in Suffolk was smaller in 1673 and 1715 than it had been during the mid-1650s.

The fluctuations in the size of the county electorate in Suffolk between the accession of Elizabeth I and the 1715 Rebellion are detailed in Table 2.1.

Table 2.1 The county electorate in Suffolk 1558–1715

Ref.[51]	Date	Estimated size of electorate
a	1558	3,000
b	1640	3,500–4,000
c	1654	6,868
d	1656	11,972 [52]
e	1673	4,500
f	1715	6,500

While the county had a uniform franchise, before, during and after the Great Rebellion, the boroughs varied considerably. In pre-Civil War days all freemen (privileged citizens) in Aldeburgh, Dunwich and Ipswich could vote. But in Bury St Edmunds and Sudbury the franchise belonged to members of the Governing Body or corporation. In Eye the vote was given to those who paid 'scot and lot'.[53] In Orford we do not know what the situation was.[54]

During the Protectorate no alterations were made in the franchise of the boroughs and the old and variegated rights of voting were retained.[55] However, Aldeburgh, Eye and Orford were disfranchised by the Instrument of Government,[56] though they regained their status as parliamentary boroughs at the Restoration.

Throughout our period, then, the electorate in the Suffolk boroughs seems to have been tiny, at least until after the Glorious Revolution.[57] We

Borough of Eye
(Engraved by T. Barber from a sketch by T. Higham in *Excursions*, II, p. 13)
This quiet and thinly populated place is a good example of a pocket borough, for the
electorate never exceeded 200 before the 1832 Reform Act. Eye's parliamentary elections
were controlled by the Bacons of Redgrave from 1571 until the mid-seventeenth century,
and by the Cornwallis family of Brome from 1640 to 1820.

Orford Castle
(Photograph: A. Hodge)
This castle was built
from 1165 by Henry II,
to offset the seemingly
menacing power of the
Bigods at Framlingham.
Under the shelter of the
castle Orford developed
as a prosperous port.
But the silting up of
harbours brought the
closure of ports like
Orford, Dunwich and
Blythburgh. Population
decline turned Orford
into a pocket borough,
characterised by strong
landlord control and
only 150 electors in 1715.
The 1832 Reform Act
disfranchised Orford,
Dunwich and Aldeburgh.

Orford Church
(Photograph: A. Hodge)
This parish church has a spacious fourteenth-century nave and aisles and a remarkable
ruined chancel probably dating from *c.* 1160. But during the prosperous fifteenth century
the parish church was not the only religious building. There were two other churches, a
house of Augustine Friars and two hospitals. But when Defoe, writing in 1722, said that
Orford 'is now decayed', only the parish church was left.

must, of course, distinguish between *actual* and *potential* voters. In Dunwich
thirty freemen voted in the election to the Short Parliament in 1640, but
later in the year, in the election to the Long Parliament, forty-seven voted.
In Ipswich only 199 adult males voted in the election to the Short Parliament.[58] Since the population of Ipswich must have been *at least* 5,000 by
1640, this seems an incredibly low figure. The *potential* voters must have
considerably outnumbered the *actual* voters.

The small number of both actual and potential voters in the boroughs
partly explains why the gentry and outsiders were able to dominate parliamentary elections. One outsider – Robert Devereux, Earl of Essex
(d. 1601) – successfully interfered at Dunwich in 1593 to secure the election
of a friend, and also at Ipswich once he had become High Steward.[59] The
large county electorate was less amenable to control, however. Even the
Duke of Norfolk lacked influence on the freehold voters from 1559 to 1572.[60]

To sum up so far, Suffolk was a county noted for divided authority and
divided loyalties before the execution of the 4th Duke of Norfolk in 1572.
Even after the abolition of the Liberty of St Edmund in 1540, the county

lacked unity because of the East-West divide. Yet by annexing the feudal and ecclesiastical liberties, the Tudor monarchy increased its power in Suffolk at the expense of the nobles and the Church. The Tudors did not try to weaken Parliament, however, and the parliamentary boroughs in Suffolk expanded in number. These boroughs were often dominated by the gentry and outsiders, partly because of their small electorates. Finally, the Tudor and early Stuart periods saw the JPs increase their authority at the county, hundred and parish level. The JPs of Suffolk, like those elsewhere, belonged to the gentry, a social group which must now be studied, along with other ranks of society.

Society

'In early modern England, belief in hierarchy was as axiomatic as belief in God'. Such is the opinion of Dr John Adamson [61] and it is hard to disagree with him. Tudor and Stuart England, like other pre-industrial societies, was socially unequal and hierarchical, though, as we shall see, there was also considerable social mobility. Table 2.2 gives a bird's eye view of the social structure of England and Suffolk in about 1600.

Table 2.2 Social Structure about 1600

England		Suffolk	
1 Nobility	*Nobilitas Maior* (Lay peers [62] & bishops) *Nobilitas Minor* (Knights, Esquires, Gentlemen, Lawyers, clergy)	1 Nobility & Barrony (lay peers) 2 Knights 3 The Gentleman	Gentry
2 Citizens		4 Townes-man	
3 Yeomanry		5 Yeomanry	
4 Copyholders & cottagers		6 The Husbandman 7 The Poore	

Source: Thomas Wilson, *The State of England 1600* [63]

Source: Robert Reyce, *The Breviary of Suffolk* (1603) [64]

Wilson and Reyce have been put into the same table because they have much in common. Both were of gentry stock,[65] both were class conscious, both believed in social and economic inequality, and both were almost exactly contemporaneous. The social categories of Thomas Wilson, a government official, are similar to those used by other well-known social commentators, such as Rev. William Harrison in 1577, Sir Thomas Smith in 1583 and Edward Chamberlayne in 1669.[66] But Smith, Harrison and Chamberlayne would not have included lawyers and clergy among the *nobilitas minor*, i.e. the gentry.[67] Nor indeed would Reyce have done. In some respects Wilson and Reyce differ. First, Wilson, like Harrison and

Smith, divided people into four sorts, whereas Reyce listed seven degrees of callings in his *Breviary*. Second, Wilson, like Harrison, Smith and Chamberlayne, did not regard peers and gentry as two separate groups, but subdivisions of a single ruling class (see Table 2.2), whereas Reyce seems to regard nobles, knights and gentlemen as distinct.[68] Third, Wilson defined Citizens narrowly, confining his attention to the town rich, especially in London,[69] whereas Reyce describes a more modest trader whose fortunes fluctuated. Finally, Wilson and Reyce seem to give *slightly* different descriptions of the lower orders. Can one equate Wilson's copyholders with Reyce's husbandman? How far were Wilson's cottagers and wage earners synonymous with Reyce's 'Poore'. However, the similarities between Wilson and Reyce are far more important than the differences. The social structure of Suffolk may not have been identical to that of England, but it was similar. Hence it is not pointless to discuss all six groups of Robert Reyce in turn.[70] For convenience they will be dealt with in this order: nobles, gentry, yeomen, husbandmen, townsmen, the 'poore'.

The Nobility

Reyce lists ancient noble families which, he lamented, were 'long since extinguished'.[71] Well might he lament, for when he wrote the *Breviary* in 1603, the nobility had indeed declined in Suffolk.

This was not the case in the early Tudor period. As MacCulloch says, 'successive magnates dominated the whole region of East Anglia from 1485 to 1547: John de Vere, 13th Earl of Oxford (d. 1513); the Howard family, Dukes of Norfolk; and Charles Brandon, Duke of Suffolk, who lost power in 1538'.[72] The power of the 3rd Duke of Norfolk was temporarily eclipsed after the execution of Catherine Howard (Henry VIII's fifth wife) in 1542, but he regained favour on Mary Tudor's accession in 1553. The Howards remained extremely powerful during the first fourteen years of the reign of Elizabeth I. The 4th Duke of Norfolk was able to influence the composition of the Bench of Suffolk JPs in 1558 and to nominate at least one MP for each Suffolk borough in nearly every parliamentary election till 1572.[73] The Duke was also an extremely wealthy man, owning nearly 17,000 sheep in the autumn of 1571, i.e. after the sale of surplus lambs. Indeed, he has been described as the greatest sheepmaster of the Elizabethan age.[74] B. W. Beckingsale and M. E. James have argued that the Howards were as much princes in East Anglia and Sussex as the Percies were in Northumberland.[75] But the 4th Duke of Norfolk allowed himself to be drawn into the Ridolfi Plot (1571) to replace Elizabeth I by Mary, Queen of Scots. He was consequently put in the Tower of London and his execution in 1572 meant the end of independent noble power in Norfolk and Suffolk. 'The fall of the fourth Duke of Norfolk', says MacCulloch, 'made Suffolk safe for knights and mere gentry'.[76]

The Gentry

The gentry were those consistently described in official documents as baronets (after 1611), knights, esquires and gentlemen and recognised as such by their contemporaries. However, a modicum of wealth was needed to sustain gentility (hence Sir Thomas Smith's well-known remark about being able to 'beare ... the charge ... of a gentleman'.[77]). Thus urban and rural 'gentlemen' whose real or personal estates were very small are not counted as gentry for the purposes of this study. In the early Tudor period 'gentlemen' holding land worth less than £5 p.a. or moveables valued at under £20 are not regarded as gentry.[78] In the Stuart period 'gentlemen' whose landed incomes were under £40 p.a. or who had fewer than five hearths also fail to qualify as gentry.[79]

Diarmaid MacCulloch believes that the Tudor period benefited the gentry, at least politically. 'During the sixteenth century Suffolk was transformed in political terms. From being part of an East Anglian region dominated by great noblemen, first the Earl of Oxford, then the Dukes of Norfolk and Suffolk, it became an increasingly self-contained county whose day to day running was in the hands of an oligarchy of Puritan-minded gentry'.[80]

But the Suffolk gentry gained at the expense of those below as well as those above themselves in the social scale. We have noticed how the JPs – drawn from the greater gentry (knights and esquires) – increased their powers over the hundreds.[81] The gentry were also able to dominate parliamentary elections as time went on. It is not surprising that the gentry were able to influence elections in the smaller boroughs. It was partly because it was expensive for a town to maintain burgesses in Parliament that it preferred to elect a gentleman who was prepared to forego his wage claims in return for a parliamentary seat. But it was also because the Suffolk boroughs had small electorates. Whatever the reason, gentry control over the boroughs increased dramatically. Taking together the boroughs of Ipswich, Dunwich, Orford, Sudbury, Eye and Aldeburgh, the proportion of 'real burgesses' attending Parliament was 49 per cent in the period 1504–58 and only 17 per cent in the period 1559–1601. By contrast, the proportion of Suffolk gentry and outsiders elected to Parliament rose from 50 per cent in the earlier period to 83 per cent in the later part of the century.[82] Even Ipswich – a community of merchants and sailors and a town noted for its independent spirit and corporate pride in its privileges – succumbed to gentry influence. The borough elected MPs like the Solicitor-General John Gosnold of Otley and other gentry like Sir Thomas Rush of Sudbourne, Knight, Sir Humphrey Wingfield of Brantham, Knight, Thomas Seckford of Woodbridge, Esquire, and Edward Grimston of Rishangles, Esquire.[83]

Socially as well as politically Suffolk saw the rise of the gentry during the sixteenth and seventeenth centuries. In the Tudor period the boroughs of Beccles, Dunwich, Eye, Hadleigh, Orford and Sudbury were each under

Seckford Hall, Great Bealings
(Engraved by E. Roberts from a drawing by T. Higham in *Excursions*, II, p. 40)
Seckford Hall, near Woodbridge, was built between 1553 and 1585, probably by Thomas
Seckford. It is noted for its long red-brick frontage with gables, fine chimneys and brick
mullioned windows. Thomas Seckford (1515–88) was in turn a lawyer, M. P. for Ipswich
and Master of Requests at Elizabeth's court.

the influence of neighbouring gentry families. Even Bury St Edmunds 'had
a host of local great men who seemed to anticipate the town's Georgian
function as the centre of a local "season".'[84] However, in the Stuart and
early Georgian periods the gentry's presence and influence in towns became
more conspicuous than it had ever been before, especially in Ipswich and
Bury St Edmunds. In 1655 Rev. Matthias Candler, Vicar of Coddenham,
said that 'many of the gentry buy or hire houses in Bury because of the
pleasantness of the place'.[85] In 1673 Richard Blome thought that 'the
scituation of the Town [Bury] is exceeding pleasant, ... in an Air as much
famed as any in England, which draws the Gentry thither from several
distant places'.[86] In 1698 Celia Fiennes briefly noted that 'there are a great
deale of Gentry which lives in the town' of Bury.[87] In 1722 Daniel Defoe
said that Bury was 'the Town of all this Part of England, in proportion
to its bigness, most thronged with Gentry, People of the best Fashion, and
the most polite Conversation'. Indeed, Defoe eulogised about Bury, calling
it 'The Montpelier of Suffolk, and perhaps of England'. Like Candler and
Blome he seemed to think that the 'pleasant Situation and wholesome Air'
caused Bury to be 'crouded with Nobility and Gentry'. As regards Ipswich,
Defoe thought that 'there are not so many of the Gentry here as at Bury',
but he hastened to add that 'there are more here than in any other Town
in the County'[88] Perhaps Ipswich had fewer gentry than had Bury because

the latter catered more successfully for the gentry's tastes. By the early Georgian period Bury had become a popular gentry leisure centre, with its assembly rooms, playhouse or theatre, and special October fairs which were attended by the Dukes of Norfolk,[89] the Fitzroys of Euston, the Herveys of Ickworth, the Cornwallises of Brome and Culford, the Cullums of Hardwick, and the Bunburys of Mildenhall and Great Barton.[90]

The Suffolk gentry increased their social control over villages and small towns as well as over the larger urban centres. MacCulloch has observed that in 1525 '67 per cent of Suffolk communities apart from Bury and Ipswich lacked a resident gentleman or influential monastic house', and that in 1568 'the percentage of Suffolk communities without a resident gentleman was still 58 per cent'.[91] However, the situation had greatly changed by the reign of Charles II. In 1680 only 33 per cent of Suffolk communities had no resident gentry.[92] For the first time in history the majority of the population were living directly under the eye of one or more members of the ruling élite.

Did the Suffolk gentry rise economically and numerically as well as socially and politically? From an economic standpoint there is insufficient evidence to generalise. No one has yet made a detailed, statistical study of the economic fortunes of the Suffolk gentry in Tudor and Stuart times.[93] But the general impression is that many were prospering. This is suggested by their estate management and building activities.

The main sources[94] show that between the 1480s and 1620s ninety-five gentry houses (usually called 'halls') were built, re-built or substantially expanded.[95] This surely testifies to the affluence of the Suffolk gentry.[96] In the early and mid-Tudor period the new gentry – former London merchants and royal officials – were prominent in building large country houses. Sir Thomas Kitson of the Merchant Adventurers Company, and Sheriff of London in 1533, built Hengrave Hall between 1525 and 1538 at a cost of £3,500.[97] Edmund, son of Paul Withipoll, merchant tailor of London, built the huge Christchurch Mansion in Ipswich in 1548–50 for an unknown sum.[98] Thomas Lucas, Solicitor-General to Henry VII, built the house of Little Saxham between 1505 and 1514 at a total cost of £1,425. Sir Nicholas Bacon, solicitor to the Court of Augmentations, built the now lost house of Redgrave Hall from 1545 to 1554 costing £1,253.[99] More examples of outsiders building houses in Suffolk and settling down as country gentlemen could be cited. But this would create a false impression. London merchants and officials formed a very small minority of those who built gentry houses in Suffolk. Far more typical were the native gentry, a few of whose names may be mentioned. George Mannock of Bures built Gifford's Hall near Stoke-by-Nayland during the reigns of Henry VII and Henry VIII. Robert Gosnold had Otley Hall built around 1500. Lionel Tollemache had Helmingham Hall – 'a grand and lovable house' – built for his family about the same year. These last three houses were a combination of brick and

Hengrave Hall
(Engraved by W. Wallis from a sketch by T. Higham in *Excursions*, I, p. 74)
This Hall was built in brick and stone *c.* 1525–38 for Thomas Kitson, a rich London
merchant. The ornate bay window above the main doorway was probably the work of
William Ponyard in 1538. John Wilbye, England's finest madrigal writer, was resident
musician from 1592 to 1628. In 1674 Hengrave was the largest house in Suffolk with 51
hearths.

Christchurch Mansion, Ipswich
(Engraved by E. Roberts from a drawing by T. Higham in *Excursions*, I, p. 124)
This mansion was re-built in 1548–50 in diaper brickwork by Edmund Withipoll, son of
Paul, a London merchant, on the site of the Augustinian Priory of Holy Trinity,
founded in *c.* 1177. The buildings were on the familiar E-plan, and the projecting wings
resembled other contemporary gentry mansions, such as Kentwell Hall, Melford Hall
and Rushbrooke Hall.

Otley Hall
(Photograph: S.R.O. (I), K400/G/25)
Otley Hall, built *c.* 1500 and enlarged in 1612, is timber-framed with red-brick nogging.
It has some beautiful oak panelling and was formerly the residence of the Gosnold
family. The most famous member was Bartholemew Gosnold (d. 1607), the explorer,
who discovered Cape Cod and founded Jamestown, Virginia. Also important was the
Royalist, Colonel Robert Gosnold, who was heavily fined and forced to sell much
property after the First Civil War.

Helmingham Hall
(Drawn and engraved by T. Higham in *Excursions*, I, p. 189)
Helmingham Hall is the largest moated house in Suffolk. Erected *c.* 1500 by Lionel
Tollemache, it was built of brick and timber-frame. The Hall has been remodelled since,
though it retains its early Tudor courtyard plan. The Tollemaches were not very active
politically during our period, except General Thomas Tollemache who died at Brest in
1694, serving William III.

timber-frame. During the Elizabethan and Jacobean periods there is still limited evidence of housebuilding by newcomers to Suffolk but considerable information on the building activities of the native gentry. Four examples will suffice. The wealthy Waldegrave family of Bures had Smallbridge Hall built before or about 1572. Two years later Robert Rookwood of Stanning-field built Coldham Hall, H-shaped, of red brick. Michael Hare rebuilt Bruisyard Hall around 1610. John Sulyard built the present mellow red-brick house in Haughley Park about 1620.[100]

Housebuilding aroused the interest of Robert Reyce. He noticed particu-larly the changing styles of building during the sixteenth century. Referring to the 'mansions and dwelling houses' of the Suffolk gentry, he said that 'I find [them] to be differing from them of the former times' which were 'ever environed with a broad and deep ditch or moat'. Moreover, 'these houses were alwayes built low nott with many rooms or aboue one or two storyes'. But, by contrast, 'our buildings at this day' [c. 1603], 'whither' [built] with 'brick, stone or timber', were 'raised high comonly with 3 and often with 4 stories'.[101]

So much for the buildings of the Suffolk gentry. What about their estate management? Robert Reyce said in 1603 that 'there bee many [gentry] which with a very wise and wary foresight doe much yearly improve and increase their estates'.[102] For an example of a prospering gentry family, take the Bacons of Redgrave. Sir Nicholas Bacon, the Lord Keeper, twice doubled the rents of Rickinghall Inferior before his death in 1578. In 1546 he raised the rents of the demesnes from £15 to £29. He doubled the rents again in 1570, creating a permanent hedge against inflation. His successors continued his rent raising policy and on their estates of Mettingham, near Bungay, their income from leases rose from £112 in 1578–79 to £702 in the early 1640s, a sixfold increase. Sir John Cornwallis, a royal courtier, was another enterprising landlord. The yield of his ten Suffolk manors increased over two and a half times, from £199 to £513 between 1558 and 1595.[103] In the early seventeenth century there also seem to have been many business-like gentry in Suffolk, according to Professor Alan Everitt. 'There were probably many families, like the Rouses of Henham, who owed their wealth to the export of Suffolk cheeses in scores and hundreds to Calais, Boulogne, and Berwick for the royal armies, or to London and the Low Countries in time of peace'. The Barnardistons of Kedington were also enterprising land-owners. 'Every week Sir Nathaniel Barnardiston or his son Sir Thomas might be seen in the market-place at Haverhill or Clare. Their purchases took them to fairs in London' and in many of the eastern counties. Furthermore, the Barnardistons were enterprising in commerce as well as in agriculture. 'All five brothers of Sir Thomas Barnardiston were merchants: Nathaniel, Samuel and Arthur in London and Pelatia and William in Turkey'.[104] However, let us end on a note of caution. Not all Suffolk landowners were business-like. Reyce remarked that 'others' were 'nott so

Smallbridge Hall
(Photograph: S.R.O. (I), K478/20)
Smallbridge Hall, in Bures St Mary, was the home of the Waldegrave family from *c.* 1380–1700, and was a large new house when Elizabeth I visited in 1578. The new house was a brick building, erected before or *c.* 1572 by the Waldegraves. During the First Civil War Sir William Waldegrave (d. 1648) was a passive Anglican Royalist.

Haughley Park
(Engraved by J. Greig from a drawing by Lady Jerningham in *Excursions,* I, p. 168)
This small, red-brick house in Haughley Park was built *c.* 1620 by John Sulyard, yet with its E-plan, crow-stepped gables and octagonal chimneys it is typical of an Elizabethan house. The manor and park remained in the hands of the Sulyard family until 1811. The family's Roman Catholicism continued for almost as long.

Kentwell Hall
(Photograph by kind permission of Patrick Phillips)
Kentwell is a red-brick Tudor house surrounded by a moat and consisting of a centre and two far-projecting wings. William Clopton, lord of Kentwell (1541–1562), was probably the builder of the present Hall. The Clopton family failed in the male line in 1641. Kentwell is today renowned for its Award-Winning Re-Creations of Tudor life.

provident' and 'doe become depressed with the alternate vicissitude of this world, and so are inforced to suffer a revolution'.[105] In short, Suffolk, like most counties, had its declining as well as its rising gentry.

Numerically, the gentry expanded during the early modern period, both nationally and locally. It has been recently argued that in England between 1524 and the end of the seventeenth century gentry numbers multiplied 'four times over while the population at large rather more than doubled'.[106] In Suffolk, too, gentry numbers greatly increased, as Table 2.3 suggests.

Table 2.3 The gentry population of Suffolk 1520s–1670s

	1520s	1603	1642	1670s
Estimated total population of Suffolk [107]	90,000	108,000	125,000	125,000
Total No. of gentry families [108]	166 [109]	406 [110]	689 [111]	577 [112]
Total gentry population (using multiplier of 4.5 persons to a household) [113]	747	1,827	3,100	2,596
Gentry as a percentage of total population of Suffolk	0.8	1.7	2.5	2.0

Table 2.3 prompts five comments. First, the Suffolk gentry multiplied four times over between the 1520s and the outbreak of the First Civil War in 1642, though the population at large increased by only 38 per cent. So the Suffolk gentry had a better expansion record than the English gentry as a whole. Second, the number of gentry families given for the 1520s is a gross underestimate because of the inadequacy and limitations of the sources. However, the trend is clear. The gentry greatly expanded during the Tudor and early Stuart period before declining during the later seventeenth century. Third, the most expansionist period was the mid and late Tudor period when the gentry more than doubled. It is therefore no surprise that Robert Reyce, writing in 1603, should say that 'I find that number of Suffolk Gentlemen as great as any other places or shires'.[114] Reyce, of course, exaggerated. Some counties in 1600 had more gentry families than Suffolk (e.g. Kent, Lancashire and Yorkshire[115]). Moreover, in about 1580 neighbouring Norfolk boasted 'at least 424 gentlemen',[116] eighteen more than in Suffolk.[117] Fourth, the number of Suffolk gentry families peaked in 1642 at 689.[118] This was indeed the golden age of the Suffolk gentry. Finally, we should note the much smaller number of gentry families in the 1670s. The numerical decline of the gentry in the later seventeenth century was not peculiar to Suffolk, however. Decline was also evident in Lancashire, Huntingdonshire and in Cumberland and Westmorland.[119] It is hard to explain the disappearance of so many gentry families. But 'the Civil War was a period of particular difficulty for landlords', involving as it did high taxation and 'the dislocation of marketing systems'. After 1664 landlords were forced to adjust to 'a long-term stagnation of agricultural prices', while rents were 'ill paid'.[120]

Between 1603 and 1642 198 families left, but 481 families joined, the Suffolk gentry. From where did the new families draw their recruits? It is hard to say. But since only sixty (12 per cent) of these 481 families were town dwellers, it seems reasonable to assume that most of them may have risen on the profits of yeoman farming. Such would have been the opinion of Robert Reyce, who said that from the rising yeomen 'are derived many noble [i.e. gentry] and worthy families'.[121]

The Yeomanry

Thomas Fuller succinctly described the yeomen as a rural group 'living in the temperate zone betwixt greatnesse and want'.[122] Although their economic condition might vary from county to county and even within counties, they undoubtedly belonged to the 'middle sort of men'. Historians are generally agreed that the yeomen were mostly prosperous farmers. Certainly in Suffolk they seem to have been affluent. Robert Reyce thought that at the end of Elizabeth I's reign the yeomen of Suffolk were the one really flourishing group: their 'continuall vnder living, saving, and the immunities from costly charge of these vnfaithfull times, do make them so to grow with the wealth of this world, that whilest many of the better sort [the gentry] ... do suffer an vtter declination, these [the yeomen] only doe arise ...' [123]

Statistical and documentary evidence supports contemporary comment. Nesta Evans, in her case-study of the nine parishes of South Elmham between 1550 and 1650, says that the detailed evidence of wills and probate inventories reveals 'a high standard of living' among the yeomen. She emphasises that the South Elmham parishes 'lay almost in the centre of the wood-pasture region of East Anglia, an area characterised by a large yeoman class who were wealthy without necessarily having a large acreage'. [124]

So much for the wealth of the Suffolk yeomanry. What about their numbers and distribution? This question is perhaps best answered by a thorough study of Wendy Goult's three volume *Survey of Suffolk Parish History* (Suffolk County Council, 1990). This detailed reference work identifies the wood-pasture and sheep-corn parishes of the county and lists the occupations of their inhabitants, giving, *inter alia*, the numbers of yeomen and husbandmen during the sixteenth and seventeenth centuries. Table 2.4, based on this work, shows that the yeomen undoubtedly rose at the expense of the husbandmen. [125]

Table 2.4 Social status of Suffolk farmers 1500–1699

	Wood-pasture parishes [126]			Sheep-corn parishes [127]		
	Yeo.	*Husb.*	*Total*	*Yeo.*	*Husb.*	*Total*
1500–49	102(36%)	182(64%)	284(100%)	36(28%)	91(72%)	127(100%)
1550–99	1,009(53%)	899(47%)	1,908(100%)	369(45%)	443(55%)	812(100%)
1600–49	2,606(77%)	798(23%)	3,404(100%)	962(66%)	491(34%)	1,453(100%)
1650–99	2,376(86%)	381(14%)	2,757(100%)	880(83%)	179(17%)	1,059(100%)

Note: In the Fenland parish of Lakenheath thirty-one yeomen and forty-nine husbandmen are recorded between 1500 and 1699.

The numbers given in Table 2.4 are not large and can only represent a small proportion of the farmers of Suffolk. Nevertheless, the trend is clear. The yeomen greatly expanded, especially during the seventeenth century.

Just as important as the numbers of yeomen is their geographical distribution. Contemporaries thought that the yeomen were conspicuous in High Suffolk (predominantly wood-pasture country). Richard Blome said in 1673 that 'High-Suffolk, or the Wood-land, is chiefly the seat of the Yeomanry, few being there either very rich, or very poor'. [128] About 1600 the anonymous Chorographer noted the '*very many* yeomen of good credit' in High Suffolk. [129] Moreover, Table 2.4 shows that almost three-quarters of the yeomen lived in wood-pasture parishes. Yet, except in the early Tudor period, the numbers of yeomen in the sheep-corn parishes of Suffolk are not insignificant. Indeed, during the seventeenth century these yeomen had overwhelming majorities over the husbandmen (see Table 2.4).

It is hard to explain the (surprisingly) strong yeoman presence in the sheep-corn parishes. But the reasons for the prosperity and numerical importance of the yeomen in the wood-pasture areas are not far to seek. First, they greatly benefited from the rise of dairy farming. The phenomenal growth of London's population during the early modern period caused a huge demand for the dairy products of High Suffolk. Second, the yeomen of the Waveney Valley were enriched by its flourishing dual economy in the seventeenth century. Many yeomen and others were not only dairy farmers but also linen weavers. In short, they had two occupations and two sources of income.[130] Third, many yeomen seem to have enjoyed favourable land tenure, holding their property either as freeholders or as copyholders of inheritance.

Freeholders had absolute security of tenure, and their chief rents, fixed centuries earlier, were nominal and unalterable. Their labour costs rose during the sixteenth century but wages lagged well behind their selling-prices. In Tudor times Suffolk probably had more freeholders than almost any other English county.[131] R. H. Tawney, analysing a sample of manors with 6,203 tenants, taken from eleven counties, found that the proportion of freeholders was highest in Suffolk. In these counties as a whole freeholders constituted 20 per cent of tenants, but in Suffolk they formed 50 per cent.[132] In 1561 in the Geldable region of Suffolk there were 1,292 freeholders, of whom one was a peer (Thomas Lord Wentworth of Nettlestead), 102 (8 per cent) were gentry, and 1,189 (92 per cent) were non-gentry.[133] That there were very many freeholders in Suffolk is undeniable. But how many freeholders were yeomen and, more importantly, how many yeomen were freeholders? It is impossible to say, but Julian Cornwall has convincingly argued that in Babergh hundred in 1525 four-fifths of yeomen were free-holders.[134]

Copyhold of inheritance was the most usual form of customary tenure in eastern England, and it gave greater security than did any other kind of copyhold. Not only were these copyholds heritable, but money rents were almost always fixed by manorial custom and fines were limited.[135] It is impossible to say how many Suffolk yeomen were copyholders of inheritance. But Nesta Evans found that in South Elmham the yeomen tenanted the greater part of the copyhold land.[136] Yeomen freeholders and yeoman copyholders had much in common. From the 1540s onwards they not only enjoyed security but were in the happy position of having relatively fixed expenses and steadily rising selling-prices. No wonder these Suffolk yeomen prospered.

The Husbandman

Husbandmen were in status one rank below the yeomanry. They were mostly, though not entirely, the poorer farmers. Reyce thought that life was hard for the husbandman. 'Though hee thriveth ordinarily well, yett he laboreth much'. Also 'the husbandman before hee can tast the fruits of his labour endureth much travel' [hard work].[137] Table 2.4 shows that numerically the husbandmen were expanding in the sixteenth century but greatly declining in the following century, especially after 1650. It is possible that some husbandmen were rising into the ranks of the yeomen, for 'compared with other parts of England, such as Oxfordshire, the term husbandman was much less commonly used in Suffolk'.[138] However, it is more likely that many were declining into the ranks of 'the poore'. Reyce gives no indication that the husbandmen were affluent. How could they have been when only a minority enjoyed security of tenure? Julian Cornwall has observed that in Babergh hundred in 1525 only about 40 per cent of them had freehold tenure.[139]

The Townes-man

Reyce seems to regard the typical 'Townes-man' as a trader of mixed fortunes. 'His trade of all sorts of diversities, which hee, fetcheth from London and other such places' enabled him 'in short time' to 'climeth to much creditt and wealth'. But Reyce thought that 'riches ... hastily got-ten ... can abide noe induring continuance' and that the trader experienced 'first decay' and 'then poverty too ...'[140] In short, Reyce implies that trade is a risky business, a view endorsed by modern historians. Professor Palliser has argued that in the later sixteenth century 'trade remained a very uncertain means of profit compared to land, for the former might yield a very high return or might fail altogether'.[141] As we have seen, trade and industry in Suffolk had mixed fortunes during our period.[142]

The Poore

Historians are divided as to the numbers and economic state of the poor in Tudor and Stuart England. Professor Palliser says that 'only a relatively small number of the population depended wholly upon wages' in Tudor times, and that 'there is little evidence of rural poverty on a large scale', though he admits that 'the system [of poor relief] broke down in towns'.[143] But Dr Keith Wrightson argues that 'population pressure and agrarian change produced both an absolute and relative increase in the wage dependent population' and that 'the life of the labourer was a constant battle for survival'.[144]

Both Palliser and Wrightson link poverty with wage-earning. Here they resemble a number of contemporary commentators. Thomas Wilson thought that some 'Copyholders and Cottagers' were 'poore' and lived 'cheefly upon contry labor workeing by the day for meat and drink and some small wages'.[145] But Dr John Pound, who has studied thoroughly the problem of poverty in one clothing area of early Tudor Suffolk, Babergh hundred, with the aid of the 1522 Muster Roll, does not find any neat equation between labourers and the poor. He shows that 28 per cent of the population of Babergh were labourers in 1522,[146] but says that under normal circumstances only 10 per cent 'lived in conditions of extreme poverty'.[147] Moreover, he adds that 'a poor man was not necessarily a destitute man'.[148] Pound is perhaps too sanguine about the extent of poverty in Babergh,[149] but some other historians have gone to the other extreme. Two Belgian scholars, Lis and Soly, have said that by the third decade of the sixteenth century 87 per cent of the inhabitants of Babergh hundred 'lived at or beneath the poverty line'.[150] This would seem to be a gross exaggeration.

Robert Reyce has a fair amount to say about the 'poore' in Suffolk. He distinguishes between the deserving poor – those 'poore by impotence or by casualty' – and 'the thriftles poore, whither hee be riotous, idle person, or vagabond', and he hopes that the 'late godly lawes' [the Poor Laws of 1597 and 1601] will 'so reform the quality of them, or diminish the number of them'. Reyce locates the worst regions of poverty. In 'those parts of this shire, where clothiers doe dwell or have dwelled, there are found the greatest number of the poor'. He seems to be referring to the textile manufacturing parts of south-west Suffolk. But in the linen manufacturing parts of the county he believed 'there are nothing so many poor'.[151]

Reyce was commenting on poverty at the beginning of the seventeenth century. But it still existed, and in fact probably increased, from the 1670s. The Hearth Tax returns of 1674 give much evidence about the amount and distribution of poverty. The Hearth Taxes were levied twice yearly, from 1662 to 1689, at the rate of two shillings per hearth, and were paid by occupiers, not landlords. If poor, people could be exempted from payment. A map by Nesta Evans, in *An Historical Atlas of Suffolk*, shows the total number of persons (that is, heads of households) listed in most Suffolk parishes. Totals include taxpayers and those exempted from the tax on grounds of poverty. With a few exceptions, all the towns which have more than 50 per cent of listed persons excused payment of tax are either ports or in the clothing districts.[152] In 1673 Blome had in mind the south-west Suffolk clothing area when he referred to the '... *decaying trade*, ... in broadcloth'.[153] Many places on the coast were impoverished by the decline of the herring industry and boat building. Blome remarked that 'the coast has been eminent for the Fishing-trade but it is now miserably decayed'. He gives Orford as an example. 'It was in former time a Town of good account for fishing, but that trade being lost, the Town cannot find itself'.[154] But the worst affected coastal town was Dunwich where the proportion exempt from the Hearth Tax on grounds of poverty was the highest in Suffolk – 73 per cent.[155]

To conclude, we may say that Tudor and Stuart Suffolk was a socially unequal society which yet experienced considerable upward and downward mobility. The most obviously rising social groups were the gentry and the yeomen, whose numbers enormously increased, at least until the First Civil War. Certain groups declined. The nobility lost power in Suffolk with the execution of the 4th Duke of Norfolk. The husbandmen greatly diminished in numbers, especially during the second half of the seventeenth century. There is a *prima facie* case for saying that the poor numerically increased during the seventeenth century because of the decay of the broadcloth industry and many east coast ports. The townsmen are a doubtful category and their rise or fall depended a lot on the economic fortunes of their particular town.

CHAPTER THREE

The Reformation in Suffolk from Henry VIII to Mary Tudor

The Protestant Reformation is arguably the most important event, or series of events, in pre-industrial Britain. Indeed, without the Reformation, it is hard to see how the Civil Wars of the 1640s and the Glorious Revolution of 1688–89 could have occurred. Later chapters will study the effects of these wars and the 'Glorious Revolution' on Suffolk. Meantime we must examine the impact of the Reformation on that county.

What was the Reformation? It was primarily a religious revolution in the sixteenth century which split the unity of Latin Christendom, set up national Protestant churches and sects, and led to religious wars. Both Protestants and Catholics [1] are agreed that the Reformation was a revolution, and Figure 1 illustrates, perhaps rather simplistically, most of the essential differences between the two religious groups.

The Reformation was sparked off by Martin Luther (1483–1546) in Germany in 1517, continued by Huldrich Zwingli (1484–1531) in Switzerland, and further advanced by John Calvin (1509–64), a Frenchman, in Geneva. Luther, Zwingli and Calvin were agreed about most Protestant doctrines and practices (e.g. Justification by Faith alone, the Bible as the basis of faith, and church services in the vernacular), but Zwingli rejected Luther's interpretation of the Eucharist, while Calvin was more extreme than either Luther or Zwingli on the question of predestination.[2] The fame of Martin Luther caught the imagination of some English followers in the 1520s. Churchmen, including Thomas Bilney (c. 1495–1531), Robert Barnes (d. 1540), and the Bible translator and controversialist William Tyndale (c. 1494–1536), reinterpreted the Reformation message. However, their support was confined to young Cambridge university students and merchants trading with the Low Countries and north Germany, and the Reformation arrived late in England.[3]

The Reformation is still a highly controversial subject – despite the ecumenical movement – and always will be while there are Protestants and Catholics. The best known advocate of the Protestant interpretation is Professor A. G. Dickens.[4] He has argued that discontent with Catholicism increased markedly in later medieval England, that devotional life was

CATHOLICS	PROTESTANTS

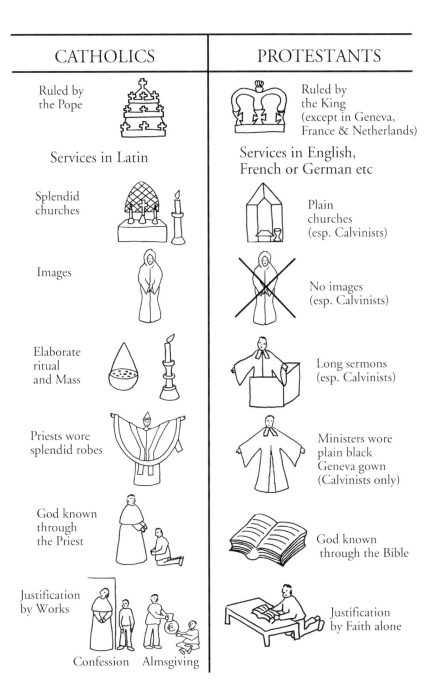

Ruled by the Pope

Ruled by the King (except in Geneva, France & Netherlands)

Services in Latin

Services in English, French or German etc

Splendid churches

Plain churches (esp. Calvinists)

Images

No images (esp. Calvinists)

Elaborate ritual and Mass

Long sermons (esp. Calvinists)

Priests wore splendid robes

Ministers wore plain black Geneva gown (Calvinists only)

God known through the Priest

God known through the Bible

Justification by Works

Justification by Faith alone

Confession   Almsgiving

Figure 1: The Reformation

characterised by much superstition (e.g. the cult of the saints), that Lollardy and anti-clericalism were widespread, and that consequently Protestantism rapidly won popular support and did not depend only on government initiative. Catholic historians, like Professors Scarisbrick and Duffy, and revisionists, such as Professor Haigh, have put forward diametrically opposed views.[5] The Catholic/revisionist argument is bluntly stated by Professor Scarisbrick on the first page of his book, *The Reformation and the English People.* 'English men and women did not want the Reformation and most of them were slow to accept it when it came'. It is contended by Scarisbrick, Duffy and Haigh that Catholicism was still flourishing on the eve of the English Reformation, and that this is shown by much church building or re-building, by the popularity of the religious guilds, and by the fact that 'the overwhelming majority of people still accepted the efficacy of the mass, prayers for the dead and the usefulness of veneration of saints'.[6] There was little opposition to the Catholic church, and Lollardy and anti-clericalism remained relatively rare. Consequently the progress of the Reformation in the sixteenth century was both difficult and slow. Protestantism lacked popular support not only in the north and west of England, but even in East Anglia.

It should be clear by now that the Reformation in England, let alone in Europe, is a vast subject. So for reasons of space this chapter will concentrate on just four topics concerning the Reformation in Suffolk: the condition of the late medieval church; the dissolution of the religious orders; the progress of Protestantism from *c.*1525 to 1558; and the early Protestants during those years.

The late medieval Church

Professor Patrick Collinson, a leading *Protestant* historian has conceded that 'early sixteenth-century English Catholicism was in many respects in a flourishing condition'.[7] Suffolk Catholicism, too, was 'in a flourishing condition', and this becomes clear when we study the parish churches, the religious guilds, the clergy and, to some extent, the Lollards.

The Parish Churches

'The parish church was the main focus of late medieval devotion: not the monasteries or the cathedrals'. It is difficult to disagree with this re-mark.[8] The parish church was the largest building in a village and many a town. Its tower was its arsenal; it displayed the village clock; and was also a political centre, where churchwardens and local officials were elected, church rates agreed and the upkeep of the church fabric and churchyard discussed. The parishioners took great pride in their local church, so it is not surprising that the fifteenth and early sixteenth centuries saw a con-siderable amount of building or re-building. Between a third and a half of the 10,000 or so parish churches in England were extensively rebuilt, normally in the magnificent Perpendicular style of Gothic architecture. In all parts of England, but particularly in the rich cloth-producing regions, church towers were built, naves enlarged and new aisles added. Many of these Perpendicular churches are nationally as well as locally famous. One only has to think of St Mary Redcliffe in Bristol, Manchester collegiate church (now the Cathedral), and some of the parish churches of the Cotswolds: Chipping Campden, Cirencester, Stow-on-the Wold. Suffolk, too, has many beautiful Perpendicular churches. Professor Eamon Duffy singles out the parish churches of Stoke-by-Nayland, Stoke-by-Clare, Southwold and Blythburgh, called 'The Cathedral of the Marshes'.[9] The last two, along with the churches of Lowestoft, Kessingland, Covehithe, Walberswick and Aldeburgh, are on the Suffolk coast and were built out of the profits of the fishing industry between the early fifteenth and early sixteenth centuries.[10]

Even more famous are the churches of the clothing towns and villages of south-west Suffolk. We have already mentioned Stoke-by-Clare and Stoke-by-Nayland, both described by Pevsner as 'large Perpendicular churches'. The building of Stoke-by-Nayland was financed by local merchants in 1439, 1440, 1441, etc., to 1462.[11] But by far the most famous late medieval churches in south-west Suffolk, indeed in the whole of Suffolk, are the Church of SS Peter and Paul, Lavenham, and the Church of the Holy Trinity, Long Melford. The latter was 'entirely rebuilt in the last half of the 15c, largely through the generosity and piety of the Clopton family'.[12] We shall describe this church more fully later. For the present a few words are needed about the parish church of Lavenham. With some exaggeration this church has been called 'one of the finest examples of Late Perpendicular in the world'.[13] It was clearly a late medieval church for, though the chancel had been constructed between 1330 and 1350, the tower, nave and aisles were built between 1486 and 1525.[14] Cautley has rightly emphasized that Lavenham Church was built 'largely through the interest and munificence of the Earl of Oxford and Thomas Spring, a rich clothier'.[15] The operative words here are 'interest' and 'munificence'. In short, piety as well as prosperity explains the extensive rebuilding of so many of the churches in late medieval Suffolk. As Professor Duffy reminds us, this building programme was 'an expression not simply of the bourgeois prosperity brought by the Suffolk wool trade, but the concern of rich graziers or cloth-merchants to use their wealth as post-mortem fire insurance'.[16]

Those leaving money to the Church were not all wealthy gentry or merchants, however. Many ordinary people also contributed. Professor MacCulloch discovered that nearly 90 per cent of Suffolk testators left something to the parish church in the half-century before the Reformation.[17] What Pevsner has called 'the Golden Age of church building in Suffolk'[18] can only have been an age of deep Catholic piety. As Professor

Church of SS Peter and Paul, Lavenham
(Drawn and engraved by T. Higham in *Excursions*, I, p. 46)
One of the glories of Suffolk, and indeed of England, this outstanding church is largely
late Perpendicular. It was re-built between 1486 and 1525, and funded mainly by profits
from the cloth industry. Inside the church the chantry chapels of the main benefactors,
the de Veres and the Springs, are the chief attraction.

Lander has said, 'People do not spend vast sums of money upon institutions of which they profoundly disapprove'.[19]

So much for church building. What about church furnishings and worship? We know something about those aspects of late medieval religion thanks to an important work by Roger Martin (*c.* 1527–1615), a gentleman of Long Melford and a Catholic recusant in the reign of Elizabeth I.[20] It was probably in the 1580s or '90s that Martin wrote nostalgically about *The State of Melford Church as I, Roger Martyn, did know it*, in which he lovingly recalls the church decorations, devotional equipment and seasonal rituals that were lost from his parish church of Long Melford in the course of the Reformation. He remembered from his childhood in the 1530s the images and furnishings of Melford Church and especially the chancel and the south aisle, 'called Jesus Ile',[21] where his own family had their burial place. He describes the roodloft and screen. Standing high in the roodloft was a large cross or 'rood' depicting the Crucifixion of Christ. The cross was flanked by images of the Virgin Mary and St John the Evangelist. On the front of the loft, facing the congregation, were paintings of the twelve Apostles. The roodloft and screen separated the chancel, where the clergy

Church of the Holy Trinity, Long Melford
(Engraved by J. Greig from a sketch by T. Higham in *Excursions*, I, p. 56)
This fine Perpendicular church, which has the proportions of a cathedral, was re-built
between *c.* 1460 and *c.* 1495. The nave was extended, porches and chantry chapels were
added, culminating in construction of the Lady Chapel. The main feature of the church
is its length, 250 feet. The building was largely funded by the profits of the cloth trade.
The greatest benefactor of the Church was John Clopton, whose descendants built
Kentwell Hall.

officiated, from the nave, where the laity were accommodated. Martin also
describes the sepulchre frame set up each year within John Clopton's great
Easter Sepulchre-cum-tomb in the north side of the chancel.[22] Martin
recalled the elaborate, carved tabernacles[23] on either side of the high altar
(where the Latin mass was celebrated) and the gilded carving of Christ's
Passion above the same altar.[24]

   Martin fondly remembered the festivals of the church's year and his
account of them shows how elaborate was late medieval worship. On Palm
Sunday,[25] for instance, the parishioners of Long Melford would solemnly
parade the 'Blessed Sacrament'[26] around their churchyard, with bell-ringing
and singing, and would kneel to adore it. On Corpus Christi 'they went
likewise with the Blessed Sacrament, in procession about the Church Green,
in copes'. Martin also recalled St Mark's day and the Rogation days, when
the litanies were sung and the parish processed with handbells and banners
'about the bounds of the town', each day's march culminating in communal
drinking.[27]

   It must be remembered that Long Melford was a very large church – a
sort of 'village cathedral' – in a prosperous clothing area and may have had

Long Melford, Holy Trinity Church tower (Photograph: A. Hodge) This is a modern view of the church tower. It was struck by lightning and set on fire in Queen Anne's reign. Its successor (1725) was brick-work. The height of the tower is now 118 feet, smaller than that of Lavenham Church.

Long Melford, Holy Trinity, south porch (Photograph: A.Hodge) This was the main entrance to the church. It may formerly have been much more ornate. At various times the Reformation put an end to much colouring, illumination and carved work.

more decorations and devotional equipment than most Suffolk churches. It certainly had more than Cratfield. The church inventory of Long Melford for 1529 included thirteen silver and gilt chalices, eleven mass books, fifty-eight altar cloths, twenty-seven antiphoners, graduals and processionals, and at least twenty corpasses.[28] By contrast, the church inventory of Cratfield for 1528 included only five silver and gilt chalices, four mass books, thirty-two altar cloths, thirteen antiphoners, graduals and processionals and seven corpasses.[29] That Cratfield had far less devotional equipment than Long Melford is not really surprising; it was after all just a small agricultural village. But considering it size,[30] Cratfield had a large supply of church goods and can be regarded as a fairly typical Suffolk parish. As for Long Melford, it was not so much an exception as an extreme case of what existed elsewhere in Suffolk.[31]

Religious guilds

After the parish, with its churches and chapels, the most important of the Catholic institutions open to laymen was the religious guild or fraternity. Professor Scarisbrick has defined a fraternity as 'an association of layfolk who, under the patronage of a particular saint, the Trinity, Blessed Virgin Mary, Corpus Christi or similar, undertook to provide the individual member of the brotherhood with a good funeral ... together with regular prayer and mass-saying thereafter for the repose of the dead person's soul'.[32]

Hadleigh Church and Deanery Tower
(Engraved by W. Deeble from a drawing by T. Higham in *Excursions*, I, p. 53)
Dominating the town of Hadleigh is the large parish church of St Mary, alongside which stands the Deanery Tower, built in 1494 by Archdeacon William Pykenham as a gateway to a great house never built. The strong clerical presence did not prevent Hadleigh from being second only to Lavenham among Suffolk cloth towns in 1500.

The Corpus Christi guildhall, Lavenham
(Photograph: A. Hodge)

The market place of Lavenham is dominated by the guildhall of the Guild of Corpus
Christi, built shortly after the foundation of this religious guild in 1529. It had a splendid
porch, varied and diversely decorated. The guildhall is one of the finest Tudor
half-timbered buildings in the country and arguably the most famous in Suffolk.

Whereas every Christian was compelled by canon law to attend his parish
church on Sundays and festivals, membership of the confraternities was
entirely voluntary, but eagerly sought.[33] The religious guilds were extremely
numerous in Suffolk and testify to the strength of religious orthodoxy in
the county. Peter Northeast has identified around 500 fraternities. However,
his map in *An Historical Atlas of Suffolk* shows that they were rather un-
evenly distributed. 'The majority of parishes in West Suffolk certainly had
gilds; most parishes in the north-east of the county also had gilds, but
conspicuously few in the south-east'.[34] It is clearly wrong, then, to say that
each parish had a fraternity. Some parishes, like Aldeburgh, Euston and
Mendham, apparently had no guilds, while others, not always the largest,
had several. Boxford parish had four guilds in 1522: St Peter, St John, the
Trinity and St Christopher.[35] Lavenham also had four: SS Peter and Paul,
Our Lady Mary, Holy Trinity and Corpus Christi.[36] Long Melford had
five: Trinity, Bachelor's, Our Lady Mary, St Peter and Jesus.[37] A large town
like Bury St Edmunds had as many as seventeen guilds in 1389.[38] From
the late fourteenth century religious guilds became very numerous and
reached their peak in the early sixteenth century. This was when a number
of timber-framed guildhalls were built in Suffolk:[39] Debenham (1500), Eye
(early *c.* 16), Hitcham (*c.* 1500), Kelsale (*c.* 1500), Laxfield (*c.* 1519) and, most
famous of all, the Corpus Christi guildhall in Lavenham (*c.* 1529).[40]

The guildhall of Hadleigh
(Photograph: S.R.O. (I), K443/62)
The timber-framed guildhall of Hadleigh – one of the oldest in Suffolk – is a tall
three-storeyed jettied building of the 1430s, with lower wings added a little later and a
rear wing of about 1460 where the town's five religious guilds met.

The main functions of the religious guilds, or fraternities, were mutual charity, general sociability (including food and drink) and religious celebrations. The religious functions were considerably more important than the social. The fraternities satisfied devout lay people who were unable to withdraw from the secular world. Their popularity can hardly be exaggerated. Thus the guild of St Peter, Bardwell, had a membership which comprised most of the adult population of the village.[41]

The religious fraternities may have been popular partly because they could hire and fire their priests and could admit women as full members in their own right and not just as wives. But despite this growing lay control, the religious guilds in Suffolk and elsewhere did *not* prepare the way for the Reformation. As Scarisbrick says, 'the theology on which the religious guild rested and which was its *raison d'être* (belief in Purgatory, the sacrificial efficacy of the mass, veneration of saints) was the very antithesis of Protestantism'.[42]

The clergy

In the half-century before the Reformation the clergy seem to have displayed high standards of morality and commitment. Christopher Haigh has argued that 'there is very little evidence that the conduct of the [English] clergy was worse than it had been in earlier centuries and a good deal to suggest that it was much better'.[43] Certainly in Suffolk there was little reason to be dissatisfied. At Cardinal Morton's visitation of Suffolk in 1499, from 489 parishes there were only eight allegations of sexual laxity against priests, and only two priests were suspended for their ignorance. Forty-eight incumbents were found to be absent from their benefices, but in all but two cases they had appointed appropriate deputies and there was no suggestion of pastoral neglect.[44] It is not surprising, then, that there was little anti-clericalism in Suffolk. The parish clergy in the diocese of Norwich (which included Suffolk) were set a good example by some of the higher clergy. Richard Nix, Bishop of Norwich from 1501 to 1535, has been described as 'among the best of late medieval bishops – resident, energetic and conscientious'.[45]

The most famous Suffolk cleric was, of course, Cardinal Thomas Wolsey. Reputedly the son of an Ipswich butcher, he was Archbishop of York from 1514 to 1530, Lord Chancellor from 1515 to 1529, a cardinal from 1515 until his death in 1530, and papal legate from 1518. Holding such a variety of posts simultaneously, he was extremely powerful both in Church *and* State. Wolsey has acquired a bad reputation. But this is quite undeserved. True, he was ostentatious, arrogant and a pluralist.[46] Yet Wolsey was also something of a religious reformer. His aim was to produce a better-trained and better-disciplined clergy. He concerned himself with the morals of parish priests, the duties of incumbents and selection of deputies for absentees. Wolsey made further attempts at reform by legislation. He tried to regulate the behaviour of sanctuary men in 1519, and in the same year he obtained sweeping powers from Rome for the reform of the secular clergy. He also attempted to reform the religious orders. The Augustinian canons were given new constitutions in 1519, the Benedictines had new statutes in 1522, and in 1525 he embarked on a more systematic rationalisation of monasteries.[47] Altogether Wolsey dissolved twenty-nine English religious houses,[48] his aim being to use their revenues to build a new college at Oxford, to be called Cardinal College (later Christ Church), and to build a grammar school with the same name in Ipswich. Wolsey particularly hoped that his college at

Thomas Wolsey (1475?–1530) by an unknown artist.
As a Cardinal (1515–30) and statesman, Wolsey has acquired a reputation for worldliness and ostentation. But he was also a church reformer and generous benefactor.

Wolsey's Gate, Ipswich
(Engraved by J. Greig
from a drawing by
T. Higham in
Excursions, I, p. 133)
This gateway is all that
remains of the Cardinal
College of St Mary
founded by Wolsey in
1527 after the dissolution
of the Priory of SS Peter
and Paul. When Wolsey
fell from power in 1529,
the college was
demolished. Its
completion would
almost certainly have
brought immense
prestige to Ipswich.

Oxford would produce a better educated clergy and 'be the engine room for reform of the English Church'.[49]

The Lollards

The Lollards were followers of John Wycliffe (*c.* 1329–84), Master of Balliol College, Oxford (1360), who denounced clerical wealth and privilege and attacked Catholic fundamentals, such as papal authority, confession, transubstantiation and monasticism. When Wycliffe was forced to withdraw from Oxford the Lollards[50] took his ideas to a wider audience. Their belief that Holy Scripture was divinely inspired and should be accessible to everyone resulted in the Lollard Bible, an English translation made in the 1390s. But Church and State retaliated and in 1401 Henry IV's Statute *De Heretico Comburendo* introduced death by burning for heresy and in 1407 the Lollard Bible was banned. After Sir John Oldcastle's abortive revolt (1414) and death (1417), the Lollards lost upper class support and relied mainly on the support of local artisans and yeoman farmers. But Lollardy survived as an underground movement, with its own priests, schoolmasters and literature.

How much support did the Lollards obtain in Suffolk? Very little compared with that received in London, Bristol, Coventry, Essex, Kent and the Chilterns.[51] However, the East Anglian Lollards were taken very seriously by William Alnwick, Bishop of Norwich (from 1425 to 1436), who prosecuted sixty men and women for heresy between 1428 and 1431.[52] Of those accused sixteen were from Suffolk and the rest from Norfolk. But the overwhelming majority lived in or near the Waveney valley.[53] This valley, at the junction of the two counties, Norfolk and Suffolk, was suspected of Lollardism, of which Earsham and Loddon in the former county, and Beccles and Bungay in the latter, were considered the chief centres. The heresy trials were mostly held in the Bishop's Palace in Norwich. The accused eventually made submission, formally abjuring their views after a most solemn fashion. In abjuring, the defendants stated very clearly what their Lollard beliefs had once been.

Devotion to the saints had been attacked by Richard Fleccher of Beccles, who said that 'every prayer shuld oonly be made unto God, and to noon other seynt'. John Skylly of Flixton, miller, when abjuring, admitted that he had said that 'prayers shuld be maad unto no seynt in hevene, but oonly to God'. John Eldon of Beccles, glover, had made a very similar remark about praying to saints. Venerating images had been denounced by Suffolk Lollards. Richard Fleccher had wanted all images 'to be destroied and do away'. John Skylly admitted that he had 'affirmed and taght that … no maner of worship owith to be do unto ony ymages of the crucifix, of Our Lady or of ony other seyntes'. Some Lollards, like John Kynget (of Nayland or Needham Market?) had stated that 'no pilgrimage oweth to be mad but only to poure peple'. John Reve of Beccles, glover, had linked pilgrimages with veneration of saints. 'No maner of pilgrimage oweth to doo to ony places of seyntes but only to pore peple'. Papal authority had likewise been attacked by Suffolk Lollards. John Skylly, Richard Fleccher, John Reve and John Eldon had all remarked that 'the pope of Rome is Anticrist'. Most serious of all, several of the Suffolk defendants had denied transubstantiation. John Eldon had said 'that no prest hath poar to make Goddys body in the sacrament of the auter, and that aftir the sacramental word is said of the prest at messe ther remayneth nothing but oonly a cake of material bred'. John Skylly, Richard Fleccher and John Reve had objected in similar terms.[54]

In their attack on prayers to saints, veneration of images, pilgrimages, papal authority and transubstantiation the Suffolk Lollards resembled the sixteenth-century Protestants. Professor Conrad Russell has indeed said that 'Lollards anticipated Protestants in almost all their key beliefs except the central Lutheran belief in Justification by Faith, which held all the rest together'.[55] But in one respect Lollards actually went further than Protestants; they questioned all seven sacraments.[56] Protestants, however, accepted Baptism and the Eucharist as sacraments.

After the Norwich heresy trials we hear little about Lollardy in Suffolk during the rest of the fifteenth century. But early in the next century, 'before the Lutheran explosion', three Suffolk Lollards were burnt at the stake for their beliefs: one man from Bungay in 1511 and between 1512 and 1515 two more from Eye and Earl Stonham.[57] These were a tiny minority, however. If we take the period 1400–1520 as a whole, we are perhaps justified in saying that East Anglia, and especially Suffolk, was not a Lollard stronghold.

Nevertheless, we would be wrong to dismiss Lollardy out of hand. The outstanding feature of the heresy trials in Norwich diocese had been the extreme sacramentarian views of the accused. The Catholic Church was clearly very concerned that the laity should accept and not reject the seven sacraments. Hence between 1449 and 1510 fourteen Suffolk churches erected carved, octagonal stone fonts depicting the seven sacraments. In Norfolk twenty-five such fonts were built between about 1460 and 1544.[58] The seven-sacrament fonts were largely a Catholic response to Lollard repudiation of the sacramental system and were mostly situated near former centres of East Anglian Lollardy.[59] It is highly likely that these particular fonts strengthened religious orthodoxy because they were 'seeable', being situated in the most prominent part of the church immediately opposite the door by which the laity entered and left the building.

The Norwich heresy trials of 1428–31 and the erection of seven-sacrament fonts suggest that the undoubtedly few Lollards in Suffolk were influential out of all proportion to their numbers. Indeed some historians have argued that Lollards influenced the English Reformation.[60] But in Suffolk there appears to have been little link between Lollards and mainstream Protestants. True they had very similar beliefs but the latter were not direct descendants of the former. None of the Lollard surnames of 1428–31 appears in the list of early Protestants in Suffolk.[61] Nor did Suffolk Lollards provide, what Professor Dickens called, 'reception-areas for Lutheranism'.[62] Indeed, there is little sign that former Lollard centres (e.g. Beccles, Bungay) became Protestant strongholds before the reign of Elizabeth I.[63] There does, however, appear to be a superficial link between Lollardy and post-Civil War Nonconformity in Suffolk.[64] As K. B. McFarlane said, 'the heirs [of the Lollards] were not Anglicans, but Brownists and Independents'.[65]

The Henrician Reformation

> The English Reformation embraces a break from the Roman obedience; an assertion of secular control over the Church; a suppression of Catholic institutions such as monasteries and chantries; a prohibition of Catholic worship; and a protestantisation of services, clergy and laity.[66]

Few would disagree with Professor Haigh's clear summary. But Haigh would be the first to admit that the English Reformation was not a single movement. It is necessary, therefore, to distinguish between the Henrician Reformation and the Protestant Reformation. The former includes the break with Rome, lay domination of the Church and the suppression of the monasteries. The latter applies to the dissolution of the chantries, the prohibition of Catholic worship and the protestantisation of services, clergy and laity.

The Break with Rome

Many years ago Sir Maurice Powicke wrote: 'The one definite thing which can be said about the Reformation is that it was an act of state'.[67] More recently Diarmaid MacCulloch has endorsed this view. 'The English Reformation was the creation of the English monarchy, more an act of state than in any other part of Europe apart from Scandinavia'. It was, MacCulloch continues, 'the result of one man's obsessive quest for a male heir, rather than a nation's search for the way back to the Church of the Apostles'.[68] To produce a male heir Henry VIII wished to 'divorce' Catherine of Aragon and marry Anne Boleyn. But Cardinal Wolsey was unable to persuade Pope Clement VII to annul Henry's marriage to Catherine. Henry's solution was to break with the Catholic Church, and establish his own, the Church of England, with himself as its head. He would then be able to grant his own divorce.

Various Acts of Parliament set aside the Pope's authority in England. In 1533 the Act in Restraint of appeals (24 Hen. VIII, cap. 12) forbad appeals to Rome. In 1534 an Act for the Submission of the Clergy to the King's Majesty (25 Hen. VIII, cap. 19) gave the crown more control over the 'national' church. Also in the same year the following acts were passed. The Ecclesiastical Appointments Act (25 Hen. VIII cap. 20) stated that no one should be presented to the Pope for appointment. The Succession Act (25 Hen. VIII, cap. 22) settled the succession on the children of Anne Boleyn. The Act of Supremacy (26 Hen. VIII, cap. 1) stipulated that the King was to be 'the only Supreme Head on earth of the Church of England'. The Second Annates Act (26 Hen. VIII, cap. 3) stated that annates or first fruits, formerly given to the Pope, were now to be paid to the King.[69] Finally the Treason Act (26 Hen. VIII, cap. 13) ordered the death penalty for anyone who denied in words any dignity or title to the King, or who called him heretic, schismatic or tyrant.

By these acts Henry cast off papal jurisdiction and asserted his authority over the Church. Easily the most important piece of legislation was the Act of Supremacy, 1534. This statute not only conferred on Henry the title of 'Supreme Head of the Church of England' but granted him full power 'to repress, redress, reform … correct … and amend all errors, heresies, abuses, offences' whatsoever by '*spiritual authority*'.[70] To confer full spiritual authority on the secular prince was, says Professor Scarisbrick, 'a radical innovation'.[71] Indeed, no English medieval monarch had claimed the title of Supreme Head of the Church, or the right to decide its doctrine. No wonder Scarisbrick calls the English Reformation 'a momentous revolution'.[72]

Christopher Haigh has said that 'however slowly and unwillingly Henry had achieved his supremacy [over the Church], once he had it he found he rather liked it'.[73] Hence Henry would brook no opposition to his supremacy. As is well-known, Sir Thomas More, former Lord Chancellor, and Cardinal John Fisher, Bishop of Rochester, were both beheaded in 1535 for refusing to acknowledge the royal supremacy and for refusing to renounce the spiritual authority of the Pope. Eight others were hanged, drawn and quartered at Tyburn in the same year for the same 'offences'. These included John Haile, a secular priest, Richard Reynolds, a Bridgettine monk, and six Carthusian monks.[74] The strong 'monkish' presence among these ten martyrs largely explains why Henry VIII saw the monasteries 'as centres ... of opposition to the break with Rome'[75] and why he dissolved them between 1536 and 1540. Henry also felt threatened by the friars, especially the Franciscan Observants, two of whom – Hugh Rich and Richard Risby – had supported Elizabeth Barton, the (dangerous) Maid of Kent, in her opposition to Henry's 'divorce'. So Henry had the Maid and her Franciscan supporters executed at Tyburn in April 1534.[76] In August he closed down the Observant houses and four years later suppressed the remaining friaries in England.

The Dissolution of the Religious Orders

Definitions

The Religious Orders consisted of monks, canons regular,[77] friars and nuns, all of whom had taken vows to follow the rule of a religious order.

Monks lived in monasteries. These were places in which devout people (usually men) lived together in an enclosed community dedicated primarily to prayer and worship. Other tasks performed by monks – manual work, teaching, tending the sick, housing travellers, maintaining the poor – were of secondary importance.[78] There were many monastic orders throughout England, but only the following were to be found in Suffolk on the eve of the Dissolution: Benedictines (Black monks), Cistercians (White monks), Cluniacs and one order of soldier-monks, the Knights Hospitallers of St John of Jerusalem.

Canons, like monks, lived a regular communal life, but unlike monks they performed the duties of parish priests. In Suffolk in 1536 there were just two such orders of canons: the Augustinians and Premonstratensians.

Friars (Latin *fratres*, i.e. brothers) did not live in enclosed communities but were generally itinerant and mendicant, i.e. they lived by begging. Unlike monks, who were usually rural based,[79] friars were mostly urban based. Friars were primarily dedicated to preaching, administering the sacraments, etc. Friaries, unlike many monasteries, had little landed endowment. There were five main orders of friars in Suffolk in the mid-1530s: Augustinians (or Austin Friars), Carmelites (White Friars), Dominicans (Black Friars), Franciscans (Grey Friars) and Friars of the Holy Cross ('Crutched' Friars). As Peter Northeast says, 'the friars were the best known and most popular of the religious orders. This was partly because of their philosophy summed up in the oft-quoted, albeit simplistic, definition: "a monk stayed in a monastery to save his soul, and a friar went into the world to save the souls of others".'[80] This would partly explain why more Suffolk people left money in their wills to friaries than to monasteries.[81]

Nuns were religious women who lived in nunneries or convents. Like monks, their main duty was to maintain the daily round of prayer and praise which was made up by the monastic hours. In Suffolk in 1536 three orders of nuns existed: Augustinian canonesses, Benedictines and Franciscans (or Poor Clares). Apparently 'the nuns were more popular recipients [of bequests][82] than any other religious group, excepting the friars'.

Numbers

In 1536 there were in England and Wales more than 800 monasteries, friaries and nunneries and within them 12,000 monks, canons, friars and nuns. Numbers of course varied from county to county. Yorkshire was saturated with religious houses and could boast thirty-five male monasteries, nineteen friaries, twenty-three nunneries, one double Gilbertine house, and two major hospitals served by the monastic order.[83] Suffolk, on the other hand, had a much more modest number of religious houses,[84] including just eighteen male monasteries,[85] eleven friaries and six nunneries (see Map 9). Moreover, the houses of Yorkshire accommodated well over 1,000 monks, canons, friars and nuns.[86] By contrast, those of Suffolk lodged only 273 inmates (see Appendix I (a)).

Of the eighteen monasteries in Suffolk the huge Benedictine abbey of Bury St Edmunds was easily the most important in the county, and indeed was famous throughout Europe. Well-known as a major pilgrimage centre, it also fascinated travellers. In 1538 John Leland, the King's Antiquary, said 'You would aver that the Abbey was a town in itself, so many gates has it, ... so many towers and a Church surpassed by none'.[87] Founded in 1020, the abbey had eighty monks, twenty-one chaplains, and 111 servants in about 1260. The number of monks had dropped to about sixty in 1535, the time of the first visitation of Henry VIII's commissioners. Henry's threatening policy had driven out a third of that number before the surrender on 4 November 1539.[88] Yet even at that date Bury could still boast a large number of monks. But Bury Abbey was exceptional, not typical. Appendix I (a) shows that among the remaining seventeen monasteries of Suffolk only three – Butley, Ixworth and Leiston – had more than a dozen inmates at the time of their dissolution[89] and that the other

Map 9: Religious Houses in Suffolk in 1536

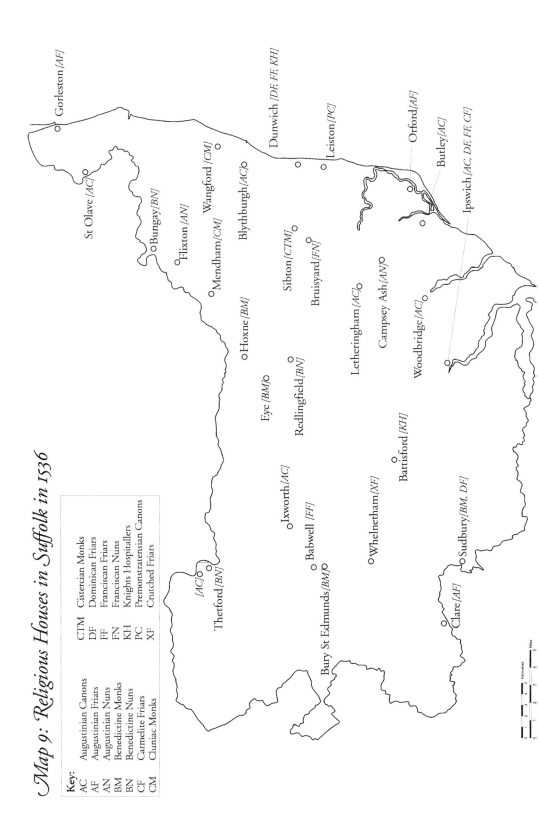

Key:

AC	Augustinian Canons
AF	Augustinian Friars
AN	Augustinian Nuns
BM	Benedictine Monks
BN	Benedictine Nuns
CF	Carmelite Friars
CM	Cluniac Monks
CTM	Cistercian Monks
DF	Dominican Friars
FF	Franciscan Friars
FN	Franciscan Nuns
KH	Knights Hospitallers
PC	Premonstratensian Canons
XF	Crutched Friars

Gorleston [AF]

St Olave [AC]

Bungay [BN]

Flixton [AN]

Mendham [CM]

Wangford [CM]

Blythburgh [AC]

Dunwich [DF, FF, KH]

Leiston [PC]

Orford [AF]

Butley [AC]

Ipswich [AC, DF, FF, CF]

Sibton [CTM]

Bruisyard [FN]

Letheringham [AC]

Campsey Ash [AN]

Woodbridge [AC]

Hoxne [BM]

Eye [BM]

Redlingfield [BN]

Battisford [KH]

Whelnetham [XF]

Ixworth [AC]

Babwell [FF]

Bury St Edmunds [BM]

Thetford [BN]

[AC]

Clare [AF]

Sudbury [BM, DF]

Bury St Edmunds Abbey
(Engraved by W. Wallis from a sketch by T. Higham in *Excursions*, I, p. 15)
After the Dissolution of the Monasteries little remained of the large Benedictine Abbey
of Bury (founded 1020), except two great gateways: the Norman Tower on the far right
of the picture and the Great Gate in the centre. The Great Gate, built after serious riots
by the Bury townsmen in 1327, wisely included many defensive features associated with
castles, such as a portcullis.

fourteen housed very small communities. St Olave had only seven monks,
Letheringham just three, and Sudbury a mere two. In short, most Suffolk
monasteries were underpopulated.

Yet Suffolk was not alone in having thinly populated monasteries. Essex
had twenty-four monasteries and three of them – Bicknacre, Berdon and
Latton – had only one inmate each when dissolved.[90]

Appendix I (a) shows that the nunneries of Suffolk were mostly rather
small communities. Campsey Ash had twenty nuns at the dissolution,
Bruisyard fifteen and Redlingfield thirteen. But none of the others had over
a dozen 'religious'.

There were eleven friaries in Suffolk in 1536, but unfortunately we know
the number of inmates in only three: Clare, Sudbury and the Dominican
friary of Ipswich.[91]

Wealth

Many years ago, the Russian scholar, Alexander Savine, reckoned that the
monastic houses held about one-tenth of the land of England.[92] However,
the amount of landed property owned by the monasteries and nunneries

varied considerably from county to county. In Suffolk the monasteries were not particularly well endowed and on the eve of their suppression only three had net annual incomes over £200: Bury St Edmunds Abbey, Butley Priory and Sibton Abbey (see Appendix I (a)). We have already observed that prior to the Dissolution Bury Abbey exercised considerable administrative and legal jurisdiction in West Suffolk.[93] But the abbey enjoyed wealth as well as power. According to the *Valor Ecclesiasticus*, its total landed income in 1535 was £1,659.[94] The prosperity of Bury Abbey can scarcely be exaggerated. That it was the richest monastery in Suffolk goes without saying. But in addition it was the fifth wealthiest Benedictine house in England, being outstripped only by Westminster, Glastonbury, St Albans and Canterbury.[95] Why was Bury Abbey so well off? Professor Gottfried has suggested that its 'prosperity stemmed … from its vast landed endowment and the profits of land ownership'. When the abbey surrendered on 4 November 1539 its estates were scattered throughout eastern England, from Lincolnshire to London. 'With the exception of the Crown, it seems to have been the largest single landholder in West Suffolk'.[96] In Babergh

Butley Priory Gatehouse
(Drawn and engraved by T. Higham in *Excursions*, II, p. 54)
Founded in 1171 for Augustinian Canons, Butley Priory was the second wealthiest monastery in Suffolk in 1536. The remains are almost entirely confined to the magnificent gatehouse, erected *c.* 1325 and decorated with 35 coats of arms of East Anglian families. After the Dissolution Butley manor was bought by William Forth, a gentleman–clothier of Hadleigh.

Sibton Abbey
(Engraved by W. Wallis from a drawing by T. Higham in *Excursions*, II, p. 97)
Sibton Abbey, the only Cistercian house in Suffolk, was founded in 1150. The abbey
ruins are close by in the woods. Before the Dissolution Sibton was the third wealthiest
monastery in Suffolk. The 3rd Duke of Norfolk obtained Sibton manor in 1536. But in
1610 it was sold to the Scriveners, future Royalists, who built a house out of the ruins.

hundred, for example, the Abbot of Bury was the richest landowner in
1522, being wealthier than men of great prestige, like Sir William Waldegrave
and the clothier Thomas Spring.[97]

The second wealthiest monastery in Suffolk – and it was a very poor
second – was Butley Priory, with a net income of only £318.[98] In 1538 the
Butley household had thirteen canons and two chaplains, but in addition
there were at least eighty lay people whose lives would be affected by
the Dissolution. These included domestic officials, 'cookes', 'Servantes in
husbandry', 'Shepperdes', 'woodmakers', etc.[99] Butley Priory was clearly a
substantial landlord and employer and the centre of a busy agricultural
estate.

The other wealthy monastery – Sibton Abbey – had an annual income
of £250, but we lack detailed information about its economic activities at
the time of the Dissolution.[100]

Appendix I (a) shows that in Suffolk a big gap separated the greater
monasteries – Bury, Butley and Sibton – from the lesser. We know the
incomes of fourteen of the fifteen lesser monasteries.[101] Of these, only three
– Eye, Ixworth and Leiston – had annual incomes between £100 and £200.
Eight were worth between £20 and £100 per annum, while three – Hoxne,

Leiston Abbey
(Engraved by T. Barber from a sketch by T. Higham in *Excursions*, II, p. 94)
Leiston was founded for Premonstratensian Canons in 1182, and re-built in the late
fourteenth century. Like the Cistercians they sought simplicity in secluded spots. On the
eve of the Dissolution Leiston had more monks than any other Suffolk monastery,
except Bury Abbey and Ixworth Priory.

Ixworth Abbey, exterior
(Photograph: S.R.O. (B), K 505/718)
'The Abbey' is Georgian in external appearance but incorporates substantial remains of
an Augustinian priory founded in *c.* 1100. On the eve of the Dissolution Ixworth had
more monks than any other Suffolk monastery, except Bury Abbey.

Mendham and Sudbury – struggled along on less than £20 a year. In short, most of the lesser monasteries of Suffolk seem to have been very poor.

The six nunneries of Suffolk also had low annual incomes (see Appendix I(a)). The richest (or the least poor) of the six – Campsey Ash – was worth £182 a year. The remaining five convents, however, had incomes below £100, though none was exceptionally poor (i.e. under £20).

As regards the friaries, we do not know their incomes since they had little landed property. Besides, most friars lived by begging.

Spirituality
What was the spiritual state of the Suffolk religious houses on the eve of their closure? The short answer is 'good', or at least 'satisfactory'. Various monasteries were subjected to *episcopal* visitations during the reign of Henry VIII, but nothing seriously wrong was found. When Woodbridge Priory was visited on behalf of the Bishop of Norwich in 1520 it was complained that the monks sang the psalms neither distinctly nor yet with devotion.[102] When Butley Priory was examined by Bishop Nix in 1532, a flood of grievances poured into his ears. There were complaints that no proper accounts had been kept for thirty years, that the Sub-Prior had taken for his own use some pewter mugs which belonged to the infirmary, and that a gluttonous young servant was eating most of the fresh vegetables which should have gone to the monks.[103] From a religious standpoint the faults of Woodbridge were not grave, while Butley was actually 'a house of higher than average disciplinary condition'.[104]

However, the *royal* visitation of 1535–36 levelled more serious charges against the religious houses. The purpose of this visitation was to examine the state of the monasteries and convents throughout England, and to produce evidence of laxity, scandal and abuses which could be used by Thomas Cromwell, the king's vicegerent in matters spiritual, as grounds for at least a partial suppression and confiscation of monastic property.[105] The evidence produced by the visitors (inspectors), although colourful, lively and sometimes amusing, can hardly be taken at face value, and this includes remarks made about the Suffolk religious houses.

On the 4th November 1535 Bury Abbey was inspected by Ap Rice and Legh, two of the royal commissioners. They wrote to Cromwell an unfavourable report. They remarked that 'thabbot ... delited moche in playing at dice and cardes, and therein spent moche money'. As a pilgrimage centre Bury had an abundance of holy relics. These were roundly condemned by the 'visitors'. 'Among the reliques we founde moch vanitee and superstition, as the coles that St Lawrence was toasted withall, the paring of St Edmundes naylles, St Thomas of Canterbury pennekyff and his bootes ...'[106] But even Ap Rice and Legh had to admit that 'As for thabbot, we found nothing suspect as touching his lyving'.[107]

The evidence suggests that Diarmaid MacCulloch is right in saying that the Suffolk monasteries as a whole were 'conscientious if uninspired'.[108] Certainly the monasteries in Suffolk compare favourably with those in Norfolk; Wymondham Abbey, Norwich Cathedral Priory and, surprisingly, Walsingham Priory were in a deplorably bad state in the early sixteenth century.[109]

If Suffolk monasteries were in generally good condition, so were the county's nunneries. Shortage of space forbids detailed examples. But Drs Gilchrist and Oliva have convincingly shown that the nuns of both Suffolk and Norfolk 'maintained a high standard of religious life', that they were greatly respected by the laity, that their hospitality was generous, and that they spent a higher proportion of their yearly budgets on alms to the poor than did most male monasteries.[110]

Dissolutions

The dissolution of the monasteries, says Professor Scarisbrick, 'was the capital event' of the English Reformation.[111] Within four years (1536–40) all the monasteries, friaries and nunneries in both England and Suffolk were swept away. Except during the short reign of the Catholic Mary Tudor (1553–58), England was henceforth to be a land without monks, friars and nuns, 'an England that had indeed turned its back on the past'.[112]

Suppressing monasteries and other religious houses was not new, however. A precedent had been set by Cardinal Thomas Wolsey. Mainly for educational reasons, he dissolved twenty-nine religious houses between 1524 and 1528.[113] Five of these establishments were in Suffolk: Dodnash, Ipswich (SS Peter and Paul), Rumburgh, Snape and Walton, near Felixstowe. These were tiny houses. Apart from Ipswich, which had seven monks, all the rest had under five.[114]

The actions of Wolsey do not begin to compare with those of Henry VIII and Thomas Cromwell, known as 'the hammer of the monks'. Wolsey had dissolved a mere twenty-nine religious houses, whereas Henry was to suppress around 800 in England and Wales. Why did Henry dissolve the religious orders? The reasons were hardly spiritual. Henry argued that they were idle, rapacious and immoral. But this was a mere pretext. Though many religious communities lacked real spiritual fervour, few were obviously disgraceful.[115] Certainly in Suffolk they were not. The religious houses were dissolved for political and financial reasons. Politically, Henry regarded the religious orders as a threat to his authority, believing they were papal garrisons. As the late Geoffrey Elton said, few monks and friars resisted the Act of Supremacy, 1534, 'but what resistance there was came largely from them'.[116] Moreover, 'the monasteries' foreign links increased their vulnerability to royal attack, for the allegiance owed by the English priories to parent houses on the continent was seen as both incompatible with the royal supremacy and a potential threat to the security of the realm'.[117] But perhaps an equally important reason for the suppression of the religious orders was Henry's serious financial difficulties. By the mid-1530s the king faced a Catholic coalition ranged against him – France, Catholic Germany, Scotland and Spain – so he had to build up his navy, repair his castles on the Scottish border, and construct new forts along the south coast. But where was the money to come from? Henry, remembering the strong opposition in 1525 to the Amicable Grant, especially in Suffolk,[118] hesitated to levy more taxes on his people. So he turned on the monks, friars and nuns.

The legislation for the dissolution of the religious orders included the Act for the Dissolution of the Lesser Monasteries, 1536 (27 Hen. VII, cap. 28), and the Act for the Dissolution of the Greater Monasteries, 1539 (31 Hen. VIII, cap. 13). An Act of 1538 officially suppressed the friaries. The Act of 1536 transferred to the Crown all the lands and property of monasteries and nunneries with an annual income of less than £200. Abbots, abbesses, priors and prioresses were to be granted pensions for life by the King. The rank and file, however, were to be pensionless, but they could either be transferred to a surviving house of their order or they could apply for a dispensation (known as a 'capacity'), releasing them from the monastic vows of poverty and obedience (but not chastity) and enabling them to pursue a fresh career outside the cloister. Many smaller houses bought from the Crown, at a very high price, leave to continue, but only one of these – Bruisyard – was in Suffolk.[119] All the Suffolk monasteries and convents, except Bury, Butley and Sibton, fell within the scope of the 1536 Act because of their lack of wealth.

The Act of 1539 vested all monastic property in the King. This act was largely retrospective in effect because many of the larger houses had been dissolving themselves under pressure from Thomas Cromwell and the royal visitors. They had been surrendering individually to the king's agents. The three richest houses of Suffolk submitted in this way: Bury Abbey on 4 November 1539; Butley Priory in March 1538; and Sibton Abbey as early as 1536.[120] From the time of the negotiated surrenders of November and December 1537 until the dissolution of the last house in England (Waltham Abbey, Essex) in March 1540, *the Letters and Papers of the reign of Henry VIII* show that most of the dispossessed monks, canons and nuns were pensioned.

The Act of 1538 for the suppression of the friaries awarded no pensions to any of the friars and no chance to transfer to another house was offered. The friars had always lived on charity. There was no need therefore, in the eyes of the government, to compensate them for the loss of a secure livelihood, for such they had never enjoyed. There was, however, a chance for ex-friars to take posts in the Church and some did, as we shall see.

The Fate of the ex-Religious
The fate of monks, friars and nuns after the closure of their religious houses has been a controversial subject. Cardinal Gasquet suggested that widespread

hardship and poverty afflicted the English monks after the Dissolution. Later Geoffrey Baskerville argued that pensions received by monks were on the whole adequate, and sometimes generous, and that a large number, perhaps the great majority, of young and middle-aged religious, found within a few years employment as chantry priests, curates and incumbents of parochial livings. G. A. J. Hodgett steered a middle course between the pessimistic Gasquet and the optimistic Baskerville, stating that the pensioned monks fared well, while the unpensioned did not.[121]

What was the situation in Suffolk? Appendix I(a) and (b) show that of the 273 ex-religious, only fifty-seven (21 per cent) received pensions from the government.[122] This is fairly similar to the position in Lancashire where thirty-three (28 per cent) out of 119 obtained pensions.[123] The pensioned religious of Suffolk consisted of all forty-four monks of the abbey of St Edmundsbury and thirteen heads of houses. The amount of the pensions varied. One of the Superiors, Elizabeth Hoth, former prioress of Thetford St George, received an annual pension of £5. This was barely above subsistence level in 1537 and would be even less adequate during the inflationary years of the 1540s. By contrast, Ela Buttery, ex-prioress of Campsey Ash, obtained a pension of £23, more than that received by any monk, with the exceptions of the Abbot and the Prior of Bury St Edmunds Abbey. Among the most fortunate of the pensioned Suffolk monks were the forty-four of Bury Abbey. All received pensions which, if not generous, were adequate, even allowing for inflation (see Appendix I(b)).

So much for the pensions of the Bury monks. What about their post-dissolution careers? Unfortunately we were ignorant of the careers of eight of those monks. Another eight – classified as 'retired' – did not seek ecclesiastical positions, either because they considered their pensions adequate or because they were too old. One of the eight – Abbot John Reve – in fact died before he could receive his exceptionally high pension of £333. Appendix I(b) shows that of the remaining twenty-eight Bury monks, twenty obtained ecclesiastical positions and another eight employment of a more secular kind. Some procured ecclesiastical preferment quickly, like Thomas Hall, who became Rector of Tuddenham St Mary in 1540. Others had to wait until the 1550s or even later.[124] However, it would be a mistake to regard these latecomers as unlucky. Success did come their way eventually. Of the eight monks who became virtually laymen, one, John Helperby, was unemployed in 1555 and another, John Sanderson, was just a weaver. However, some did well for themselves. John King obtained the highly prestigious position of High Master of Bury School, while Thomas Rought became a notary of Bury.

Let us now turn to the less fortunate, the unpensioned ex-religious. These consisted of all known friars, plus monks and nuns who, by the Act of 1536, received no financial help.[125] Apart from the rank and file, six heads of monasteries and two heads of nunneries apparently received no pensions (see Appendix I(a)). It is hard to explain why, but not all were ruined. Thomas Manning, ex-prior of Butley, though not pensioned, was appointed Warden of Mettingham College (housing secular priests) in about 1539.[126] The unpensioned monks and friars of Suffolk, like those elsewhere, were able to seek capacities. That is, they could apply for ecclesiastical positions. Thus in September 1536 William Reeve, a canon of the Premonstratensian abbey of Leiston, applied 'for a dispensation to hold a benefice with complete change of habit', and from 1537 to 1552 was Vicar of Corton and perpetual curate of Leiston.[127] William Downaby, a canon of the Augustinian house of Woodbridge, received his dispensation in February 1537, and from 1539 to 1554 was Rector of Iken.[128] Of the friars, the most successful were John Bale, Peter Brinckley and John Hodgkin. Bale, prior of the Carmelite house of Ipswich from 1533 to 1538, became Bishop of Ossory, Ireland, in 1548.[129] Dr Brinckley, the last warden of the Franciscans of Babwell, became Rector of Great Moulton, Norfolk, from 1540 to 1543.[130] Dr Hodgkin, an ex-Dominican of Sudbury, obtained the vicarage of Walden, Essex, in 1541.[131] But those unpensioned monks and friars are examples of the fortunate few. If we take all 142 unpensioned male ex-religious (116 monks and twenty-six friars), we find that only thirteen (9 per cent) received ecclesiastical posts. However, the situation was better in Suffolk than in the diocese of Lincoln where apparently 'only about 4 per cent of those leaving religion in 1536 and 1538 obtained ecclesiastical preferment'.[132]

But arguably the most unfortunate of the ex-religious of Suffolk were former nuns. Except for four heads of houses, none received an annual pension. Moreover, in a male dominated society, where the ordination of women was unthinkable, no nun became a parish or chantry priest. Perhaps worst of all, ex-nuns were forbidden to marry until 1549. However, the situation was not disastrous for all ex-nuns. Some procured life-time support. Nicholas Hare purchased Bruisyard after its suppression, and in his will of 1557 he directed his wife Katherine to continue to support Margaret Loveday, Florence Rouse, Florence Scuteler, and Jane Wentworth, all ex-nuns of the abbey. Other former nuns had to rely on their own initiative. Two from Campsey Ash, Isabella Norwich and Bridget Cocket, ran a school together in Dunwich. Several ex-nuns moved to towns in search of greater economic opportunities. Elizabeth Hoth, the last prioress of Thetford St George, and Ela Buttery, the last superior of Campsey Ash, both moved to Norwich.[133]

The disposal of monastic and convent lands[134]

The Dissolution of the Monasteries involved the largest confiscation and redistribution of land and property since the Norman Conquest. When Henry VIII confiscated the monasteries and nunneries he hoped to increase his revenue considerably. Indeed, Thomas Cromwell thought that the dissolution would make Henry 'the richest prince in Christendom'. But

Henry could not wait for the long-term benefits of the dissolution to be felt. Having nationalised monastic property, he soon decided to privatise it. From the very first the need for ready money was pressing, and, with the outbreak of war with Scotland in 1542 and France in 1543, became more pressing still. So between 1536 and 1547 Henry, through the Court of Augmentations,[135] sold about two-thirds of monastic property in England, raising about £780,000 in the process,[136] most of it going on military supplies and soldiers' wages. The sales began as a trickle in the late 1530s and became a flood after 1542.

Henry VIII made 1,593 grants of land to about 1,000 grantees during his reign.[137] There were very few gifts: forty-one cases only out of 1,593 grants.[138] The gifts were granted to win or reward political support. These fortunate recipients included great magnates like the king's brother-in-law, Charles Brandon, 1st Duke of Suffolk, and Thomas Howard, 3rd Duke of Norfolk,[139] who had crushed with severity the most dangerous rebellion of Henry's reign, the Pilgrimage of Grace (1536–37). Another twenty-eight grants were a combination of gifts with sale or exchange,[140] from which both crown and grantee benefited. For example, in 1538 the king granted several valuable manors in Suffolk to Richard Codington, of an ancient Surrey family, in exchange for the manor of Nonesuch, where he soon erected his famous royal palace.[141] So much for gifts and exchanges. But it must be emphasised that the overwhelming majority of grants were outright sales, especially during the 1540s when Henry desperately needed ready cash for his wars. Most monastic property was not cheap. Indeed, during Henry's reign most lands sold at twenty years' purchase, that is a capital sum of twenty times their current net annual value.[142] Thus when Sir Edmund Bedingfield bought the Bedingfield family nunnery at Redlingfield, Suffolk, in 1537 his total liability of £561 19s. 0d. was almost exactly twenty years' purchase of the net annual value.[143]

What social and occupational groups obtained monastic and convent land in Suffolk? Table 3.1 attempts an answer.

Some comments on Table 3.1 are necessary. Five nobles were granted monastic manors in Suffolk: Thomas Cromwell, Earl of Essex; Thomas Darcy, Lord Darcy of Chiche; John de Vere, 16th Earl of Oxford; Charles Brandon, 1st Duke of Suffolk; and Thomas Howard, 3rd Duke of Norfolk. Appendix I(c) shows that Cromwell and de Vere only obtained one manor each, that Lord Darcy was more fortunate in gaining three manors, and that Charles Brandon and Thomas Howard were granted far more manors than any of the other grantees. However, the nobility – at least in East Anglia – did not hold on to their acquisitions for long. Dom David Knowles has said that 'most of the grantees at court either sold part of their land almost at once to pay for the expenses of their careers, or fell into disgrace in conspiracies, thus causing their land to escheat in part or in whole to the crown'.[146] Charles Brandon procured large grants of miscellaneous

Table 3.1 Persons granted monastic and convent land in Suffolk 1536–47

Grantees	Numbers	Manors obtained[144]
Anne of Cleves	1 (1.6%)	1 (0.7%)
Nobility		
(a) Suffolk	2 ⎤	15 ⎤
(b) Norfolk [145]	1 ⎬ 5 (8.1%)	16 ⎬ 35 (24.0%)
(c) Other	2 ⎦	4 ⎦
The Church	2 (3.2%)	2 (1.4%)
Lawyers	2 (3.2%)	2 (1.4%)
London merchants	4 (6.5%)	11 (7.5%)
Norwich merchant	1 (1.6%)	1 (0.7%)
Royal officials	8 (12.9%)	25 (17.1%)
Officials of peers	3 (4.8%)	7 (4.8%)
Gentry		
(a) Suffolk	26 ⎤	42 ⎤
(b) Norfolk	3 ⎬ 31 (50.0%)	3 ⎬ 56 (38.4%)
(c) Other	2 ⎦	11 ⎦
Uncertain status	5 (8.1%)	6 (4.0%)
Total	62 (100.0%)	146 (100.0%)

property in Suffolk and elsewhere in England,[147] but he sold as soon as possible.[148] It would seem that Brandon may 'have been pressurised (by the King?) into abandoning his native county (Suffolk) and extending his (landed) interests in Lincolnshire'. Thus from 1538 he no longer played an important part in Norfolk and Suffolk affairs.[149] The Duke of Norfolk lost many of his acquisitions for rather different reasons. In 1542 the disgrace of his niece, Catherine Howard, the King's fifth wife, weakened his position at court and in 1546 he was convicted of treason. So not surprisingly several monastic manors, which Henry had granted him, escheated to the crown and were re-granted to other people. Two examples will suffice. Henry granted the duke Sibton Abbey in 1536 and Butley Priory in 1538. But after the duke's attainder, Sibton reverted to the crown and in 1547 the King granted the lordship to Sir Anthony Denny. Three years previously Henry had granted the Manor of Butley to William Forth of Hadleigh for the sum of £910.[150]

Closely allied to the Crown was the Church. But despite this, the latter obtained very little ex-monastic land. The Dean and Chapter of Ely were granted the manor of Lakenheath, which had belonged to the former abbey, while the Dean and Chapter of Norwich obtained the manor of Hopton, hitherto part of the priory (See Appendix I(c)).

Only two local lawyers acquired former monastic property in Suffolk. Sir Humphrey Wingfield of Brantham got Creping Hall manor, Stutton, in 1537, while Henry Payne of Bury St Edmunds was granted the manor of Nowton in 1545 for £648.[151]

Like cathedral clergy and local lawyers, merchants comprised only a few of the purchasers of ex-monastic property. One was a provincial merchant, William Rede of Norwich. He was granted the manor of Beccles between 1540 and 1542, paying at least £120.[152] Appendix I(c) shows that only four London merchants obtained ex-monastic land in Suffolk. They included Sir Thomas Gresham, who was to become a famous financier under Edward VI, Mary I and Elizabeth I. He acquired St John's manor, Battisford, in 1543 for an unknown sum. Adam Winthrop, a clothier, was granted the manor of Groton for £409 in 1544.[153] Paul Withipoll, merchant tailor, obtained Holy Trinity, Ipswich, in 1546, for an unknown sum, and his son, Edmund, later built Christchurch Mansion on the site of the former priory.[154] Easily the most outstanding London purchaser was Sir Thomas Kitson of the Merchant Adventurers Company and Sheriff of London in 1533. In 1521 he bought the manor of Hengrave and between 1525 and 1538 built Hengrave Hall at a cost of £3,500. It has been called 'a monument of his magnificence'. Kitson also purchased considerable estates in Devon, Dorset, Somerset and Nottinghamshire. Not content with these acquisitions, he took advantage of the sale of monastic lands to extend his domain in Suffolk. In 1540 he bought eight monastic manors for £3,710.[155] In spite of, or

Sir Thomas Kitson of Hengrave Hall (1485–1540) by an unknown artist. (Photograph: S.R.O. (B), K 505/2972) Sir Thomas was a wealthy London merchant in the 1530s, engaging in extensive mercantile transactions. Also desiring to be a country gentleman, he built Hengrave Hall, near Bury, and purchased eight monastic manors in Suffolk, as well as much property elsewhere. He probably obtained more land than any of his Suffolk gentry contemporaries, except Sir Nicholas Bacon of Redgrave.

perhaps because of, his extensive purchases, Kitson was an investor, not a speculator, and his family was to establish itself among the ranks of the Suffolk gentry during the later sixteenth century. The Redes, Winthrops and Withipolls also settled down as country gentlemen.[156]

More numerous among the purchasers than Londoners were royal officials: courtiers, councillors, office-holders and gentlemen of the King's household. Lawrence and Jeanne Stone have argued that during the sixteenth and early seventeenth centuries 'the principal means of acquiring great wealth leading to swift upward mobility ... was office-holding'.[157] Certainly officials engaged in the royal administration were well placed to benefit from the sales of monastic lands. Although not necessarily guilty of corruption, they must have had valuable inside information about the land market which was denied to outsiders. This was especially likely to be the case if they were members of the Court of Augmentations. Thus Sir Robert Southwell, a solicitor to that court in 1537,[158] obtained two monastic manors in Suffolk (see Appendix I(c)). More successful was Nicholas Bacon. The younger son of a yeoman from the Drinkstone area of Suffolk, he was a solicitor to the Court of Augmentations from 1537 to 1546 and acquired seven monastic manors, mostly in the Bury area (see Appendix I(c)). In 1546 Bacon became Attorney to the Court of Wards and Liveries and obtained monastic lands in several counties.[159] When he died in 1578 Bacon had become Lord Keeper of the

Sir Nicholas Bacon of Redgrave, Knight (1509–79) by an unknown artist c. 1579. The younger son of a Suffolk yeoman, Bacon acquired great wealth through office-holding and the purchase of monastic lands.

Great Seal (1558), a successful landlord,[160] and the possessor of over thirty manors, half of them in his native Suffolk.[161] Nicholas Bacon was rather exceptional, and not all royal officials gained as much from the Dissolution of the Monasteries. John Gosnold obtained only the manor of Coddenham Priory, while three other administrators – Sir Anthony Denny, Gentleman of the Privy Chamber, Sir Richard Gresham, Gentleman Usher-Extraordinary in the royal household, and Sir Nicholas Hare, Master of Requests – gained just two manors each. However, Sir Edmund Bedingfield, a courtier, was more fortunate and acquired four Suffolk manors in 1537, while Sir Anthony Wingfield, a Privy councillor, obtained five.[162]

E. A. Wasson has rightly said that families could rise high by earning the personal favour of magnates as well as monarchs.[163] But only three officials of the peerage obtained monastic manors in Suffolk. Sir Anthony Rous, Treasurer to the 3rd Duke of Norfolk, got four manors, spending a total of at least £3,876.[164] Sir Arthur Hopton, servant of the 1st Duke of Suffolk since 1523, acquired two valuable manors near his home. But Sir Richard

Freston, Comptroller of the same duke's household, only obtained the manor of Wickham Skeith.[165] Despite the expensive purchases of Sir Anthony Rous, the transactions of monastic land suggest that servants of the nobility were rather less successful than servants of the King.

The gentry, mostly Suffolk men, formed exactly half the number of those purchasing monastic land. Yet Table 3.1 rather understates the number of gentry grantees. The two lawyers[166] and at least seven office-holders were of gentry stock.[167] If we add those to the thirty-one gentlemen in the table, then the gentry total is forty (64 per cent). Suffolk undoubtedly resembled Devon, Lancashire and Norfolk with its large proportion of gentry pur-chasers, though it differed somewhat from Essex, where many buyers were royal civil servants.[168] Concentrating on the twenty-six mere gentry of Suffolk,[169] it would appear that most made modest purchases, composed of one or two monastic manors. Only five gained three or more. These were Thomas Bacon of Hessett, Sir William Drury of Hawstead, Sir John Jenny of Brightwell, Sir Thomas Jermyn of Rushbrooke and Robert Spring of Lavenham. Moreover, just four – William Forth of Hadleigh, Sir Thomas Jermyn of Rushbrooke, and Sir John and Robert Spring – apparently spent over £1,000 on monastic land, though two gentlemen – Henry Jerningham of Somerleyton and John Tasburgh of Elmham St Peter – paid almost that

Redlingfield Nunnery remains
(Photograph: S.R.O. (I), J I 11/2/3618)
Just south of the parish church is a barn of flint with buttresses and fragments of windows. This forms part of the Benedictine nunnery of Redlingfield founded in 1120. On the eve of the Dissolution Redlingfield was the third largest convent in Suffolk and was bought, for a high price, in 1537 by Sir Edmund Bedingfield, a royal official.

amount.[170] Another point worth emphasising is that while most purchasers were gentry, most gentry were not purchasers. Of the 166 gentry families of Suffolk in the 1520s, only thirty-one (19 per cent) at most bought monastic property in the period 1536–47.[171] Thus, while the Dissolution of the Monasteries may have been one reason for the rise of the gentry in sixteenth-century Suffolk, it was by no means the only one nor the most important.

Finally, what was the religious outlook of those buying monastic land? It is hard to identify the faith of many individuals during years of uncertainty, and indeed we are ignorant of the religion of seventeen of our sixty grantees.[172] But it would be quite wrong to regard the other forty-three as a class of land-hungry Protestant exploiters, eager to dismantle the Catholic Church and enrich themselves on the proceeds. In fact only twenty grantees or their descendants were or became Protestants or conformists, while as many as twenty-three belonged to families which were to remain Catholic or conservative in religion.[173] But why did devout Catholics such as Bedingfield, Cornwallis, Hare, Jerningham, Rookwood, Rous and Tasburgh buy monastic land, often in large quantities and at great expense? It is hard to say. Perhaps the most convincing explanation is that given by Dr Woodward, who says:

> [No] distinction [can] be drawn between a 'protestant' and a 'catholic' attitude towards the purchase of lands once devoted to the maintenance of the religious orders. For men of all religious sympathies such purchases were straightforward business deals into which considerations of faith or sentiment did not enter.[174]

The Protestant Reformation
The progress of Protestantism 1525–58

Suffolk's robust Catholicism of 1500 was replaced by radical Protestantism by 1600. Such a fundamental change is surprising even in the course of a century. The most common explanation given is that prosperity, trade and commercial links with the Low Countries tended to make East Anglia, and especially Suffolk, accept religious change more readily than the more conservative north and west of England. This seems highly likely. However, Bishop Nix, surveying the state of his Norwich diocese in 1530, blamed Cambridge clerics as well as overseas traders for disaffection towards the Church.[175] That Cambridge educated clergy played an important part in spreading Protestant ideas in Suffolk is undeniable, and it is worth saying a few words about the more important of them.

Thomas Bilney (1495?–1531) is the first reformer who springs to mind. Born in Norfolk, educated at Corpus Christi College, Cambridge, and ordained a priest in 1519, he attributed his 'conversion' to reading Erasmus's

Latin version of the New Testament. He was also an admirer of William Tyndale's English New Testament (printed 1525–26), one of the motors behind the Reformation. Bilney is important because he converted both Robert Barnes and Hugh Latimer to his reforming views. Some historians deny that Bilney was a Lutheran,[176] even though he stressed Justification by Faith alone. But he remained orthodox on the Papal Supremacy, the authority of the church and the doctrines of transubstantiation and confession. However, he totally rejected pilgrimages and the worship of saints. Bilney was burned as a relapsed heretic in Norwich in 1531. But, as Dr Craig says, 'his preaching, particularly against images, was not without fruit' and his influence 'in the region of Hadleigh can be seen in the wave of iconoclasm which spread across the Stour valley in the early 1530s'.[177]

Another Protestant preacher who had some influence in Suffolk and elsewhere was John Bale (1495–1563). Born at Cove, near the east coast of Suffolk, he entered the Carmelite friary at Norwich when only twelve. Two years later he entered Jesus College, Cambridge, and had a distinguished academic career. In 1533 he became prior of the Carmelite house at Ipswich. It was probably in Suffolk that he attracted the notice and patronage of Thomas, Lord Wentworth, who converted him to Protestantism. Bale then left his order and became a curate at Thorndon, Suffolk, where he preached inflammatory sermons against the Catholic religion. Bale's fame rests mainly on his propagandist plays, which strengthened the Protestant cause by vigorously attacking the papacy and monasticism.[178]

Bale and other reformers received a boost during the late 1530s when the First Protestant Reformation in England took place. In July 1536 the Ten Articles were adopted by Convocation at the wish of Henry VIII. The articles have been described as 'blatantly heterodox' because they mentioned only three sacraments – baptism, penance and the altar – and implied that the other four – confirmation, matrimony, ordination and extreme unction – were to be discarded. Furthermore, 'much of what [the Articles] said, about justification for example, derived almost verbatim from Lutheran theology'.[179] In 1538 the Second Royal Injunction of Henry VIII exhorted the clergy (as in the First Injunctions of 1536) to teach the laity the Lord's Prayer, the Creed and the Ten Commandments in English. Even more important, the Second Injunctions ordered every parson to provide an English Bible in his church, with free access to readers.[180] The Great Bible was published in April 1539. This was indeed a landmark in the history of the English Reformation because in Protestant eyes the bible is the basis of faith.

How did Suffolk respond to these religious changes? Services in the vernacular were welcomed in some quarters, and in 1538 the parish churches of Hadleigh and Stratford St Mary illegally used English in the Mass, being among the first places in England to do so.[181] More importantly, when did Suffolk churches acquire English bibles? It is very hard to say, though the churchwardens' accounts throw some light on the subject. Boxford church and Bungay St Mary both acquired English bibles in 1541. But the list of Church Goods, 1541, belonging to the church of the Holy Trinity, Long Melford, makes no mention of a bible.[182] The differences may perhaps be explained by the fact that Protestant tendencies were almost certainly stronger in Boxford and Bungay than in more traditional Long Melford.

Meanwhile Henry had stopped the embryonic Protestantism of the 1530s in its tracks. In June 1539 the Act of Six Articles (31 Hen. VIII, cap. 14) reasserted Catholic doctrine on disputed points. The Act upheld transubstantiation, communion in one kind, clerical celibacy, the binding character of vows of chastity, private masses and auricular confession. The Act was to be enforced by draconic penalties. This reactionary policy was no doubt partly due to the fact that Henry had been 'shaken by the Pilgrimage of Grace (1536–37)' when 40,000 of his subjects had taken up arms against Thomas Cromwell and "the heretics". 'Fear of internal disorder', says Christopher Haigh, 'now strengthened his distrust of innovation'.[183] Henry continued his anti-Protestant policy until 1543, if not later. The King's Book of that year was pointedly anti-Lutheran, emphasising the importance of transubstantiation, communion in one kind and justification by works.[184] 'By the spring of 1543 the Protestant elements in the first Reformation had been reversed; only the break with Rome and the suppression of the monasteries survived'.[185]

What difference did Henry's more conservative policy make to Suffolk Protestants? Very little it seems. Only seven Suffolk people can be shown to have been in trouble with the authorities between 1539 and 1547, including John Kirby and his wife, both of Mendlesham, who were burnt at the stake in 1546.[186] But most Suffolk Protestants and other heretics who suffered for their faith did so between 1525 and 1538 and in the reign of Mary Tudor.[187]

During the reign of Edward VI (1547–53) the Second Protestant Reformation in England occurred, leading to major changes in worship, doctrine and liturgy. The first important statute was the Chantries Act, 1547 (1 Edw. VI, cap. 14). This dissolved the secular colleges and religious guilds as well as the chantries. England had about 140 secular colleges – communities of secular priests who lived together and staffed 'collegiate' churches or chapels – on the eve of their suppression.[188] But only six of these were in Suffolk. They were located at Bury St Edmunds, Denston, Stoke-by-Clare, Sudbury, Mettingham and Wingfield. The first three survived until 1548, but the other three were suppressed before the Act of 1547. Sudbury was dissolved in 1545 and Mettingham and Wingfield as early as 1542. This is rather surprising because Mettingham and Wingfield were perhaps the most reputable secular colleges in the county, and apparently had educational as well as religious functions. Mettingham College was founded for a master and eight priests, but it also supported fourteen boys giving them education, board, lodging and clothes. Wingfield College in its heyday had a master, nine priests and three choral scholars.[189] As regards the religious guilds, these had reached their peak in Suffolk in the early sixteenth century.[190] But by the time they were dissolved under the 1547 Act, many had already ceased to funtion.[191] Even so, the suppression of the confraternities can hardly have been popular in Suffolk, either with religious or non-religious laymen. As Dr Oxley says, 'the disappearance of the gilds must have removed what, at best, were instruments of spiritual well-being, at worst, pleasant "get-togethers" for parishioners'.[192] Finally, let us consider the chantries, those endowments which maintained priests to chant masses for the soul of the founder and other designated individuals after their deaths. Chantries existed in only a minority of parishes and their numbers varied from one county to another. Lancashire had ninety-one chantries by the 1540s, Essex sixty-four by 1535, and Suffolk apparently had as many as seventy-nine in 1542.[193] What was the reaction of Suffolk folk to the abolition of the chantries? We do not know, but it can hardly have been favourable since their dissolution deprived many people of their only reliable means of coming to terms with death.[194] The 1547 Act, by suppressing chantries, religious guilds and colleges, denied by implication purgatory and prayers for the dead, and clearly set the Edwardian régime on the path towards Protestantism.

During the brief reign of Edward VI a series of parliamentary statutes ushered in major doctrinal and liturgical change. In 1547 Parliament passed an Act for Receiving in Both Kinds (1 Edw. VI, cap. 1), which meant that in the communion service the laity were to receive both bread and wine. Two years later the First Act of Uniformity (2 & 3 Edw. VI, cap. 1) was passed. The Act made the First English-language Prayer Book the prescribed liturgy. The Book was conservative in many ways (e.g. it allowed auricular confession, extreme unction and vestments). Nevertheless, says Professor Culkin, 'the first Book of Common Prayer [was] the first attempt to change the sacrifice of the Mass into a simple communion service'.[195] In the same year Parliament passed an Act to take away all positive laws against Marriage of Priests (2 & 3 Edw. VI, cap. 21). Many clergy took advantage of the Act and it can be tentatively suggested that the incidence of clerical marriage between 1549 and 1553 is a very rough index of religious sympathies. In Lancashire, the most religiously conservative shire in England, less than one in twenty priests married. In more Protestant-inclined London, however, one in three parish clergy did so. London was closely followed by Essex, Norfolk and Suffolk where at least a quarter of priests married. Indeed, Suffolk spearheaded the movement towards clerical marriage as early as 1536–37.[196]

So much for religious change in the early years of Edward VI. But change was even more pronounced in the King's later years. In 1550 a new Ordinal, introduced by the Edwardian régime, stipulated that the chalice and paten were no longer to be handed to the newly-ordained priest, but merely a bible. The Ordinal in effect turned a sacramental priesthood into a preaching ministry. This was a decisive move towards Protestantism. But more extreme changes were to follow. In 1552 Parliament passed the Second Act of Uniformity (5 & 6 Edw. VI, cap. 1) making church attendance compulsory on Sundays and imposing a new Prayer Book. This Second Prayer Book, unlike the first, gave the Church of England an unmistakable Protestant liturgy. Transubstantiation was discarded. Vestments were abolished, apart from the rochet and surplice. The so-called 'Black Rubric' denied that kneeling at communion implied any adoration of bread and wine, or the presence therein of Christ's natural body. Moreover, the language of this Prayer Book was significantly Protestant. 'Minister' was substituted for 'priest', and 'table' for 'altar'. In short, the ancient Mass gave way to the new Holy Communion. The following year Thomas Cranmer, Archbishop of Canterbury, compiled the Forty-two Articles of Religion with royal approval, giving the Church of England a definite Protestant theology. The Articles accepted justification by faith alone and Calvinist predestinarian teaching, while condemning the sacrificial concept of the Mass, the doctrine of purgatory and the adoration of saints and images.

The religious changes of Edward VI's reign were not all due to parliamentary legislation; they were also enforced by Injunctions and royal commissioners. In July 1547 the government of Protector Somerset issued Injunctions ordering the destruction of all 'shrines', paintings and pictures of saints. In February 1548 the Privy Council ordered the elimination of *all* religious images from churches. In 1550 Injunctions ordered the removal of altars from parish churches.[197] It is not surprising that the period 1547–50 is sometimes referred to as 'The Great Pillage'.

During the reign of Mary I England became Catholic again, at least officially. Papal supremacy over the Church, the Latin mass and Catholic doctrines (expounded in the Act of Six Articles, 1539) were restored. In 1553 Parliament's First Statute of Repeal (1 Mary, Stat. 2, cap. 2) abrogated Edward VI's Protestant Statutes and thus restored the legal situation obtaining in the last year of Henry VIII. In 1554 Mary's Injunctions condemned symbolic (i.e. Zwinglian) interpretations of the Eucharist and ordered the removal of married priests from their benefices.[198] Also in 1554 Mary's third Parliament agreed to revive the heresy laws (1 & 2 Philip and Mary, cap. 6) and to pass the Second Statute of Repeal (1 & 2 Philip and Mary, cap. 8), which revoked Henry VIII's anti-papal legislation and restored the situation of 1529. This last act did not, however, repeal the Dissolution Acts of 1536 and 1539. This is not surprising; restoring monastic lands would have been impracticable because many had changed hands too often since they were first sold.

So much for the religious statutes and injunctions of Edward VI and Mary I. The churchwardens' accounts from 1547 to 1558 show how far they were enforced in three selected, but perhaps representative, Suffolk parishes: Boxford, Bungay St Mary, and Long Melford. The churchwardens' accounts – our principal evidence for the ritual and ornamentation employed in parochial worship – shows that our three parishes were generally obedient to the commissioners attempting to enforce royal policy. In Edward's reign the main targets of the Protestant reformers were images, tabernacles, roodlofts and altars. In 1547 'certayn [unspecified] ymags were soldd' by the churchwardens of Bungay for 1s. 2d. In Long Melford 'the greateste image[s] about the chyrche & chapelles' were sold by the churchwardens to William Clopton of Kentwell Hall for 3s. 0d. In 1547 the churchwardens 'had down the tabarnaculs' in Boxford church. Tabernacles were also 'takyn down' at Bungay and Long Melford in the same year. The roodloft was taken down at Boxford in 1547 when its sale was recorded. Ralph Borom, a carpenter, removed the loft in Long Melford in the same year. Altars, both high and low, suffered particularly badly. The stone side 'awlters' were destroyed at Boxford in 1550. In the same year 'ye lowe Altar' [side altar] was 'takyn Down' at Bungay. At Long Melford in 1548 'the hyghe alter' was 'takyng down' along with the 'funt' [font]. At Bungay in 1550 'ye highe Alter' was ruined when 'ye Stone & Lyme' were 'taken down'.[199]

Alongside the destruction,[200] the Protestant reformers endeavoured to inculcate their new faith, but apparently with less success. In 1549 the churchwardens of Boxford, Bungay and Melford bought copies of the new 'servyce books' [The First Book of Common Prayer] without delay. It is not clear if Boxford purchased the Second Book of Common Prayer of 1552, but Bungay and Long Melford certainly did. In 1548 Boxford obediently bought a copy of Desiderius Erasmus's *Paraphrases* (commentaries on the New Testament), but there is no sign that Bungay or Long Melford did so. The following year Edward Mole was paid 2d. for 'makyn A lecthorne [lectern] for the bible' in Bungay church. The accounts of this church also reveal that Mole was paid 7s. 0d. in 1551 'for tymber for ye com'vnyon table, & for makyng the same'. This is an early, but not the earliest, mention of the communion table. Indeed, there are signs that in Boxford in 1549 Robert Hall made a simple communion table, in place of the high altar, probably to stand lengthwise, i.e. east-west, in the chancel. Orders for this to be done were not made general until the 1552 Prayer Book. Thus one is almost tempted to say that both Boxford and Bungay accepted and at times anticipated the Reformation. One cannot say this about Long Melford.

When Mary Tudor came to the throne in 1553, Catholic worship was restored throughout the land. There are no signs that Boxford or Bungay offered any resistance. But few parishes can have enforced Mary's religious measures as enthusiastically as did Long Melford, partly because the two leading churchwardens – Richard Clopton and Roger Martin – were very devout Catholics. The accounts for 1554–57 show that Melford parishioners witnessed the restoration of the Easter Sepulchre, the refurbishing and 'paynting of the hye awlter', the obliteration of Protestant inscriptions or 'vayn scrybylyng uppon the churche walles',[201] the 'makyng ... payntyng & gyldyng of the roode', which included 'makying of the ymagys of Marye & John', ' the makyng' of 'greate organs', the 'mendyng' of 'organs in the quere' [choir],[202] 'the payntyng of the banner clothes',[203] and the buying of new ceremonial gear such as censer,[204] 'alter clotthe', 'vestimentes', 'holye water sprycle' [sprinkler] and a 'pewter pyxe'.[205] Clopton and Martin were also involved in repairing the 'grete crosse on [Melford] grene'.

In Boxford and Bungay the churchwardens were fairly quick in restoring Catholic furnishings and worship. In Bungay in 1553 a craftsman was paid an unspecified sum for 'makyng the high Alter', the communion table being discarded. In 1554 a certain 'Turner of Ersh'm' was paid an unspecified amount for 'making ye canopy over the sacrament'.[206] That time-serving artisan, Edward Mole, was paid 4d. for supplying 'ii holie water strenkills' [sprinklers]. In 1555 'a clothe of lynnen ... was hung before the crucifix in Lent'. In 1557 Mole and 'his man' were paid 5d. for 'setting uppe the ymages of St Marie and St John on the Rood loft'. In Boxford the return to Catholicism was just as evident as in Bungay. The restoration of the Catholic faith in Boxford was reflected in the purchase of service books and the many items needed for the ceremonial of the pre-Reformation type of worship. Thus in 1554 payments were made for 'a mestboke [massbook or missal], ... a preseshenary [processionary][207] ... a chales [chalice] ... a pyex'. In 1555 payment was made for 'a sense [censer] & a paske' [pax].[208] In late 1557 money was provided 'for making the sepulchre ... for the makyng of Images'. These changes were made just in time, for the death of Queen Mary in late 1558 was to usher in the Third English Reformation under Elizabeth I and another round of destruction.[209]

The churchwardens' accounts show how obedient the people of Suffolk were during a time of fundamental religious change. As Professor Hutton has said, 'the machinery of coercion and supervision deployed by the government was so effective that for most parishes passive resistance was simply not an option'.[210] Thus the churchwardens' accounts leave us little the wiser about the *true* religious beliefs of ordinary Suffolk people. Reading between the lines, it can perhaps be said that Long Melford was strongly Catholic and traditionalist and that Boxford and Bungay were slightly more willing to conform to the Protestant régimes of Edward VI and Elizabeth I. But this can be little more than a guess. What is clear is that Protestants in Suffolk were a definite minority of the population between 1525 and 1558. It is now time to study this minority.

The early Protestants

We can never know the exact number of Protestants in Suffolk, or indeed any other English county, during the sixteenth century. The general consensus among historians seems to be that before the reign of Elizabeth I Protestants were not only a small minority of the population, but a small minority in most places where they were to be found. However, their importance was out of all proportion to their numbers, so it behoves us to find out what we can about them. We are fortunate in possessing a useful list of around 3,000 known and named Protestants occurring between 1525 and 1558.[211] This is the unpaginated *Biographical Register of Early English Protestants and others opposed to the Roman Catholic Church 1525–1558*, compiled by Dr John Fines.[212] Fines used the following sources: John Foxe, *Actes and Monuments*, popularly known as the *Book of Martyrs*,[213] ecclesiastical archives, especially bishops' registers and the surviving act books of the church courts; governmental records such as the Domestic State Papers and the *Acts of the Privy Council*; and Miss Garrett's *Marian Exiles*.[214] The Fines *Register* does not necessarily list a typical cross-section of all English Protestants and other anti-Catholics during the period 1515–1558. Even so the *Register* deals with 'the persecuted minority of the Protestants, the risk-takers, activists, martyrs, exiles, the people who get into trouble and consequently into the official archives and martyrologies'.[215] Although the *Register* represents only the visible tip of the Protestant iceberg, it should very roughly indicate the geographical and social distribution of the new religion.[216]

Geographical distribution

Ecclesiastically, Suffolk was part of the diocese of Norwich and was divided between the western Archdeaconry of Sudbury and the eastern Archdeaconry of Suffolk. The archdeaconries were divided into rural deaneries and the latter into parishes. Thus, for example, the parish of Felixstowe formed part of the deanery of Colneis which in turn was under the ecclesiastical jurisdiction of the Archdeaconry of Suffolk. Another feature of the county was that it contained four peculiars (see Map 10). Moulton, Monks Eleigh and Hadleigh were directly under the jurisdiction of the Archbishop of Canterbury and outside that of the Bishop of Norwich. The peculiar of Freckenham was controlled by the Bishop of Rochester.[217] The Fines *Register* has the names of 112 heretics for Suffolk Archdeaconry, seventy-three for Sudbury Archdeaconry and twelve for the peculiar of Hadleigh (see Map 10). Seventeen heretics, though clearly Suffolk people, cannot be located in any particular parish. The figures suggest that during the Reformation Protestants were much more numerous in Suffolk Archdeaconry than in Sudbury Archdeaconry, just as during the First Civil War (1642–46) Puritans were to be much more conspicuous in East than in West Suffolk.[218]

Professor MacCulloch has argued that Protestantism was 'remarkably localised' in Suffolk,[219] and that it took root in three main areas: the Stour valley, the area around Hadleigh and the 'High Suffolk' country in the centre of the county.[220] To these might be added Ipswich. Let us deal with these four regions in turn.

Map 10: Distribution of Protestants and other Heretics (1525–58) in Archdeaconries, Deaneries and Peculiars pre 1837

(based on the Fines Register)

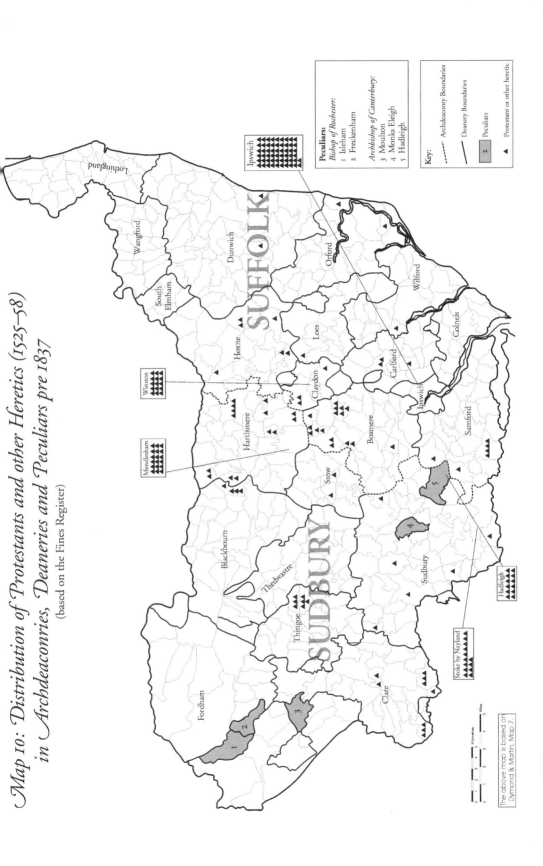

Peculiars:

Bishop of Rochester:
1 Isleham
2 Freckenham

Archbishop of Canterbury:
3 Moulton
4 Monks Eleigh
5 Hadleigh

Key:

·/·/·	Archdeaconry Boundaries
/ / /	Deanery Boundaries
▨ 2	Peculiars
▲	Protestant or other heretic

The above map is based on Dymond & Martin, Map 7.

In the Stour valley Protestants were to be found in cloth manufacturing parishes, such as Haverhill, Stoke-by-Clare, East Bergholt and, above all, Stoke-by-Nayland. The latter possibly, though not certainly, had links with the Lollards. Moreover, the absence of a prominent Catholic gentry family in Stoke-by-Nayland may have encouraged independence of mind.[221] The parish priest of Stoke-by-Nayland was also sympathetic to the Protestants.[222] But whatever the reasons, the Fines *Register* has more names of Protestants for Stoke-by-Nayland than for any other clothing centre in the deaneries of Clare, Sudbury and Samford (see Map 10). Under Mary Tudor Stoke-by-Nayland experienced prosecutions for religious dissent and vigorously resisted the Marian reaction. John Foxe claimed that three years after Queen Mary's accession, only two people were prepared to risk the wrath of their fellow villagers by receiving communion in the Catholic manner.[223] However, the craftsmen-clothiers were not bound to be Protestant and Professor MacCulloch has said that they 'could demonstrate their piety either in the building of splendid churches for the practice of the traditional liturgy or in the espousal of corrosively radical doctrines'.[224] Two important cloth towns, Long Melford and Lavenham, with their magnificent parish churches, showed few signs of Protestantism. The Fines *Register* names only one Protestant in Long Melford – Roger Coo, shearman – and one in

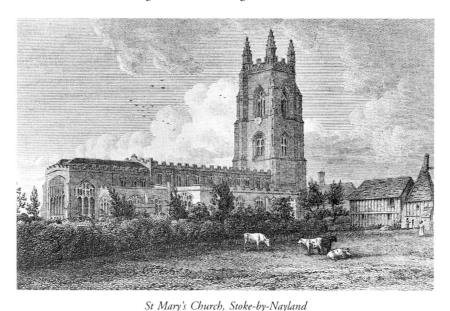

St Mary's Church, Stoke-by-Nayland
(Engraved by W. Deeble from a sketch by T. Higham in *Excursions*, I, p. 70)
St Mary's is a large fifteenth century Perpendicular church, 168 ft. long. The Tower is 120 ft high and very ornate. The building was financed by local merchants between 1439 and 1462. Despite this devotion to the late medieval Catholic Church, there were later to be more Protestants in Stoke-by-Nayland than in any other cloth centre in south-west Suffolk.

Lavenham, Grace Wrighton, spinster.[225] It is no surprise that Long Melford was traditionalist in its religious outlook. But the apparent submissiveness of Lavenham *is* surprising. MacCulloch has shown how prominent Lavenham men were in the Amicable Grant Rebellion, 1525, Ket's Rebellion, 1549, and in the local rising of 1569.[226] Furthermore Lavenham was to be a Roundhead stronghold during the First Civil War (1642–46).[227] Yet Lavenham was not then a Puritan centre and indeed, like Long Melford, was to show few signs of advanced Protestantism until the early eighteenth century.[228] The conclusion must be that until the end of our period Lavenham was politically radical but religiously conservative.

Hadleigh has been regarded as the archetypal Protestant cloth town, perhaps largely because of John Foxe's description of the place. Foxe wrote that

> a great number of that parish [Hadleigh] became exceeding well learned in the holy Scriptures, as well women as men, so that a man might have found among them many, that had often read the whole Bible through, and that could have said a great sort of St Paul's epistles by heart, and very well and readily have given a godly learned sentence in any matter of controversy. Their children and servants were also brought up and trained so diligently in the right knowledge of God's word, that the whole town seemed rather a university of the learned, than a town of cloth-making or labouring people; and (what most is to be commended) they are for the most part faithful followers of God's word in their living.[229]

The Protestant religion made headway in Hadleigh not just because of the piety of the town cloth workers but also because it was helped by four outstanding preachers: Thomas Bilney, Thomas Rose, Nicholas Shaxton and, most notably, Rowland Taylor, a future martyr. Furthermore Hadleigh's status as a peculiar of the Archbishop of Canterbury meant that it was exempt from the authority of the Bishop of Norwich. Thus Hadleigh became 'a benefice of refuge for some of Thomas Cranmer's protégés and early reformers'.[230] It is not surprising then that the Fines *Register* names more Protestants in Hadleigh than in any other cloth centre in south-west Suffolk, except Stoke-by-Nayland (see Map 10). However, the strength of Protestantism in Hadleigh may have been exaggerated by Foxe for propaganda purposes. Hadleigh was in fact a very divided place and 'not all the preaching' it heard 'was of the reforming tendency'. Indeed, Dr Craig has said that 'the group of committed Protestants in Hadleigh … remained a minority until the settled years and unhindered opportunities afforded by Elizabeth's reign'. Moreover, by the turn of the century, Hadleigh did not become a Puritan centre like so many other Protestant parishes in Suffolk, such as East Bergholt, Boxford, Bildeston and Ipswich. Instead it provided 'fertile ground for later Arminians'.[231]

Dr Taylor rebuking a Popish Priest who was about to say Mass in Hadley Church.

Religious conflict in Hadleigh
(From John Foxe, *Book of Martyrs* (1732 edn), p. 156)
The above scene is a later artist's reconstruction of a dramatic confrontation between Dr
Rowland Taylor, Rector of Hadleigh, and a Catholic priest intent on saying mass. It led
to the martyrdom of the former in 1555. Yet despite Taylor's fate, Hadleigh during the
Reformation was not a Protestant stronghold but a very divided town.

Central Suffolk, which included the deaneries of Hartismere, Hoxne,
Bosmere and Claydon, had more Protestants than the Stour valley (see
Map 10). Protestants were particularly numerous in Mendlesham and
Winston (see Map 10). The strength of Protestantism in mid-Suffolk might
surprise sociologically-minded historians because, in the sixteenth century
at least, the area was predominantly rural with few towns and industries.
On the other hand this region formed part of High Suffolk, a large
wood-pasture area with weak manorial organisation and limited gentry
control. 'The classic central Suffolk case is Mendlesham', says Professor
MacCulloch. 'This was a large village', he continues, 'with several prosperous
yeomen; the gentry landlords of the village, the Knyvetts, had long been
absentee, living at Buckenham Castle in Norfolk. It was perhaps this which
enabled the village to develop a startling radical organisation'.[232] If Stoke-
by-Nayland lay at the heart of dissident religious activity in the Stour valley,

Mendlesham was equally prominent in central Suffolk. Indeed, it seems to have harboured a brotherhood of Lollards in 1531, so it is likely that 'the Lollards of Mendlesham found Edwardian religion fully satisfying, believing as they did in clerical marriage, the royal supremacy, and in the Bible as their sufficient doctrine'.[233] In addition to Mendlesham, Winston was an important centre of Protestantism, though it appears to have had no Lollard antecedents. Both Mendlesham and Winston suffered from the fierce persecution of Sir John Tyrrell of Gipping who forced thirteen to flee from Winston and twenty-one from Mendlesham.[234] Moreover, the law was no respecter of persons. Joan Seman, aged sixty-six, and mother of a humble husbandman, was forced to leave her home in Mendlesham in 1556. In the same year Mrs Alice Thwaites, though a gentlewoman over sixty, was driven from her home in Winston, accompanied by two servants.[235]

Ipswich has often been called 'the cradle of the English Reformation'. This it was not because the English Reformation began in London.[236] Nevertheless, there was a very strong Protestant presence in Ipswich from 1530 at the earliest, perhaps because of the port's trading contacts with the Low Countries.[237] Bishop Nix almost certainly had the port of Ipswich in mind in 1530 when he condemned as disaffected to the Church, not only Cambridge clerics, but 'marchantes and suche that hath ther abyding not farr from the see'.[238] Nix was unlikely to have been thinking about the lesser ports of Suffolk. Professor Dickens has said that Dunwich, Aldeburgh and Orford revealed a Protestant presence between 1520 and 1558.[239] But the evidence hardly supports this view. The Fines *Register* names only one Protestant for each of these ports. By contrast, fifty-six inhabitants of Ipswich appear in the *Register*. However, this was the tip of the Protestant iceberg. In 1556 Catholic supporters at Ipswich drew up a list of ninety-eight inhabitants who were in hiding for, or otherwise exhibited, Protestant sympathies, including five clergy.[240] No wonder Professor MacCulloch says that 'the strength of Ipswich Protestantism in Mary's reign is unmistakable'.[241] Under Elizabeth I Ipswich would become the capital of Protestantism, indeed of Puritanism, in Suffolk.

So much for the main centres of Suffolk Protestantism. What about the strongholds of the traditional faith? Professor MacCulloch has remarked that in the Archdeaconry of Sudbury the fen and sheep-corn area to the north of Bury St Edmunds showed little sign of religious dissidence. In the Archdeaconry of Suffolk the sheep-corn area along the coast showed little trace of heresy and would show little inclination to Protestant activism under Elizabeth. How does one explain the religious conservatism (or was it religious indifference?) of the Fielding and the Sandlings? MacCulloch has suggested that 'perhaps the light-soil communities, with their sparser population and tighter manorial structure, were easier to control than the tough-minded yeoman farmers of the wood-pasture country'.[242] It is hard to disagree with this hypothesis.

Social composition[243]

We must now examine the social structure of Protestantism in Suffolk between 1525 and 1558. To maintain a sense of perspective the status and occupations of Protestants in a neighbouring county – Norfolk – and in a remote and backward county – Lancashire – will also be studied, though in less detail. Table 3.2 gives a statistical analysis of these Protestants.

Table 3.2 Some English Protestants 1525–58: A social analysis[244]

Status or Occupation	Suffolk	Norfolk	Lancashire
Nobility [245]	1 (0.5%)	–	–
Gentry	5 (2.3%)	4 (5.8%)	1 (2.0%)
Professionals	29 (13.6%)	30 (43.5%)	21 (43.8%)
Traders and craftsmen	58 (27.1%)	7 (10.1%)	6 (12.5%)
Husbandmen	10 (4.7%)	–	–
Labourers and servants	14 (6.5%)	–	–
Others [246]	2 (0.9%)	–	–
Unknown	95 (44.4%)	28 (40.6%)	20 (41.7%)
Total	214 (100.0%)	69 (100.0%)	48 (100.0%)
	(74 women,[247] i.e. 34%)	(7 women, i.e. 10%)	(5 women, i.e. 10%)

Table 3.2 shows that large groups in Suffolk, Norfolk and Lancashire consisted of 'unknowns'. Here we must heed Christopher Haigh's warning that the 'large number of heretics whose social status is not known weakens any calculation, especially as higher ranks were more likely to be recorded, and the unknowns may have been poor'.[248] On the other hand Dr Cliftlands has argued that 'we should not assume that historical obscurity is synonymous with social obscurity'.[249] The Fines *Register* names eighteen Protestants in Mendlesham, but records the occupations of only three. One of those Protestants whose status is not recorded is William Shepherd. Yet he was clearly a member of a yeoman family,[250] and what we know of the history of Mendlesham suggests that most of the named Protestants in the parish were of yeoman stock. In short, we must accept that 'unknowns' could include men and women of variable status or occupation.

It has been said that 'Protestants were recruited from throughout the social scale, but disproportionately from the middling and prosperous sectors'.[251] If we exclude the 'unknowns', we can indeed say that in Norfolk and Lancashire the Protestants were recruited from the more prosperous sectors, that is the gentry and professionals (see Table 3.2). In Norfolk and Lancashire, and indeed in Suffolk, the vast majority of professionals were former secular priests or ex-religious.[252] Table 3.2 shows that in percentage terms the gentry were less well-represented among the Protestants in Suffolk than they were among those in Norfolk.[253] Lancashire, in percentage terms, seems to be like Suffolk (see Table 3.2). Only one person – Sir William Charlton – was an indubitable gentleman. However, if we study the twenty-one professionals in detail, we find that eight of them were of gentry stock.[254] Among the tradesmen-craftsmen category, two merchants – George and Thomas Heaton of Heaton Hall – were also of gentle birth.[255] So if we take social *origins* into account, it could perhaps be argued that 23 per cent of Lancashire Protestants were gentry.

But if Protestantism was socially top-heavy in Norfolk and Lancashire, this was not the case in Suffolk. There the largest single group, excluding 'unknowns', consisted of artisans (see Table 3.2). Craftsmen and their wives numbered fifty-eight, including twenty-eight people involved in the textile industry,[256] fifteen in the leather trades,[257] four in woodwork occupations,[258] two in metal working,[259] and nine in miscellaneous occupations.[260] By contrast, artisans were poorly represented among the Protestants of Norfolk and Lancashire, as Table 3.2 shows. This same table shows two other major differences between the Protestants of Suffolk and those of Norfolk and Lancashire. In the last two counties husbandmen, labourers and servants are conspicuous by their absence, whereas in Suffolk they are very much in evidence.[261] The other major difference is that women formed only one-tenth of Protestants in Norfolk and Lancashire, but comprised a third of those in Suffolk. However, females were clearly a minority of heretics in all three counties. Perhaps the main reason was the high rate of illiteracy among women,[262] who would hardly have been attracted to a Bible-based religion.

The Marian martyrs
Artisans formed the backbone of Suffolk Protestants in the period 1525–58. This was even more the case among the most committed Protestants, the martyrs who died for their faith under Mary Tudor. Table 3.3 shows their social composition.

Table 3.3. Protestant and other martyrs in Mary Tudor's reign: A social analysis[263]

Status or Occupation	Numbers
Professionals	4
Traders and craftsmen	18
Husbandmen	2
Labourers	3
Servant	1
Unknown	2
Total	30
	(5 women, i.e. 17%)

Table 3.3 suggests that no Suffolk gentleman was burned for his faith. Only four professionals were burned, including three ex-priests and a former royal servant, Thomas Spurdance. One husbandman, William Seman of Mendlesham, and Margaret Dryver of Grundisburgh, the wife of

a husbandman, died for their beliefs. Three labourers suffered: William Allen of Somerton, Roger Barnard of Framsden and Thomas Spicer of Winston. So did Elizabeth Folkes, a maidservant of Stoke-by-Nayland. The occupations of two of the martyrs – James Ashley and Elizabeth Lawson, widow of William of Bedfield – are unknown. Clearly the most prominent martyrs were the eighteen tradesmen and craftsmen, the lower 'middle sort', who formed 60 per cent of the total.

Suffolk endured the full force of the Marian persecution. John Foxe wrote that 'the rage and vehemence of this terrible persecution in Queen Mary's reign did *chiefly*[264] light in London, Essex, Norfolk, Suffolk and Kent'.[265] Foxe exaggerated the situation in Norfolk, where only six people are definitely known to have suffered martyrdom under Queen Mary.[266] However, he was correct about the other four counties. According to the Fines *Register* Kent produced fifty-six Marian martyrs and Essex fifty-five. London had forty-four martyrs[267] and Suffolk came some way behind with thirty, though this may be an underestimate.[268] However, Suffolk's known total of thirty was the fourth largest among English counties and something of which local heretics could be proud,[269] though they might have been surprised that the county produced only fourteen Protestants who were exiles abroad during Mary's reign.[270]

So much for the numbers and social range of the Marian martyrs of Suffolk. But there are other important questions to be answered. Where did the thirty martyrs reside? What were their ages when burned? Where and when were they burned, and, most important of all, *why* were they burned? Appendix I(d) attempts to answer these queries.

The residences of the martyrs and their places and dates of execution are given in Appendix I(d). But some brief comment on their ages is necessary. Susan Brigden has argued that the 'Marian martyrs were very often young' and she names many heretics who were under thirty when they died.[271] Unfortunately we know the ages of only ten of the thirty Suffolk martyrs and our small sample cannot be statistically significant. Nevertheless, for what little they are worth, the figures show that six were aged thirty or under – Margaret Dryver (30), Elizabeth Folkes (20), Adam Foster (26), Robert Lawson (30), William Seman (26), Thomas Spicer (19) – and that of the remaining four, two were middle aged – Alexander Gooch (36) and Rowland Taylor (c. 46) – and two were elderly: Elizabeth Lawson (60) and Richard Yeoman (70).

We can speak much more confidently about the heresies than the ages of our Marian martyrs. The main heresies were refusal to accept the Mass and auricular confession, because they gave so much power to the priesthood. The Mass, the sacrament of the altar, is a re-enactment of Christ's sacrifice. Catholics then and now believe that at every celebration of the Mass a miracle occurs: the consecrated elements of the bread and wine are transformed, by the working of God's grace in the priest, into the very body and blood of Christ. It was this miracle of transubstantiation which the Protestants attacked most vehemently because they believed that Christ's sacrifice had been made once and for all and could not be repeated. Moreover, the Catholic priesthood had long held great power over the laity in confession and absolution, because every Christian who had reached the age of discretion was to confess privately his sins to a priest at least once a year. 'So vehement and widespread were attacks upon auricular confession at the Reformation.', says Susan Brigden, 'that it seemed as if it was almost a reason in itself for abandoning the old faith'.[272]

In Suffolk twenty-five of the thirty martyrs attacked the doctine of transubstantiation and by implication the Mass (see Appendix I(d)).[273] The situation was similar in London where thirty-seven of the forty-four martyrs denied the Mass.[274] Among the Suffolk martyrs was James Abbes, shoemaker of Stoke-by-Nayland, who said 'that the Sacrament of the Altar is but brede and that whosoever doth worship the sacrament committeth Idolatry'.

The burning of John Noyes at Laxfield (From John Foxe, *Book of Martyrs* (1732 edn), p. 824.) A later artist's reconstruction shows the terrible death suffered by John Noyes in his own village of Laxfield. Like most Protestant martyrs in Marian Suffolk, Noyes was of humble status.

Thomas Cobbe of Haverhill, a strong biblicist, 'saith he hath not lerned by the Scripture that Christ shuld be in the Sacrament' of the Altar. John Noyes of Laxfield, when asked 'whather he believed the body of our Lord Jesus Christ to be in the sacrament of the altar, under the forms of brede and wine, after the words of the consecration', answered that 'he thought natural the body of Christ to be only in heaven, and not in the sacrament'. Joan Trunchfeld, wife of an Ipswich shoemaker, argued on Zwinglian lines, saying that 'the sacrament of the altar YS brede only, and but a *memory*[275] of Christ's passion', adding that 'Masse is Idolatrye'. Thomas Spurdance was examined before the Chancellor of Norwich, who announced that 'the mass is a sacrifice for the quick and the dead'. Spurdance replied that 'it is no sacrifice for St Paul saith that Christ made one sacrifice once for all'. Rowland Taylor, Rector of Hadleigh and the most distinguished victim of persecution after the Oxford martyrs (Cranmer, Latimer and Ridley), denied transubstantiation because the body of Christ is in heaven and cannot be in two places at once.[276]

Twelve Suffolk martyrs refused to go to confession (see Appendix I(d)). Among them was William Allen of Somerton, who defiantly refused to be confessed. Roger Barnard of Framsden admitted that he had not been to Mass nor confessed his sins to a priest, but added: 'I have confessed my sins to Almighty God'. Thomas Spurdance refused to go to the confessional because he too had confessed directly to God.[277] Appendix I(d) shows that eight Suffolk martyrs rejected papal supremacy, some using strong language. Richard Yeoman, Rowland Taylor's curate at Hadleigh, was 'required to submit himself to the holy father the pope'. But he refused, saying 'I defy him and all his detestable abominations. I will in no wise have to do with him, nor anything that appertaineth to him'. Dr Taylor himself prayed to be delivered from the 'tyranny of the bishop of Rome, and all his detestable errors, idolatries and abominations'.[278]

Appendix I(d) shows that at least seven of our Marian martyrs despised the elaborate religious ceremonies which had been so popular in the late medieval church. Elizabeth Lawson of Bedfield held that the ceremonies of the church were not good. William Allen of Somerton refused to come to church because none of the services was edifying. Philip Umfrye of Onehouse thought that the ceremonies of the church were abominable. John Dennye, Edmund Poole and Thomas Spicer believed that 'ceremonies used in the church' did not encourage religious devotion. Thomas Spurdance told Bishop Hopton of Norwich that 'the ceremonies in your church' were 'inventions and imaginings out of your own brain, without any word of God to prove them'.[279]

Appendix I(d) identifies five individuals whose beliefs were extremely radical. James Ashley, John Cooke, Alexander Lane and Robert Miles did not, like most Protestants, confine themselves to attacking transubstantiation, the Mass, confession, papal supremacy and church ceremonies; they also denied the humanity of Christ. Thomas Cobbe not only denied transubstantiation but rejected baptism as a sacrament. These five radicals are best described as 'other heretics'. The other twenty-five martyrs can be regarded as mainstream Protestants.

Clerical and gentry supporters

By attacking the central beliefs of the Marian church – transubstantiation and the Mass, auricular confession, papal supremacy, church ceremonies – twenty-five Suffolk Protestants and five other heretics condemned them-selves to burning at the stake. These martyrs included not a single gentleman and only three priests (see Appendix I(d)). However, Professor MacCulloch attributes the eventual triumph of Protestantism in Suffolk to the support of influential local men (ie. nobles and gentry) and to charismatic preaching by renegade priests.[280] The role of these committed individuals was indeed of vital importance.

The reforming clergy, though a minority, must bulk large in any account of early Protestantism in Suffolk. As MacCulloch rightly says, 'Thomas Bilney's personal crusade of the 1520s ... was probably of great importance in stimulating popular disenchantment with traditional Catholicism'.[281] We have noticed that Bilney was succeeded at Hadleigh by three outstanding preachers: Thomas Rose, Nicholas Shaxton and, above all, Rowland Taylor, perhaps the most powerful Protestant preacher in mid-sixteenth century Suffolk. Rose preached against saint and image worship, transubstantiation and auricular confession, and may have introduced an English mass in about 1538. Shaxton stressed man's impotence for good and believed that priests might marry. Rowland Taylor not only denied transubstantiation and papal supremacy, but stoutly defended clerical marriage. Many other clergy did much to advance the Protestant cause in Suffolk. One thinks of Robert Barnes, who helped to infect Bury Abbey with heresy; Thomas Robertes, an anti-papal propagandist in Ipswich where he was parish priest of St Mary at the Elms; Thomas Bacon, active in Ipswich and arrested in 1540 for sermons preached in Norwich diocese; William Leiton, monk of Ely, executed in 1538 for advocating communion in both kinds; and John Bale, curate of Thorndon, and Matthew Parker, dean of Stoke-by-Clare college and future Archbishop of Canterbury, both of whom preached in favour of justification by faith.[282]

So much for the clergy. What about the nobility and gentry? In 1530 Bishop Nix of Norwich was of the opinion that 'gentilm ... be not greatly infect' by heresy.[283] But as MacCulloch says, ' this situation was to change over the next decade when gentry support ... began to emerge'.[284] The most active upper class Protestants in mid-Tudor Suffolk were Charles Brandon, 1st Duke of Suffolk; Thomas, 2nd Lord Wentworth; Sir William Waldegrave of Bures; and Edward Grimston of Rishangles. Charles Brandon (d. 1545) protected Protestant clergymen. He allowed Thomas Rose, formerly of

Hadleigh, to preach at Stratford St Mary, a benefice held by Brandon himself. During the later 1530s and 1540s the Brandons included among their chaplains a number of definite reformers, such as the Scots ex-friar Alexander Seton, or the first Elizabethan Bishop of Norwich, John Parkhurst. Thomas, 2nd Lord Wentworth (d. 1551) had a genuine zeal for reform. Indeed, John Bale, former prior of the Carmelite friars at Ipswich, attributed his own conversion to Protestantism to Wentworth's influence. Sir William Waldegrave (d. 1554) was second to none in his devotion to the Protestant cause. In 1538 he was having to be restrained in his enthusiasm for promoting church services in English in the area of his home at Bures. Edward Grimston (d. 1599), a gentleman pensioner of Henry VIII and three times an MP for Ipswich, clearly had strong Protestant inclinations; otherwise in 1549 the town schoolmaster of Ipswich would not have dedicated to him a translation of the works of Zwingli.[285]

Charles Brandon, 1st Duke of Suffolk (d. 1545) by an unknown artist. Brandon greatly helped the Reformed religion in Suffolk by protecting and encouraging Protestant clerics.

Professor MacCulloch rightly says that such 'gentry support was vital for sustaining (though not necessarily creating) a vigorous grass-roots Protestantism'.[286] But generalising about England, W. J. Sheils has noted that 'before 1558 the number of Protestant gentry remained small'.[287] This may also have been true of Suffolk for, as MacCulloch says, 'the Marian régime ... enjoyed ... powerful support among the county magistrates'.[288] Without strong upper class support, the Protestants were doomed. However, support for Protestantism became more widespread from the late sixteenth century in Suffolk and elsewhere. In France, for example, 'Protestantism initially made its biggest impact on the lower orders of society. By the mid-sixteenth century, however, Calvinism had begun to make deep inroads into the nobility'.[289] In Suffolk the situation was strikingly similar. As we have observed, the early Protestants were mostly of lower or, at best, lower-middle class stock. But in the Elizabethan and early Stuart period humble Protestants would enjoy considerable gentry support and leadership. The importance of the Protestant gentry, including the 'hotter sort', will be apparent in the next chapter.

Conclusion

What general conclusions can be drawn about the Reformation in Suffolk? First, we can agree with Christopher Haigh that 'it was the break with Rome which was to cause the decline of Catholicism, not the decline of Catholicism which led to the break with Rome'.[290] For on the eve of the Reformation the Church in Suffolk was in a flourishing condition, and this is particularly shown by the large amount of church building or re-building, the popularity of the religious guilds, the high standards of morality and commitment among the clergy, and the small amount of anti-clericalism and Lollardy in the county. The break with Rome was imposed from above and the people of Suffolk looked on helplessly as Henry VIII assumed the title of 'Supreme Head of the Church of England'.

The breach with Rome led almost inevitably to the Dissolution of the Religious Orders because Henry regarded them as a threat to the royal supremacy. In Suffolk most monasteries, friaries and nunneries were easy targets for they were neither numerous, nor large, nor wealthy. The great Benedictine abbey of Bury St Edmunds, with many monks and much landed wealth, was exceptional. Within four years (1536–40) all the religious houses in Suffolk (except the few secular colleges and a dozen hospitals[291]) were swept away. It is hard to generalise about the fate of the ex-religious. Most heads of houses, together with the monks of Bury abbey, received adequate pensions. Moreover, several of the Bury monks had successful post-dissolution careers, mostly in the Church. But the unpensioned male ex-religious, except for a fortunate few, did badly, only 9 per cent receiving ecclesiastical posts. Much monastic and convent land in Suffolk was sold between 1536 and 1547. Apart from a few London merchants and some office-holders, the main beneficiaries of the dissolution in Suffolk were the gentry. The purchasers included Protestants, Catholics and 'neuters' alike.

The progress of Protestantism was slow in Suffolk from the 1520s until the death of Mary Tudor. The First Protestant Reformation (1536–39) witnessed few religious changes in the county. But the Second Protestant Reformation (1547–53) saw the disappearance of the secular colleges, religious guilds and chantries. Clerical marriage became more common in Suffolk under Edward VI. But Suffolk, like the rest of England, was re-catholicised under Queen Mary. On the whole the churchwardens' accounts from 1547 to 1558 show how obedient the Suffolk people were to authority, whether that authority was enforcing Protestantism under Edward VI or Catholicism under Mary I. Clearly it was a case of *cuius regio, eius religio*.

Finally, it must be emphasised that the Protestants in Suffolk were a very small minority. However, their importance was out of all proportion to their numbers. Protestantism was localised in Suffolk, being found mainly

in the Stour Valley, central Suffolk and Ipswich. Socially, the early Protestants received their strongest support from artisans. These humble folk,
and especially the martyrs, strongly resented priestly power, hence their
vigorous and articulate attacks on transubstantiation, the Mass, auricular
confession, papal supremacy and church ceremonies. But such people could
not supply to the Protestant cause strong leadership. This was provided by
the Protestant clergy and gentry, and in the Elizabethan and early Stuart
period it resulted in a firm alliance between 'magistracy and ministry'.

CHAPTER FOUR

Papists and Puritans in Elizabethan and early Stuart Suffolk

The Elizabethan Church Settlement

The Third English Reformation is associated with the Elizabethan Church Settlement which made England irrevocably Protestant. The legal basis of that settlement was laid down in the 1559 Acts of Supremacy and Uniformity but also in the Thirty-Nine Articles of Religion, passed in the Convocation (general assembly of the clergy) of 1563 but not part of statutory law until 1571.

The Act of Supremacy (1 Eliz., cap. 1) gave Elizabeth I the new title of 'Supreme Governor' of the Church of England. This finally repudiated the Pope's jurisdiction. Like her father, Henry VIII, Elizabeth was determined to keep religion firmly under the control of the Crown. Her attitude was symbolised by the placing of the royal coat of arms within the parish churches in the place where the rood had once stood as an object of communal worship. One of the best examples is to be found in the parish church of Preston, Babergh Hundred. During Elizabeth's reign Robert Reyce set up in that church royal arms and commandments and texts arranged on triptychs.[1]

The Act of Uniformity (1 Eliz., cap. 2) imposed a fine of one shilling on all who absented themselves from Church of England services on Sundays and Holy Days (e.g. Easter). More importantly, it authorised a new English-language Prayer Book, which contained a few changes from its 1552 predecessor. The most important modifications lay in the communion service and the Ornaments Rubric. The 1552 communion service was modified in the new Prayer Book to add the words of administration in the 1549 book to the 1552 words: 'the body of our Lord Jesus Christ, which was given for thee, preserve thy body and soul unto everlasting life (1549). Take and eat this in remembrance that Christ died for thee, and feed on him in thy heart by faith with thanksgiving' (1552). By joining together the two formulae it allowed the possibility of belief that Christ's body and blood were really present in the bread and wine, so important to Catholics, while at the same time asserting the memorial aspect of the service, which conformed to Zwinglian theology. The Third Prayer Book of 1559 also omitted the so-called 'Black Rubric' in the 1552 Prayer Book, which had contained a clear denial of the corporeal presence in the bread and wine. The Ornaments Rubric stipulated that the ornaments of the churches should be those in use 'by authority of parliament' in the second year of Edward VI's reign. Hence churches were allowed to keep their crucifixes, candlesticks and other furnishings. The sign of the cross in baptism and the ring in marriage were also permitted. The clergy were expected to wear the alb and cope (Catholic vestments traditionally worn at Mass) at communion and a white surplice at all other services. This was a concession to traditionalists and was clearly less Protestant than the 1552 book which had abolished all vestments except the surplice.

The Thirty-Nine Articles of Religion were and are the official doctrines of the Church of England. About one-third of the Articles expressed ecumenical Christian beliefs, six refuted the alleged teachings of the Ana-baptists (radical Protestant sects), and the remainder were either positively Protestant or anti-Catholic. Article Thirty-One strongly attacked the Mass, which Catholics regard as the central act of worship. But the Article considered that 'the sacrifices of Masses ... were blasphemous fables and dangerous deceits'. Article Twenty-Eight condemned transubstantiation be-cause it 'cannot be proved by holy writ'. Article Twenty-Two repudiated 'The Romish Doctrine concerning purgatory ... as well as Images as of Reliques' which was 'grounded upon no warranty of Scripture, but rather repugnant to the Word of God'. As for basic Protestant beliefs, these, with one exception, were stated with great clarity. Article Twelve said that 'we are justified by Faith alone'. Article Thirty strongly advocated communion in both kinds. Article Thirty-Two allowed clerical marriage. Only one Protestant doctrine was not clearly stated: predestination. Article Seventeen, says Susan Doran, 'was deliberately ambiguous' on this subject 'in order to be acceptable to both Lutherans and the Swiss Reformed Churches'.[2] Finally, it is worth noting Article Thirty-Six. This approved of bishops and, by implication, a clerical hierarchy. It was to offend some of the more Calvinistic Protestants, who noted that in Calvin's Geneva ministers were equal.

It is no longer fashionable to regard the Elizabethan Church Settlement as a *via media*, a middle way between Rome and Geneva.[3] But the Church was undoubtedly of a hybrid nature. Christopher Hill has argued that the Church Settlement offered 'protestant doctrine for the intellectuals, catholic ceremonies for the masses'.[4] Professor Conrad Russell has opined that the state church of Elizabeth was one 'which looked Catholic, and sounded Protestant'.[5] This was indeed the problem. The catholic ceremonies (e.g. the Ornaments Rubric) and, to a lesser extent, the church hierarchy were to be unacceptable to hard-line Protestants (called Puritans), while the mainly Protestant Thirty-Nine Articles and the royal supremacy over the Church were to be anathema to hard-line Catholics (called Papists). Let us now deal with these opponents of the Elizabethan Church Settlement, the Papists and the Puritans.

Papists

'Papist' was a contemporary, abusive term applied to Roman Catholics who recognised the Pope as head of their church. In the middle and later years of Elizabeth's reign and in the early Stuart period Papists were generally divided into three categories by contemporaries: 'recusants' (Latin *recusare*, to refuse) [6] who would not attend the established Anglican Church;[7] 'non-communicants' who attended Anglican services but did not take communion; and 'schismatics', who took communion while remaining at heart in sympathy with Catholicism. A member of either of the last two groups may be described as a 'Church Papist'. However, little attention will be paid to 'Church Papists' because, important though they were, they are extremely difficult to identify and 'defy statistical analysis'.[8] Instead, we shall concentrate mainly on the ascertainable, open and committed Catholics: the 'popish recusants'.

The first recusants appear in 1568, if we can believe Sir Edward Coke. They were three Suffolk gentlemen: 'Cornwallys, Beddingfield and Sily-arde ..., they absolutely refusing to come to our [Anglican] churches. And untill they in that sort began, the name of recusant was never heard of amongst us'.[9] But they were rare birds, and Coke emphasised that until about 1570 'all Papists came to our [Established] Church and service without scruple'.[10] This is not surprising. In a church-going society, to cease attending the parish church was unthinkable. What largely changed the situation was Pope Pius V's bull of 1570, *Regnans in Excelsis*, excommunicating and deposing Elizabeth. Catholics now had to choose between loyalty to the Queen or to the Pope. If they chose the former they would have to attend the Anglican Church; if the latter they would not. The long-term result was that a majority of Catholics defected to Protestantism, while a committed minority became Catholic recusants.

There was much anti-Catholic hysteria in the Elizabethan and Stuart periods. One would therefore expect the recusants in Suffolk and elsewhere to have been persecuted. The Papists were regarded as disloyal subjects, in league with the Papacy and Spain, the leading Catholic power and spearhead of the Counter-Reformation. Catholics were indeed regarded as lackeys of Spanish imperialism. They were also 'the enemy within' and Catholics as a whole were to be unjustly blamed for the Gunpowder Plot of 1605, the execution of Charles I in 1649, the Great Fire of London of 1666 and the Popish Plot of 1678. But despite this fierce anti-Popery, Catholics were not continuously persecuted, but only intermittently – in times of crisis, such as during the 1580s, which saw plots and conspiracies against Queen Elizabeth and the sailing of the Spanish Armada; during the few years following the Gunpowder Plot of 1605; during the run-up to the First Civil War, in 1640–42; and during the Popish Plot years of 1678–81. It was mainly during these crises that Catholics suffered heavy recusancy fines, imprisonment or death.

In Suffolk there does not seem to have been much persecution. Diarmaid MacCulloch has observed that no Suffolk gentleman was executed for recusant offences during Elizabeth's reign, except Mountford Scott of Ipswich, a Jesuit missioner.[11] He was hanged, drawn and quartered in Fleet Street, London, on 1st July 1591.[12]

Not many Suffolk Catholic gentry were imprisoned in the late sixteenth century and those who were suffered far less than might be expected. Sir Thomas Cornwallis of Brome Hall (1519–1604), apparently a recusant in 1568, was vigorously interrogated about his religious and political views and imprisoned between 1 October 1569 and 30 September 1570. However, he was not treated with any harshness and was allowed to maintain contact with his family and friends. During most of the 1570s he was a Church Papist but towards the end of that decade he ceased to conform to the Anglican Church and became a recusant again. He was imprisoned once more in 1587–89, but his confinement was in the comparative ease of the house of family and friends in London.[13] Other Suffolk recusant gentry were also treated with consideration. During August 1578 Elizabeth and her Court came on progress into East Anglia. Later twenty-three prominent Catholic gentlemen of Norfolk and Suffolk were ordered to appear before the Privy Council. Nine were sentenced to imprisonment for refusing to conform to the State religion. In practice, however, John Daniel of Acton, Henry Drury of Lawshall, Michael Hare of Bruisyard and Roger Martin of Long Melford were confined, not in prison, but in the houses of certain reliable citizens in Bury St Edmunds and Ipswich. Of the five others, four, including Edmund Bedingfield of Denham and Henry Everard of Linstead, were allocated to houses in Bury and one, Edward Sulyard of Haughley, went to Ipswich.[14] Sulyard was shown equal consideration in 1588. In that year he was 'imprisoned' at the London house of Thomas Tyrrell during the Armada scare, but, as MacCulloch says, 'his ordeal cannot have been very severe; Tyrrell was his brother-in-law'.[15] MacCulloch has also noted that 'time and time again recusant prisoners were released or transferred to house arrest to regain their health or to avoid an outbreak of plague'.[16] The Suffolk Catholics were indeed fortunate because for most of their co-religionists imprisonment in Elizabeth I's reign was often an extremely unpleasant experience.[17]

The financial penalties for recusancy were legally savage. Under an Act of 1581 (23 Eliz., cap. 1) convicted recusants could be fined £20 for every month they stayed away from Church of England services, a vast sum for all but the richest Catholics.[18] By an Act of 1587 (29 Eliz., cap. 6) Catholics defaulting on payment could have all their goods and two-thirds of their lands seized by the Crown. In practice, these penalties were not rigidly enforced and only a tiny number of Suffolk gentry seem to have paid heavy fines for popish recusancy under Elizabeth I. As MacCulloch reminds us, just three attempted to pay the statutory £20-a-month fine for non-churchgoing for any length of time: Edward Sulyard of Haughley, Edward Rookwood of Euston, and Michael Hare of Bruisyard.[19] In addition, they had to pay their pre-1587 arrears of recusancy fines to the Exchequer. Sulyard was heavily mulcted and by 27 November 1587 he had paid £1,380.[20] Hare paid the same amount by 16 November 1587.[21] However, he does not seem to have been unduly worried. According to Professor MacCulloch 'Hare clearly regarded his burden of fines as a spur to a dynamic policy of estate management'.[22] The least fortunate of the trio was Rookwood. His fine of £940, paid by 28 November 1589,[23] apparently took a heavy toll of his resources.[24] But his downfall may have been caused less by recusancy fines than by building 'the biggest house in the county of Suffolk', Euston Hall.[25] Another Suffolk recusant who paid heavily for his beliefs was the devout Roger Martin of Long Melford. Indicted as a recusant in 1574, Martin was fined nearly £200 ten years later 'for not cominge to Church'. Moreover, from 1587 he was deprived of income from lands which he owned.[26] Sulyard, Rookwood, Hare and Martin probably suffered more, financially, than any other Suffolk recusant gentry during Elizabeth's reign.

Since few were victims of cruel persecution, it is hardly surprising that 'the overwhelming majority of the Suffolk recusant gentry were vocal and sincere in their protestations of loyalty to the Crown'.[27] At any rate only two Suffolk Catholic gentlemen seem to have been found guilty of treason. Charles, son of Philip Tilney of Shelley, was executed in St Giles Fields, London, for his part in the Babington Plot of 1586, and Ambrose Rookwood of Coldham Hall was executed, along with Guy Fawkes, in Old Palace Yard, Westminster, for his involvement in the Gunpowder Plot of 1605.[28]

We must not, however, paint too rosy a picture of the situation, either in the Elizabethan or early Stuart periods. As Dr Mullett has rightly emphasised, 'the crown had a direct pecuniary interest in the enforcement of the penal laws'.[29] In 1627 Charles I restored the practice of composition. This was a contract between government and recusant whereby the latter agreed to compound, that is to pay an annual rent based upon the assessed value of two-thirds of his landed property, often in *lieu* of arrears of recusancy fines. Though not as heavy as the fines themselves, the compositions were onerous. In Suffolk recusant revenue rose from £103 4s. 0d. in 1627–28 to a staggering £728 in 1633–34, though after that date there was a small decline.[30] The heavy composition fines paid by Suffolk recusants must at least partly explain why during the First Civil War (1642–46) few of the Catholic gentry supported Charles I and why most apparently opted for neutrality.[31]

So much for the loyalties and persecution of the Suffolk Catholics. Let us now study the numbers, social structure and geographical distribution of the Catholic recusants from the 1590s to the eve of the First Civil War, and then examine the part played by the Suffolk gentry in the survival of Roman Catholicism.

Coldham Hall, Stanningfield
(Photograph: S.R.O. (I), J I 11/2/2743)
Coldham Hall was built by Robert Rookwood *c.* 1574. It is an H-shaped house of red
brick. The windows are mullioned. Above the hall all along the house runs a long
gallery. The Hall had a secret hiding-place for Catholic priests. Robert Rookwood's son,
Ambrose, was one of the Gunpowder Plotters.

We shall never know the exact number of Catholics during the early seventeenth century. The sources either overestimate or underestimate their strength. Gondomar, the Spanish ambassador at the court of King James, estimated that there were as many as 300,000 recusants in England in 1617.[32] On the other hand, the communicant returns record minute numbers of recusants in 1603. In that year enquiries were directed to the parish clergy by the Archbishop of Canterbury concerning the numbers of communicants, recusants and dissenters ('they that do not receive' communion). Unfortunately, many incumbents gave 'rounded' estimates rather than exact counts of communicants and others. Many also under-represented the numbers of recusants and non-conformists in an attempt to present a good picture of the religious state of their livings.[33] Perhaps the most reliable estimates of the numbers of Catholic recusants in the early Stuart period are those given by Professor Bossy. He says that in England and Wales the total size of the Catholic community was about 40,000 in 1603 and above 60,000 in 1641. Thus in 1600 Catholics formed 1 per cent of the population of England and in 1641 1.2 per cent.[34]

What was the situation in Suffolk? It is almost impossible to say. But in 1606 355 people were indicted for recusancy, and if we use the commonly accepted multiplier of 4.5 persons to a household, papists formed about

1.5 per cent of the total population of Suffolk, which was 108,000. This percentage was above the national average. In 1641 ninety-five persons were presented for recusancy. Using the same multiplier, it would seem that popish recusants comprised a mere 0.3 per cent of the county population, which was 125,000. This percentage was well below the national average.[35] Contrast Lancashire where in 1641 recusants formed 9 per cent of the total population.[36]

Table 4.1 gives more details of the numbers of Catholic recusants in Suffolk and examines their social composition in 1592, 1606 and 1641.[37]

Table 4.1 Suffolk Catholic recusants: A social analysis[38]

Status or Occupation	1592	1606	1641
Gentry	30 (31%)	93 (26%)	34 (36%)
Professionals	–	2 (1%)	–
Traders and craftsmen	5 (5%)	14 (4%)	–
Yeomen	23 (24%)	77 (22%)	33 (35%)
Husbandmen	2 (2%)	4 (1%)	–
Labourers and servants	–	8 (2%)	–
Others	21 (22%)	78 (22%)	5 (5%)
Unknown	15 (16%)	79 (22%)	23 (24%)
Total	96 (100%)	355 (100%)	95 (100%)
	(35 women i.e. 36%)	(164 women i.e. 46%)	(34 women i.e. 36%)

Two main conclusions emerge from our study of Table 4.1. First, the numbers of recusants fluctuated, reaching their peak in 1606, but this was not necessarily because recusancy found more favour among Catholics but rather because of greater vigilance on the part of the authorities. In the aftermath of the Gunpowder Plot the government made a determined effort to rope in as many recusants as possible. However, there is no denying the dramatic fall in the numbers of recusants between 1606 and 1641,[39] and this is particularly noticeable among the gentry. Some families, like the Jerninghams of Somerleyton, moved to Norfolk,[40] some, like the Hares of Bruisyard, failed in the male line, while others, like the Waldegraves of Smallbridge Hall, near Bures, conformed to the Church of England.[41] By 1641 only thirty-four Suffolk gentry families can be confidently called Catholic[42] (See Map 11).

Second, the Catholic recusant gentry were nevertheless important. Indeed, Table 4.1 shows that in 1592, 1606 and 1641 they were the largest single group.[43] Moreover, in 1606 and 1641 (and probably in 1592) the proportion of gentry in the Catholic recusant community was considerably larger than the proportion of gentry in the population at large. The gentry comprised 1.7 per cent of the total population of Suffolk in 1603 and 2.5 per cent in 1642.[44] But the gentry formed 26 per cent of the recusant population in 1606 and 36 per cent in 1641.[45] We are therefore justified in saying that

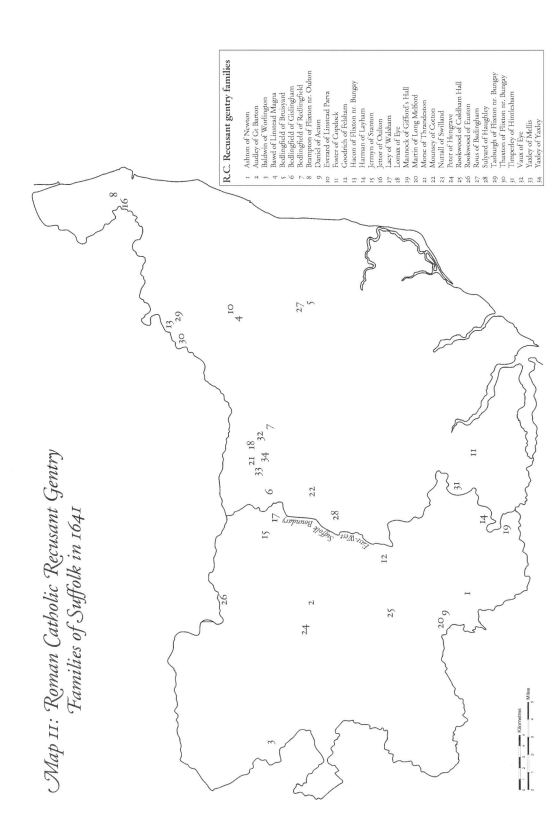

Map II: Roman Catholic Recusant Gentry Families of Suffolk in 1641

R.C. Recusant gentry families

1. Ashton of Newton
2. Audley of Gt Barton
3. Baldwin of Worlington
4. Bawd of Linstead Magna
5. Bedlingfield of Bruisyard
6. Bedlingfield of Gislingham
7. Bedlingfield of Redlingfield
8. Brampton of Flixton nr. Oulton
9. Daniel of Acton
10. Everard of Linstead Parva
11. Foster of Copdock
12. Goodrich of Felsham
13. Hacon of Flixton nr. Bungay
14. Harman of Layham
15. Jermyn of Stanton
16. Jettor of Oulton
17. Lacy of Walsham
18. Lomax of Eye
19. Mannock of Gifford's Hall
20. Martin of Long Melford
21. Morse of Thrandeston
22. Mounsey of Cotton
23. Nuttall of Swilland
24. Peter of Hengrave
25. Rookwood of Coldham Hall
26. Rookwood of Euston
27. Rous of Badingham
28. Sulyard of Haughley
29. Tasburgh of Flixton nr. Bungay
30. Thaxton of Flixton nr. Bungay
31. Timperley of Hintlesham
32. Vaux of Eye
33. Yaxley of Mellis
34. Yaxley of Yaxley

Roman Catholic recusancy was essentially seigneurial. In this respect Suffolk was a typical and not an exceptional county, as Table 4.2 suggests.

Table 4.2 Gentry and plebeian Catholics in 1641[46]

Status	EAST			SOUTH	
	Suffolk	*Norfolk*	*Essex*	*Oxfordshire*	*Sussex*
Gentry	34 (36%)	28 (41%)	83 (28%)	50 (39%)	88 (17%)
Plebeians	61 (64%)	40 (59%)	211 (72%)	79 (61%)	428 (83%)
Total	95 (100%)	68 (100%)	294 (100%)	129 (100%)	516 (100%)

Status	MIDLANDS		NORTH
	Staffordshire	*Warwickshire*	*Lancashire*
Gentry	206 (19%)	30 (36%)	616 (7%)
Plebeians	863 (81%)	53 (64%)	8,056 (93%)
Total	1,069 (100%)	83 (100%)	8,672 (100%)

Table 4.2 shows that it was Lancashire which was the exceptional county. This was a shire where Catholicism was essentially popular. The differences between the seigneurial Catholicism of East Anglia and the popular Catholicism of Lancashire were graphically portrayed by Father John Gerard, a Jesuit priest of Lancashire extraction, who operated in East Anglia in the 1590s. It is worth quoting Gerard's remarks in full:

> There is a great difference between these counties where I was now working [East Anglia] and other parts of England. In other places, where a large number of the people are Catholics and nearly all have leanings towards Catholicism, it is easy to make many converts and to have large congregations at sermons. For instance, in Lancashire I have seen myself more than two hundred present at mass and sermon. People of this kind come into the Church without difficulty, but they fall away the moment persecution blows up. When the alarm is over, they come back again. By contrast, in the districts I was living in now, Catholics were very few. They were mostly from the better classes; none, or hardly any, from the ordinary people, for they are unable to live in peace, surrounded as they are by most fierce Protestants.[47]

Let us now examine the geographical distribution of the Catholic recusants in Suffolk. Referring to Catholics as a whole, Joy Rowe has said that 'By the end of Elizabeth's reign a pattern of Catholic community had been established in Suffolk, scattered across the county but with the greatest concentration in High Suffolk and the Liberty of St Edmund'. They were also to be found 'along the valley of the River Waveney forming the Suffolk-Norfolk border'.[48] The recusant gentry were similarly distributed on the eve of the First Civil War (see Map 11). They were particularly strong in the heavy wood-pasture lands of High Suffolk. Here they greatly differed from the recusant gentry of Elizabethan Norfolk, where 64 per cent lived in the sheep-corn area.[49] Map 11 shows that many parts of Suffolk were untouched or barely touched by recusancy. The recusant gentry were practically non-existent in the Breckland, in Risbridge hundred, in Ipswich and especially in the Sandlings, except Lothingland.

Lothingland has been called 'a Suffolk Lancashire'[50] because of its topography, powerful gentry and strong Catholicism. MacCulloch says that Lothingland was 'a microcosm of the changing fortunes of Catholicism in Suffolk'.[51] This coastal hundred was practically an island, bordered by marshes and Broadland to the north and west and by the sea to the east.[52] Catholics seemed safe here as they were dominated and protected by the powerful family of Jerningham. But in 1584 John Jerningham was removed from the Bench of magistrates[53] and he lost his authority to Protestant JP's, one of whom was John Wentworth. Under the early Stuarts, Wentworth's son, Sir John of Somerleyton, apparently almost extirpated Catholicism in Lothingland for it was said that 'he brought good preachers into that Island of Lothingland, and ther was the chief patron of religion and honestye in his time'.[54] So in Lothingland Catholicism was replaced by advanced Protestantism.

Catholicism undoubtedly declined in numbers and influence during the late Elizabethan and early Stuart periods, but, except possibly in Lothingland, it was not obliterated. Was this largely due to the gentry? Professor Scarisbrick would answer with an emphatic yes. He has said that

> The survival of the old faith would have been impossible without the country houses which acted as mass-centres, created communities of Catholics consisting of families, servants and dependants, and sheltered priests as tutors, chaplains or itinerant missionaries smuggled in or hidden from ransacking pursuivants and sent on to their next destination with food, money and possibly escort. The laity [i.e. gentry] nourished and protected their clergy ...[55]

Joy Rowe has criticised some of Scarisbrick's views, saying that 'In the parishes of central Hartismere Deanery ... the Catholic community does not appear to have been dependent on its proximity to gentry houses'. Moreover, Catholic priests 'seem to have been peripatetic missioners rather than chaplains resident in gentry houses'. Rowe admits that Jesuit priests tended to remain at a single house. 'In 1590, John Gerard S J spent a year with Edward Rookwood at Euston before moving the 15 miles to Lawshall where he remained for a similar period with Henry Drury'. But secular priests in Suffolk were 'constantly on the move'.[56]

It is difficult to disagree with these comments. However, let us not throw out the baby with the bathwater. We have noted that during the late Elizabethan and early Stuart periods the gentry formed the largest single group among Suffolk recusants. Furthermore, they gave much spiritual support to their faith. It was thanks largely to the gentry that the Catholic Church in Suffolk was provided with mass centres, priests and nuns.

Rowe's map, in *An Historical Atlas of Suffolk*, shows the mass centres of the county, including those around 1600.[57] There were eighteen such centres and all but two – Bury and Wetherden – were provided by the gentry. Mass centres were, of course, exceptionally important because to Catholics mass was the central act of worship.

Thirty-five Suffolk men were ordained Catholic priests, or took their professions as regular clergy, between 1588 and 1642.[58] Of these thirty-five, twenty (57 per cent) were of gentry stock. Two-thirds of these gentry-priests joined religious orders. Eleven gentlemen were ordained as Jesuits: Henry and Edward Bedingfield of Redlingfield (between 1606 and 1611 and in 1622 respectively), Thomas Bedingfield (pre-1635),[59] Thomas Everard of Linstead Parva (1592), Robert and Bartholemew Foster of Copdock (1615, 1616), Henry Lanman of Westhorpe (1603), John Mannock of Gifford's Hall (pre-1621), Robert Rookwood of Coldham Hall (1604), Andrew Sulyard of Haughley (1634), and Henry Morse of Thrandeston (1624). The latter was martyred for his faith in 1645. Three Suffolk gentry became Benedictines. These included Dunstan Everard of Linstead Parva, who made his profession in 1616, and two urban gentry: Bartholemew and James Roe of Bury St Edmunds. James was professed in 1626, while his elder brother, Bartholemew, was professed in 1612, ordained in 1615 and martyred in 1642.[60] Finally, six gentlemen were ordained as secular priests: William Everard of Linstead Parva (in 1615), William and Henry Mannock of Gifford's Hall (1605, 1612), Robert Rookwood of Euston Hall (1621), Anthony Rous of Dennington (1592), and Thomas Short of Bury St Edmunds (1641).[61]

By providing a fair number of priests, the Catholic gentry helped to ensure the very survival of the old faith in Suffolk, for without priests there can be no Roman Catholicism. It is also difficult to visualise Roman Catholicism without nuns. Fourteen Suffolk women became choir nuns in continental convents between 1600 and 1642, and *all* were from gentry families. Exactly half the gentry-nuns joined the most prestigious religious order, the Benedictines. Three – Margaret Yaxley of Yaxley (professed in 1623), Anne and Eleanor Timperley of Hintlesham (professed in 1625 and 1630 respectively) – became nuns at Cambrai. Two-Tecla and Eugenie Bedingfield of Redlingfield (1630, 1633) – were nuns at Ghent. One – Dorothy Mannock of Gifford's Hall (1619) – became a nun in Brussels. Mary Yaxley of Yaxley, professed at Brussels in 1621, was one of three nuns lent by that convent to initiate the community at Cambrai. Four Suffolk ladies joined the Poor Clares at Gravelines: Dorothy Yaxley of Yaxley (professed in 1619), Margaret and Ann Bedingfield of Redlingfield (1624, 1640), and Mary Rookwood of Coldham (1640). Finally, three Suffolk gentlewomen became nuns at St Ursula's convent in Louvain: Agnes

Tasburgh of Flixton (professed in 1622), and Helen and Grace Bedingfield of Redlingfield (1622, 1635).[62] It is noticeable that six of the fourteen Suffolk nuns were provided by the Bedingfield family of Redlingfield. They were probably the most devout Catholic family in early Stuart Suffolk.

To sum up so far, the evidence suggests that Catholicism in Suffolk under Elizabeth and the early Stuarts was numerically weak and declining but not dying, and was essentially seigneurial. Was Puritanism in Suffolk in the same period in a stronger position and was it also gentry-dominated? This will be the concern of the next part of this chapter.

Puritans

In 1576 Chief Justice Wray wrote to Lord Burghley saying that the Elizabethan Church Settlement was accepted everywhere except in Norfolk and Suffolk. 'There is no county in England so far out of order as these two ... many were obstinate Papists, but *the most*[63] of them wilful and indiscreet precisians' [i.e. Puritans].[64] Justice Wray exaggerated the strength of Roman Catholicism in East Anglia, but he was certainly correct about the strength of Puritanism. Later Thomas May, historian of the Long Parliament, described the Diocese of Norwich, which embraced Norfolk and Suffolk, as 'a Diocese in which there were as many strict Professors of Religion (commonly called Puritans) as any part of England'.[65] Most modern historians would agree with Wray and May about the Puritans. Professor MacCulloch has called Suffolk 'the heart of East Anglian Puritanism, where so many of the leading gentry were enthusiastic for radical reformation'.[66] Dr Cliffe, in his book, *The Puritan Gentry*, regards Devon, Essex, Northamptonshire and Suffolk as the most Puritan counties in England, certainly as regards the gentry.[67]

Who were the Puritans? It is generally agreed that they were those Protestants who thought that the Reformation had not gone far enough and called for further 'purification' of the Church of England. The term 'Puritan', like 'Precisian', was often used in a derogatory sense by their opponents. But their friends referred to them as 'the godly'. Whichever term is used, the Puritans were undoubtedly the more committed Protestants. Percival Wiburn said in 1581 that 'the hotter sort of Protestants are called puritans'.[68] This seems as good a definition as any. The differences between Catholics and Protestants were differences of kind, but the differences between Puritans and Anglicans 'were differences of degree, of theological temperature ... rather than of fundamental principle'.[69] Professor Coward has endorsed this view, stating that in many ways Anglicans and Puritans were similar. Both stressed the importance of predestinarian theology, Bible reading, preaching, and a learned and godly ministry.[70]

However, there *were* some important differences between Puritans and Anglicans. Dr New has defined the latter as 'those generally satisfied with the Church [of England's] doctrine, organisation and ceremonial'.[71] But the Puritans were not generally satisfied with the Established Church. According to Paul Hentzner, who visited England in 1598, the 'PURITANS ... according to the doctrine of the Church of Geneva, reject all ceremonies antiently held, and admit neither organs nor tombs in their places of worship and entirely abhor all differences in rank among churchmen, such as Bishops, Deans, etc.' [72] Hentzner exaggerated the differences, but he was basically correct. It was mainly because of their hostile attitudes to ceremonial and, at times, to the hierarchy of the Church that Puritans differed from Anglicans.

But despite their criticisms, Puritans wished to reform the Church of England from within and not to break away from it. Indeed, Hentzner emphasised that the Puritans 'do not live separate, but mix with those of the Church of England'.[73] They should not be confused with the Separatists, those extreme Protestants who wished to sever all connection with the Church of England and found their own independent, voluntary congregations. There is in fact little sign of Separatism in Suffolk before the Civil Wars,[74] except in a few places, such at Stoke, Ipswich, Mildenhall, Thetford and, above all, Bury St Edmunds.[75] The most famous of the sectaries, the Brownists, were active in and around Bury. Their leader, Robert Browne, was imprisoned in 1581 for seditious preaching at Bury. After being set free by Lord Burghley, Browne took refuge in Holland. He returned to England in 1584 and in 1591 he became an Anglican parson in Northamptonshire, and remained one until his death in 1633.[76] Browne's defection to Anglicanism and his death did not mean the end of the Brownists. Their spiritual descendants – the Congregationalists or Independents – were to be active and important in Suffolk and elsewhere during and after the Interregnum.[77]

Since the Puritans were not Separatists but members of the Church of England, albeit the more radical members, they are, like the Church Papists, very hard to identify. So no attempt will be made at quantification until we reach the Civil War period.[78]

The main characteristic of Suffolk Puritanism was that clergy and gentry closely co-operated. There was a clear alliance between 'magistracy and ministry'. Queen Elizabeth remarked: 'Now I have learned why my county of Suffolk is so well governed, it is, because the magistrates and ministers go together'.[79] However, for convenience I shall mostly deal with the Puritan clergy and gentry separately.

The Clergy

The Puritan Robert Reyce referred to the 'great number of religious, grave, reverend, and learned ministers of God's holy word, which are planted in this shire [Suffolk], travelling to the Lord's harvest, with sound doctrine and upright life'.[80] These Puritan clergy felt very strongly about their faith and were highly sceptical about parts of the Elizabethan Church Settlement.

They disliked particularly the ceremonial of the Church, especially the surplice. Certain parts of the Book of Common Prayer were also viewed with misgivings. Some of the more extreme Puritans were opposed to episcopacy and wished to set up a Presbyterian system of church government, though other Puritans showed less enthusiasm. But all Puritans were agreed about the importance of preaching.

The surplice was one of the vestments worn by priests of the Roman Catholic Church, so it is hardly surprising that the Puritan clergy objected to wearing it. But refusal or failure to use it could be interpreted as opposition to the constituted authority in Church and State. It is understandable therefore that when Elizabeth I visited Ipswich in 1561, she took great offence at the refusal of some town ministers to wear the surplice.[81] Opposition to this garment continued during her reign. In 1593, when the Archdeaconry of Sudbury was subject to an episcopal visitation, eighty-three clergy were reported for not wearing the surplice.[82] Four years later, when William Redman, Bishop of Norwich, organised an episcopal visitation of his diocese, it was stated that in the Archdeaconry of Suffolk eighty-one ministers 'weareth not the surples'.[83] The 164 incumbents not wearing the surplice during the 1590s amounted to one-third of the 500 or so beneficed clergy of Suffolk,[84] an indication of the strength of local Puritan feeling.

So much for the surplice. What about opposition to the Prayer Book? There are signs of this in 1582 when John Knewstub, Rector of Cockfield and doyen of the Suffolk Puritan preachers, held a secret conference in Cockfield of 'threescore ministers' from Suffolk, Norfolk, Essex and Cambridgeshire. The aim was to examine the Prayer Book and decide 'what might be tolerated, and what necessarily to be refused in every print of it; apparel, matter, form, days, fasting, injunctions, etc.'[85] In 1584 there was more opposition by Suffolk Puritan ministers to the Prayer Book. This was because of the policy of John Whitgift, Archbishop of Canterbury from 1583 to 1604. Whitgift was determined to enforce uniformity in the Church of England. To this end he drew up a set of three articles for subscriptions by all ministers of the Church. The real sticking-point in these articles was the second, which demanded that ministers assent to the proposition that the 1559 Book of Common Prayer and the Ordinal 'containeth nothing ... contrary to the word of God'. As Professor Collinson says, 'this touched the conscience of all precisions [puritans] in the most tender place'.[86] The upshot was that sixty-four Suffolk ministers were suspended for refusing to subscribe to Whitgift's 'articles'.[87]

A minority of Puritans in Suffolk and elsewhere desired to change the structure of the church, substituting a presbyterian order for episcopacy. Instead of bishops in charge of dioceses directly appointed by the Queen, the Presbyterians wished to substitute congregationally chosen ministers and lay elders administering the church through local, provincial and ultimately national councils. The system was oligarchic rather than democratic, but it

Church of St Mary, East Bergholt
(Engraved by W. Wallis from a sketch by T. Higham in *Excursions*, I, p. 152)
East Bergholt's parish church is entirely Late Perpendicular and very impressive. The
large stone tower was begun in 1525, but never completed, perhaps because of a
downturn in the local cloth industry, or Wolsey's fall from power. East Bergholt became
a strongly Protestant village in the 1580s, and the local minister, John Tilney, regularly
attended meetings of the Dedham *classis*.

consorted ill with monarchy, and Queen Elizabeth was rightly alarmed. Some Puritan clergy put themselves under the discipline of a *classis* or local committee of presbyters who wielded considerable power. The best known of the *classes* was the more formal series of assemblies held at Dedham, Essex, between October 1582 and June 1589. About twenty Puritan clergy, but no laymen, regularly attended the meetings, including six from Suffolk: Bartholomew Andrews, minister of Wenham; William Bird, living at Boxford; Richard Dowe, dwelling at Stratford St Mary; Edmund Salmon, a resident of Erwarton; Henry Sands, living at Boxford and perhaps beneficed there; John Tilney, living at East Bergholt.[88] The Presbyterian Classical Movement was not spread throughout the country and its active members were few. Only in Cambridge, Essex, London, Northamptonshire, Oxford, Warwickshire and Suffolk were there groups directly involved in the national movement. This was one, but only one, reason why the Presbyterian system faded away. It would not appear in Suffolk again until the late 1640s when lay elders as well as ministers would be nominated members of the *classes*. The fate of the Presbyterian system in this later period will be discussed in Chapter 6.

While not all Puritan clergy favoured a Presbyterian system, all were agreed about the supreme importance of preaching the Word of God. Some

Puritan ministers were in fact over-enthusiastic about preaching. The episcopal visitations of the 1590s reported that set forms of worship and the wearing of the surplice were being neglected because the minister was too busy preaching. Bishop Redman's visitation of 1597 reported that the curate of St Margaret's Church, Ipswich, 'doth usually omitt some parts of service, letanie [litany] and other pt of common prayer ... for that he usuallie preacheth both forenoon and afternoon on Saboth daies'.[89] During the visitation of 1593 it was noted that some ministers did not read parts of the Prayer Book so that they would have more time for preaching. Thomas Carew, Rector of Bildeston, apparently 'readeth not the whole service when he preacheth'. Likewise Thomas Chambers, Rector of Boxford, 'readeth not the whole service by reason that he preacheth'. Thomas Nicholson, Rector of Groton, apparently did 'leave out part of the service when he preacheth'.[90] As well as racing through the Prayer Book, these four ministers did not wear the surplice.

During the reign of James I there was less friction between Puritans and Anglicans than there had been during the reign of Elizabeth I. This is hard to explain, but there are two possible reasons. First, the Church of England seemed strongly and genuinely Protestant, giving Puritans little cause to complain. Indeed, Collinson has said that 'Calvinism can be regarded as the theological cement of the Jacobean Church'.[91] Furthermore that Church agreed with the Puritans about the importance of a preaching ministry. Hence the reign of King James saw a notable upsurge in pulpit-building. In Suffolk at least eighty-five pulpits were built.[92] Among parish churches acquiring pulpits for the first time were Ashfield (in 1619), Boxted (1618), Cratfield (1617), Great Redisham (1619), Martlesham (1614), Occold (1620), and Stonham Aspall (1616)[93] Some of the Jacobean pulpits were raised to a great height, like the three-decker pulpit at Kedington, and topped by impressive sounding-boards in order both to emphasise the importance of the sermon and to make the preacher visible above the rows of high-backed pews.

Second, the character of Puritanism changed. With the collapse of the Presbyterian movement, Puritanism became more moderate and less political, taking an inward turn. Its main characteristics were household religion, sabbatarianism, and an emphasis on discipline, preaching and strict morality, especially the latter. Indeed, Jeremy Goring has argued that 'In the half century before the Civil War ... the word "puritan" came to have a definite moral connotation'.[94] This seems worth emphasising because there has been a tendency among some historians to play down the moral tone of Puritanism.[95] It is, of course, true that Puritanism was not just a movement for sober living, and in defining Puritans Henry Parker mentioned not only 'ethical puritans' or 'puritans in morality', but also 'ecclesiastical puritans', 'puritans in religion' and 'puritans in State' (i.e. politics).[96] And yet some leading Puritans said that their religion was defined

Kedington Church pulpit
(Photograph: S.R.O. (I), SPS 8835)
Kedington is famous for its pulpit. Dated *c.* 1619, the pulpit is an uncommonly complete
three-decker with canopy and hour-glass stand. It was mainly from this three-decker
pulpit that Rev. Samuel Fairclough vigorously preached his puritanical sermons.

in ethical terms. Mrs Lucy Hutchinson said that '. . . whoever was zealous
for God's glory or worship, could not endure blasphemous oathes, ribald
conversation, prophane scoffes, Sabbath breach, derision of the word of
God, and the like . . . were Puritans'. Rev. Richard Baxter wrote that his
father was 'reviled by the name of Puritan, Precision and Hypocrite' because
he had reproved 'Drunkards and Swearers'.[97]

Puritans were deeply concerned about moral reform. But few could have
been more worried than Rev. Samuel Ward (1577–1640), Town Preacher
of Ipswich since 1604.[98] Ward preached a strongly-worded sermon, *Woe to
Drunkards*, and published it in 1622, 1624 and 1627. The last version of
the sermon ran to fifty-three pages. Ward considered that a drunkard was
worse than 'The Adulterer and Usurer' because they 'desire to enjoy their
sinne alone, but the chiefest pastime of a drunkard is to heat and overcome
others with wine'. He said that 'the wine of Drunkards is the wine of
Sodom and Gomorrah'. Expecting to be asked why 'Drunkenness is not
specially prohibited in any one of the tenne Commandments', Ward said
that drunkenness was 'not the single breach of any one, but in effect the
violation of all and everyone'. Drunkenness was 'no one sinne, but all
sinnes . . .'. Moreover, drunkenness was dangerous not just to the individual
but to the nation. It was 'a Nationall wo to be feared and expected of a
Nation overrun with drunkennesse'. Ward thought that this 'Sinne' was

not being taken seriously enough by those in authority. 'I wish the Magistracy, Gentry and Yeomanry would take it to serious consideration'. Ward believed that the 'best course' of action was for the 'great persons' to 'first begin through reformation in their own families, banish the spirits of their butteries, abandon that foolish and vicious custome ... of drinking healths'. The 'countryman' could not be expected to give up drunken habits unless the gentry gave a lead. Drunkenness should 'be out of fashion and grace in Gentlemens tables, butteries and cellars'. Above all, the 'clergie' should by 'care and devotion' suppress the vice of drunkenness 'for the common good'.[99]

Samuel Ward was not just an 'ethical puritan'. He is in fact much more famous as an ecclesiastical and political opponent of the early Stuarts. 'Silver-tongued' Ward, as he was called because of his persuasiveness in the pulpit, first clashed with the government in 1621. In that year he was sent to prison for a short spell by the Privy Council for publishing an anti-Spanish and anti-Papal cartoon which offended Gondomar, the Spanish ambassador, and the English government at a time of difficult negotiations with Spain. The following year he was prosecuted in the Consistory Court of Norwich for nonconformity, but shortly afterwards released. In 1626, after the dissolution of Charles I's second parliament, Ward was said to have 'tuned' the pulpits of Ipswich against the King's main adviser, the Duke of Buckingham. Seven years later Richard Corbett, Bishop of Norwich, reprimanded Ward for opposing 'significant ceremonies' during divine service. So far Ward had been fairly leniently treated, thanks to the pro-Puritan outlook of George Abbott, Archbishop of Canterbury from 1611 to 1633. However, the situation changed when Abbott was succeeded by William Laud. At Laud's insistence Ward was censured in the Court of High Commission on 2 November 1635. He was found guilty of preaching against bowing at the name of Jesus and against the Book of Sports on the Lord's day and of attacking church government. He was suspended from his ministry before being imprisoned. The inhabitants of Ipswich declined to ask the

Rev. Samuel Ward (1577–1640)
by an unknown artist *c.* 1620.
Town Preacher of Ipswich from 1604,
Ward was a strong Puritan. The
inscription 'WATCH WARD' and the
Armada beacon portray the archetypal
defender of the Protestant cause.

Bishop of Norwich to appoint another Town Preacher as they were 'resolved to have Mr Ward or none'. There is little more to be said about Ward, except that his silencing by the court of High Commission in 1635 led to serious rioting in Ipswich the following year, a problem that Matthew Wren, the new Bishop of Norwich, had to cope with.[100]

The Puritans of Ipswich, and indeed of Suffolk, did not take kindly to Bishop Matthew Wren, uncle of the future architect, Sir Christopher Wren. Why was this? A number of reasons may be suggested. First, he apparently had an unpleasant personality. The future Royalist Earl of Clarendon described him as 'a man of a severe, sour nature'.[101] Next to Archbishop Laud, he became the most hated of all bishops. Second, he was an Arminian.[102] This meant that he rejected the predestinarian theology of Calvin [103] and agreed with the Dutch theologian Jacobus Arminius (c. 1559–1609), who emphasised the role of free will in attaining salvation. This Arminian doctrine caused consternation. As Nicholas Tyacke says, 'for many people in the early seventeenth century the basic issue as between Protestantism and Catholicism was that of divine determinism versus human free will'.[104] No wonder Puritans equated Arminians with Papists. Third, he enforced with vigour the High Church policies of Charles I and Archbishop William Laud (1633–45).

Wren was Bishop of Norwich for just over two years, but during that short time he made a deep impression on the diocese. Indeed, he was probably the most thorough and conscientious of Laud's bishops. The 'orders, directions and remembrances', issued by Wren at his primary visitation (inspection) of his diocese in 1636, comprised twenty-eight articles. All were designed to promote the reverence, decency and good order in church services for which Laud consistently strove. Like Laud, Wren was determined to enforce the King's authority in the Church, and to impose liturgical and doctrinal uniformity and a strict conformity to it by the clergy. However, more was involved than decency and discipline.

Wren emphasised the importance of ceremonial more than his prelatical predecessors, such as Bishop

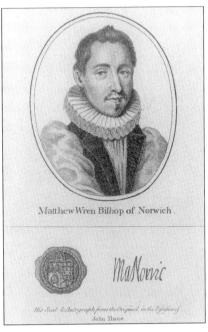

Matthew Wren Bishop of Norwich.

His Seal & Autograph from the Original in the Possession of John Thane.

Matthew Wren (1585–1667)
by an unknown engraver.
When Bishop of Norwich (1635–38) Wren greatly antagonised the Puritans in his diocese by his High Church policies.

Redman, had done. Wren's visitation articles ordered the clergy in Norfolk and Suffolk to use the surplice. But at least fourteen ministers (ten from Suffolk, four from Norfolk) were brought to his notice in 1636 for not wearing this garment when reading prayers or when preaching. 'Failure to wear a surplice'. says D. W. Boorman, 'was almost entirely a Puritan practice'.[105] Wren also ordered the clergy in his diocese to show 'lowly reverence ... at the name of Jesus', but nine ministers (seven Suffolk, two Norfolk) did not do so. One of them – Richard Prowde of Thrandeston – 'did not bowe his body or bend his knee' and, along with six others, was censured by the Consistory court.[106] Such defiance is not surprising. As Professor Seaver reminds us, 'Bowing at the name of Jesus seemed little short of idolatrous to most Puritans'.[107]

Puritan clergy in Norfolk and Suffolk objected strongly to Wren's emphasis on ceremonial, but they were probably even more annoyed about his hostility to Sabbatarianism. Puritans strongly believed that the whole of Sunday should be spent in worship. This would involve morning and afternoon sermons, religious discussions and family prayers and bible-reading. On the other hand many people undoubtedly agreed with the Book of Sports which allowed lawful recreations after Sunday morning service.[108] The first Book of Sports was issued in 1618 by James I but remained a dead letter. However, its re-issue in 1633 by Charles I was followed by general enforcement. The parish clergy were ordered by the King to read and commend the Book from their pulpits.[109] Wren gave the Book every encouragement, but in his Norwich diocese at least nineteen ministers (fifteen Suffolk, four Norfolk) refused to read it aloud to their congregations.[110]

The Puritan divines in the diocese of Norwich also disliked Wren's apparent lack of enthusiasm for preaching. Puritans believed that preaching the Word was the chief means of salvation, and that the sermon was the centrepiece of the church service. Wren, however, was concerned about the content of the sermons and feared they might be doctrinally erroneous or politically seditious.[111] Hence he discouraged preaching by emphasising the need for catechising and by suppressing or regulating lecturers. In 1633 Archbishop Laud ordered the clergy to teach the catechism and not preach on Sunday afternoons. In 1636 when Wren visited his diocese about seven clerics were presented because they had preached on Sunday afternoons instead of Catechising. Wren suspended them from exercising their ministerial office.[112] More abhorrent to Wren than non-catechising clergy were the lecturers. Dr Christopher Hill has aptly called them 'free-lance clergy'.[113] They were in fact non-beneficed ministers and bishops had less control over them than over parochial clergy, especially when lecturers enjoyed the support of town corporations or influential gentlemen. In December 1636 Wren told Archbishop Laud that when he first arrived at Norwich diocese 'Lectures abounded, especially in Suffolk. Not a bowling green, or an ordinary could stand without one', and many lectureships were 'set up by private gentlemen at their pleasure'.[114] Moreover, 'the lectureship was essentially a Puritan institution ... and it was staffed predominantly by Puritan preachers'.[115] This is not surprising since the purpose of the lectureship was the provision of sermons. To Wren the proliferation of (mostly Puritan) lectures was a situation which could not be tolerated, so he made a determined effort to abolish the 'ratsbane of lecturing', stopping all weekly lectures in his diocese. Wren later followed Archbishop Laud in forbidding any afternoon sermons at all.[116] Eventually most of the lecturers in Norfolk and Suffolk, at least for a time, were brought to submission and conformity.[117] Clearly Wren had struck a severe blow against the Puritan lecturers and their preaching.

Finally, we must consider Wren's altar policy. This involved a change in the position of the communion table. Since Elizabethan times the table in most parishes had stood in the main body of the church. But Wren in his third visitation article of 1636 ordered the conversion of communion tables into altars, which were to be permanently railed in at the east end of chancels. As Tyacke says, 'the altar now became the focal point of worship'.[118] This emphasis on the altar, as opposed to the pulpit, angered the Puritans because it upgraded the sacraments and downgraded the sermon. Wren also annoyed the Puritans by ordering communicants to 'come up reverently and kneel before the [altar] rail', instead of receiving the sacrament from the minister in their seats.[119] There can be little doubt that 'none of the Laudian reforms caused deeper suspicion and resentment than' the altar policy.[120] Statistically it is difficult to say how many Puritan clergy expressed open hostility to Wren's policy. But there are some interesting individual cases. Nicholas Beard, minister of St Peter's, Ipswich, 'administered ye commn to many not kneeling and (they say) to few otherwise. Mr Broughton of Chilesfor [Chillesford] did carry to Holy Commyon up and down, though ye chancell is rayled & prepared'. At Groton James Alderson, who was schoolmaster of Boxford, administered Holy Communion in the middle of the church.[121]

We must not exaggerate the extent of opposition to Wren's policies in the 1630s by the Puritan divines of Suffolk. D. W. Boorman found the names of only forty-six Suffolk ministers who clashed with Wren and his officials on doctrinal or ceremonial grounds, out of a total of perhaps 500 clergy in the whole county, that is, a mere 9 per cent.[122] Numbers were not everything, however. Wren's clerical Puritan opponents were formidable, being sustained by their strongly-held beliefs and by much local support. Wren had good reason to be worried. Nevertheless, the late Ketton-Cremer was probably correct in saying that 'most of Wren's clergy were quiet conformists'.[123]

Not only has opposition to Wren been overstated, but so also has the argument that his religious persecution drove large numbers to seek refuge abroad. Many migrants went to Holland, but most risked their lives by voyaging to North America. During the 1630s 790 Suffolk people emigrated to New England; no other eastern county produced as many migrants.[124] But, as Professor Kevin Sharpe says, 'in the absence of official records of those leaving, we will never be able to conclude how many were *religious* exiles'.[125] However, Wren's ecclesiastical policies turned at least some East Anglians into religious refugees. Dr N. C. P. Tyack has said that in Suffolk Puritan nonconformity 'from 1620 to 1640 seems to have centred mainly in Haverhill, Sudbury, Ipswich and Wrentham ... These centres, and their influence, were a major concern to Bishop Wren ... the majority of New England emigrants from these towns and villages ... appears to have been driven out by the whiplash of religious persecution'.[126] Wren, defending himself before the House of Commons in 1642, denied the charge of persecution and argued that the main cause of emigration, at least to Holland, was low wages. 'The chiefest Cause of the Departure, was the small Wages which was given to poor Workmen, whereby the Workmasters grew rich, but the Workmen were kept very poor'.[127] Wren's arguments have been endorsed by modern historians who emphasise economic hardship in the cloth centres of eastern England during the 1630s as the main reason for emigration.[128]

The Gentry

Puritanism was never a movement of clerics alone. The Puritan Robert Reyce noted with approval that many of the Suffolk gentry were 'crowned with the purity of true religion and godly life'.[129] We do not know the number of Puritan gentry families in the period 1558–1640, but thanks to the work of scholars such as Professor Collinson and Dr Cliffe, we know how important a role they played in sustaining and strengthening their faith.[130] Their influence exceeded their numbers. As previously stated, the Puritan gentry closely co-operated with the Puritan clergy. Collinson has said that 'the primary bond between the magistrates and the ministers was one of patronage'.[131] We must now briefly study this subject.

As owners of advowsons,[132] Puritan gentry helped their cause by appointing like-minded ministers to the benefices in their gift. Without these gentry patrons, it is hard to see how there could have been Puritan ministers preaching to a wider public. During the reign of Queen Elizabeth Sir Robert Jermyn of Rushbrooke, one of the godliest as well as the most powerful of the gentry, appointed clergy to no less than ten livings.[133] Another zealous Puritan, Sir John Higham of Barrow, presented to four.[134] Six other puritans among the local magnates and gentry presented to livings during the same period. Lord North presented to seven benefices, Edward Lewkenor of Denham to one, Sir Nicholas Bacon of Redgrave, junior, to ten, Sir William Spring of Pakenham to two, Robert Ashfield of Stowlangtoft to three, and John Clench of Holbrook to two.[135] 'In few

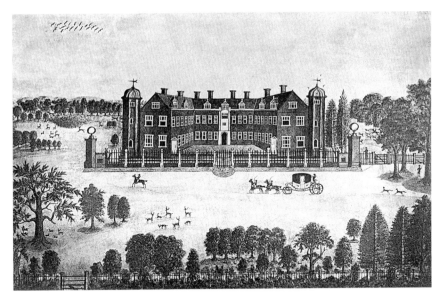

Rushbrooke Hall

This painting shows Rushbrooke Hall as it appeared before the eighteenth-century
alterations. The will of Sir Thomas Jermyn (d. 1552) suggests that this building was
largely of the late 1540s and 1550s (MacCulloch, *Suffolk*, plate 2c). Rushbrooke was
associated with the history of sixteen generations of Jermyns. The family was mostly
Puritan under Elizabeth I, but strongly Royalist in the Civil War period.

other counties', wrote Professor Collinson, 'did the Puritan Movement own
such whole-hearted and powerful patrons'.[136]

As magistrates, the Puritan gentry strongly supported the clergy on
religious and moral issues. In February 1579 four Puritan JPs – Robert
Jermyn of Rushbrooke, Robert Ashfield of Stowlangtoft, John Higham of
Barrow and Thomas Andrews of Bury – drew up and exhibited in the
churches a code of discipline for the parishioners of St Mary's, Bury St
Edmunds. Dr Craig argues that 'the greater significance of this code lay in
its uncompromising challenge to recusants and conservatives' within the
parish. Punishments were ordered for any who kept 'monuments of idolatry
or superstition', for 'any ... Papiste or a mayntener of poperie', for all who
heard or said mass secretly. Absence from church services, disturbance of
prayers and sermons, railing at 'magistrates and preachers', blasphemy and
witchcraft, all were punishable offences. However, penalties were also stipulated for moral offences, such as gaming, usury, drunkenness and, especially,
fornication.[137] In short, the Puritan JPs of the Bury area were equally
concerned about popery and 'the reformation of manners'.

As soldiers, some of the Puritan gentry of Suffolk joined the Earl of
Leicester's expedition in 1585 to fight for the Protestant cause in the Low
Countries. They feared that if the Spaniards won the war in the Netherlands,

not only the Dutch Protestants but the English Church would be doomed. Sir Robert Jermyn of Rushbrooke, and half-brother Henry Blague of Horringer, sailed with Leicester's forces, accompanied by their brother William Jermyn and the veteran West Suffolk Protestant Thomas Poley of Icklingham. Lord North also joined the expedition. Sir Robert prayed that Leicester's soldiers would be 'valiant in the Lords cause and fight his battailes with corage'. Lord North and Sir Robert were certainly active 'in the Lords cause', the former leading a retinue of twenty-two and the latter a retinue of thirty-two, before returning to Suffolk to raise more volunteers.[138] Not until the First Civil War (1642–46) would the Jermyns and Blagues take up arms again, and then it would be *against* the Puritan cause![139]

During the early Stuart period the Puritan gentry of Suffolk still continued to present clergy to benefices. Among the more important patrons were Sir John Wentworth of Somerleyton, Sir Nathaniel Barnardiston of Kedington and Brampton Gurdon of Assington Hall, senior. Sir John Wentworth, who had succeeded to Somerleyton in 1618, not only almost eradicated Catholicism in Lothingland by bringing 'good preachers into the island',[140] but he also became principal landowner in the hundred, and patron of five benefices: Ashby, Bradwell, Flixton, Lound and Somerleyton. The most notable of his ministers was John Brinsley, junior (1600–1665), who was presented to the livings of Somerleyton and Ashby around 1632. Brinsley was the author of various theological works and an excellent preacher whose powerful and lucid sermons gained him a large following. Sir Nathaniel Barnardiston was just as good a patron of Puritan clergy as Wentworth. Sir Nathaniel had four livings in his gift: Kedington, Barnardiston, and Great Wratting in Suffolk, and Great Coates in Lincolnshire. His most famous minister was Samuel Fairclough (1594–1677), who he appointed Rector of Barnardiston in 1623 and Rector of Kedington in 1630. Fairclough was described by a fellow divine as 'an admirable preacher ... mighty in the scriptures ... serving the Lord day and night with incessant prayer'. Brampton Gurdon appointed Nathaniel Rogers (1598–1655) to the living of Assington. Rogers had recently been dismissed as curate of Bocking, Essex, for performing a burial service without a surplice. Rogers was, however, such an excellent preacher that Assington church was often unable to accommodate all who wished to hear him preach.[141] There can be little doubt that the Puritan gentry of Suffolk used their patronage to good effect.

Like the Catholic seigneurs, the Puritan gentry provided their cause with leadership and support. Similarly, Puritan like Catholic gentlemen practised household religion.[142] Catholics did so because they were forbidden to worship publicly. But household religion was 'stressed by the Puritans as a remedy for the shortcomings of the state church'.[143] 'Family prayers and family catechising', says Christopher Hill, 'offered an alternative to public worship, especially when the worship itself left so much to be desired as that of the Laudian Church'.[144] One of the best examples of godly household

religion was to be found at Kedington Hall, owned by the wealthy Sir
Nathaniel Barnardiston, future leader of the Suffolk Parliamentarians during
the Civil Wars. Rev. Samuel Fairclough said that his patron, Sir Nathaniel,
as 'governour and master of a family: ... permitted no known profane
person to stand before him, or wait upon him ... He had at one time ten
or more such servants of that eminency for piety and sincerity, that I never
yet saw their like at one time, in any family in the nation ...' Under Sir
Nathaniel Kedington Hall was 'a spiritual church and temple, wherein were
daily offered up the spiritual sacrifices of reading the Word, and prayer,
morning and evening, of singing psalms constantly after every meal, before
any servant did rise from the table ...'[145] Psalm-singing was not confined
to Kedington Hall, however. There also seems to have been much psalm-
singing in the godly household of Sir Simonds D'Ewes of
Stowlangtoft.[146]

Apart from being the head of a spiritual household, D'Ewes, like Rev.
Samuel Ward of Ipswich, is a good example of an ethical Puritan. Like
Ward, D'Ewes roundly condemned drunkenness and reflected sadly that
'Those that accustome themselves to drinking are never able to leave it'.
But in an age before tea and coffee D'Ewes was against *excessive* drinking,
not drinking alcohol itself in *moderation*. D'Ewes complained that when
an undergraduate at St John's College, Cambridge, from 1618 to 1620 there
had been not only too much drinking but also too much 'swearing ...

Effigies of Sir Nathaniel Barnardiston and Jane his wife
These effigies, photographed by G. F. Cordy, are in Kedington parish church.
Sir Nathaniel leans out of the opposite aisle, one hand on his wife's, their disengaged
hands propping their heads uneasily. Long before the Civil War Sir Nathaniel was a
patron of Puritan clergy and a strong supporter of godly household religion. He died
in 1653 and his wife in 1669.

rioting and hatred of vertue and pietie ...' D'Ewes also strongly disliked gaming with dice, which, like card-playing, was sinful and displeasing to God. He favoured games of skill, like bowls, chess and draughts, but not games of chance or gambling.[147] D'Ewes believed that the remedy for immorality was Puritan piety. 'For piety', he declared on 27 July 1641, 'we know the way to maintain it is to abolish whoring, swearing and drinking and to increase preaching and praying'.[148]

Puritans like D'Ewes were certainly very worried about what they believed to be a general decline of morals. But they were even more disturbed by the rise of the High Church party, which included many Arminians. Sir Simonds D'Ewes relates that during the reign of Charles I 'many ... popishly affected divines and schollers in both universities and elsewhere mainteined in the schooles and pulpits justification by workes, free-will, Christ's bodily presence in the sacramente of the Lord's supper and a world of other corrupt and noisesome tenents'.[149] D'Ewes may have exaggerated the Arminian threat, but he was not alone in doing so. An aged Suffolk countryman, comparing Bishop Wren's policy to Queen Mary's, apparently remarked that he had 'lived to see the old religion restored again'.[150] To both D'Ewes and the old countryman, Arminianism seemed indistinguishable from Roman Catholicism.

The Church of England bishops were blamed for Arminianism, so the Puritans campaigned for the abolition of episcopacy. This was a sea-change in Puritan opinion. As Christopher Hill says, 'in 1604 most Puritans acknowledged the spiritual leadership of the bishops, and wanted to remain within the church. But by the late 1630s the breach was becoming absolute'.[151] In June 1641 a bill was introduced in the House of Commons to abolish episcopacy 'root and branch'. One of the strongest supporters of this bill was an MP for Sudbury, Sir Simonds D'Ewes.[152] Another eminent Puritan who attacked episcopacy on the eve of the First Civil War was Sir Philip Parker of Erwarton, one of the MPs for the county of Suffolk. In January 1641 he presented a petition from Puritan ministers in that county asking relief from the burdens of the hierarchy, by which they meant 'Superstitions' introduced by Bishop Wren. The petition also asked for a reform of the Prayer Book and a diminution of the ceremonies.[153]

It is clear from the events described that Puritan attitudes had hardened during the 1630s, mainly due to the ecclesiastical policies of Archbishop Laud and Bishop Wren. Indeed, Professor Lawrence Stone has said that 'Laud may be regarded as the most important single contributor to the cause of Puritanism in the early seventeenth century'.[154] As for Wren, it would be wrong to exaggerate the strength of Puritan opposition to him since he only held the bishopric of Norwich from 1635 to 1638. Nevertheless, there can be no doubt that his activities played a major part in alienating public opinion in Suffolk during the later years of Charles I's Personal Rule. In Ipswich in 1640 some Puritans showed what they thought of

Wren's altar policy by ripping out the communion rails in St Lawrence Church and burning them with broom faggots.[155] There was indeed great fear that Archbishop Laud's policies were taking the Church back to Rome and that the Protestant cause was threatened. 'First, bring in Arminian doctrines, then the popish will easily follow', said Matthew Newcomen, Puritan lecturer at Dedham in 1636.[156] Fear of Laudianism and popery strengthened Puritanism. 'The party of the Puritans ... has increased enormously', said the Venetian ambassador in 1637. A year later a new Venetian ambassador reckoned that 'the Puritans' were 'the strongest party in the Kingdom'.[157] These diplomats were referring to England and unfortunately we have no estimates of Puritan numbers in our region. However, it is highly likely that, despite some emigration to north America, Puritans would have been more numerous in Suffolk in 1640 than in 1630. We shall probably never know the number of plebeian Puritans. But we can estimate roughly, tentatively, hesitatingly, and extremely cautiously the number of Puritan gentry in Suffolk during the Civil War period.

For obvious reasons, the Puritan gentry present a much greater problem of identification than the Catholic recusant gentry: there is no equivalent of the official lists of Catholics presented for recusancy and other breaches of the penal laws. Puritans who appear in visitation records tend to be clerical offenders. Nevertheless, the evidence is fairly substantial, though inevitably diffuse. The following gentry, then, may be classified as Puritan: those appointing or financially assisting Puritan ministers or lecturers;[158] those employing Puritan chaplains in their households; dedicatees of Puritan works; those serving on puritanical religious committees, whether locally or in the House of Commons; those appointed Presbyterian elders to the county of Suffolk on 5 November 1645 and on 18 February 1648;[159] and those shown to be Puritans by their wills,[160] correspondence or the opinions of their contemporaries. On the basis of these criteria it has been calculated that during the Civil War period there were 102 Puritan gentry families in Suffolk.[161] This is not as large a number as might be expected.[162] But it would be wrong to call them, in the words of Professor Kevin Sharpe, 'a small and beleaguered minority'.[163] Moreover, the Puritan gentry were clearly in a much stronger position than the Catholic gentry, who numbered only thirty-four families. We have seen, too, that Catholic gentry families were non-existent in some regions of Suffolk (see Map 11). By contrast, the Puritan gentry were conspicuous in most parts of the county (see Map in Appendix II). The Puritan gentry were to be the main driving force among the Suffolk Parliamentarian families during the First and Second Civil Wars. It is to these wars that we must now turn.

Map 12: John Blaeu's
Map of Suffolk, 1645

CHAPTER FIVE

Suffolk and the First Civil War: Parties and issues

The English Civil War is one of the most controversial subjects in history. At the risk of gross oversimplification we may say that until the late 1970s there were three main interpretations: the Whig, the Marxist and the localist. Whig historians regarded the Civil War as essentially a struggle over religious and constitutional principles. Parliament's victory in the Civil War, confirmed in 1688–89, laid the foundations of constitutional government and religious liberty.[1] Marxist or neo-Marxist historians asserted that the 1640s and 1650s saw a successful bourgeois revolution, that the 'middling sort' formed the backbone of the Parliamentary party and that fear of the populace was a major cause of Royalism.[2] Localist historians interpreted the Civil War in terms of localism, emphasising the strength of county awareness among the gentry, their preference for local over national politics and, above all, their reluctance to be involved in the conflict.[3] However, the Whig, Marxist and localist interpretations are no longer fashionable, and during the last twenty years or so other arguments have dominated the debate on the Civil War. Professor John Morrill regards the struggle as mainly a 'war of religion', Dr John Adamson as largely a 'baronial conflict', and Professor Conrad Russell as primarily a 'problem of multiple kingdoms in Britain'.[4] We shall discuss more fully the issues at stake in Suffolk in the concluding part of this chapter. But first let us consider the Civil War allegiances and activities of the local gentry and commoners.

Allegiance and activities

Suffolk has been regarded as a battle-free zone and Roundhead heartland during the First Civil War of 1642–46. Certainly there was no serious fighting in the county. Apart from the so-called siege of Lowestoft in March 1643, which lasted only about one hour, there was no important military action. The Parliamentarians incompletely fortified Ipswich and took charge of the powder magazines at Bury St Edmunds and Landguard Fort, near Felixstowe, in 1642. Later there were a few minor skirmishes (e.g. at Crow's

Hall, Debenham, in 1643). Otherwise, Suffolk during the Civil War was militarily quiet. Here Suffolk greatly differed from the battle-torn Midlands, described as 'the Belgium of the English Civil War'.[5]

Most historians consider Suffolk to have been a Parliamentarian stronghold. Alfred Kingston, a late Victorian historian, assumed that Suffolk, like the rest of East Anglia, was a centre of Parliamentarianism and Puritanism. Modern historians have largely agreed. Professor Alan Everitt stated that 'probably in no other shire was support for Parliament more widespread' and that 'Suffolk deliquents [Royalists] were so few'. Paul Fincham said that 'Suffolk supported Parliament overwhelmingly'. Dymond and Northeast say that Suffolk Royalists were 'not numerous', though they do not dismiss them out of hand.[6] If referring to the total population of Suffolk, those authors are probably correct. But are they correct about the local gentry?

The gentry

Were the Suffolk gentry predominantly Parliamentarian or Royalist?[7] They were neither, and probably mainly neutral. Of the 689 families in 1642, only 182 (26 per cent) had one or more members who participated in the First Civil War, though this is a conservative estimate. Some of the other 507 (74 per cent) gentry families were probably Parliamentarians or Royalists whose activities are undocumented, or those whose allegiances are not clear.[8] But very large numbers must have been neutral, like Henry Lambe, Gentleman and Lord of the manor of Tostock. The possibility of large numbers of neutrals should not surprise us. After all, the Royalist Earl of Clarendon said that during the English Civil War 'the number of those who desired to sit still was greater than of those of either party; so that they were generally inclined to articles of neutrality'.[9] Why was there so much possible neutralism in Suffolk? There are many likely reasons: apathy, escapism, laziness, cowardice, localism, indifference to national politics, or maybe fear that civil war would threaten the social hierarchy. But perhaps the most plausible reason is that Suffolk was not one of the major theatres of war, and therefore most gentry were not forced to choose sides.

But what about the Suffolk gentry who did take sides? Who exactly were the Royalist and Parliamentarian gentry? They were those who, at some time or other between 1642 and 1646, served either the King or Parliament in a military or civil capacity. The Royalists, popularly known as 'Cavaliers', called themselves 'the king's party', while their enemies generally labelled them 'delinquents' if moderate, and 'malignants' if extreme. The Suffolk Royalists included those in arms, persons 'adhering to' or 'assisting' the king, unspecified 'delinquents', and *generally* such officials as commissioners of array and of 'inquiry into Rebellion'. The Parliamentarians, popularly known as 'Roundheads', called themselves 'the well-affected', while their opponents dubbed them 'rebels'. The Suffolk Parliamentarians included soldiers, civilian officials like county committee-men, sequestration agents, assessors, receivers, collectors, treasurers, and also those voluntarily contributing men or money to their cause. Besides Royalists and Parliamentarians there was a small number who changed sides. Leaving aside this last group, how many Suffolk gentlemen were Royalist or Parliamentarian?

Unfortunately it is easier to define than to identify and enumerate Royalists and Parliamentarians. They were not monolithic 'parties'. Between the two poles of firm Royalists and firm Parliamentarians there was a vast gradation of different shades of opinions and attitudes. Moderates on both sides had more in common with each other than they had with their own extremists. A big gulf separated a hard-line Cavalier like Henry Jermyn of Rushbrooke [10] from a moderate Royalist like William Glover of Frostenden, who lent £10 to the Parliamentary cause on 11 November 1642,[11] though from 1643 onwards he apparently 'clove as faithfully to the king as to the church'.[12] Likewise there were great differences between a dedicated Parliamentarian like John Gurdon of Great Wenham and a more lukewarm one like Sir Simonds D'Ewes of Stowlangtoft. The former, an MP for Ipswich from 1640 to 1653, supported the War Party in 1643–45 in the House of Commons, while the latter, an MP for Sudbury from 1640 to 1648, adhered to the Peace Party.[13] Nevertheless, once the Civil War was really under way Jermyn and Glover were united in their hostility to the Parliamentary cause, while Gurdon and D'Ewes could both oppose, in their own ways, the common Royalist enemy. In short, it *is* possible to divide the combatant gentry of Suffolk into Royalists and Parliamentarians, despite the differences within their ranks.

The three maps and lists of families in Appendix III and Table 5.1 below show that only small numbers supported either side and that the Parliamentarians outnumbered the Royalists by over three to two.

Table 5.1 Civil War allegiances of Suffolk gentry families

Region of Suffolk	Parliamentarian	Royalist	Sidechangers /Divided	Neutral/ Unknown	Total No. of families
East	80 (18.1%)	42 (9.5%)	9 (2.0%)	310 (70.4%)	441 (100.0%)
West	25 (10.1%)	22 (8.9%)	4 (1.6%)	197 (79.4%)	248 (100.0%)
Total	105 (15.2%)	64 (9.3%)	13 (1.9%)	507 (73.6%)	689 (100.0%)

A close examination of this table shows that Parliamentarian dominance was particularly evident in East Suffolk, while the maps in Appendix III show that this superiority was most marked in the northern and extreme southern parts of the region. However, a different situation pertained in West Suffolk, for there the Parliamentarian majority was almost negligible. The thirteen gentry families who divided, or whose members changed sides, are

named and located in Map iii in Appendix III. But since they formed only
2 per cent of the total families and just 7 per cent of the combatant families,
we can safely ignore them and concentrate on the Parliamentarians and
Royalists.

To get a full picture of Civil War allegiances it is of course necessary
to classify the Suffolk gentry on an individual as well as on a family basis,
for two reasons. First, some families sent more of their members into battle
than others. Both Sir Thomas Glemham of Little Glemham and his son,
Sackville, fought for King Charles I. But among the Cutlers of Ipswich,
Benjamin, head of the family, was in arms against Parliament at Newark,
while his son and brother apparently remained neutral. Second, split
families did not always divide evenly between the two sides. The Soame
family of Little Thurlow divided evenly, Sir William being an active
Parliamentarian while his son Stephen 'tooke part with K. Charles agt the
Parliament'.[14] The Le Hunts of Little Bradley did not divide evenly.
Sir George Le Hunt and his sons, John, Robert and William, were
Royalists, but his other son, Richard, was a major in the army of the
Parliamentarian Eastern Association. If, then, we classify the Suffolk gentry
on an individual basis, the following picture emerges of their Civil War
loyalties (see Table 5.2).

Table 5.2 Civil War allegiances of individual Suffolk gentry

Region of Suffolk	Parliamentarian	Royalist	Changed Sides
East	104	53	5
West	38	36	1
Total	142	89	6

Once again it will be noted that in the county as a whole the Parliamentarian gentry outnumbered the Cavaliers by three to two. In East Suffolk,
however, it was a two to one majority. In West Suffolk, on the other hand,
the Parliamentarian majority over the Royalists was tiny. The negligible
number of sidechangers in the county can of course be ignored.

So much for the numbers and distribution of the Parliamentarian and
Royalist gentry of Suffolk. What about their Civil War involvement? The
individual gentry on both sides may be divided into the 'active' and the
'passive'. The 'active' were those who were prepared to risk their lives and
limbs as soldiers and/or who were ready to undertake much drudgery as
civilian officials or as MPs. By contrast, the 'passive' tended to be faint-
hearted. They usually avoided fighting, even if holding military rank, were
content to give or lend small sums of money to their cause and, if nominated
as officials, served either infrequently, reluctantly or not at all. Table 5.3
shows the political involvement of individual Cavalier and Roundhead
gentry of Suffolk.

Table 5.3 Civil War involvement of individual Suffolk gentry

Region of Suffolk	The Active		The Passive	
	Parliamentarian	Royalist	Parliamentarian	Royalist
East	49	30	55	23
West	24	22	14	14
Total	73	52	69	37

Concentrating on the activists, two conclusions emerge. First, the Parliamentarians had a comfortable, but by no means overwhelming, majority over the Royalists in Suffolk as a whole. Second, the Parliamentarians outnumbered their enemies by five to three in East Suffolk, but had only a wafer thin majority in West Suffolk.

Why these regional differences in allegiance between East and West Suffolk? A geographical explanation seems obvious but is unconvincing. Although it was easier for Royalist sympathisers in West than in East Suffolk to join the King's army, most of the more active Royalist gentry soldiers happened to come from East Suffolk. Religion is a more likely explanation. The Parliamentarians may have been less dominant in West than in East Suffolk because – except in the Stour valley – Puritan influence was weaker. During the Civil War period there were sixty-four Puritan gentry families in East Suffolk, but only thirty-eight in West Suffolk (see Appendix II). A social explanation is also possible. Did the Stour valley riots of 1642 perhaps drive several West Suffolk gentry into the arms of the King? We shall discuss this more fully later.

The statistics in Tables 5.1–3 [15] concerning the allegiances of the gentry – at least in West Suffolk – may surprise the modern reader, but they would not have surprised contemporaries. Thomas May, writing in 1647, said of the eastern counties of Suffolk, Norfolk and Cambridgeshire that 'it were certain that many of the chief Gentry in these Counties bended in their affections to the King's Commission of Array'. Later on, referring to Suffolk, Norfolk, Cambridgeshire, Essex, Hertfordshire and Huntingdonshire, May said that there was affection to Parliament 'especially among the common people', but by contrast 'a great and considerable number of the Gentry, and those of the highest ranks among them were disaffected to the Parliament; and were not sparing in their utmost indeavours to promote the King's Cause'. [16] Richard Baxter (d. 1691), a Roundhead army chaplain, said that 'a very great part of the Knights and Gentlemen of England ... adhered to the King: except in Middlesex, Essex, *Suffolk*, [17] Norfolk, Cambridgeshire'. But he thought that if the King's army had come to East Anglia 'it's like it would have been there as it was in other places'. [18] In short, the gentry of East Anglia (including Suffolk) would have been predominantly Royalist, or at least they might well have been in West Suffolk.

Let us now examine in detail the actual civil and military activities of the Parliamentarian and Royalist gentry of Suffolk. Table 5.4 suggests that the Parliamentarians were more prominent as officials and the Royalists as soldiers.

Table 5.4 Civil War activities of individual Suffolk gentry

	Parliamentarians	Royalists
Officials only	83 (58.5%)	13 (14.6%)
Soldiers only	10 (7.0%)	44 (49.4%)
Soldiers and officials	22 (15.5%)	12 (13.5%)
Other supporters	27 (19.0%)	20 (22.5%)
Total	142 (100.0%)	89 (100.0%)

In Table 5.4 those described as 'other supporters' may be quickly dismissed. All were fairly passive individuals. Those on the Parliamentary side included twenty-five who merely subscribed small sums of money to their cause. Those on the Royalist side included several who just appear in the papers of the Committee for Compounding as unspecified 'delinquents'. Some, like George Lumley of Stanstead, Babergh, are vaguely described as having taken 'pt with K. Charles agt the Parliament',[19] while others, like William Barker of Sibton, are simply called 'loyall to his Kinge'.[20]

Table 5.4 shows that twenty-five (28 per cent) of the eighty-nine Suffolk Cavaliers were appointed officials by the King. Twenty-two of those were nominated Commissioners of Array in 1642,[21] being responsible for raising forces for the Royalist side. Also in 1643 four were named as commissioners 'to inquire within the County of Suffolk of the Estates of such psons as are or have been in Rebellion agt his Matie within the space of one yeare last'. Unfortunately it is not known whether any of these commissioners – of array or of inquiry – actively served the King.

One hundred and five (74 per cent) of the 142 Suffolk Roundhead gentry were officials. Some were deputy lieutenants, others were MPs, but most were members or agents of the County Committee.[22] Parliament could hardly have won the Civil War if it had relied solely on existing local officials, such as the sheriffs and justices of the peace. For financial, political and military reasons new organs of local government had to be created. So from 1643 onwards various county committees were set up by Parliamentary ordinances: committees for assessment, for the sequestration of delinquents, for the militia and for various other purposes. In theory, those committees were separate institutions; in practice, since membership was often the same, they were collectively known as the 'County Committee'.

The Suffolk County Committee met at Bury St Edmunds. As county committee members or agents the Roundhead gentry raised taxes, soldiers and horses for Parliament and sequestered Royalist estates. Between 1642 and 1648 they collected an average of £56,000 a year.[23] Of course not all members of the County Committee were equally conscientious. Eighty-five meetings of the County Committee were held between September 1643 and October 1645. Some Parliamentarians were industrious. Thomas Cole of Haverhill attended twenty times, Nathaniel Bacon of Friston twenty-five times and Edmund Harvey of Wickham Skeith thirty-eight times.[24] But others were idle. Edward Malby of Stonham Aspall, though nominally on the County Committee, attended no meetings; nor did Philip Parker of Erwarton, who apparently 'lacked zeal for the cause'.[25] When it came to signing documents, some Parliamentarian gentlemen were also less active than others.[26] Indeed, some seem to have been exceptionally lazy. Wiseman Bokenham of Thornham Magna signed only six documents, while Robert Reynolds of Ampton signed just two. William Cage of Ipswich signed no documents, although this was probably because he was busy as one of the town's two MPs. Parliament thus relied heavily on the conscientious county committeemen. Among these were Edmund Harvey of Wickham Skeith signing eighty-four documents and Francis Bacon of Ipswich signing ninety-two. Easily the most committed of all the Parliamentarian officials was the latter's elder brother, Nathaniel. A well educated barrister, Nathaniel Bacon was elected Recorder of Ipswich in December 1642 and later became chairman of the standing committee of the Eastern Association, which met

Erwarton Hall
(Engraved by E. Roberts from a sketch by T. Higham in *Excursions*, I, p. 149)
The great hall dates from the late sixteenth century, but the tunnel-like red-brick gateway is probably Jacobean. This was the main dwelling of Sir Philip Parker, lord of Erwarton, who during the Civil Wars showed himself to be a strong Puritan but a lukewarm Parliamentarian.

Little Wenham Hall
(Engraved by J. Greig from a sketch by T. Higham in *Excursions*, I, p. 151)
During the seventeenth century Little Wenham Hall was acquired by the Thurstons of
Hoxne, passive Parliamentarians in the First Civil War. The Hall, built *c.* 1270–80, is the
earliest brick house left in England. It is not a keep but a fortified manor house.
Arguably it laid the foundations for the development of the English manor house.

at Cambridge. As Chairman Nathaniel signed a staggering total of 864 documents between April 1644 and March 1645. Perhaps his Puritan zeal spurred him on. Rev. Cave Beck regarded him as a very pious, prudent and learned man.[27] But whatever the reason, Bacon's industry was exceptional even among the activists.

What about the military activities of the Suffolk gentry? Here the Parliamentarians seem to have been far less active than the Royalists. Only thirty-two (22 per cent) out of 142 Parliamentarian gentlemen were soldiers as compared with fifty-six (63 per cent) out of eighty-nine Royalists. One possible explanation is that the Royalists were younger than the Parliamentarians. Of the 118 Civil War contestants who were sixteen or over in 1642,[28] 23 per cent of Parliamentarians but as many as 43 per cent of Royalists were under thirty.[29] Even so, it is surprising that there were so few Parliamentary gentry soldiers since the army of the Eastern Association was raised all over East Anglia. Oliver Cromwell's 13th Troop of Horse (captained by Ralph Margery) was raised in Suffolk and so originally were the infantry regiments of Colonels Francis Russell of Cambridgeshire and Valentine Walton of Huntingdonshire. Yet Professor Clive Holmes found only two Suffolk gentleman-officers in the Eastern Association army:

Lieutenant-Colonel John Deynes of Coddenham and Major Richard Le Hunt of Little Bradley.[30] Likewise Professor Ian Gentles found just two Suffolk gentleman-officers in the New Model Army – Captains Henry Fulcher of Eye and Stephen Winthrop of Groton[31] – and it is doubtful if either of them served in the First Civil War. The most militarily active Suffolk Roundhead gentleman in that war was undoubtedly John Deynes, Lieutenant-Colonel of Foot. He was at the sieges of Reading and King's Lynn in 1643, at the taking of Lincoln (1643) and at the battles of Horncastle (1643), Marston Moor (1644) and Second Newbury (1644).[32] Deynes towered above his military colleagues and was not a typical Suffolk Roundhead gentleman. Altogether only thirteen (41 per cent) of the thirty-two Parliamentary gentry soldiers showed outstanding bravery or held high military command as field officers. On the other hand, at least forty-nine (87 per cent) of the fifty-six Royalist gentry soldiers were outstanding in rank or courage.

It is perhaps worth mentioning some of the more notable Royalist gentry army officers.

Sir Frederick Cornwallis of Brome Hall, Baronet (1610–62)

He was a Lieutenant of Horse[33] and famous for having rescued Lord Wilmot from the Roundheads at the Battle of Copredy Bridge in June 1644. He was so courageous that it was said 'no fear came into his thoughts'.[34]

Sir John Pettus of Cheston Hall, Baronet (1613–84)

He was a field officer of Horse, possibly Colonel of his own regiment. Taken prisoner at the siege of Lowestoft in 1643, he frankly admitted his Royalism to Oliver Cromwell, who seems to have respected his honesty. Released eleven months later, he continued to fight for the King and was at Bristol when Prince Rupert surrendered the city to Parliament in 1645.[35]

Henry Jermyn of Rushbrooke, Gentleman (1604–84)

Third son of Sir Thomas Jermyn, Knight, he was Colonel of Queen Henrietta's Lifeguard regiments of Horse and of Foot during the First Civil War. 'Bred from the Cradle in the Court', he become vice-chamberlain to the Queen in 1628 and her Master of the Horse in 1639. As a courtier he had a vested interest in the Royalist cause and lacked clear principles in religion and politics. Indeed the Royalist Earl of Clarendon said that Jermyn 'in his own judgement was very indifferent to all matters relating to religion'.[36] The Parliamentarians called him 'Butcherly Jermyn, contemptible Harry'. But he was brave, being wounded at Auburn Chase at the head of the Lifeguard of Horse in late 1643. Charles I appreciated his loyalty and services, making him Baron Jermyn of St Edmundsbury in 1643 and Governor of Jersey in 1644.[37]

Henry Jermyn of
Rushbrooke (1604–84) by
Sir Peter Lely
An active but irreligious
Royalist, Henry Jermyn,
a younger son, was well
rewarded by the Stuart
monarchy, both in the
1640s and at the
Restoration.

Sir Thomas Glemham of Little Glemham, Knight (c. 1590–1649)
A Colonel of Foot, Glemham was the most famous of all the Suffolk
Royalists and very like the Cavalier of fiction. Indeed Clarendon called him
a man of 'courage and integrity unquestionable'.[38] He was a professional
soldier and fought in the Thirty Years War on the continent and against
the Scots in 1639. During the First Civil War Glemham was successively
governor of York, which he had to surrender in 1644, governor of Carlisle,
which he also had to surrender in 1645, and finally governor of Oxford,
the Royalist headquarters in England. In 1646 the Privy Council ordered
Glemham to surrender Oxford. He protested vigorously, but like a good
soldier eventually obeyed his orders. In the Second Civil War of 1648
Glemham helped Sir Philip Musgrave, a Cumbrian Royalist, to capture
Carlisle. He died in exile in 1649. Incidentally, Glemham was, according

Glemham Hall

(Engraved by J. Webb from a drawing by T. Higham in *Excursions*, II, p. 81)
The original Hall was probably built by Sir Henry Glemham (d. 1632), father of the
Cavalier. Hereafter it was the main residence of the Glemham family until 1709. It was
then sold to Sir Dudley North, merchant. He substantially altered his Tudor style house
at Little Glemham in 1720, giving it a decidedly early Georgian appearance, as the plain
façade shows.

to a contemporary, 'the first man that taught soldiers to eat cats, dogs, etc.'[39] Finally, was Glemham a typical Cavalier? In his bravery and loyalty he undoubtedly was. But in one respect he was a rare bird – he had Puritan sympathies, having helped distressed Puritan ministers.[40]

The commoners

Let us now turn our attention to the common people, especially the townsmen and countrymen, and then examine the extent of popular Royalism in Suffolk.

Townsmen

In 1642 about a dozen towns in Suffolk had over 1,000 inhabitants: Beccles, Bungay, Bury St Edmunds, Hadleigh, Ipswich, Lavenham, Long Melford, Lowestoft, Mildenhall, Sudbury, Woodbridge and, possibly, Aldeburgh. Unfortunately, the allegiance of most of those towns is unknown.[41] Indeed, it is exceptionally difficult to discover the balance of political opinion in towns. Thus the late Philip Styles wrote: 'When we say that a particular town was Royalist or Parliamentarian in the Civil War we are speaking in terms of military control rather than of opinion'.[42] Lowestoft is an example.

In March 1643 eighteen 'Strangers' (mostly Norfolk and Suffolk gentry) took control, their aim being to fortify the port for Charles I, get arms from abroad and then attack the Eastern Association army. But we have no hard evidence about the attitudes of the townsfolk. However, owing to Lowestoft's long-standing fishing rivalry with nearby Great Yarmouth, which was 'wholly committed to the Parliament',[43] they are most unlikely to have had Roundhead sympathies.

We can be rather more positive about the political outlook of the other towns named in Map 13. Bury St Edmunds, a declining industrial town but not yet a gentry leisure centre, was politically divided. It appears to have been strongly Roundhead at first, being one of only twenty-two places in England which raised volunteers for the Parliament *before* the raising of the royal standard at Nottingham on 22 August 1642.[44] However, there was also a powerful Royalist faction in Bury.[45]

Three Suffolk towns were clearly Parliamentarian in sympathy: Ipswich, Lavenham, and Aldeburgh. The port of Ipswich was not only fortified against the Royalist fleet in 1642, but in 1643 the corporation loaned £450 to the Parliament.[46] Lavenham, still an important cloth town, had many inhabitants who were enthusiastic for the Parliamentary cause. Over 100 men volunteered either to serve as soldiers or to supply horses, muskets or corslets.[47] As far as we know, only one Lavenham man – John Hunt – was a Royalist soldier. Aldeburgh, a temporarily thriving port, raised a foot company for Parliament.[48] Indeed, in 1647 General Thomas Fairfax, commander-in-chief of the New Model Army, said that in Aldeburgh the support given his forces 'had exceeded that of all other towns in Suffolk', a compliment gratefully acknowledged by the bailiffs by 'ringing the church bells when the Lord Fairfax was in town' a few months later.[49]

Some of the most active Parliamentarians in Suffolk were townsmen. Thomas Chaplin, linen draper and alderman of Bury St Edmunds, was the second most active Suffolk official, signing ninety-four documents as a county committeeman. Other active plebeian county committeemen were Robert Dunkon, bailiff and tanner of Ipswich; Thomas Gibbs, alderman of Bury St Edmunds; and Samuel Moody, cloth merchant and also Bury alderman. Peter Fisher, an Ipswich woollen draper, held the responsible post of 'register' of the Suffolk Accounts Committee. All these commoners were Puritans as well as Parliamentarians.

The countrymen

What were the allegiances of the Suffolk farmers? There is little sign of Royalism among them. On the contrary, Thomas May believed that 'the Free holders and Yeomen' in Suffolk, Norfolk and Cambridgeshire 'in general adhered to the Parliament'. John Rushworth noted that 'many of the Chief Gentry of those Counties', together with those of Kent, Sussex, Surrey and Middlesex, 'were for paying Obedience to his Majesty's Commission

Map 13: Civil War Allegiances of Suffolk Towns

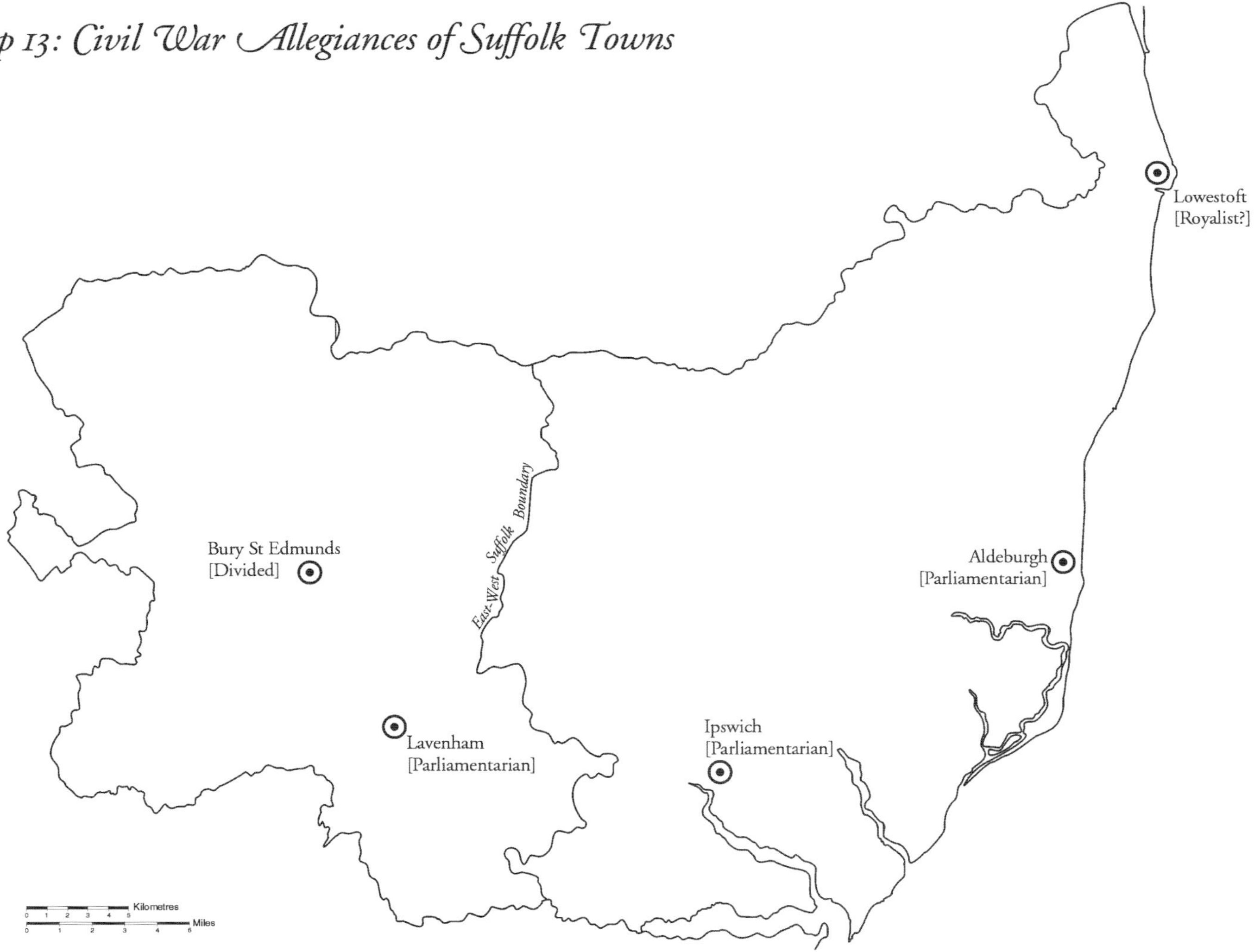

Lowestoft
[Royalist?]
Aldeburgh
[Parliamentarian]
Bury St Edmunds
[Divided]
East-West Suffolk Boundary
Lavenham
[Parliamentarian]
Ipswich
[Parliamentarian]
Kilometres
0 1 2 3 4 5
Miles
0 1 2 3 4 5

of Array', and he contrasted them with 'the Freeholders and Yeomen' who were 'generally of the other [Parliamentary] side'.[50]

That there was considerable support for Parliament among the farmers is suggested by the generous contributions to the propositions for raising money and horses in 1642. A total of £995 was raised in Wangford hundred in north-east Suffolk for the Parliamentary cause, and this included sums of over £100 from quite small villages like Mettingham and South Elmham All Saints and St Nicholas.[51] Villages in West Suffolk, like Alpheton, Cockfield and Shimpling, also supplied plenty of men, money and muskets for the Parliamentary cause.[52]

Perhaps the most active Parliamentarians among the Suffolk yeomen were Ralph Margery of Walsham-le-Willows, the famous 'plain russet coated captain' of Oliver Cromwell's 13th Troop of Horse;[53] John Base of Saxmundham, who held the important post of solicitor-general for sequestrations in Suffolk from 1643 to 1657; and above all William Dowsing, Provost Marshall General of the Eastern Association army and famous iconoclast.[54] Margery, Base and Dowsing were all Puritan Roundheads.

An impressionistic survey, then, suggests that there was much popular support for Parliament in Suffolk, especially among the 'middling sort'. Let us now see how much popular support there was for Charles I.

Popular Royalism

To assess – at least partially – the extent of popular Royalism in Suffolk we need to examine, very cautiously, the maimed soldiers' petitions among the Quarter Sessions Order Books. An act of 1662 required justices of the peace to pay small pensions to maimed or indigent former Royalist soldiers or their widows. Unfortunately the petitions seldom give the status or occupations of the petitioners, but they do relate mostly to common soldiers and NCOs and thus give a good indication of the extent of popular Royalism during the 1640s. David Underdown studied the maimed soldiers' petitions for 1662–67 and found as many as 815 former Royalist soldiers in Dorset and 327 in Wiltshire.[55] I have studied the Quarter Sessions Order Books for Suffolk for the longer period 1662–83 [56] and found only fifty-three former plebeian Royalist soldiers.[57] Besides these fifty-three maimed soldiers, I have found twenty-three other commoners who were apparently Royalists in the Civil War, of whom only ten were activists. But this total of seventy-six is unimpressive and it would seem that, with the possible exception of Bury St Edmunds, popular Royalism was extremely weak in Suffolk during the First Civil War.

I have located fifty-six of those seventy-six plebeian Royalists as well as 106 plebeian Parliamentarians.[58] Map 14 confirms Underdown's thesis – at least for Suffolk – that Royalist commoners tended to be strong in sheep-corn areas and Parliamentary commoners in wood-pasture districts.[59] If we combine the two sheep-corn areas of Suffolk (the Fielding and the

Map 14: Distribution of Royalist and Parliamentarian Commoners in Suffolk

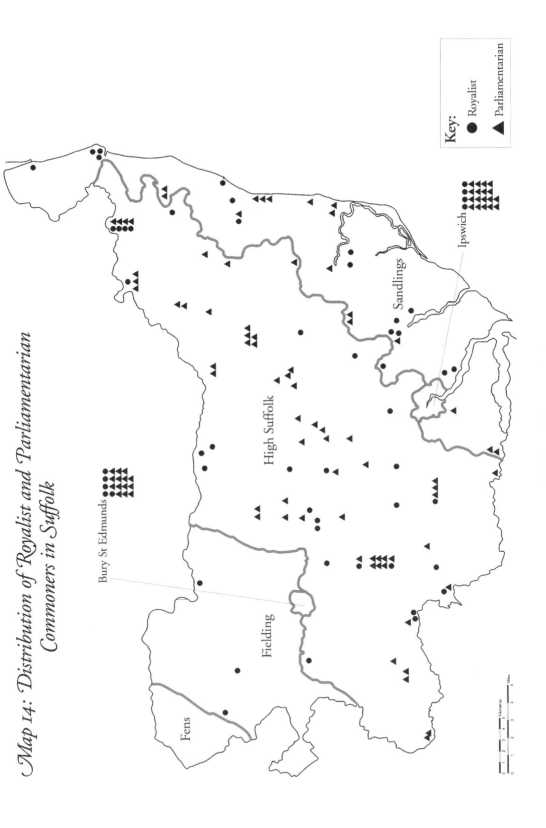

Key:
● Royalist
▲ Parliamentarian

Bury St Edmunds

Fens

Fielding

High Suffolk

Sandlings

Ipswich

Sandlings), we find that the Royalists very slightly outnumbered the Par-liamentarians. Those areas had nucleated villages where a manorial system still dominated agriculture. On the other hand the Parliamentarians easily predominated in the wood-pasture region (High Suffolk), which was weakly manorialised, had dispersed villages, 'very many yeomen of good credit'[60] and rural industries, especially in the Stour valley. Likewise the Parliamentarians had overwhelming majorities in the two main towns: Bury St Edmunds and Ipswich.

The issues

Let us deal with the main issues in Suffolk during the Civil War. The 'British problem', so strongly emphasised by Professor Conrad Russell, was hardly an issue to most Suffolk folk. Nor can Dr Adamson's 'baronial conflict' have concerned them, since the three peers who held land in Suffolk – two Royalists, the Earl of Cleveland and Lord Windsor, and one Parliamentarian, Lord Willoughby of Parham – were neither influential nor resident in the county. However, it is pertinent to consider the social, local, constitutional and religious issues.

Parham Moat Hall
(Engraved by W. Wallis from a sketch by T. Higham in *Excursions*, II, p. 79)
This is a moated early sixteenth century timber-framed house with substantial brick parts. A major contribution of the Moat Hall is in bay window design. The Willoughbys were the first known possessors of the Moat Hall. The 5th Baron Willoughby of Parham was an active Parliamentarian in the First Civil War and an equally active Royalist in the Second.

Social

According to Professor Brian Manning fear of the populace was a major cause of Royalism.[61] Manning stated that in 1643 'moderate nobility and gentry began to side with the King out of fear of social revolution and in defence of the social order'.[62] Manning was referring partly to anti-enclosure riots, refusal to pay rents and attacks on the property of Roman Catholics in 1641–42. There were certainly attacks on Papists or suspected Papists in Suffolk and Essex in August and September 1642. In the Stour valley, a wood-pasture area where there was much unemployment in the cloth trade, mobs attacked and plundered the houses of the Countess of Rivers at St Osyth in Essex and at Long Melford in Suffolk. The house of another Papist, Sir Francis Mannock at Stoke-by-Nayland in Suffolk, was also raided. Later the mob got out of hand and plundered 'as well protestants as papists'.[63]

Recently John Walter has implied that those riots were inspired by fear of Catholics rather than by hatred of the upper classes.[64] But whether expressions of anti-Catholicism or of class hatred, those attacks, far from driving large numbers of Suffolk gentry into the arms of the King, drove many into the arms of Parliament. Professor Robert Ashton has said that

Melford Hall
(Engraved by E. Roberts from a sketch by T. Higham in *Excursions*, I, p. 58)
Melford Hall is a turreted brick Tudor mansion. Like Christchurch Mansion, Rushbrooke Hall and Kentwell Hall, it has two far-projecting wings. In the summer of 1642 Melford Hall, owned by the Countess of Rivers, was attacked by a mob 'for no other ground than that she was a papist'.

Gifford's Hall, Stoke-by-Nayland
(Engraved by E. Roberts from a drawing by T. Higham in *Excursions*, I, p. 71)
The Hall was probably built between *c.* 1480 and 1500 judging by the style and type of
carving and ornamentation. The fine brick gatehouse, no higher than two storeys, with
angle turrets, was probably built in the 1520s. Gifford's Hall was owned by the Roman
Catholic Mannocks. Their house was attacked by anti-Papist mobs during the Stour
Valley riots of 1642.

'fear of popular disorder was as likely to work in favour of the King's
opponents who in some areas appeared as the only effective guardians of
public order'.[65] The Parliamentary gentry under Sir Nathaniel Barnardiston
endeavoured to put down the disorders in the Stour valley.[66] So it could
perhaps be argued that in Suffolk it was the Parliamentary gentry rather
than the Royalists who were able to pose as champions of law and order
against lower class violence. However, the fact that in West Suffolk – where
the riots took place – the Royalist gentry were almost as numerous as the
Parliamentarian gentry suggests that there may be at least some truth in
Professor Manning's thesis.

Local

It was once fashionable to interpret the English Civil War in terms of
localism. Professor Roots defined this as 'a priority given to the apparent
needs of a community smaller and more intimate than the state or nation ...
Hence it was local rather than national politics that men revelled in' and
'rebellions, including the Great Rebellion itself, were emphatically local
movements'. Everitt said about the Suffolk gentry that 'their primary sphere

of activity was the local community: their "country" was the shire'.[67] There is indeed a *prima facie* case for emphasising the parochialism and localism of our seventeenth century ancestors. Local feelings and local loyalties were bound to be strong among all social groups in an age when transport facilities and communications were poor and when a journey from Ipswich to London might take anything up to three days.

However, in Suffolk local issues do not seem to have been of great importance during the Civil War. There are certainly some examples of localism. The likely Royalism of Lowestoft would have been due less to its love of the King's cause than to its traditional fishing rivalry with neighbouring Yarmouth, which was strongly Parliamentarian. Indeed, had Yarmouth been Royalist, Lowestoft might well have been Parliamentarian through sheer local cussedness.

Some Civil War historians have said that localism was shown by a reluctance to fight outside one's own county.[68] The Suffolk Parliamentarians have been described as men 'who were always reluctant to fight far from home' and 'who frequently grumbled about marching to distant parts of the realm'.[69] This seems hard to believe because Colonel Russell's, largely Suffolk, regiment fought at Marston Moor in 1644 as part of the army of the Eastern Association.[70] Yet the fact remains that only seven (22 per cent) of the thirty-two Suffolk Roundhead gentry soldiers definitely fought outside their county during the First Civil War.

The Suffolk Cavaliers present a very different picture. Of the fifty-six Royalist gentry soldiers, at least forty-one (73 per cent) fought outside their native county. This more national outlook may perhaps be partly explained by the fact that the Royalists married further afield than did the Parliamentarians. Thirty-nine per cent of Roundhead gentry marriages, but as many as 56 per cent of Cavalier marriages, were with women from outside Suffolk.[71] But whatever the reason, Suffolk Royalist gentlemen saw military action at Alresford, Ashby-de-la-Zouch, Auburn Chase, Bristol, Burton-on-Trent, Carlisle, Copredy Bridge, Edgehill, Exeter, Faringdon, Gainsborough, King's Lynn, Naseby, Newark, First and Second Newbury, Oxford, Pontefract, Reading, Rowton Moor, South Wales, Tewkesbury, Wallingford, Wetherby, Winchester, Woodstock and York.

None of this is surprising. There is little reason why localism should have been strong in Suffolk. It was not an isolated county, having no strong natural frontiers. The sea was a highway, not a barrier. The rivers Waveney and Little Ouse do not separate Suffolk from Norfolk in the way that the Mersey separates Lancashire from Cheshire. Nor is the river Stour a great barrier between Suffolk and Essex. The East Anglian Heights do not separate Suffolk from Cambridgeshire in the way that the Pennines separate Lancashire from Yorkshire.

Constitutional [72]

There was much constitutional opposition in Suffolk to the arbitrary government of Charles I. Suffolk MPs like Sir Nathaniel Barnardiston of Kedington, Sir Simonds D'Ewes of Stowlangtoft and Sir Philip Parker of Erwarton, strongly championed the privileges of Parliament. All became Roundheads in the Civil War.

Many gentry throughout England were prepared to suffer imprisonment rather than submit to arbitrary taxation. Among those Suffolk men deprived of their liberty in 1627 for resisting the forced loan was Sir Nathaniel Barnardiston, the future Roundhead leader in Suffolk.[73]

In 1629 Charles I dissolved Parliament and ruled without it for 11 years. Sir Simonds D'Ewes referred to the dissolution as 'the most gloomie, sadd and dismall day for England that had happened in 500 yeares space last past'.[74]

Arbitrary taxation continued during the Personal Rule of Charles I and particularly resented was Ship Money. Today few living in an inland place, like Bury St Edmunds, would object to paying taxes for the upkeep of the navy, but before 1635 it was expected that only coastal towns, like Ipswich, would pay Ship Money. Thus Charles I aroused resentment by imposing Ship Money on inland and coastal areas alike, hence the famous refusal to pay in 1637 by John Hampden, a gentleman from Buckinghamshire, an inland county. Ship Money was demanded annually from 1635 and, though a coastal county, Suffolk showed a notable reluctance to pay. By 1640 only £200 was raised out of an annual assessment of about £8,000. This may have been partly because of 'the decay of trade' but also because Ship Money threatened to become a permanent tax levied without Parliamentary approval. If Parliament did not approve taxes, its *raison d'etre* was threatened. Thus Sir Simonds D'Ewes, exaggerating as usual, referred in his autobiography to Ship Money as 'the most

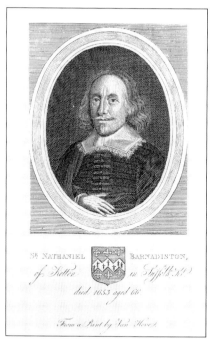

Sʳ NATHANIEL BARNADISTON,
of Ketton in Suffolk Kᵗ
died 1653 aged 66.

From a Print by Van Hove.

Sir Nathaniel Barnardiston of Kedington (Ketton), Knight (1588–1653) by Van Hove, engraver.
A devout Puritan and champion of Parliamentary privilege, Sir Nathaniel led Suffolk into the Roundhead camp when the First Civil War began.

deadlie and fatall blow ... to the libertie of the subjects of England ... in 500 yeares last past'.[75]

Apart from Ship Money, the war against Scotland, started in 1639, was very unpopular in Suffolk and led to a soldiers' mutiny at Bungay and a transport strike at Ipswich.

When Charles I at last had to summon the 'Long' Parliament in 1640 strong opponents of his rule were elected, like Sir Nathaniel Barnardiston, Sir Simonds D'Ewes and Sir Philip Parker.

The Long Parliament ended arbitrary taxation, arbitrary justice and non-parliamentary rule, but much bitterness remained and memories of Ship Money and other non-parliamentary taxes must have caused many a Suffolk man to support Parliament in the Civil War. The Long Parliament later split over religion. Many MPs wanted the abolition of episcopacy and petitions from nineteen counties in 1641 supported this demand. One of those counties was Suffolk.[76]

Religious

It is now as fashionable to emphasise religion as a Civil War issue as it was to stress localism in the 1960s and 70s. Professor Morrill has called the English Civil War 'the last of the Wars of Religion'. Professor Fletcher has said that what 'distinguished the two armies' – and presumably the two sides – in the Civil War was 'the sharp contrast between their religious attitudes'. Even the cautious Conrad Russell says that 'many people, and very many of the first activists, did fight for religion'.[77]

Table 5.5 shows that among the Suffolk gentry there was a close correlation between Civil War alignments and religious loyalties.

Table 5.5 Religion and Civil War allegiances of Suffolk gentry families

	Parliamentarian	Royalist	Sidechangers/ Divided	Neutral/ Unknown	Total No. of families
Roman Catholic	Nil	6 (9.4%)	Nil	28 (5.5%)	34 (4.9%)
Puritan	61 (58.1%)	5 (7.8%)	9 (69.2%)	27 (5.3%)[78]	102 (14.8%)
Anglican	44 (41.9%)	53 (82.8%)	4 (30.8%)	452 (89.2%)	553 (80.3%)
Total	105 (100.0%)	64 (100.0%)	13 (100.0%)	507 (100.0%)	689 (100.0%)

As Table 5.5 shows, the overwhelming majority of the Royalist and Neutral/Unknown families were Anglican, and so were a substantial minority of Parliamentarian families. But how many of these families were devout and how many were indifferent cannot be quantified. The Anglican or non-Puritan Parliamentarians are unlikely to have been staunch supporters of the established church. The Anglican Royalists are far more likely to have been, but exactly how many of them actually fought in the Civil War mainly to defend episcopacy and the Prayer Book, it is impossible to say.

Since Suffolk was a strongly Protestant county by 1642, it is hardly surprising that so many Royalist gentry families were Anglican and that so few were Roman Catholic. Indeed Table 5.5 shows that the link between Catholicism and Royalism was extremely weak. Of the thirty-four Catholic families, only six (18 per cent) supported Charles I during the Civil War,[79] and those six in turn comprised just 9 per cent of the sixty-four Royalist gentry families of Suffolk.[80] Contrast Yorkshire where 35 per cent, and Lancashire where at least 68 per cent, of Cavalier families were Roman Catholic.[81]

Table 5.5 shows, not surprisingly, that a majority of the Suffolk Parliamentarian gentry were Puritan: sixty-one (58 per cent) of the 105 families.[82] Eighty-three (58 per cent) of the 142 individual Parliamentarian gentry were also Puritan. Moreover, these are conservative estimates. Yet, rather surprisingly, there were fewer Puritan Parliamentarian gentry in Suffolk than in Lancashire. There 71 per cent of Parliamentarian families were Puritan during the Civil War.[83] However, if we concentrate on the Roundhead activists in Suffolk, the link between Parliamentarianism and Puritanism is indeed close. Forty-nine (67 per cent) of the seventy-three most committed individual Parliamentarian gentlemen were Puritan. Of the fifty-six most active members or agents of the County Committee, thirty-six (64 per cent) were Puritan. Of the thirteen most outstanding Parliamentary gentry soldiers, nine (69 per cent) were Puritan. Of the seventeen Parliamentarian gentlemen who *actively* served as *both* soldiers and officials, as many as fourteen (82 per cent) were of the same faith.

Numbers were not everything, however. What mattered most was that almost all the Suffolk Parliamentarian leaders were Puritan. These included such gentlemen as Sir Nathaniel Barnardiston of Kedington, county boss who led Suffolk into the Roundhead camp in September 1642; Thomas Cole of Haverhill and Edmund Harvey of Wickham Skeith, county committee activists; and Nathaniel Bacon of Ipswich, the vigorous chairman of the standing committee of the Eastern Association. Without such Puritan leaders it is hard to see how the Suffolk Parliamentarian gentry could have won control of their county so quickly and decisively.

Conclusion

Although Suffolk was a militarily quiet county controlled by one party throughout the Civil War, studying the region has not been a pointless exercise. We have been forced to question some widely held views, such as that Suffolk was a Roundhead heartland. We have found that the Civil War allegiances of a majority of the gentry, and indeed of the commoners, are unknown. More importantly, perhaps, we have noticed that among the combatant gentry the Parliamentarians had a large majority over the Royalists only in East Suffolk and that in West Suffolk the two sides were almost evenly matched. Moreover, a majority of both the Parliamentarian and Royalist gentry of Suffolk *actively* supported the war effort of their own side, and were by no means parochial.[84] About three-quarters of the Roundhead gentry were officials during the First Civil War, raising men, money and horses for the *national* Parliament and sequestering Royalist estates, though not all were conscientious. In the same war Suffolk Royalist gentry saw military action in twenty-six different places *outside* the county.

Among the commoners of Suffolk, and especially among the 'middling sort', there seems to have been much active support for Parliament. By contrast there appears to have been little popular Royalism in the county.

Finally, it has been hard to discover what motivated the Suffolk gentry to support one side or another. But it would seem that social, local and even political factors were only of limited importance. As in Lancashire, religion appears to have been the issue which principally divided the two sides in the Civil War.

CHAPTER SIX

Suffolk and the Second Civil War: Origins and outcome

The Second Civil War of 1648, like the First Civil War of 1642–46, is a controversial topic. Some historians actually deny that 1648 saw a civil war. Barry Coward considers that 'the series of unco-ordinated risings [in East Anglia, Kent, South Wales and the Fleet] hardly deserves being called a war'. He also states that there is 'little evidence of ardent royalist fervour among the rebels of 1648'.[1] Professor John Morrill rejects 'the assumption that the first and second Civil Wars can be treated as a unit ... for the issues are arguably totally different and in some ways unrelated'. He has stressed that 'the great majority of those who rose for Charles I were reacting against Parliament and centralisation, not for the king'.[2] The late Bryan Lyndon disagreed with both Coward and Morrill, arguing that 'the Second Civil War of 1648 was ... the perpetuation of ideological and political conflict which, since 1642, had divided Royalist and Parliamentarian'.[3] Lyndon particularly emphasised the royalism of the New Model Army's opponents. Professor Robert Ashton has recently put forward the most convincing and balanced arguments. In his *Counter-Revolution* he has established beyond any doubt that the First and Second Civil Wars were quite distinct.[4] At the same time he has stressed the widely differing views to be found among the enemies of the New Model Army. 'The risings in the Second Civil War were at best tenuous coalitions', consisting of 'disgruntled ex-parliamentarian soldiers ... moderates alienated by [county] committee tyranny ... and thoroughgoing Cavaliers ...'[5]

Ashton's book throws much light on the Second Civil War and also on its background. Like some historians Ashton regards high taxation, arbitrary rule by low-born county committeemen and disorders provoked by the army as major causes of the war. But in addition he has emphasised the revival of political and religious conservatism. Fiscal, constitutional and social factors were not of paramount importance in Suffolk during the period 1646 to 1648, but religious factors undoubtedly were. This chapter will therefore concentrate on the religious background to the Second Civil War and conclude by examining the part played by Suffolk people in that war.

The religious background

Since the First Civil War was primarily a 'war of religion', it is hardly surprising that important religious changes accompanied the Parliamentarian victory. The mid and late 1640s witnessed attempts to stamp Puritan ways of life upon Suffolk. This involved, *inter alia*, stricter enforcement of the Sabbath, the outlawing of Christmas celebrations and a new system of church government. As regards the Sabbath, Puritans believed that the whole day should be spent in worship and that Sunday afternoon games in the spirit of the early Stuart Declarations of Sports should be sternly forbidden. The Puritan outlook is clearly demonstrated by an order of the Ipswich corporation, issued on 7 March 1644. It is worth quoting at some length:

> Forasmuch as the Lord's Day nowe is and of late hath been much prophaned within this towne, by usinge diverse pastimes and recreations, children sportinge and playinge in the streetes, and a great parte of that day after the publique worshipp of God ended wastefully and vainely spent in idle and needles sitting at doores, walkinge at the Key, in the feildes, and other publique places, to the great dishonour of God and the increasinge of the giult which lies upon this nation for the sin of sabaoth breakinge: nowe for the better sanctyfyinge of that day and the more strict and due observinge of the fast dayes, and to the intent that after the publike service of God ended each family apart may spend the remainder of those dayes in the exercise of religious duties: it is ordered and agreed that all persons inhabitinge within this towne that after the twentieth day of March next shall prophane the Lord's Daye by sportinge or playinge at any games, walkinge at the Key, in the feildes, or other publique places in or neere this towne, by unnecessary roweinge in boates, washing themselves in the somer time, rydeinge of horses out further than to the neerest water, and leapinge, runninge, or otherwise sportinge with the said horses; and all masters and parents that shall suffer their apprentices, servants or children to comitt any of the said offences or to bee playeinge and idleinge in the streetes upon the Lord's Day or fast dayes, shall for the first offence forfeit 12*d*. And for every time soe offendinge afterwards 2*s*. ... and that the money hereuppon raised and levyed shall bee to the use of the poore of the parishe where the said offence shall bee committed ... And it is desired that this order bee published in the severall churches of this towne the next Lord's day ...[6]

Whether this order was successfully enforced in Ipswich, is unknown. But it would be surprising if it did not arouse at least some opposition and resentment.

Opposition was certainly aroused by the Puritan attempt to enforce the Parliamentary ordinance of 19 December 1644 prohibiting the celebration of Christmas,[7] the most popular Church festival. Serious disturbances occurred in the main Suffolk towns. In Bury St Edmunds in 1647 a Puritan attempt to enforce the ordinance led to a popular riot which was seen as 'a horrid plot and bloudy conspiracie'.[8] In Ipswich on Christmas Day 1647 there were riots against the same ordinance. However, the ringleaders were all safely locked up by 27 December, and among the casualties was a man named Christmas 'whose name seemed to blow up the coales of his zeale to the observation of the day'.[9] If there was strong opposition to the anti-Christmas ordinance in the two main Puritan strongholds of Suffolk, there must have been considerably more in the other, less puritanical, parts of the county, though as yet there is no positive proof.

Puritan rule during the 1640s was not entirely negative. The Puritans of Suffolk hankered after a new system of church government. Many wished to replace episcopacy by Presbyterianism. So on 19 August 1645, in place of the Elizabethan Church, Parliament sanctioned a Presbyterian system of church government for the nation.[10] On 5 November Suffolk was divided into fourteen classical Presbyteries with 104 ministers and 259 lay elders. An extra sixteen ministers and forty-three lay elders were named on 18 February 1648.[11] Suffolk is one of only twelve of the forty English counties whose Presbyterian lists have survived.[12] The Presbyterian system might be expected to have succeeded in Suffolk because Presbyterian ministers were numerous in the county and in December 1648 the vast majority of the Puritan MPs preferred Presbyterianism to Independency.[13] Moreover, there seems to have been a strong popular demand for the strict enforcement of Presbyterianism, judging by a Suffolk petition of 16 February 1647 to the House of Lords.[14] However, 'there is practically no trace of the [Presbyterian] system working' in the county. 'This' says Professor Yule, 'is puzzling'.[15] But is it? The Presbyterian system was bound to fail when it was not given the central government backing necessary for enforcement. As John Morrill reminds us, 'the will of Parliament to enforce the Presbyterian scheme disappeared in effect from the time of the Army's first occupation of London in August 1647'.[16] It can perhaps be speculated that there was also a social reason for the failure of Presbyterianism in Suffolk. Enemies of Presbyterianism said that many lay elders were men of 'meane quality'.[17] This was of course a gross exaggeration, yet of the 302 individual Presbyterian elders nominated for Suffolk in 1645 and 1648, 198 (66 per cent) were commoners. Only 104 (34 per cent) can be identified as gentry in 1642. Perhaps, in this deferential age, the Presbyterians of Suffolk might have had more success had there been a higher proportion of gentry among them. After all, the strength of Suffolk Puritanism before the First Civil War had depended largely on the alliance between 'magistracy and ministry'.[18]

On the whole, the Puritans of Suffolk were more destructive than creative during the 1640s. This is shown by their treatment of 'scandalous' and 'malignant' ministers, by the iconoclasm of William Dowsing and by the witch-hunting of Matthew Hopkins. Let us first examine the case of the 'scandalous, malignant priests'. These were Anglican clergy expelled from their livings by the triumphant Parliamentarians. Some 2,780 out of at least 8,600 Church of England clergy were harassed by the authorities between 1641 and 1660. About 1,600 clerics were dispossessed before the execution of King Charles I, while another 320 were ejected during the Interregnum.[19] Concentrating on the 1640s, it would seem that the highest percentages of expulsions were in strongly Parliamentarian areas, such as London, Cambridgeshire and Suffolk and lowest in the more solidly Royalist areas of England.[20] In Suffolk 129 Anglican clergy out of a total of at least 517 [21] were sequestered by the Puritans between 1643 and 1646, while at least another seven were severely harassed.[22] The charges against eighty [23] are known, so let us concentrate on them and ignore the other fifty-six.[24] Some of our eighty Suffolk clergy suffered at the hands of Parliament's Committee for Plundered Ministers set up in December 1642 under the active chairmanship of John White, a devout Puritan. But a majority of clerics were victims of two Suffolk committees commissioned by the Earl of Manchester in March 1644.[25] The ultimate aim of all these committees was to replace 'scandalous' by 'godly' ministers. Local committeemen and parishioners, whose social standing varied, accused the clergy of being either 'scandalous in Doctrine', 'scandalous in Life' or 'malignant'. If found guilty, the incumbents were expelled from their livings and their entire property was sequestered, reserving only one-fifth for the benefit of their wives and children.[26] The ejected ministers had to seek an alternative living, ranging from teaching to begging.[27] Many of the charges against these priests were gossipy and malicious, but they make fascinating, and sometimes amusing, reading. Accusations against ministers can be divided, for convenience, into three categories: the religious, the moral and the political.[28] Several clergy were, of course, accused under all three heads (e.g. Lionel Playters, Rector of Uggeshall).

Let us begin with religious accusations. Among our sample of eighty Suffolk clergy listed in Appendix IV, sixty-seven (84 per cent) were accused of religious offences, mostly of being 'scandalous in Doctrine'. This phrase meant preaching false doctrine or introducing new forms of worship, i.e. ritualism. Only a small minority of our clergy were accused of preaching unsound doctrine. Allegations of Arminianism were levelled against just four priests: Theodore Beale, James Buck, Robert Cotesford and Jeremiah Ravens.[29] The former had argued that 'Christ must save the greatest parte of people otherwise he can be no Saviour'.[30] Eight parsons were charged with favouring auricular confession: William Aldus, James Buck, Seth Chapman, Alexander Clarke, Robert Cotesford, Thomas Geary, Anthony Sparrow and Watts of Mildenhall's curate, Mr Blower.[31] Two ministers –

Cuthbert Dale and Thomas Tyllot – were accused of advocating prayers to saints and angels.[32] Three priests – James Buck, Lionel Playters and William Walker – were alleged to have positively praised the Church of Rome, the latter affirming that 'the papists be as good orthodox Divines ... as wee, bowing to Images only excepted'.[33] Most of our eighty clergymen were not neo-Papists, however. Yet neither were they moderate Anglicans. Fifty (62 per cent) were accused of having been ceremonalists or ritualists in the 1630s.[34] Certain stock allegations were constantly repeated: observing and urging Bishop Wren's 'innovations'; insisting on the congregation receiving communion kneeling at the altar rails; bowing at the name of Jesus. John Ferror was considered guilty of all three offences. He was 'a conformist to popish and superstitious Innovations enioyned by Bishopp Wrenn', he had 'refused to give to a poor widow the sacrament of the Lord's supper because shee refused to kneele at the rayles' and he 'bowed towards the east at the name of Jesus'.[35] Lionel Playters likewise 'conformed himselfe to all Bishop Wren's iniunctions' and 'made obeysance and many leggs and cringings before the communion table and [altar] rayles'.[36]

Other important religious accusations were brought against our clergy. A charge levelled against fifteen priests was reading *The Book of Sports*,[37] which, by allowing stipulated activities on Sundays, was utterly obnoxious to Puritan Sabbatarianism. Also repugnant to the Puritans – though this had been a complaint since Elizabeth I's reign – were those clergy deemed guilty of general negligence. Thirty-six of our Suffolk sample were accused of this.[38] The negligent clergy comprised mostly pluralists, non-residents and 'dumb dogs'. The latter were condemned for lacking the ability or inclination to 'preach the Word' regularly. William Pratt was alleged to have 'seldom preached and then read his sermons wholly'. Edmund Mayor did likewise. Edward Barton had 'an inaudible voice' and his sermons 'lasted only half an hour'.[39] However, let us keep a sense of proportion. Of our sample of eighty clerics, only sixteen were condemned as inadequate preachers.[40] This is fewer than expected. A possible explanation is that seventy-seven of our eighty clergymen were university graduates,[41] so most would have been articulate in the pulpit.

Of our eighty clergy, at least forty-three (54 per cent) were accused of immorality or, to use contemporary jargon, of being 'scandalous in Life'. This mainly involved allegations of drunkenness, swearing and sexual immorality, which were an echo of the campaign waged by the Puritans against unsuitable clergymen under Elizabeth I and James I. Thirty-eight of our sample were charged with drunkenness.[42] Thomas Newman was called 'a frequent haunter of Alehouses' and was accused of returning 'home drunke behaveing himself like a madman'. Thomas Geary was 'often drunke, even to spewing', while John Wells, 'a common drunkard', had 'in drunkenness layne abroad in the fields, lost his hat and fallen into ditches'.[43] Thirteen of our priests were said to be swearers.[44] John Wells was alleged to be a 'common swearer of very great Oathes'. More specifically, Thomas Geary was accused of uttering 'most Prophane bloody oathes as God damme me'.[45] Fifteen ministers were accused of sexual immorality.[46] Nicholas King was charged with 'attempting the chastity of a woman'. William Gibbons, it was deposed, had 'in a suspitious and lustfull manner putt his hands under the clothes of Susan Scott, a noted harlott'. More seriously, Samuel Scrivener was accused of 'adultery with Margaret the wife of George Woods'.[47] Some of the accusations against the clergy are laughable. Lionel Playters was charged with 'Eating Custard after a scandalous manner'.[48] Custard denoted rich food and Playters was in fact being accused of high living, hardly surprising since he belonged to a well-known Suffolk gentry family, the Playters of Sotterley. However, such indulgence was condemned by the Puritans and this was apparently one of the main reasons why Playters was ejected from his living.[49] Many of the above accusations were false, unjust or greatly exaggerated.[50] Indeed, the 'sinnes' of the 'scandalous' ministers in the 1640s were probably as exaggerated as those of the monks had been in the 1530s. Certainly some contemporary sources,

West Stow Hall
(Engraved by E. Roberts from a sketch by T. Higham in *Excursions*, I, p. 77)
This famous Hall is part of a large building owned by the Crofts family. The
three-storey red-brick gatehouse, built *c.* 1525, has corner-turrets and pinnacles and carries
the arms of Mary Tudor, sister of Henry VIII. This gatehouse is often compared with
that of Giffords Hall. The Crofts family (both lay *and* clerical) were active Royalists in
the First Civil War.

such as the Puritan John White's *First Century* (1643), are not always reliable as to the moral character of the sequestered clergy. However, even if we cannot believe all the charges, we can at least record them. As Jim Sharpe has said, 'a more active and demanding Christianity had made its impact' by the mid-1640s and the depositions imply that higher standards of morality were now expected from the clergy.[51]

'Malignancy' was the third main charge levelled against the sequestered and harassed Anglican clergy. Of our eighty priests, at least fifty-eight (72 per cent) were accused of being 'malignant', a term of abuse often applied to hard-line Royalists. But not all 'malignant' clergy were in fact hard-liners and there were varying degrees of 'malignancy' or Royalism. At one extreme were those parsons supporting Charles I in a military capacity. John Crofts, John Gordon, Edmund Hinde and Philip Parsons seem to have served as fighting men in the royal army, while Edmund Boldero, Lionel Gatford and John Pearson were chaplains to the Marquis of Montrose, the King's army in the West and Goring's army respectively.[52] At the other extreme were six clerics, who, though not actively Royalist, were apparently unenthusiastic about Parliament's cause. Samuel Alsop, James Buck, John Gregson and Nicholas King were charged with expressing 'great malignancy agt the Parliament',[53] but this 'malignancy' was unspecified and there is no other evidence that they were ever Royalists. William Franklin was merely 'suspected of malignancy'.[54] Robert Large took the Vow and Covenant but 'only as far as the law allowed'. This grudging support for Parliament was enough to ensure his ejection from his living by the Earl of Manchester in 1644.[55]

Between the two extremes of 'malignancy' were forty-five clergy who were decidedly anti-Parliamentarian, if not overtly Royalist.[56] Twenty-five apparently opposed Parliament by their deeds.[57] Some would not lend money to Parliament, others did not observe the Parliamentary fasts, while others were accused of refusing to take such loyalty oaths to Parliament as the Vow and Covenant or the Solemn League and Covenant.[58] Thirty-five opposed Parliament by their words, being charged with speaking out against the Roundheads or their Scottish allies.[59] There was indeed great fear of outspoken 'ill affected clergie' and in January 1644 Parliament was warned by its supporters in Suffolk of the harm they were doing.[60] One of the most outspoken priests was Miles Goltey who was accused of having 'wished the king and his Cavilyers were in Suffolk, [then] all wrongs would be righted'. Some of the 'ill affected clergie' were accused of smearing Parliament and its leaders. Theodore Beale had said that 'the two houses [of Parliament] were full of Anabaptists, naming the Lord Say and Sir Nathaniel Barnardiston', the Suffolk Roundhead leader. Beale was also alleged to have said that 'the Earle of Strafford dyed uniustly' after his trial, a bold remark since the Parliamentarians believed that the earl had deserved his fate for attempting to establish absolute monarchy. Just as hated as Strafford had been was the Earl of Newcastle. William Walker was alleged to have said that he was 'a zealous protestant'.[61] This was also a defiant remark because Newcastle and his 'popish' army were regarded as a serious threat to the Eastern Association in 1643. The above remarks seem to have been made in private conversation or informally. However, at least eight of our parsons were alleged to have denounced Parliament or supported the king from their pulpits.[62] This was serious. As organs of public instruction and indoctrination, pulpits were inevitably involved in the struggle for power in seventeenth-century England. From the pulpit Parliament's Scottish allies were attacked. William Walker was alleged to have 'publicly in his preaching rayled upon our brethren the Scotts upon their first comming, calling them Rebells'. William Alcock was accused of having made similar remarks 'openly in the congregation'. But of all the preaching 'malignant' ministers none was as vociferous as Lionel Playters. The uncle of Thomas Playters of Sotterley, a Royalist colonel of Horse and of Foot, Lionel was devoted to the king's cause. 'In his preaching' he was accused of having said that 'such as have or shall take upp armes' against the king were to 'receyve to themselves damnation'. Worst of all, he was charged with having remarked that 'a king was not to be resisted in any cause, although he should be a tirant'.[63]

It has been important to end with the political allegations against the ejected clergy. The fact that almost three-quarters of our sample of ministers were accused of some form of 'malignancy' surely suggests at least some link between Anglicanism and Royalism, between religion and politics in seventeenth-century Suffolk.[64] Moreover, our evidence has endorsed the view of Professor Ashton that 'Royalism was a more common Anglican characteristic than ritualism'.[65]

Finally, how much support and sympathy did the 'suffering' clergy of Suffolk receive from their neighbours? It is very hard to say. William Raymond, a preacher of considerable repute, was helped after his sequestration by a group of local gentlemen. They allowed him to preach in their houses, where his ex-parishioners came to hear him. Henry Rolinson also received a great deal of support from his parish. John Crofts, ejected from his parish in 1644 by the Earl of Manchester, found when he returned to Suffolk in 1647 that he had a substantial party of followers. In November John Legate, the 'intruded' Puritan minister of Barnham, complained to a Parliamentary Committee that not only had Crofts arrested him for detaining the tithes, but had forcibly seized the Church, while at harvest time 'the violence of Dr Crofts *and his Adharents*'[66] had forced Legate to 'garrison' his house with men hired in Norfolk.[67] William Short and Thomas Rogerson are also interesting cases. William Short had his rectory of Euston sequestered in 1645 and two years later he tried to divert the payment of tithes to himself from the 'intruded' Puritan minister, Robert Stafford. Although the Committee for Plundered Ministers supported

Stafford and ordered that his tithes should be 'forthwith paid' to him, Short had come within an ace of success because he had 'the combinacon [support] of several of the parishioners', including Edward Rookwood, the Catholic Royalist lord of the manor of Euston.[68] Thomas Rogerson, ejected from his living in 1643, had the sympathy of 'the Neighbouring Gentry and Clergy and the Inhabitants of the Parish, who petitioned the Committee for Plundered Ministers and the Assembly that he might be restored, testifying withal his abilities, orthodoxy and good life; but they were deaf to anything of that kind'.[69] So the petition failed, but the evidence, though somewhat biased, suggests that Rogerson's ejection had not been popular with his parishioners. Do the above cases represent growing opposition to Puritan rule in Suffolk? We cannot say, but the likelihood should not be ruled out.

The vehemence of the Suffolk Puritans was not confined to action against Anglican clerics; it blazed forth against places of worship. During the 1640s Suffolk produced the most renowned iconoclast in England: William Dowsing of Stratford St Mary, Yeoman (1596–1668).[70] For a short time Dowsing was Provost Marshall General of the Eastern Association army[71] and had seen military action at the siege of King's Lynn in 1643.[72] But he clearly found his iconoclastic activities much more to his liking. He was quite convinced that he was doing God's work when he deliberately damaged at least 147 (28 per cent) of the 517 Anglican parish churches in Suffolk, not to mention 96 churches in Cambridgeshire.[73] On 28 August 1643 a Parliamentarian ordinance ordered that altars, crucifixes, crosses, images and pictures should be demolished in, or removed from, churches.[74] On 19 December 1643 Dowsing was officially commissioned by the Earl of Manchester, commander-in-chief of the Eastern Association army, to eradicate all those 'relics of popery' in the parish churches of the counties of the Association.[75] In 1644 he carried out his instructions with zest. He kept a journal of his crusade of destruction in Suffolk and it is worth quoting a few extracts. At Frostenden Dowsing destroyed '20 superstitious pictures,[76] one Crucifix and a Picture of God the Father'. At Walberswick 'we brake down 40 superstitious Pictures'. At Southwold 'we brake down 130 superstitious Pictures'. At Bures ' we brake down above 600 superstitious Pictures, 8 Holy Ghosts, 3 of God the Father and 3 of the Son'. At Clare 'we brake down 1,000 Pictures superstitious; I brake down 200'.[77] The round figures that feature in the journal suggest inflated totals and arouse suspicion. Even so, the destruction wrought by Dowsing seems considerable.

We must not paint too black a picture of William Dowsing, and a number of points may be made in his favour. First, Dowsing was a discriminating iconoclast. This is shown by his sparing secular memorials[78] and objects of artistic beauty.[79] Second, Dowsing was a bureaucratic Puritan. If something was in the ordinance, it was removed or ordered to be removed.

Church of the Holy Trinity, Blythburgh
(Engraved by W. Deeble from a sketch by T. Higham in *Excursions*, II, p. 119)
Known as 'the Cathedral of the Marshes', Blythburgh was a huge parish church built
mainly in the later fifteenth century. It suffered at the hands of William Dowsing in
1644 when he and his men destroyed '20 superstitious pictures', tethered their horses in
the nave, and probably used the beautiful angel roof for target practice.

If not, it was left behind. Thus stained glass containing coats of arms or
royal insignia were not touched. Dowsing, the yeoman-farmer, waged
religious, not class, war. Third, Dowsing was a well-educated man, though
he had not attended university. He could translate Latin and had an
encyclopaedic knowledge of the Bible. That he was a cultured man is shown
by his substantial library, so graphically described by John Morrill. Fourth,
Dowsing was not, like some Parliamentarian soldiers, a mindless van-
dal,[80] but a man driven by personal conviction. His iconoclasm was part
of a wider programme of godly reformation. Hence his principal targets
were those pictures and images which distracted the worshipper from paying
attention to the Word of God.[81]

How much support and opposition did Dowsing meet in his work of
destruction? Margaret Aston has said that Dowsing was given 'unsolicited
help by nameless hands' and that in some places they visited, Dowsing and
his deputies had their work already done for them. At Haverhill two
hundred 'superstitious pictures' had been broken before Dowsing got
there.[82] On a few occasions Dowsing 'says or implies that he met with a
warm and eager response, that is with a party eager to cleanse its church
but waiting for external authority to arrive so that the work could be

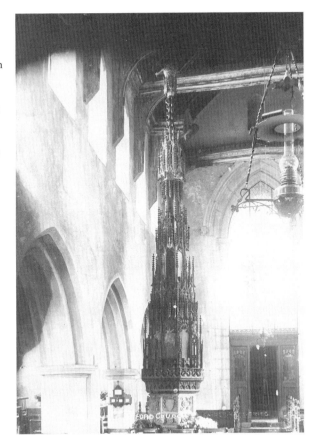

Ufford Church font
(Photograph: S.R.O (I),
K 400/B/9)
In this church there is an
eighteen feet high
canopied font cover,
dating from the fifteenth
century and in the
Perpendicular style.
Cautley has called it 'the
most beautiful in the
world'. It was spared by
William Dowsing for its
artistic beauty.

undertaken'.[83] But Dowsing met resistance as well as co-operation. At Ufford a united front of churchwardens, constable and sexton denied the keys of the church to Dowsing and his deputies, and kept them out of the building for over two hours. At Covehithe the people refused to help them to raise ladders to destroy the glass in the windows and the cherubim in the roof. At Great Cornard a churchwarden, John Pain, refused to pay the fee which Dowsing expected from every parish, and was taken away by the constable to appear before the Earl of Manchester.[84] Were these isolated incidents or the tip of an opposition iceberg? It is hard to say. On the whole Dowsing was successful, but this was probably because he apparently operated mainly in puritanical East Suffolk.[85] But could he have succeeded in, more Anglican, West Suffolk? Moreover, we must remember that in 1644 the whole of Suffolk was under the complete control of the Earl of Manchester and the Eastern Association. Also Dowsing was 'at least some times accompanied by ... soldiers'.[86] In short, successful resistance was almost impossible. But resentment was not.

If William Dowsing destroyed church property, Matthew Hopkins

Church of St Andrew, Covehithe
(Engraved by John Greig from a drawing by T. Higham in *Excursions*, II, p. 129)
Often called 'a ghost church', Covehithe was a small seventeenth-century church
within the ruins of a large fourteenth-century church. But the latter eventually
became too big for the dwindling number of parishioners, so in 1672 it was largely
dismantled. In 1644 William Dowsing and his assistants destroyed 200 sacred images
in the older church.

destroyed individual lives and was far more dangerous. Hopkins was born
about 1621, son of James Hopkins, Vicar of Great Wenham, Suffolk. But
around 1644 he was residing in the parish of Mistley-cum-Manningtree, so
strictly speaking he was an Essex man during the Civil War period.[87]
However, no account of Suffolk can ignore him. This former shipping
clerk[88] acquired notoriety as a brutal persecutor of so-called witches in
several eastern counties from 1645 to 1647. Assuming the title of Witchfinder
General, he extorted confessions from suspects, or discovered witches by
searching and torture.

Most of his victims were poor, elderly women of strange appearance and
quirky habits who had fallen out with their neighbours. Susan Marchant
of Hintlesham confessed to making a neighbour's sow lame, to having
consorted with the devil, and to possessing three 'familiars' or 'imps'.[89] But
arguably the worst case was the persecution of John Lowes, 80 year old
vicar of Brandeston. Lowes had antagonised his parishioners who were
persuaded by Hopkins to regard him as a witch. During his interrogation
the old man was kept awake for several nights, forced to run until he

St Mary's Church, Woolpit
(Engraved by W. Deeble from a sketch by T. Higham in *Excursions*, I, p. 174)
St Mary's has a 140 ft high spire and a stone porch built 1439–51. The nave is
fourteenth century and crowned by a hammerbeam roof with spread-winged angels
decorating the beam ends. Within the nave are carved pews and a lectern (given by
Elizabeth I?). William Dowsing had 80 of St Mary's statues and paintings destroyed
during the 1640s.

collapsed and then 'swum' in a pond. He finally confessed under pressure
that he had two 'imps', one of which he had sent to sink a ship near
Harwich. He was accordingly hanged, having read the burial service on his
own behalf prior to his execution.[90]

Susan Marchant and John Lowes were, of course, only two of the many
victims of Hopkins. Called 'the hangman of Manningtree', Hopkins began
his reign of terror in his adopted county – Essex – and in July 1645 he
had thirty-six suspects, all women, tried for witchcraft at the Assizes held
at Chelmsford. Of these nineteen were almost certainly executed. Hopkins
also had sixteen suspects, again all women, hanged for witchcraft in Norfolk
in 1645. Hopkins also had a small number of witches hanged in Huntingdonshire, Northamptonshire and the Fens of Cambridgeshire and the Isle
of Ely. But it was Suffolk that provided him with by far the largest number
of witches (see Table 6.1). The 124 suspects (including 96 women) in Suffolk
were tried at the Assizes in Bury St Edmunds in August 1645. The table
shows that well over half met their deaths. These figures clearly support
the view that 'the worst period for Suffolk [as regard witch-hunts] was
undoubtedly during the First Civil War'.[91]

Table 6.1 Prosecutions and executions for witchcraft in eastern England 1645–47[92]

County	Numbers accused	Numbers hanged
Suffolk	124	68
Essex	36	19
Norfolk	16 (at least)	16
Cambs.	14	7
Hunts.	9	8
Northants.	3	1
Total	202	119

By autumn 1646 there was 'a steadily mounting campaign of criticism' against Hopkins.[93] His most courageous, rational and forthright critic was Rev. John Gaule of Great Staughton, a moderate Puritan. Gaule complained that 'every old woman with a wrinkled face, a furr'd brow, a hairy lip, a gobber tooth, a squint eye, a squeaking voice, or a scolding tongue … is not only suspected, but pronounced for a witch'.[94] In 1647 Hopkins' cruel methods were exposed and public indignation forced him to abandon his witch-hunts.[95] But, contrary to popular belief, Hopkins was not himself hanged as a witch. He apparently died from tuberculosis in 1647.[96]

It is not for the historian to pass moral judgements and the witchcraft prosecutions and executions must be placed in their historical context. During the sixteenth and much of the seventeenth century many people, including the well-educated, believed in witches who consorted with the Devil and they accepted literally the words of Exodus 22:18, 'Thou shall not suffer a witch to live'. Persecution of witches and wizards was widespread in many countries and counties. Catholics and Protestants alike committed atrocities. In Catholic Würzburg 160 people, 25 per cent of whom were children, were executed as witches between 1627 and 1629.[97] However, it has been convincingly argued that persecution of witches was 'more fanatical in Protestant than Catholic areas'.[98] Fanaticism was particularly strong among the 'hotter sort of Protestants', or Puritans, and it is not surprising that the witchmania reached its height during the Puritan Revolution of the 1640s. Sir Keith Thomas has observed that 'there were notable [witch] trials in Essex in 1582 … and in Lancashire in 1612 … and 1633' but has argued that 'the *most acute period*[99] was 1645–47 when the [anti-witch] campaign was led by Matthew Hopkins and his associates'.[100] However, Thomas and his former pupil, Alan Mac-Farlane, deny that Hopkins himself was a Puritan, while admitting that his assistant, John Stearne, was one.[101] Indeed, Hopkins may have been motivated mainly by greed.[102] Nevertheless, Hopkins' campaign had strong Puritan backing. His clerical allies were 'all Puritans of the extremer kind' [103] and these included well-known ministers like Samuel Fairclough, 'who preached two sermons on witchcraft at the opening of the [Bury] assize', and Edmund Calamy, the elder, who was on the commission of oyer and terminer.[104] Hopkins also had the support of very influential Puritan laymen, such as Robert Rich, 2nd Earl of Warwick, Sir Harbottle Grimstone, MP for Harwich, and Nathaniel Bacon, Recorder of Ipswich and chairman of the Central Committee of the Eastern Association. 'None of these people would have hindered Hopkins in his career as witch-finder'.[105] Perhaps A. L. Rowse only slightly exaggerated when he wrote that 'the rise of persecutors of witches in Puritan East Anglia needs no explanation'.[106]

The Second Civil War

It is hard to believe that the Puritans did not alienate many people in Suffolk by their strict sabbatarianism, their suppression of Christmas celebrations, their attempt to set up a Presbyterian system (signifying stern religious discipline), their persecution of 'scandalous, malignant priests', their iconoclasm and their witch-hunting. However, it is hard to prove that those religious changes *directly* caused a royalist revival and a second Civil War. But whatever the reasons, Suffolk people *did* participate in the insurrections of 1648. During the Second Civil War some supported the King and others his enemies, but, even more than in the First Civil War, many remained neutral. Let us, however, concentrate on the combatant gentry and commoners.

Before discussing the part played by the Suffolk gentry and commoners, we must remind ourselves of the main events in the Second Civil War. Royalist insurrections were apparently almost nationwide.[107] But they were most serious and important in South Wales, Kent and eastern England. In the last named region Royalist risings occurred at Colchester, Chelmsford, Norwich, Thetford, Linton, Cambridge, Bury St Edmunds, Newmarket and Stowmarket.[108] Apart from Colchester, we are only concerned with the last three places, which are in Suffolk. The disturbances in Stowmarket are scarcely worth recording. Apparently drums were beaten and 'many tumultuously assembled' but they were soon suppressed by the action of the Parliamentarian authorities.[109] In Newmarket the situation was not very serious either. The Royalists met 'under pretence of horse-racing'. Matters came to a head on 15 June when three Royalist colonels – Scudamore, Stewart and Thornton[110] – rode into the market-place and, it was said, declared

> That all gentlemen whatsoever that had a desire to serve his Majestie, for the defence and preservation of his royall Person, the Protestant Religion, the fundamental Laws of the Kingdom and the Libertie of the Subject should repair to the King's Arms, there to receive present

Entertainment and advance Money ... whereupon divers resorted thither, protesting to live and die in the Cause.

But this announcement was leaked to the Parliamentary commander, Captain Pickering, and he, with twelve men, after the exchange of some bullets, arrested the three colonels, thus ending the abortive rising in favour of Charles I.[111]

In Bury St Edmunds the situation seemed much more dangerous. On 12 May a defiant crowd, resentful of the Puritan attack on the festive culture of 'Merrie England',[112] erected 'a May-pole' when a troop of Lord Fairfax's own cavalry regiment rode into the town. To shouts of 'For God and King Charles' the crowd chased the soldiers out of town. They then seized control of the powder magazine and began to put Bury into 'a posture of defence'. Their numbers swelled to 600 armed men and another 100 on horseback. The Bury incident was a spontaneous eruption of Royalist and anti-Puritan sentiment, but, compared with events in Essex, it was never a serious military threat. On 15 May the rising was easily suppressed by the local trained bands assisted by troops from the New Model Army, the rioters 'yeelding to mercy'.[113]

The most important feature of the Bury rising was the large number of Royalists involved. Moreover, the rioters seem to have acted independently of the local gentry. Referring to the First Civil War Dr Mark Stoyle only slightly exaggerated when he argued that 'in ... Suffolk popular Royalism was almost non-existent'.[114] But the Bury rising of 1648 shows that it was clearly a force to be reckoned with during the Second Civil War.[115]

Royalism in Suffolk in 1648 was essentially a plebeian phenomenon. This contrasts with the Royalism of the First Civil War which had been gentry dominated. But only three Royalist gentlemen of Suffolk can be shown to have participated in the Second Civil War: Sir Thomas Glemham of Little Glemham; Roger, a younger brother of Sir Simonds D'Ewes; and John Morden of Great Bradley. The last two appear to have been quiescent in 1642–46. But in 1648 Lieutenant Roger D'Ewes helped to defend Colchester for the king, while John Morden took part in the rising at Linton, Cambridgeshire.[116] Sir Thomas Glemham had been extremely active in supporting Charles I during the First Civil War. But he was also heavily involved in the Second. As we have seen, Glemham helped Sir Philip Musgrave, a Cumbrian Royalist, to capture Carlisle for the king.[117] Another East Anglian county which had few Royalist gentry in 1648 was Norfolk. There the only Cavaliers who participated in the Second Civil War 'were younger sons with little to lose, such as Roger L'Estrange and Edmund Hobart of Holt'.[118]

Why were the Royalist gentry so quiescent in Suffolk and perhaps in Norfolk in 1648? It is very hard to say. One reason may have been that from the mid-1640s many Royalists had to endure the sequestration of their lands or goods and had to pay composition fines to regain possession. Even if these fines were not always heavy,[119] they must have deterred several Cavaliers from supporting the king for a second time. For many it was a case of 'once bitten, twice shy'. In any case it could perhaps be argued that the mere act of compounding indicated acquiescence in defeat.

If most Royalist gentry were quiescent in 1648, many Parliamentarian gentry were the opposite. Of the 142 individual Parliamentary gentry participating in the First Civil War, forty-two openly continued to support their cause in 1648, and are listed in Appendix V. In addition, eight helped Parliament in 1648 who had not done so during the First Civil War.[120] Moreover, in Suffolk former Parliamentary gentry did not defect to the king during the Second Civil War,[121] as happened in Kent and Westmorland.[122] As in the First Civil War, the overwhelming majority of Suffolk Parliamentarians were Puritan.[123] Most of the 'godly' wanted to build a 'New Jerusalem' and making peace with the king was unthinkable to them. Also, as in the First Civil War, most opponents of the king served their cause in a civil capacity, acting as members or agents of the county committee. A majority of these were activists.[124] In 1648, as in the period 1642–46, only a small proportion of Parliamentarian gentry were soldiers.[125] But at least seven of them were active at the siege of Colchester.

Colchester in Essex, one of the largest provincial towns in England,[126] was occupied by about 5,600 soldiers under George Goring, Earl of Norwich, on 12 June 1648.[127] It was then besieged by Lord Thomas Fairfax, commander-in-chief of the New Model Army. The famous siege lasted from 13 June until the surrender of the garrison on 28 August.[128] This was not a particularly long siege. Yet it was 'perhaps the bitterest episode of either civil war'.[129] It was marked by fierce fighting, heavy bombardment, high casualties,[130] much property destruction,[131] and, ultimately, starvation within the walls.[132] The surrender 'to mercy' led to the imposition of a huge fine – £11,000 [133] – on the citizens, the taking of 3,391 prisoners,[134] the shipping of many as slaves to the West Indies and the summary execution of two leading Cavaliers, Sir Charles Lucas and Sir George Lisle.

Let us examine the part played by the Parliamentary gentry and commoners of Suffolk at the siege of Colchester. During the siege General Fairfax had at least 9,000 soldiers under his command. Of these, 4,160 belonged to the New Model Army, 2,640 were Essex militia men, and the rest consisted of four foot regiments and seven troops of horse from Suffolk. The Suffolk cavalry was commanded by Colonel Brampton Gurdon of Assington, junior, and the infantry regiments were led by Sir Thomas Barnardiston of Kedington, William Blois of Grundisburgh, James Harvey of Wickham Skeith and John Fothergill.[135] These Suffolk troops were divided between the siege lines and the defence of the Essex/Suffolk border, and amounted to 3,600 men; but on 24 June 2,000 Suffolk foot and five troops of horse were engaged at Colchester.[136] During the siege Fairfax

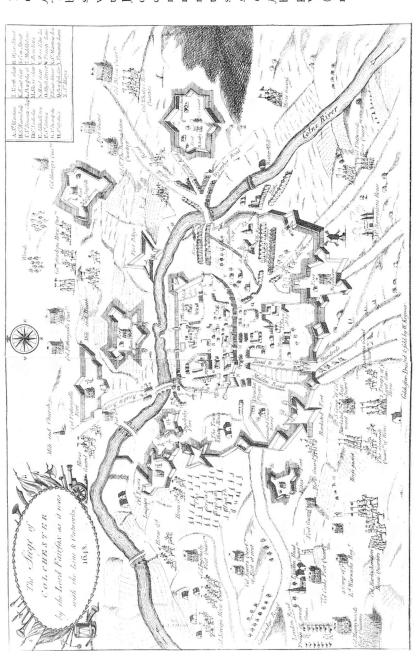

The Siege of Colchester, 13 July–26 August 1648 This contemporary bird's eye view shows the siege works as they were towards the end of July. The quarters of the five Suffolk colonels and their men are to the north and north-east of the town. For details see Plan of the siege of Colchester by Parliamentary forces, from a broadsheet published by W. Keymer (British Museum ref. 1872–11–0–171).

built ten forts and drew a 'line of circumvallation' around the town, thus cutting it off from the outside world. These forts were probably earthen banks ringed with ditches and defended by lengths of wattle fencing reinforced with earth. The Suffolk men co-operated fully with Fairfax's plan and erected three of the four forts north of the town, named Fothergill, Bloys and Suffolk.[137] The active part played by the Suffolk militia at Colchester can hardly be exaggerated. There is no doubt that the Suffolk troops were highly regarded by the New Model Army and that they greatly contributed to the victory of General Lord Fairfax.[138] Could this have been because of good gentry leadership?

The Parliamentary gentry of Suffolk certainly played an important military role during the siege of Colchester[139] and were also prominent at the surrender. On 27 August the surrender terms were signed by commissioners appointed by both sides. No Suffolk men figure among the Royalist commissioners, but among the ten commissioners acting on behalf of Lord Fairfax were three Suffolk gentry: William Blois of Grundisburgh, Giles Barnardiston of Clare[140] and the younger Brampton Gurdon of Assington. These three gentlemen were obviously considered important enough to be named commissioners alongside such famous New Model Army officers as Colonels Sir Thomas Honywood, Thomas Rainsborough, Edward Whalley, Isaac Ewer and General Henry Ireton.[141]

After the surrender of Colchester came retribution. The ugly mood of the Second Civil War was exemplified by the summary trial and immediate execution by firing squad of two eminent Royalist leaders, Sir Charles Lucas and Sir George Lisle. The story of their bravery and defiance in the face of death is too well known to need repeating. But it may interest readers that one of those who served on the courts-martial of Lucas and Lisle was that hyper-active Suffolk Parliamentarian, Brampton Gurdon of Assington, junior.[142] This puts Gurdon in a rather unfavourable light and makes him partially responsible for the judicial murder of these two courageous Cavaliers.

However, the actions of Gurdon must be placed in their historical context. There were perhaps two

Brampton Gurdon of Assington, junior (1609–69) by N. Marloe.
A Puritan-Parliamentarian activist, Gurdon fought at Naseby and the siege of Colchester, where he was partly responsible for the execution of the Royalist leaders, Lucas and Lisle.

main reasons why Gurdon and many other Parliamentarians approved of the execution of Lucas and Lisle. First, the laws of war justified the action. Lucas had broken his parole given in 1646 not to bear arms against Parliament in future.[143] But Lisle had given no parole undertaking. So why was he shot? This brings us to the second reason, a religious one. Brampton Gurdon and many other devout Puritan-Parliamentarians in Suffolk and elsewhere believed that those who tried to re-open the war in 1648 were attempting to overturn a victory (in the First Civil War) for which God had been responsible. Royalists, like Lucas and Lisle, who had participated in the Second Civil War had therefore committed sacrilege.[144] But the most sacrilegious person of all was King Charles I. He had allied with the Scots in December 1647 and had caused the suffering and bloodshed of the Second Civil War. 'Charles Stuart, that man of blood', had to be brought to account for his crimes. The shooting of Lucas and Lisle prepared the way for the execution of Charles I, the abolition of monarchy and the establishment of the British Republic.

CHAPTER SEVEN

Suffolk during the Interregnum

After the battle of Stow-on-the-Wold, in 1646, which saw the defeat of the last Royalist army in England in the First Civil War, the old Norfolk Cavalier, Lord Jacob Astley, said to his Roundhead captors: 'You have now done your work, boys, and may go play, unless you fall out among yourselves'.

The Roundheads did indeed fall out among themselves and between 1646 and 1648 many parts of England were racked by serious feuds between the more conservative Parliamentarians (mostly Presbyterians) and the more extreme Parliamentarians (mostly Independents). But in Suffolk the Parliamentarians seem to have presented a fairly united front, and this was shown by the lack of defections to the Royalist side during the Second Civil War.[1] However, divisions among the Suffolk Parliamentarians appeared during the crisis from December 1648 to January 1649: Pride's Purge, the trial and execution of King Charles I. As we shall see, the more moderate Suffolk Parliamentarians were horrified at the King's execution. This is not surprising for the public execution of a King on 30 January 1649 was a quite unprecedented act. In March monarchy and the House of Lords were formally abolished, and in June a republic was set up. A real revolution had taken place.

The new Republic, or Commonwealth as it was first called, soon defeated its remaining enemies: the Irish and Scottish Royalists on the right and the Levellers and Diggers on the left. Oliver Cromwell crushed the Irish in 1649 and defeated the Scots at the battles of Dunbar (1650) and Worcester (1651). The non-purged part of Parliament – the Rump – and the Council of State meanwhile governed the nation, but the new republican government was considered too conservative by the New Model Army and by the more radical Puritan sectaries. So Cromwell – pushed on by the Army radicals – dissolved the Rump Parliament in April 1653. In July 1653 a nominated Assembly – the Barebones Parliament – was set up, but it collapsed five months later. Thus ended the Commonwealth. This was succeeded by the Protectorate of Oliver Cromwell, who at last became head of state.

At first Cromwell tried to rule constitutionally but the uprising of Penruddock and threats from other Royalists in 1655 led him to introduce the rule of the Major-Generals. Their rule ended in 1657 and Cromwell tried to govern constitutionally again, and indeed his power was more limited after the Humble Petition and Advice.

After Oliver Cromwell's death on 3 September 1658, his son, Richard, who succeeded him as Lord Protector, lost the support of the Army, and the Republic – after surviving Booth's rebellion in August 1659 – disintegrated. This and the Restoration of Charles II in May 1660 came as a surprise to most British people at the time; it was expected that the Republic would last considerably longer.

Such is the national background. What was the situation in Suffolk during the Interregnum from 1649 to 1660? Did the Parliamentarians seriously split during the Revolution of 1648–49? Who supported the Republic? Did important social changes take place in local government? How much church, crown and Royalist property was obtained by men of Parliamentary loyalties and/or lower social status? How serious was the Royalist threat, especially in 1655–56? To what extent did the Royalists suffer economically? What was the religious situation?

The political situation

Many Suffolk Parliamentarians were appalled at the execution of Charles I. Among those was that most active of Roundheads, Nathaniel Bacon of Ipswich, an MP for Cambridge University since 1645. He concluded his famous *Annalls of Ipswiche* with this remark: 'The last day of Jan: puts a sad period into my penn'.[2] The last day of January of course referred to the King's execution. Another important Suffolk Roundhead opposed to Charles I's execution was Sir Thomas Bedingfield of Darsham, a Judge of the Common Pleas in 1648 and a nominated county committeeman in 1647 and 1648. He was one of six judges who, after the execution of the sovereign, 'were not satisfied to hold' under the new commissions from Parliament and he retired from the Bench until, just after the Restoration, he was made a Sergeant-at-Law by Charles II.[3]

Nathaniel Bacon of Ipswich (1593–1660) by an unknown artist.
Bacon was the most active Suffolk official on the Parliamentarian side during the Civil Wars. Appalled by the execution of Charles I, he nevertheless served the Republic in an administrative capacity.

Not only Bacon and Bedingfield but most of the Suffolk Members of Parliament opposed the revolution

Fleming's Hall, Bedingfield
(Photograph: S.R.O. (I), K 478/1)
Fleming's Hall was the home of the Bedingfields of Bedingfield from before 1300. The
Hall was rebuilt in *c.* 1586. A very fine building, it has a brick ground floor and a
timber-framed upper floor. A Judge Thomas Bedingfield of Fleming's Hall and Darsham
supported Parliament during the Second Civil War. But he opposed the execution of
Charles I and so retired from the Bench.

of 1648–49, including Pride's Purge. What was Pride's Purge? It denoted
the arrest of forty-five MPs and the seclusion from Parliament of 186 more
MPs by soldiers under Colonel Thomas Pride on 6 December as a means
of halting negotiations between Parliament and Charles I. The surviving
MPs, known as the Rump, passed an ordinance (28 December) for the
King's trial. In his book, *Pride's Purge*,[4] Professor David Underdown divided
the 471 MPs for England and Wales into five groups: (1) the active
revolutionaries who supported Pride's Purge, the trial and execution of the
King; (2) the *conformists* who avoided formal commitment at the time of
the purge but accepted the *fait accompli* in February 1649 when they could
no longer be incriminated in the execution of the King; (3) the *abstainers*
who were not actually secluded by Colonel Pride but showed their opposition by staying away from Parliament at least until the spring of 1649;
(4) the *secluded* who were not allowed to take their seats; (5) the *imprisoned*
who were the hard core of the Army's enemies. Details of the Suffolk MPs
in relation to Pride's Purge are given in Table 7.1.

For convenience we may call the imprisoned, the secluded and the
abstainers conservatives and the conformists and the revolutionaries radicals.
It is clear from Table 7.1 that only three of the fifteen were radical, while
just one of those – Edmund Harvey – was a revolutionary.[5] Twelve of the

Table 7.1 Suffolk Members of Parliament and Pride's Purge

Name	Constituency and date of election	Category	Religion	Whether served the Republic
BACON, Francis	Ipswich 1646	Secluded	Presbyterian?	Yes
BACON, Nathaniel	Camb. U.1645	Sec.	Pres.	Yes
BARNARDISTON, Sir Nathaniel	Suffolk 1640	Abstained	Pres.	Yes?
BARNARDISTON, Sir Thomas	Bury St Ed. 1645	Abs.	Pres.?	Yes
BARROW, Maurice	Eye 1645	Sec.	Pres.?	Yes?
BENCE, Alexander	Aldeburgh 1640	Abs.	Pres.?	Yes?
BREWSTER, Robert	Dunwich 1645	Conformist	Independent	Yes
D'EWES, Sir Simonds	Sudbury 1640	Imprisoned	Pres.	No
GURDON, Brampton, Jun.	Sudbury 1645	Abs.	Pres.?	Yes
GURDON, John	Ipswich 1640	Conf.	Pres.	Yes
HARVEY, Edmund	Gt. Bedwin 1646	Revolutionary	Pres.-Ind.	Yes
NORTH, Sir Roger	Eye 1640	Sec.	Pres.?	Yes?
PARKER, Sir Philip	Suffolk 1640	Sec.	Pres.?	Yes
PLAYTERS, Sir William	Orford 1640	Sec.	Pres.?	No
SPRING, Sir William	Bury St Ed. 1645	Sec.	Pres.?	Yes?

Source: Underdown, *Pride's Purge*, pp. 367–9, 371, 375, 381–3, 386.

Suffolk MPs were conservative in religion as well as in politics, that is, they were definite or possible Presbyterians. But perhaps the most surprising fact revealed by the table is that of the twelve conservative Parliamentarians five certainly and another five almost certainly served the Republic at some time or other during the Interregnum.[6]

It is not surprising that the three radicals – Robert Brewster, John Gurdon and Edmund Harvey – were to serve the Republic,[7] but it is surprising that nearly all the conservatives seem to have become collaborators, including Nathaniel Bacon who had been secluded from Parliament by Pride's Purge and so saddened by the King's execution. Most interesting of all, however, is Sir Thomas Barnardiston of Kedington. Although opposed to the Regicide, he was to become the leading supporter in Suffolk of the rule of the Major Generals (October 1655 – January 1657). Their rule involved a new 'decimation' tax on some old Royalists and the introduction of 'commissioners for securing the peace of the commonwealth'. Sir Thomas actively headed the Suffolk commissioners[8] and showed himself willing to impose the hated 'decimation' tax on his fellow gentry. It would seem that puritanical Sir Thomas supported the Major-Generals mainly in the interest of 'godly reformation'.[9]

Sir Thomas Barnardiston may be an extreme example of a collaborator, but the fact is that there was considerable continuity of administration in Suffolk between the Civil War years and the end of the Interregnum. Take the magistracy. Of the thirty-eight individuals [10] who served Parliament as justices of the peace sometime during the period 1642–48, twenty-seven (71 per cent) continued to act under the Republic.[11] These included the more conservative Parliamentarians, such as Sir Butte Bacon of Mutford, Arthur Jenny of Knodishall and Francis Theobald of Barking as well as the more radical, like Robert, Francis and Humphrey Brewster of Wrentham. If we look at the lists of nominated county committeemen,[12] the story is virtually the same. Of the seventy-eight Suffolk men [13] appointed to various county committees between 1643 and 1648, fifty-six (72 per cent) were later nominated to Interregnum committees.[14]

Sir William Spring of Pakenham, Bart. (1613–54) by an unknown artist. (Photograph: S.R.O. (B), K 505/3214) Sir William Spring was a direct descendant of Thomas Spring III, the 'Rich Clothier' of Lavenham, who died in 1523. During the Civil Wars Sir William was a Puritan-Parliamentarian activist. He was also a snob. Like the wealthy Maurice Barrow of Barningham, he objected that Ralph Margery, who had raised a troop of horse for the Parliament's service, was not a gentleman, and therefore was ineligible for such a command.

Even more surprising is the fact that some of those who served the Republic were actually ex-Royalists. Sir William Hervey of Ickworth, Sir Robert Coke of Huntingfield and Sir John Barker of Trimley served as High Sheriffs of Suffolk in 1650–51, 1652–53 and 1654 respectively.[15] Yet this is perhaps not so astonishing when one realises that these three gentlemen had been only passive Royalists in the First Civil War. Moreover, the shrievalty was a 'less politically sensitive' post,[16] and one also finds ex-Royalists acting as sheriffs in other counties.[17] However, let us not understate our case. As Professor Ann Hughes remarks, 'the Civil War and its aftermath saw the politicisation of local government',[18] and the fact that a number of Suffolk gentlemen from ex-Royalist families served as JPs during the Interregnum cannot be overlooked.[19] Nor can we ignore the fact that Sir John Pettus of Cheston Hall, an *active* Cavalier, made his peace with the Republic in 1655 and was then appointed deputy-governor of the former royal mines by Oliver Cromwell.[20]

Why did so many conservative Parliamentarians and even some ex-Royalists serve a Republic which they so obviously disliked in principle? It is impossible to give a definite answer. But in most cases it must surely have been because they wanted peace and stability after the insecure Civil

War years, and were prepared to support any government which could grant this peace and stability. Thomas Edgar of Ipswich, the most active Suffolk magistrate during the Interregnum,[21] stated the case for co-operation very clearly to his fellow JPs:

> Those in public employment in a Commonwealth must not desert government because the way or form doth not like them. Though one kind of government be better than another, yet take that is next rather than none.[22]

Edgar's views – that any government was better than none – are strikingly similar to those of Thomas Hobbes and other *de facto* theorists.[23]

However, let us not exaggerate our argument. The fact remains that the most enthusiastic and positive supporters of the Republic – especially during the Commonwealth period of 1649–53 – were often the most politically and religiously radical. Certainly some of the most active Suffolk JPs had radical tendencies, and these included John Brandling of Ipswich, Edmund Harvey of Wickham Skeith, Gibson Lucas of Horringer and Robert, Francis and Humphrey Brewster of Wrentham. Radicals were definitely appointed to the Suffolk militia commissions of 1655 and 1659. They comprised civilians like John Gurdon of Great Wenham and Robert and Francis Brewster. Military officers nominated included some radicals such as Colonels Edmund Harvey and Humphrey Brewster and Captain John Moody.[24] Radicals were also regularly appointed to the local assessment committees,[25] and embraced such men as John Gurdon, Edmund Harvey, the three Brewsters and four Ipswich bailiffs: John Brandling, Jacob Caley, Robert Dunkon and Peter Fisher. Two of these bailiffs – Jacob Caley and Robert Dunkon – were members of Congregational churches in Ipswich and also radical members of Barebones Parliament in 1653. Indeed, Caley was actually a Fifth Monarchist, belonging to that extremist sect which believed that the Kingdom of Christ was about to be established on earth and that the godly should exercise a dictatorship over the reprobate.[26]

However, granted that the radicals were probably the strongest supporters of the Republic, the fact remains that there was considerable political continuity in Suffolk between the 1640s and 1650s, moreso than in most English counties.

County Government and Social Change

Was there also social continuity? Some contemporaries doubted it. The Royalist Earl of Clarendon declared that after the Civil War local power passed from the county elite to men of lower social status. 'A more inferior sort of the common people ... who were not above the condition of ordinary inferior constables six or seven years before, were now the justices of the peace, sequestrators and commissioners'.[27] Clarendon, not for the first time, exaggerated. Yet during the Interregnum Suffolk witnessed what appears to have been a minor social revolution in government, as did several other English counties.[28] For over a century prior to the Great Rebellion county government had been dominated by the greater gentry, who were regarded as the 'natural' rulers of county society.[29] The Interregnum saw this monopoly broken and, as happened in England after the Great Reform Act of 1832, the greater gentry had to share power with socially inferior groups. This is particularly evident in the Suffolk magistracy, the county assessment commission and the militia commission.

Ninety-one Suffolk men served as JPs at some time or other between the First Civil War and the eve of the Restoration. A study of these individuals suggests that the social composition of the magistracy varied from year to year. Nevertheless, Table 7.2 shows that until the 1650s the greater gentry (baronets, knights, esquires) dominated the magistracy, but that during the Interregnum they lost not only their near-monopoly of the Bench, but, at times, their majority on it. David Underdown has, however, remarked that 'in 1657, in the commission of peace ... the old families came drifting back in much larger numbers than before'.[30] But Suffolk, like Hampshire and Sussex,[31] seems to have gone against the national trend because 1657 was the nadir of greater gentry influence.

Table 7.2 Social Composition of the acting Suffolk magistrates, 1642–59[32]

Year	Greater gentry	Lesser gentry	Plebeians	Total
1642–43	26 (96%)	1 (4%)	–	27 (100%)
1644	26 (90%)	3 (10%)	–	29 (100%)
1645	19 (100%)	–	–	19 (100%)
1646	19 (79%)	5 (21%)	–	24 (100%)
1647	16 (84%)	3 (16%)	–	19 (100%)
1648	24 (83%)	5 (17%)	–	29 (100%)
1649	20 (87%)	3 (13%)	–	23 (100%)
1650	19 (76%)	4 (16%)	2 (8%)	25 (100%)
1651	14 (70%)	1 (5%)	5 (25%)	20 (100%)
1652	27 (67.5%)	7 (17.5%)	6 (15%)	40 (100%)
1653	25 (62.5%)	10 (25%)	5 (12.5%)	40 (100%)
1654	22 (58%)	11 (29%)	5 (13%)	38 (100%)
1655	25 (61%)	8 (19.5%)	8 (19.5%)	41 (100%)
1656	23 (53%)	12 (28%)	8 (19%)	43 (100%)
1657	18 (44%)	13 (32%)	10 (24%)	41 (100%)
1658	22 (49%)	14 (31%)	9 (20%)	45 (100%)
1659	20 (51%)	13 (33%)	6 (16%)	39 (100%)

To maintain a sense of perspective, it is worth examining the social composition of the Suffolk Bench from the pre-Civil War period to the Restoration. Table 7.3 gives details.

Table 7.3 Social status of acting magistrates, 1627–65

Status	The Suffolk Magistracy[33]			
	1627, 1639 – June 1642	Oct. 1642–48	1649–59	1660–65 [34]
Baronets	6 (12%)	3 (7%)	2 (3%)	9 (13%)
Knights	11 (21%)	7 (15%)	6 (8%)	12 (18%)
Esquires	30 (59%)	31 (67%)	35 (49%)	45 (65%)
Gentlemen	4 (8%)	5 (11%)	17 (23%)	3 (4%)
Plebeians	–	–	12 (17%)	–
Total	51 (100%)	46 (100%)	72 (100%)	69 (100%)

It will be noted that in every period, except the Interregnum, approximately nine in ten acting magistrates belonged to the greater gentry. Under the Republic, however, the greater gentry formed only six out of ten justices. The lesser gentry were far more prominent than hitherto, but more important was the fact that for the first time nearly one-fifth of the magistrates were of plebeian stock. Some of these plebeian justices were very assiduous. Thomas Chaplin and John Clarke, two aldermen of Bury St Edmunds, and Barnaby Bowtell, a radical immigrant from Lincolnshire,[35] attended thirty, twenty-two and twenty-seven quarter sessions respectively during the 1650s. However, let us not exaggerate those social changes. Not only were the greater gentry seldom outnumbered by other social groups, but they *dominated* the Bench. Of the twenty-nine magistrates who attended twenty or more quarter sessions during the Interregnum, seventeen were esquires or above, nine were gentlemen and only three were plebeians.

Let us now briefly examine the personnel of the Suffolk assessment committee from the late 1640s to the Restoration. Local assessment committees had raised property taxes for Parliament since 1643, but it was not until the disappearance of the County Committee in 1650 that they came to the fore. The assessment commissioners were both numerous and socially mixed, as Table 7.4 shows.

Table 7.4 Social status of the nominated Suffolk assessment commissioners, 1647–61 [36]

Date of Committee	Greater gentry	Lesser gentry	Plebeians	Total
1647 June	42 (70%)	7 (12%)	11 (18%)	60 (100%)
1648 February	39 (71%)	7 (13%)	9 (16%)	55 (100%)
1649 April	39 (63%)	10 (16%)	13 (21%)	62 (100%)
1650 November	45 (62%)	12 (16%)	16 (22%)	73 (100%)
1652 December	38 (52%)	16 (22%)	19 (26%)	73 (100%)
1657 June	35 (36%)	22 (23%)	39 (41%)	96 (100%)
1660 January	23 (45%)	11 (22%)	17 (33%)	51 (100%)
1661	92 (70%)	20 (15%)	20 (15%)	132 (100%) [37]

Table 7.4 shows that before the Second Civil War and just after the Restoration the greater gentry comprised an overwhelming majority of the nominated assessment commissioners, that their majority greatly declined during the Commonwealth period and that in 1657 they formed only one-third of those named, as they did in Devon.[38] No more in the assessment commission than in the commission of the peace did the old families come 'drifting back' in large numbers in 1657,[39] despite the fact that this was the year when Oliver Cromwell's government was at its least radical. Indeed, the most interesting feature of the 1657 assessment commission is that plebeians formed the largest single group, lending perhaps a certain credence to Dr Aylmer's tentative suggestion that the Great Rebellion was a 'middle-class revolution'.[40]

However, it is important not to exaggerate the social changes in the assessment commissions. Old families, like Barnardiston of Kedington, Blois of Grundisburgh, Brewster of Wrentham, Gurdon of Assington and North of Mildenhall, were well represented among the commissioners throughout the period, but as more men were needed in the government of Suffolk during the Interregnum, the balance of power inevitably shifted towards those families who normally took little part in county affairs. But the 'new men' were supplements to, rather than substitutes for, the older families.[41] Finally it is important to remember that the assessment commissioners were *nominated* by Parliament and, in the absence of an assessment book in the Suffolk Record Office and elsewhere, we have no means of knowing how many of them *acted.*

Appointment to the local militia commission also did not necessarily mean active service. However, it is worth examining the social and military composition of the commissioners. Socially, important changes occurred during the Interregnum. The greater gentry were in a large majority in the militia commission appointed immediately before Pride's Purge and also in that nominated just before the Restoration. But in 1655 their majority among the commissioners was very small, while in the 1659 commission they were easily outnumbered by minor gentry and plebeians. Table 7.5 gives details.

Table 7.5 Social status of the nominated Suffolk militia commissioners, 1648–60[42]

Date of Committee	Greater gentry	Lesser gentry	Plebeians	Total
1648 December	30 (75%)	3 (7.5%)	7 (17.5%)	40 (100%)
1655	12 (52%)	5 (22%)	6 (26%)	23 (100%)
1659 July	21 (39%)	14 (26%)	19 (35%)	54 (100%)
1660 March	44 (70%)	14 (22%)	5 (8%)	63 (100%)

The military presence was also clearly visible during the 1650s. In 1655 nine (39 per cent) of the twenty-three militia commissioners were military officers. In 1659 these officers formed eleven (20 per cent) of the fifty-four commissioners. By contrast, not one of the militia commissioners of 1648 and 1660 was a military officer.

To sum up so far, Suffolk saw some important social changes in the personnel of local government during the Interregnum. However, these changes, especially in the magistracy, were very limited compared with those in some other English counties, such as Warwickshire.

The land purchases of the Parliamentarians

If there was no large scale transference of office from one social group to another, was there a great transfer of property? Some contemporaries seemed to think so. They portrayed the period from 1646 to 1660 as one when 'new men' of lower social status obtained the confiscated estates of the crown, church and Royalists and established a new landed class. The Levellers lamented that 'Parliament men, Committee men and their kinsfolkes were the only buyers' of episcopal lands.[43] Thomas Fuller noted with disapproval that a new gentry had emerged, that 'many upstarts in our late civil wars' had 'injuriously invaded the arms of ancient families'.[44] Whether or not a new gentry did emerge will be examined more fully in the next chapter. Meanwhile we must ask whether in Suffolk men of lower social status and/or Parliamentarian allegiance bought up large amounts of church, crown and Royalist property. This is an important question, whether or not one agrees with Professor Gwynne Lewis that 'revolutions, whether they are Russian, French, Latin American or English, always have the question of land at their core'.[45]

The post-Civil War period in England certainly saw the greatest transfer of land since the Dissolution of the Monasteries. The victorious Parliament confiscated the estates of the established church, the crown and the leading or more recalcitrant Royalists, but sold off most of them in a vain attempt to achieve financial solvency and settle its mounting debts. Bishops' lands were ordered to be sold in 1646, cathedral lands in April 1649, crown lands in July 1649 and crown fee-farm rents in 1650. Finally three Acts in 1651 and 1652 ordered the sale of lands of those remaining Cavaliers who had refused to compound or who, on account of their Roman Catholicism or high position in the Royalist party, were not permitted to do so.[46] Also from October 1650 delinquents [i.e. Royalists] were allowed to sell land privately in order to pay their composition fines.[47]

Who bought these lands in Suffolk? Let us begin with church lands. I have examined all twenty-three deeds of bargain and sale of church lands in Suffolk, belonging mainly to the dioceses of Norwich and Ely.[48] These lands were sold for a total of £17,543 16s. 9¾d. to thirty-two purchasers, five of whom were tenants.[49] But only one of the buyers was a former Suffolk Roundhead.[50] He was John Sicklemore, an Ipswich gentleman, previously just a nominal member of the County Committee.[51] In May

1650 he bought capitular property in Brook Street, Ipswich, for a mere £62 6s. 8d.[52] Moreover, only three of the thirty-two purchasers were of humble origins. Three yeomen of Lakenheath – Francis Bugg, Robert Church and Robert Denton – bought pasture land in their neighbourhood in September 1650 for only £72 13s. 4d.[53] The other twenty-eight purchasers comprised one peer (Viscount Hereford), twelve gentry, eleven Londoners, three clerics and one widow. So the number of purchasers in Suffolk was not particularly large. However, three Suffolk Roundheads bought church property outside the county. Robert Brewster of Wrentham, Esquire, a radical MP, bought in March 1650 the manor of Hindleveston, Norfolk, for £3,705 1s. 8d. and Ludham, Norfolk seat of the Bishop of Norwich, for £1,000.[54] Edmund Harvey of Wickham Skeith, Esquire, another radical MP, obtained in 1647 the manor and palace of Fulham, formerly belonging to the Bishop of London, for £7,617 2s. 10d.[55] Samuel Moody of Bury St Edmunds, a plebeian Roundhead, bought capitular property in Gaywood, near King's Lynn, Norfolk, for just £350.[56]

Only ten Suffolk men bought crown land in the county and elsewhere during the Interregnum.[57] Not one was a former Parliamentarian gentleman. Of the ten plebeians four were Roundhead soldiers – Daniel Dale and William Disher, both of Ipswich, Ralph Margery of Walsham-le-Willows[58] and John Moody of Bury St Edmunds[59] – and the remainder were civilians, possibly 'neuters' in the Civil Wars. The total purchases of the ten Suffolk plebeians amounted to £5,292 19s. 11d., hardly enough to establish a new landed class in the county.

Finally, not a single Parliamentarian gentleman or commoner seems to have bought any Royalist land in Suffolk from the Treason Trustees,[60] partly because so little was forfeited and publicly sold.[61]

So if we take the sales of confiscated church, crown and Royalist property together, we find, surprisingly, that only three purchasers were former Parliamentarian gentry, and that these three formed just 2 per cent of the 150 individual Parliamentarian gentlemen.[62] Fourteen purchasers were apparently commoners, but these must have formed an infinitesimal proportion of the total plebeian population. In short, there was no land revolution in Suffolk during the Interregnum.

Suffolk Parliamentarians seem to have been keener to acquire land in distant Ireland than in their native county. From 1642 onwards Englishmen who lent money to finance the reconquest of Ireland were to be granted Irish land once the island had been secured again. Four Suffolk Roundhead gentry adventured and drew Irish land. Sir Thomas Barnardiston of Kedington invested £200 in March 1642 and £50 in the 'sea adventure' the following month. In the adventurers' lotteries held at Grocers' Hall, London, in 1653 and 1654 he drew 2,221 acres in county Meath. Alexander Bence of Benhall invested £600 and drew 2,777 acres in county Tipperary. John Fiske of Rattlesden invested £100 and drew 666 acres in county

Waterford. Philip Sparrow of Wickhambrook invested £50 and later drew
111 acres also in Waterford.[63] Like many London investors, those four
Suffolk gentry were 'godly militants'.[64] Another 'godly militant' obtaining
much Irish land was Samuel Moody, cloth merchant of Bury St Edmunds.
After investing £200 in the original adventurers' scheme and a further
£600 in the 'sea adventure', Moody drew 888 acres in the Irish baronies
of Coshmore and Coshbride.[65] If there was a land revolution in Ireland
during the Great Rebellion, Suffolk Puritan-Parliamentarians made at least
a modest contribution towards it.

The Royalist threat

We must now turn our attention to the main opponents of the British
Republic, the Royalists. David Underdown, a leading authority on the
Royalists during the Interregnum, has argued that they 'were the most
intractable internal problem of every government between 1649 and 1660'.[66]
The reason for this, he says, is that after the execution of Charles I on 30
January 1649, 'Royalism was transferred from the planes of military and
political action to that of conspiracy ... The Royalists were faced with the
choice of throwing up the sponge or working for the Restoration of the
monarchy by conspiracy'.[67] Underdown states that 'a significant number
chose the second course'.[68] But this was not the case in Suffolk, where only
a few conspirators are known to have existed.

Perhaps the most famous Royalist conspiracy was the second Gerard plot
of May 1654 to assassinate Oliver Cromwell.[69] But as far as we can tell,
not a single Suffolk Royalist participated, except possibly Thomas Partridge
of Needham Market, a plebeian. However, a few Suffolk gentry engaged
in other conspiracies against the Republic. The most important of these
plotters were Thomas Blague of Horringer, Roger Coke of Thorington and
William Rolleston of Kettleburgh.

Colonel Thomas Blague was a dedicated Royalist He had fought at Edgehill in 1642, in Cornwall in 1644 and been Governor of Wallingford Castle
from 1643 to 1646. He was to fight for Charles II at Worcester in 1651,
along with Lord Francis Willoughby of Parham,[70] and against Cromwell's
Ironsides at the battle of the Dunes in 1658.[71] But in 1650 he was the main
organiser of a conspiracy in Norfolk, which the government was able to forestall
because of its intelligence network. Indeed, the conspiracy was a fiasco.[72]

Two other Suffolk Royalist plotters – Colonel William Rolleston and
Roger Coke – were active in 1657. Coke, a grandson of the famous
constitutional lawyer, Sir Edward Coke, recalled long after the plot how
he was approached by Rolleston (who had fought gallantly in the First
Civil War) with news that 'the King was making great Preparations to land
in England and that Cavaliers were intending to rise ... to assist him'. At
Rolleston's suggestion Coke went to London to buy arms, which were

secretly conveyed to his house in Suffolk by ship. Two days later the place was searched, and although the arms were not discovered, Coke's father and brother were arrested. So the plot failed.[73]

About the time of Sir George Booth's rising in 1659 – occurring mainly in Lancashire and Cheshire – Sir Lionel Tollemache of Helmingham Hall, though not a conspirator himself and a neutral and invalid in the First and Second Civil Wars, allowed the Sealed Knot to meet in his house, where officers were enlisted by Colonel William Rolleston and Sir Lionel Fanshaw.[74] The Sealed Knot was a Royalist secret society working to restore the monarchy. It had come into being before the end of 1653 and had strong connections with East Anglia.[75] Two eminent Suffolk gentlemen, Robert Naunton of Letheringham, an ex-Royalist activist, and Sir Robert Wingfield of Easton, son of a neutral, were heavily implicated in the plotting of the Sealed Knot, providing money and promising horses.[76]

Royalist conspiracy during the Interregnum alarmed the government, and with some justification. The most dangerous year was 1655. Royalist risings planned for March failed in North-East England, Yorkshire and the Welsh border through lack of effective support. But in southern England John Penruddock's rising was a much more serious affair.[77] It was, however, crushed and afterwards Oliver Cromwell set up the rule of the ten Major-Generals, each in charge of a district.

The Major-Generals were instructed to take security for good behaviour from all suspected Royalists. In 1656 they drew up lists of suspects which gave the names of people believed to have royalist sympathies, and in most cases the domiciles, status and occupations of the Royalist suspects are mentioned. Lists were drawn up in the eastern counties, even though these had been largely quiescent in 1655.[78] The lists of suspects provide valuable information about Royalism in the mid-1650s. Some suspects, or their relatives, had already served Charles I in the First Civil War, while others were 'new sprung up Cavaliers',[79] like Henry Lambe of Tostock and Hitcham and Anthony Yaxley of Yaxley. The Suffolk and Norfolk lists also show the numerical weakness of Royalism in 1656,[80] especially among the commoners (see Table 7.6).

Table 7.6 Status and occupation of Royalist suspects in 1656[81]

Status or occupation	Suffolk	Norfolk
Gentry	19	19
Clergy, professionals	4	–
Traders and craftsmen	4	3
Yeomen	–	3
Husbandmen	–	–
Labourers	–	–
Unknown	1	–
Total	28	25

Note that in 1656, as in the First Civil War, there was little popular Royalism in Suffolk and Norfolk. In the Suffolk list of suspects six described as gentlemen were of doubtful gentility, but even if we add those six to the four traders and craftsmen and the one 'unknown', the plebeian total is eleven at most, that is under 40 per cent. East Anglia contrasts sharply with Lancashire and the West County where large numbers of Royalists were named, and where plebeians formed 80 per cent of suspects in the former county and 90 per cent in the latter region.[82]

Shortly before the Restoration Suffolk Royalists were also few and elitist. In 1658 Roger Whitley, a famous Royalist plotter, drew up a 'List of Reliable Royalists' throughout England and Wales. Of the twenty-four Suffolk Royalists named, only five were plebeians; the rest were gentlemen or above.[83] Politically, those Royalists were a mixed bunch. Some, like Sir Frederick Cornwallis of Brome Hall and Thomas Blague of Horringer, had fought for the King in the First Civil War; others, like Nicholas Bacon of Shrubland and Francis Bacon of Ipswich, had been Parliamentarians in the 1640s;[84] while a few, like Thomas Soame of Hundon, Gentleman, and Sir Lionel Tollemache, were ex-Neutrals. What held together the old and the new Royalists in 1658 was undoubtedly an aversion to the republican government.

The economic fate of the Royalist gentry

Royalists engaged in plots and uprisings were an activist minority. As David Underdown says, 'the great majority who had fought for Charles I in the Civil War lapsed into political inaction afterwards, though nearly all remained loyal at heart, even if only passively so'.[85] Few were prepared to challenge outright the republican government, with its network of spies and overwhelming military force. The traumatic experience of defeat in 1646, in 1648, and, for a few, in 1651 did not encourage activism. But economic as well as psychological factors explain the passivity of most Royalists. Sequestrations, compositions, confiscations and the decimation tax were a considerable deterrent to conspiracy. Let us deal with these penalties in turn, beginning with sequestration.

Sequestration was the most common fate which befell the Royalists. On 27 March 1643 an ordinance demanded the seizure of personal and real estates of all who took arms against Parliament, contributed to the King's army or otherwise assisted his cause, and also two-thirds of the estates of all Roman Catholics.[86] Sequestration was not confiscation; the enemy landlord still retained legal title to his estate. But it meant that his lands were withheld by the local sequestration committee, which collected rents and fines and assigned leases. In short, sequestration reduced the income of the 'delinquent' [Royalist] or 'papist' [Neutral Catholic]. It is hard to say exactly how much suffering sequestration caused in Suffolk. Professor

Alan Everitt argued that 'less than 10 per cent of the gentry of Suffolk were sequestrated'. Yet he went on to say that 'the yield from sequestrated estates in the county between 1643 and 1649 was higher than anywhere else'.[87]

Sequestration could be permanently lifted in return for payment known as a composition fine.[88] Surprisingly, only thirty Suffolk Royalist gentry seem to have regained their property by paying composition fines. The amount and burden of the fine varied considerably from one family to another. Royalists were fined according to the degree of their delinquency at one-tenth, one-sixth or one-third of the capital value of their estates. A Royalist whose fine was fixed at one-tenth of the capital value paid two years' annual value; at one-sixth he paid three years' and at one-third or one quarter he paid five years' annual value. Unfortunately we do not know the *rates*, as opposed to the *amounts*, of the fines imposed on thirteen of our Suffolk gentry compounders. But the fines levied on the other seventeen gentlemen were by no means burdensome. Seven delinquents were fined at the rate of one-tenth, another seven at one-sixth, while two were leniently fined at the rate of one-twentieth. Just one was heavily fined at the rate of one-third.[89]

Some fines were lenient because a few Royalists managed to persuade the Parliamentary authorities to reduce them. For example, in October 1646 the fine of Sir Charles Gawdy was fixed at £1,789, but on his settling £150 a year on the church, it was reduced to £529. Three years later Sir Charles asked for his fine to be 'reduced to one year's value, his estate being for life'. Accordingly the fine was finally fixed at only £165.[90] Other Royalists, or their heirs, paid low fines because they deliberately undervalued their property. Such deceit was not surprising because the fine was based on the compounder's own statement of his income and liabilities and, as Sir John Habakkuk has reminded us, the possibilities of evasion were considerable.[91] In 1648 Richard Gooding of Bury St Edmunds told the Committee for Compounding that his father's lands were worth only £50 per annum,[92] whereas in fact a more objective source – the lay subsidy roll for 1641 – valued his property at three times that amount.[93] In 1650 Francis Chesney of Eye deliberately understated his landed income, saying that it was a mere £26 per annum, whereas other sources suggest that it was between £200 and £300.[94]

Since most composition fines in Suffolk were tolerable, few Royalists had to resort to private land sales, sales which were not invalidated at the Restoration.[95] Yet some contemporaries saw a close link between composition fines and 'voluntary' private sales. Clarendon said that the Parliamentary authorities forced the Royalists to compound at 'so unreasonable rates, that many were compelled to sell half, that they might enjoy the other toward the support of their families'.[96] Some modern historians have echoed Clarendon. Dr Christopher Hill has suggested that Royalists must have sold a considerable amount of land in order to pay composition fines.[97] Dr H. E. Chesney considered that private sales were extensive and that these were partly caused by composition fines.[98] Frank Walker argued that land sales caused by the Civil War itself and heavy compounding fines brought about a minor social revolution in south-west Lancashire.[99]

No such revolution occurred in Suffolk. Here there seems to have been little direct connection between private sales and composition fines. Of the thirty Royalist gentry compounders, only four (13 per cent) definitely sold land before the Restoration.[100] Richard Bowle paid a fine of £144 in 1648 and the following year sold his lease of the manor of Kersey Priory to John Berners, a Hertfordshire gentleman.[101] Robert Gosnold of Otley paid a heavy fine of £600 in 1646 and about 1650 sold his manor of Burwash in Witnesham to Thomas Edgar, Esquire, Recorder of Ipswich and strong supporter of the English Republic.[102] The evidence suggests that the fines paid by Bowle and Gosnold were responsible for their sales. But it is not so easy to explain the sales by Benjamin Cutler of Ipswich and Edward Rookwood of Euston Hall. Cutler compounded for £750 in 1646 and in 1650 conveyed his manor of Saxmundham to John Base, a local Parliamentarian yeoman.[103] But the fact that Cutler's debts in 1647 amounted to £1,500 [104] suggests that his composition fine was not entirely responsible for his sale. Rookwood, 'a Popish Recusant, compounded his Estate £700' in 1652 and in 1655 his patrimonial estate passed to George Fielding, Earl of Desmond.[105] However, Rookwood's economic collapse may not have been solely due to his composition fine. He was already in serious financial difficulties in pre-Civil War days when he was outlawed for debt.[106] Finally it is worth noting that composition fines did not always force even indebted Royalists to sell. John James of Layham was fined £180 in 1646, and in 1651 was in debt to the tune of £446.[107] Yet he apparently sold not an acre of land before the Restoration.

If a Royalist could not or would not compound, his lands either continued under sequestration or were put up for sale. Three Acts of Parliament in 1651–52 ordered the confiscation and public sale of the lands of 780 Royalists in England and Wales. No Suffolk men were named in the first two acts and only four were mentioned in the third Act of Sale, 18 November 1652: Thomas Allin of Lowestoft, Mariner, Henry Fernes of Walberswick, Mariner, Anthony Mounsey of Cotton, Gentleman, and Thomas Webb of Cowling, Gentleman.[108] There is no record of the sale of the property of Henry Fernes. The other three had their lands sold but apparently recovered them. Indeed, Mounsey's son, Tudor, appears to have regained his father's estates almost immediately because they were purchased from the Treason Trustees in October and December 1653 by a former Royalist, Francis Chesney of Eye, and a Royalist sympathiser, Robert Tyrell of Gipping.[109] Exactly when Thomas Webb regained his deceased father's estate is unknown. It is possible that it was obtained on Webb's behalf in 1653 by Thomas Knyvett of Ashwellthorpe, a well-known Norfolk Royalist, who (successfully ?) claimed from the Committee for Removing Obstructions 'An Interest in the Moiety of the Mannor of Cowling'.[110] At any rate Webb was clearly in possession of his small property by 1674 when, according to the Hearth Tax returns, he had four hearths in Cowling.[111] It is also uncertain when Thomas Allin regained his property in Lowestoft, but he was by no means ruined during the Interregnum, and after the Restoration he was to become an admiral and naval hero, with a seat at Somerleyton.[112] Insofar as the economic effects of their Royalism were not calamitous, the Suffolk Cavaliers – despite their much smaller numbers – compare with those of Lancashire, Yorkshire and South-East England where few families effectively lost their confiscated estates.[113]

Before concluding our discussion of the economic fate of the Royalist gentry after the First Civil War, we must not forget the Decimation Tax. This was a discriminatory tax imposed in 1655–56 on the wealthier Royalists or suspected Royalists to maintain the new county militia, established by the Major-Generals after Penruddock's rising. Royalists had to pay an annual tax of 10 per cent on lands worth £100 a year and £10 on every £1,500 of personal property. In Suffolk a list of fifty-six delinquents was drawn up, but twenty-six of them were too poor to be taxed.[114] Of the thirty who did pay the decimation tax, seven were not residents of Suffolk and so can be ignored. I have also discounted William Castleton of Bury, Esquire, since he was taxed solely on his personal estate.[115] Among the remaining twenty-two seventeen were gentry, three possible gentry and two were Anglican clergy. Of the twenty gentry, twelve were underassessed by the county commissioners, four overassessed, two accurately assessed, while two were doubtful.[116] Two examples of underassessment will suffice. Sackville, son of the famous Cavalier Sir Thomas Glemham of Glemham, paid £40 in tax, suggesting that his total real estate was valued by the authorities at £400 p.a. In fact the Glemhams' true income was at least £625 p.a., even though they were a financially declining family.[117] Richard Everard of Hawkedon, probably an ex-Neuter, paid £10 for his real estate, the commissioners apparently considering that he was worth £100 p.a. In fact his total annual income was probably £250.[118] Low assessments such as these perhaps largely explain why only two of the twenty Royalist gentry were ruined: Edward Rookwood of Euston and Richard Chapman of Livermere. These two were in fact overassessed.[119] Chapman paid £50 for his real and personal estate. This was unfair because his annual landed income was only £100 in 1652.[120] It is not surprising that the Chapman family disappeared from the Suffolk gentry before the Restoration. Edward Rookwood, we have seen, had to sell his patrimonial estate in 1655 and was in financial difficulties before the Civil War.[121] The 1640s apparently saw no improvement in his economic condition and in 1651 his debts exceeded the capital value of his estate. His decimation tax of £30 was more than one-tenth of his annual income of £268 [122] and must have contributed to his downfall. However, Rookwood and Chapman were exceptional cases and it would seem that the decimation tax was as harmless to most Suffolk Royalist gentry as the sequestrations, compositions and confiscations had been.

The religious situation

Let us now turn our attention to the religious history of Suffolk during the Interregnum. In Chapter 6 we discussed the failure of the Presbyterians to set up a classical system of church government after the First Civil War. 'By the end of 1649 Presbyterian hopes had been dashed' [123] and it was clear that an alternative to a narrow Presbyterian settlement was required. So in 1653 a broad national Protestant Church was set up, supported by tithes and patrons and retaining its parochial structure. The Church of England was *not* disestablished, but officially there were to be neither bishops nor Prayer Book. This Cromwellian Church included proportionately a greater number of clergy and laity than did the post-Restoration church. 'It was a union of Congregationalists, moderate Presbyterians and Calvinist Baptists'.[124] Yet despite its comprehensive character some clergy and even more of the laity quite deliberately excluded themselves from the national church. Cromwell's government openly tolerated the separatist churches of the more radical Protestants. Moreover, 'even the minority of high-church Episcopalians and Catholics in England were given remarkable freedom from persecution by Cromwell's government, as long as they did not threaten public order'.[125] 'So in practice, on the periphery of the very broad national church, a collection of churches existed in a condition of partial or total isolation'.[126] Two of these religious groups need special attention because of their importance in Suffolk during the 1650s: the Congregationalists and the Quakers.

The Congregationalists, or Independents as they were usually called in the later seventeenth century,[127] rose to their greatest influence during the 1650s under the aegis of Oliver Cromwell, who dominated that decade. In Suffolk only three Congregational churches existed before the death of Charles I: at Walpole,[128] Wrentham [129] and Bury St Edmunds.[130] But during the Interregnum at least fourteen others were formed. Independent churches were either separatist or non-separatist. Only three separatist churches apparently existed in Suffolk before the Restoration: at Market Weston, Rattlesden and Bury, an old Brownist centre.[131] The latter is the most famous and 'from its formation was Separatist to the core and remained so'.[132] The church in Bury was set up with the help of London missionaries, Katherine Chidley and her son Samuel. In their covenant they declared frankly that they were 'convinced in conscience of the evil of the Church of England, and of all other states which ware contrary to Christ's institution' and were thus '*fully separated* ... from them'.[133] The other fourteen

Walpole Old Chapel
(Photograph: S.R.O. (I),
SPS 18583)
Walpole Congregational
Chapel is one of the
oldest places of
nonconformist worship
in England. A
congregation certainly
existed in 1647, if not
earlier. Note the central
position of the pulpit,
with sounding board,
which is hardly
surprising since to
Protestants in general,
but to
Congregationalists in
particular, the sermon
was the centrepiece of
the church service.

Independent churches in Suffolk were of the non-separating kind.[134] Their adherents believed in a decentralised *national* church. Indeed, in the 1650s 'the outstanding characteristic of East Anglian Congregationalism is the holding by the ministers of livings in the Established Church concomitantly with their pastorates of Congregational Churches'.[135] These beneficed clergy served both the entire parish composed of the regenerate and unregenerate and their gathered church of visible saints. John Manning was Vicar of Sibton and also pastor to a nearby gathered church at Rendham. Thomas Spurdance was Rector of Rushmere and pastor of a Congregational church at neighbouring Henstead. At Wrentham John Phillip was Rector but, true to his Congregational beliefs, he limited church membership and the sacraments to the godly, while not denying others the right to attend.[136]

Although the Independents (both separatist and non-separatist) in Suffolk were not numerous, they enjoyed complete security and freedom of worship during the Interregnum. The same cannot be said about the Quakers, who were brutally persecuted. But first, who were the Quakers? The Quakers were the most extreme of the Protestant sects in England. Quakerism, based upon the doctrine of the Inner Light, was averse from institutional religion and found no place for either ministry or sacraments. The Quakers originated in the North of England, but from the spring of 1655 their missionaries, led by George Whitehead of Orton, Westmorland, arrived in Suffolk. How much *numerical* support these 'Friends of the Truth'[137] received in the county, it is hard to say.[138] But in 1657 Suffolk was apparently the fourth largest *financial* contributor to the Quaker cause.[139] But whatever their numbers or wealth, the Quakers aroused considerable opposition, from magistrates, ministers and mobs. Prior to the Restoration, the early Friends in Suffolk seem to have been prosecuted and persecuted for three main 'offences': vagrancy, harassment of ministers and non-payment of tithes.

The Vagrancy Act (39 Eliz. cap. 4) was used by magistrates in an effort to contain Quakerism. It was aimed particularly at Quaker missionaries, many of them northerners. 'North-country men and women', says Dr Reay, 'were whipped out of southern towns'.[140] This is no exaggeration. In 1655 Richard Clayton, a Quaker from Gleaston in Lancashire, was 'publickly whipt as a Vagrant and sent out of the Town [Bures]'. Two years later another northern Quaker – George Whitehead from Orton – was ordered 'to be whipp'd at Nayland ... till his Body be bloody' and to return to Orton within two months.[141] Xenophobia, or at least parochialism, seems to have played some part in the harsh treatment of Clayton and Whitehead. As Dr Reay says, 'the average villager ... and many town dwellers, in the Southern and Home Counties, the West Country and *East Anglia*,[142] would have had few contacts with northerners'.[143] Ignorance reinforced prejudice.

Harassment of ministers was a more frequent charge against the Quakers than vagrancy, at least in Suffolk. 'Quakers waged a guerilla war against the clergy'.[144] Many Friends were prosecuted for disturbing ministers and interrupting church services, offences punishable either by an Act of Mary Tudor's reign (1 Mar., St 2 cap. 3) or by the provisions contained in Cromwell's proclamation of 1655 which was specifically aimed at Quakers. In 1655 George Whitehead, John Harwood and Richard Clayton were indicted at the Bury Quarter Sessions as 'Common Disturbers of Magistrates and Ministers'. William Seaman of Mendlesham and Elizabeth Lockwood ' were committed to Ipswich Gaol, for speaking to a Priest[145] after he had ended his Sermon in the Place of publick Worship at Mendlesham'. In 1659 George Fox the Younger of Charsfield, Suffolk,[146] was 'put out of Town' by the Bailiff after preaching in the Market place at Aldeburgh. Not to be deterred, he preached 'to the People in the Steeple-house'[147] at Southwold, after the minister had finished his sermon. But to his dismay 'his Christian Concern for the people was ill requited by the ruder Sort, who beat him, threw him violently upon the stones'. Clearly the mob supported the minister. Quakers were also openly abusive to the clergy. In August 1655 'Joseph Laurence was committed to the County Gaol at Ipswich, being charged with Railing against the Ministers of God's Word, and calling the worship of God, Babylonish'. In the same year Richard Clayton, with two other Quakers, fixed to the 'Steeple-house' door at Bures a document full of the strongest abuse of ministers of religion, couched in biblical language. For this Clayton was whipped and expelled from the village, while his companions were sent to Bury gaol.[148]

Refusal to pay tithes was perhaps the most common 'offence' committed by the Quakers in Suffolk and elsewhere. Tithes involved the compulsory payment of one-tenth of a parishioner's income or produce to the local parson or lay impropriator. Tithes fell very heavily on the poor and were widely resented. Indeed, they became such a strong political issue that radical members of Barebones Parliament in 1653 sought (unsuccessfully) to abolish them. However, we are concerned primarily with the religious reasons for hostility to tithes. All Separatists, and not just the Quakers, opposed tithes, believing that their abolition would undermine the national church and substitute a voluntary system. However, 'the Quakers formed the vanguard of popular agitation against tithes'.[149] Anti-tithe activity was often a cause as well as a result of Quakerism. When the Quakers arrived in Suffolk, 'they enjoyed a measure of success among tithe-resisters'. George Sherwyn of Debenham, Thomas Judy of Ashfield, William Warne of the vicarage of Brundish and Tannington, Arthur Goddard of Clopton, Arnold Nunn and John Caston of the villages of Aldham and Elmsett, were involved in anti-tithe activity *before* they became Quakers in the mid-1650s.[150] After embracing the teachings of George Fox they of course continued their stand against tithes.[151] In several other counties[152] many Quakers had a background of anti-tithe activity and continued their resistance after conversion. However, continuity should not be exaggerated. Most Suffolk men and women do not seem to have resisted tithes *until* they became Quakers: people like John Simpson of Kenton, Joseph Laurence, Richard White of Mendlesham, Anthony Kettle of Edwardstone, Yeoman, John Fryer and James Norton, both of Felixstowe, John Eastling, Thomas Bircham, Thomas Bond, John Coleman, Widow Posford of Clopton, William Driver and Thomas Pinson, both of Trimley, William Burroughs of Great Finborough, Anne Shipman of Cretingham, Lucy Oxe, Widow, Christopher Sharp and Lucy his wife.[153] All the above-named Quakers were severely treated for refusing to pay tithes. Twelve suffered imprisonment, nine distraint of goods and three both penalties. Why was there such hostility to Quaker anti-tithe activity from clergy and gentry? It was because tithes were the main source of income for a minister and often formed a sizeable portion of a lay impropriator's revenue. But the main fear of the gentry was 'that landlords rent and tithe rent will stand and fall together'.[154] In short, basic property rights seemed threatened.

Conclusion

Despite the problem of the Quakers, Suffolk was noted for its high degree of stability during the Interregnum. There was considerable political continuity. A majority who had served as JPs in the 1640s continued to do so in the 1650s, and the evidence tentatively suggests that most county committeemen of the Civil War years also served the Republic during the Interregnum. Large numbers of conservative Parliamentarians, including opponents of the Regicide, and even a few ex-Royalists, seem to have supported the republican governments in the interests of peace and stability. However, the radicals appear to have been the strongest supporters of the Republic, though they were able to work alongside the more conservative officials. There was less social than political continuity, however. Indeed, there seems to have been something of a minor social revolution in government. The greater gentry were far less, and the minor gentry and plebeians were far more, conspicuous on the county assessment and militia commissions during the late 1650s than they had been earlier. However, the greater gentry continued to dominate the Bench of active magistrates during the Interregnum. If there was no large scale transfer of office from one social group to another, neither was there a great transfer of property. Extremely few Suffolk Parliamentarian gentry and commoners acquired confiscated church, crown and Royalist property. Indeed, Suffolk Parliamentarians seem to have been more eager to acquire land in Ireland than in their home county.

So much for the Parliamentarians. What about the Royalists? Many years ago Professor Everitt wrote that 'in Suffolk at least royalism remained a largely underground movement ... until the Restoration'.[155] This is an exaggeration. Although the Sealed Knot had strong connections with East Anglia, there were few Royalist plotters in Suffolk. Lists of Royalists in England and Wales were drawn up in 1656 and 1658, but they included few Suffolk men. Royalist conspiracy and armed rebellion were probably discouraged by sequestrations, compositions, confiscations and the decimation tax. Yet most Royalist gentry in Suffolk do not seem to have been financially harmed by those penalties. Not many appear to have sold land privately as a result of composition fines, while the very few whose estates were publicly sold regained them, probably before the Restoration. Likewise the Decimation Tax caused few social casualties among Royalists or suspected Royalists.

From a religious standpoint, the Interregnum in Suffolk was, in general, a time of tolerance for all except Roman Catholics and Quakers. But Catholics were apparently only harassed in 1657,[156] though Quakers were very harshly persecuted from 1655 onwards. Persecution of religious minorities would be even harsher after the Restoration.

CHAPTER EIGHT

Suffolk and the Restoration 1660–85

The gradual disintegration of the British Republic after the forced resignation of Richard Cromwell in May 1659 led to a fear of anarchy and to a belief that this could only be prevented by a restoration of the Stuart monarchy. On this historians are generally agreed. But was the Restoration of Charles II in 1660 a compromise, or was it a 'vengeful' affair?[1] The answer depends on whether one is dealing with the First Restoration Settlement of the Convention Parliament, or the Second Restoration Settlement of the 'Cavalier' Parliament.[2] Broadly speaking, the first settlement was desired by Charles II and the moderate, constitutional Royalists[3] and the second by the more extreme Cavaliers.

The First Settlement of 1660 was generous. Only nine regicides, and three or four others, were executed.[4] The New Model Army was paid and largely disbanded. The land question was settled by a compromise. The confiscated estates of the Crown and the Church were restored. Royalists also regained their confiscated lands (if they had not already done so), provided they took the necessary legal action. But Royalist lands sold privately to pay composition fines, or to raise money for the King, were not returned because they were regarded as 'voluntary' sales. This angered the Cavaliers. What also annoyed them was that the king seemed to be rewarding his former supporters inadequately and his former enemies too generously. Indeed, it was said that the Act of Indemnity and Oblivion meant 'Indemnity for his enemies and oblivion for his friends'.[5] There was much truth in this complaint. Charles rewarded only 9 per cent of the Royalist gentry in Lancashire and just 11 per cent in Yorkshire.[6] On the other hand he generously rewarded former Parliamentarians who had made his restoration possible, such as General George Monck who became Duke of Albemarle and received huge grants of crown land and a palace. Moreover, Charles appointed a mixed Privy Council of sixteen Royalists, four former supporters of Oliver Cromwell (including Monck) and eight wartime Parliamentarians who had opposed the Republic.[7] In retrospect these were sensible, conciliatory measures. However, as John Morrill reminds us, 'the greatest source of weakness in the [first] Restoration Settlement was that while Charles created a comprehensive political settlement, he failed in his attempt to create a comprehensive religious settlement'.[8]

The Second Restoration Settlement was the work of the 'Cavalier' Parliament elected in April 1661. But this Parliament, unlike Charles II, did not even attempt to establish a comprehensive religious settlement and instead imposed a narrow, vengeful one. Such a settlement was prompted by Venner's Fifth Monarchist rising in London in January 1661.[9] The uprising caused contemporaries to equate religious dissent with political subversion, and this was the main reason for the establishment of a standing army of 'Guards and Garrisons' and the passage of the 'Clarendon Code', for which the 'Cavalier' Parliament is perhaps best remembered.

The 'Clarendon Code'[10] is the collective name given to the four Acts of Parliament which re-established the Anglican Church and restricted the activities of the Protestant Dissenters: the Corporation Act 1661, the Act of Uniformity 1662, the Conventicle Act 1664 and the Five Mile Act 1665. Easily the most important was the Act of Uniformity which restored the Anglican faith as the official religion of the State. Almost 1,000 of the 9,000 parish ministers were deprived of their livings for refusing to accept the Act.[11] Thus most Puritans were driven out of the Church of England.[12] 'Henceforth', says Dr Christopher Hill, 'there were in England two Protestant nations [Anglicans and Dissenters] as well as the Roman Catholic minority'.[13]

Persecution of Dissenters on a national scale seems to have been most severe between 1664 and 1666, but by the end of the 1660s it died down. In 1672 Charles II, for various reasons, issued a Declaration of Indulgence which suspended, by royal prerogative, the penal laws against Protestant Dissenters and Roman Catholics. Dissenters were allowed to worship publicly but Papists only privately. The Declaration caused such an outcry in Parliament that Charles had to withdraw it in 1673. This opposition is hardly surprising. As the late Professor Geoffrey Holmes emphasised, there were 'two extremely powerful phobias' in seventeenth-century England, especially between 1670 and 1700. 'One was the fear of Popery; the other was the fear of Puritan fanaticism'.[14] During the 1660s and much of the 1670s the main phobia was fear of Puritan fanaticism. But from the mid-1670s this was gradually replaced by fear of Popery. Why? There were many reasons, but perhaps the most important was the conversion of King Charles II's brother, James, Duke of York, to Roman Catholicism in 1669. This caused alarm, for James was the heir presumptive and it was feared that as King he could easily suppress Protestantism and re-impose Roman Catholicism, as indeed Mary Tudor had done.

Anti-Catholicism reached its peak at the time of the so-called Popish Plot of 1678. This was a fictitious Jesuit conspiracy to assassinate Charles II, massacre Protestants and enthrone the Catholic Duke of York. These lies were spread by the scoundrel Titus Oates and caused widespread panic. Thus during the years 1679–81 Catholics were fiercely persecuted. Priests were arrested (some being put to death) and laymen also suffered. So great was the fear of Popery that the House of Commons introduced three Exclusion Bills between 1679 and 1681 to exclude James, Duke of York, from the throne and thus safeguard the Protestant religion. Fortunately for Charles II time was on his side. His opponents – the Whigs – overplayed their hand, while his supporters – the Tories – played upon the fears of another civil war.[15] The Tory slogan '41 is here again' was most effective. Thus during the final three years of Charles II's reign hatred was directed away from Catholics towards Dissenters, who were again persecuted severely.

It has been necessary to dwell at some length on national events so that the situation in Restoration Suffolk can be seen in perspective. Locally, we shall consider three main topics: the social, economic and political condition of the gentry, especially the Cavaliers; the Protestant Dissenters under Charles II; and the Roman Catholics under the same monarch.

The gentry

How did the Restoration land settlement affect the Suffolk gentry? The answer is hardly at all. We have seen that during the Interregnum no land revolution occurred in the county. Few Roundhead gentry gained and few Cavaliers lost land. Nationally the Royalists disliked the land settlement, but in Suffolk there was little cause for dissatisfaction.

However, in Suffolk, as elsewhere, the Royalists or their heirs expected rewards from Charles II. The rewards granted by the King in the three years after his return consisted of titles, bounty and offices. Let us begin with titles. As regards peerages, the Suffolk Cavaliers certainly had reason to be grateful. Frederick Cornwallis of Brome was created Baron Cornwallis of Eye in 1661. Henry Jermyn, already Baron Jermyn of St Edmundsbury since 1643, was elevated to the rank of Earl of St Albans in 1660, while William Crofts of Little Saxham had actually been granted the title of Baron Crofts of Saxham two years before the Restoration.[16] No Suffolk Parliamentarian or Republican received a peerage.

Baronetcies, however, were more evenly distributed. Five Royalists – Robert Broke of Nacton, Gervase Elwes of Stoke-by-Clare, Edward Gage of Hengrave, Sir Charles Gawdy of Crow's Hall, Debenham, and John Warner of Framlingham and Parham – were granted Baronetcies.[17] But so were five Parliamentarians – Sir Thomas Barnardiston of Kedington, Samuel Barnardiston of Brightwell, Robert Cordell of Long Melford, Thomas Cullum of Hawstead and Philip Parker of Erwarton – and two ex-Republicans: Thomas Darcy of Kentwell Hall and Sir George Reeve of Thwaite.[18]

As for Knighthoods, Royalists must have been extremely disappointed. Only two recipients – Edward Barker of Sibton and John Pooley of Boxted – were former Royalists, while five were either ex-Parliamentarians or ex-Republicans: Robert Brooke of Cockfield Hall, William Blois of

Little Saxham Church, exterior
(Photograph: A. Hodge)
The tower is Norman, the south side and porch are perpendicular. In the Stuart period
the patrons of the church were the strongly Royalist Crofts family.

Grundisburgh and Yoxford, George Reeve of Thwaite, Emanuel Sorrell of Ipswich and George Weyneve of Brettenham.[19]

Financial aid apparently benefited just one non-Royalist in Suffolk: Sir George Reeve, an ex-Republican, who received £500 'as royal bounty' in October 1663.[20] But only three from Cavalier families had cause for gratitude.[21] Sir John Pettus of Cheston Hall was given a pension of £300 a year and it was said that 'All his estate is under extent'.[22] Perhaps the pension saved him from complete bankruptcy. Sir Henry Felton of Playford also got a pension in the bailiwick of Bosmere and Claydon and the hundred of Samford.[23] Mary, widow of Thomas Blague of Horringer, was granted a £500 annuity in March 1661.[24]

As regards offices, only one Parliamentarian, Sir Thomas Bedingfield of Darsham, benefited. He was made a Serjeant-at-Law in 1660.[25] By contrast nine Royalists obtained paid offices from Charles II. Thomas Blague was confirmed as Groom of the Bedchamber in 1660.[26] Frederick Cornwallis became a privy councillor in the same year and was appointed Treasurer of the King's household in 1661.[27] William Crofts was made Gentleman of the Bedchamber as early as 1652 and was confirmed in that post in 1661.[28] John Hervey of Ickworth was appointed Treasurer to Queen Catherine of Braganza, wife of Charles II, in 1660.[29] John Pooley of Boxted was

Little Saxham Church, monument in Crofts Chapel
(Photograph: S.R.O. (B), K 505/372)
This monument is in honour of William Lord Crofts of Little Saxham, and his wife Elizabeth. It refers to William's barony and court office, granted for services to the Crown before the Restoration. During the First Civil War William had been a Lt. Colonel of the Queen's Lifeguard of Horse and had fought at Burton-upon-Trent (1643), second Newbury (1644) and Shelford House (1645).

appointed Gentleman Usher of the Privy Chamber in 1661.[30] Sir Lionel Tollemache of Helmingham was made Keeper of Richmond Park in 1660.[31] Except for Tollemache, these Royalists were given mainly court offices. But some were granted military offices in the new standing army. John Le Hunt of Little Bradley was made a Lieutenant in the Earl of Lindsey's regiment in 1662.[32] William Rolleston of Kettleburgh was made a captain in the King's Own Regiment of Foot Guards in 1661 and commissioned major in 1665.[33] The Suffolk Royalist receiving by far the greatest number of offices was Henry Jermyn. He became privy councillor, ambassador to Paris and joint registrar of Chancery in 1660. A year later he was made Captain of the Island of Jersey. Next year he was appointed keeper of Greenwich House and Park, and the following year he became Grand Master of the Freemasons.[34]

At first glance it would appear that Suffolk Royalists were quite well rewarded at the Restoration. However, royal munificence should not be exaggerated. Of the sixty-five Royalist gentry families in Suffolk who served Charles I in the 1640s, only thirteen (20 per cent) were rewarded by his son after the Restoration.[35] The Cavaliers in Suffolk were certainly much better treated than their brethren in Lancashire and Yorkshire. Yet far more than one-fifth must have expected to receive royal favours, and they must have been angry at the awards of baronetcies and knighthoods to their old enemies. Moreover, though, apart from Sir Thomas Bedingfield, former Suffolk opponents of the Stuarts did not acquire paid offices at the Restoration, many obtained unpaid local government positions, as Table 8.1 shows.

Table 8.1 Selection of post-Restoration officials (by Civil War Loyalties)[36]

Ref.[37]	Position	Date	Civil War Allegiances					Totals
			Parl.	Roy.	SC	Rep.	Neut. /Unk.	
a	MPs	1660	6	4	1	1	0	12
		1661	5	5	1	1	0	12
b	JPs	1660–65	21	17	2	11	18	69
c	Deputy Lieuts.	1662	4	6	1	0	2	13
d	Sheriffs Commissioners	1660–70	5	0	0	1	6	12
e	Army and Navy	1661	32	24	1	16	59	132
f	Voluntary Gift	1661	33	24	2	10	29	98
g	Lay Subsidies	1663	31	24	2	15	60	132

The above table shows that Royalists were in a majority only among the deputy-lieutenants. This was, of course, important because control of the lieutenancy meant control of the militia. But it must have been galling for the Suffolk Cavaliers to see ex-Parliamentarians and ex-Neutrals dominating the magistracy, the shrievalty and commissions for assessment, the voluntary gift and the lay subsidy. As Drs Heal and Holmes have said, 'in 1660 the élite sought both the immediate recovery of their local power, and the opportunity to employ it against those who had triumphed over them in the [civil] war'.[38] But Cavalier hopes (except perhaps in corporate towns[39]) were dashed. Appointments of local officials made in 1660 were of the most prominent leaders of their communities, virtually irrespective of their past politics. During the Interregnum seventy-two served on the Suffolk Bench but twenty-four (33 per cent) were re-employed at the Restoration.[40] The situation in Suffolk was similar to that in Hampshire, where 36 per cent of Interregnum justices remained on the Bench during the early 1660s.[41] This continuity with the 1650s may have been the intention of Charles II, but it can hardly have appeased the Royalists. The domination of the magistracy – the lynch-pin of local government – by former Parliamentarians, Republicans and Neutrals must have particularly angered them. Suffolk Cavaliers probably had little objection to sharing power on the Bench with conservative Parliamentarians like Isaac Appleton of Great Waldingfield or John Sicklemore of Ipswich. But they would almost certainly have hated working with Thomas Edgar of Ipswich, who had very actively supported the Republic, and even more with Edmund Harvey of Wickham Skeith, a Puritan revolutionary *par excellence*.

Limited rewards and limited power: these were major grievances among the Suffolk Royalists. But another cause for concern was the emergence of new gentry families of plebeian or non-local origins who had supported Parliament in the Civil Wars or the Republic afterwards. There were thirty-seven such families in Suffolk.[42] The outsiders included three from wealthy London merchant families: Sir Samuel Barnardiston of Brightwell, Sir Robert Cordell of Long Melford and Sir Thomas Cullum of Hawstead. All three had received baronetcies at the Restoration.[43] Samuel Barnardiston, a younger brother of Sir Thomas Barnardiston of Kedington and, according to legend, the first person to be called 'Roundhead',[44] made so much money in London commerce that he was able to buy Brightwell Manor, near Ipswich. In 1663 he built, or remodelled, Brightwell Hall, which became an extensive and impressive building.[45] Robert Cordell, son of a successful London merchant, loaned over £2,600 to the Parliamentary cause and in 1654 bought Melford Hall for £28,959.[46] Thomas Cullum, a City draper and alderman, played an essential part in Parliament's victory as a Commissioner

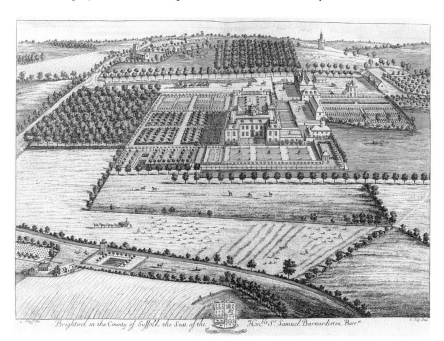

Brightwell Hall
(Engraving by Johannes Kip in *Britannia Illustrata* (1707), p. 52)
Built or remodelled, *c.* 1663, by Sir Samuel Barnardiston, Bart., former City merchant and leader of the Suffolk Whig MPs from 1678 to 1702. The picture shows the vastness of Barnardiston's mansion and estate.

of Excise, spent over £10,000 on London property, and in 1656 bought the large Hawstead estate near Bury St Edmunds for about £18,000.[47] Native newcomers to the gentry included men like Thomas Chaplin, linen draper and alderman of Bury St Edmunds, George Groome of Rattlesden, a former chandler, and John Base of Saxmundham, yeoman. All three had been prominent supporters of Parliament.[48] Base is a particularly good example of what Thomas Fuller called an 'upstart in our late civil wars' who had 'injuriously invaded the arms of ancient families'.[49] Contemporaries said that Base 'had not above £20 per annum left him by his father, a yeoman in high-Suffolk, but he hath beene well increased by a rich widow too'. Perhaps it was his wife's wealth that enabled him in about 1650 to buy the manor of Saxmundham, where he apparently built 'a comely house'. But whatever the reason, his new found wealth meant that he was recognised as a gentleman at the Herald's Visitation of Suffolk between 1664 and

Sir Thomas Cullum, Bart. (1587?–1664) by an unknown artist.
(Photograph: S.R.O. (B) K 505/3040)
Sir Thomas was one of the new gentry of Suffolk during the Interregnum. Previously a City draper and alderman, who financially supported Parliament during the Civil Wars, he later settled in Suffolk, where he bought the large Hawstead estate for a vast sum. Created a baronet in 1660, he was regarded as armigerous at the Herald's Visitation of Suffolk between 1664 and 1668.

1668.[50] The vendor of Saxmundham Manor – Benjamin Cutler of Ipswich, Gentleman, – can hardly have taken pleasure in disposing of his property since he had been on the opposite side to Base during the First Civil War; he had helped defend Newark for the King.[51] Nor would William Glover of Frostenden, Gentleman, an Anglican Royalist, have enjoyed selling his manor of Morehall, Campsey Ash, in 1654 to John Sheppard of Mendlesham, a strong Republican of doubtful gentility, 'to the great ruin of his fortunes'.[52]

Not only did it seem that upstart Roundheads were buying up the lands of gentlemanly Cavaliers; but it appeared that the very survival of the Royalist gentry was at stake. As Dr Seward has remarked, 'the Royalist gentry were unsure whether they would be able to re-establish their social dominance' after the Civil Wars and Interregnum.[53] The Cavaliers seemed to have just cause for concern. Between the outbreak of the Civil War in

1642 and the early 1660s twenty-one (32 per cent) of the sixty-five Royalist families[54] disappeared from the ranks of the Suffolk gentry.[55] This was considerably worse than the situation in Lancashire where only thirty-eight (21 per cent) of the 177 Cavalier families lost their gentility between 1642 and 1664.[56] But the situation in Suffolk must be seen in perspective. Not all the twenty-one Cavalier families can have lost their gentility because they had taken the losing side. The fact is that the Civil War years were economically harmful to *all* gentry groups. The Parliamentarian gentry may not have been, like the Cavaliers, victims of sequestrations, composition fines, confiscations or decimation taxes, but they had to pay extremely heavy taxes to the local Roundhead committee and suffered severely from loss of rents. Indeed, it has been estimated that anything up to a third of the rentals of the East Anglian gentry went to pay for the war.[57] So it is hardly surprising that sometime between the outbreak of the Civil War of 1642 and the Heralds Visitations of 1664 thirty-five (31 per cent) of the 112 Parliamentary gentry families[58] disappeared into social obscurity.[59] Indeed, there were gainers and losers among all groups of Suffolk gentry between the outbreak of the Civil War and the Restoration, as Table 8.2 shows.

Table 8.2 The new and disappearing Suffolk gentry, 1642–64[60]

Political groups	Families entering the gentry between 1642 and 1664	Families disappearing from the gentry between 1642 and 1664
Parliamentarians/Supporters of the Republic[61]	37 (18.0%)	35 (8.9%)
Royalists	4 (2.0%)	21 (5.3%)
Sidechangers	–	1 (0.2%)
Neutrals/Unknown	164 (80.0%)	338 (85.6%)
Total	205 (100.0%)	395 (100.0%)

The above table suggests that families sending support to both sides guaranteed their social and economic survival. The one disappearing family – Wentworth of Somerleyton – failed in the male line in 1651.[62] Not surprisingly, only four new families were ex-Royalists, and three of them – Elwes of Stoke-by-Clare, Gage of Hengrave and Wood of Loudham Hall – were newcomers to Suffolk.[63] Also unsurprisingly, new families were far more numerous among Roundheads and Republicans. Yet they formed only 18 per cent of the 205 new gentry families who arose between the outbreak of the Civil War and the early 1660s. Thomas Fuller was right when he said that a new gentry had emerged after the Civil War. But in Suffolk, as in Lancashire,[64] they seem to have belonged mostly to those who may have 'sate still' during the Great Rebellion. Finally, it is worth noting that the total number of disappearing families was almost twice as great as the total number of new families.[65] Numerically at least, the Restoration in Suffolk hardly witnessed the 'triumph of the gentry'.[66]

Mock Beggar's Hall, Claydon
(Engraved by T. Barber from a drawing by T. Higham in *Excursions*, I, p. 179)
The red-brick manor house with Dutch gables was erected in 1621, probably by Samuel
Aylmer, eldest son of John Aylmer, Bishop of London (1577–94). Samuel's son, Edward,
was a Royalist clergyman who compounded for delinquency in 1646. He was apparently
the only Suffolk-born Royalist who rose to gentility during the Interregnum, perhaps
because of his inherited wealth.

So much for the new and disappearing gentry. What about the perdurable
gentry, those families which were gentry in both 1642 and 1664? Among
this group the ex-Royalists need not have feared social demotion, for in
the 1660s and early 1670s they were just as wealthy as the ex-Parliamentarians, if not more so. This is shown by the size of their houses and the
size of their incomes. For house size the Hearth Tax returns are the most
important source. The Hearth Tax, or chimney money, was levied twice
yearly, from 1662 to 1689, at the rate of two shillings per hearth, and was
paid by occupiers, not landlords. The returns list, under each parish, both
taxpayers and non-payers with the number of hearths possessed by each
household. These details broadly reveal the relative size of houses, which
in turn are a very crude guide to wealth.[67] Table 8.3 compares the wealth
of the former Parliamentarian and Royalist gentry as expressed by house
size in 1674.

   Table 8.3 shows that in both absolute and relative terms the Royalists
included far more rich gentry. The Cornwallis family had the largest house,
Brome Hall, with forty-five hearths.[71] On the Parliamentarian side, Sir
Edmund Bacon had the largest house, Redgrave Hall, with forty-one

Table 8.3 House size[68] and Civil War allegiances

No. of hearths[69]	Ex-Parl. families	Ex-Roy. families[70]
20+ (large houses – prosperous)	7 (9.1%)	12 (27.3%)
10–19 (modest houses – middling)	36 (46.7%)	12 (27.3%)
9 or under (small houses – poor)	24 (31.2%)	8 (18.1%)
Unknown	10 (13.0%)	12 (27.3%)
Total	77 (100.0%)	44 (100.0%)

hearths.[72] Among those owning houses of between thirty and forty hearths, only one, Maurice Barrow with thirty-three hearths at Barningham, was a former Roundhead, while four – Naunton of Letheringham (thirty-seven hearths), Jermyn of Rushbrooke (thirty-three), Crofts of Little Saxham (thirty-one) and Pooley of Badley (thirty) – belonged to ex Royalist families. Judging by house size, then, the Cavaliers undoubtedly had most of the rich gentry on their side. But among both middling and poor gentry Parliamentarians outnumbered Royalists by three to one.

So much for house size. What about income? Here the utmost caution is needed, for there is considerably less source material on gentry incomes in the 1660s than in 1642.[73] The lay subsidy rolls for 1663 are particularly disappointing. They cover Bury St Edmunds and only four Suffolk hundreds: Babergh, Blything, Risbridge and Thedwastre.[74] Contemporary estimates of some Suffolk gentry incomes appear in the Royal Oak list of 1660[75] and others are given by Rev. Matthias Candler in 1655–57.[76] These are better than nothing. But far more valuable are Dr Cliffe's recent calculations of the landed wealth of twelve ex-Parliamentarian and fourteen ex-Royalist families in Suffolk in Charles II reign.[77] Yet Table 8.4 shows that among the perdurable Parliamentarian and Royalist gentry those whose incomes are known were not numerous.

Table 8.4 Income and Civil War allegiances

Annual income from land c. 1664 £	Ex-Parl. families		Ex-Roy. families	
2,000 and over	6	} 13 (16.9%)	4	} 16 (36.4%)
1,000–1,999	7		12	
750–999	1	} 16 (20.8%)	2	} 11 (25.0%)
500–749	3		4	
250–499	12		5	
100–249	5	} 6 (7.8%)	3	} 3 (6.8%)
Under 100	1		–	
Unknown	42 (54.5%)		14 (31.8%)	
Total	77 (100.0%)		44 (100.0%)	

For what they are worth, the above statistics show that there was a far higher percentage of rich gentry (with landed incomes of £1,000 p.a. upwards) among the Royalists, though the Parliamentarians included in their ranks Maurice Barrow of Barningham whose annual income of £6,000 made him not only the wealthiest man in Suffolk, but 'one of the richest landowners in England'.[78] The percentages of middle-income families were fairly similar on both sides, but in absolute terms there were twice as many poor gentry families (under £250 p.a.) among the Parliamentarians than among the Royalists.

Tables 8.3 and 8.4 show that the reality of Cavalier prosperity differed from the illusion of Cavalier impoverishment. However, in community relations it is beliefs, not facts, which matter, and the Royalists *did* believe that their world was being seriously threatened, especially by the Protestant Dissenters, who were seen as potential rebels or republicans, especially if Baptists and Quakers. Sir John Holland, a Norfolk squire with much power in Suffolk, told Parliament in the early 1660s that, if government was shaken, 'wee must unavoidably fall into the hands of ... a Phanatick[79] Generation of People, who in hatred to Monarchy, Magistracy and Ministry, would soon destroy all the Nobility, Gentry, Persons of Interest and Quality throughout the Nation'.[80] As late as 1678 Edmund Bohun of Westhall, a Suffolk magistrate and ex-Puritan, still believed that the Dissenters' 'ultimate object was the destruction of the monarchy and the bringing in a republic'.[81] To Bohun monarchy was the keystone of the social arch, any shaking of which might cause the collapse of the gentry. The fears so forcibly expressed by Holland and Bohun do much to explain the persecution of Dissenters in Charles II's reign.

The Dissenters

Dissenters were those Protestants who refused to accept the 1660–62 reimposition of episcopacy and the Prayer Book in the Church of England: such church bodies as the Presbyterians, Independents, Baptists and Quakers. For all those groups, except the Quakers, 'Cromwellian England' had been 'a haven of religious freedom'.[82] But after the Restoration they were to be persecuted.

The first blow was struck in 1660 when twenty-three intruded Puritan ministers in Suffolk lost their livings as ejected Royalist clergy were restored.[83]

But it was not enough to get rid of Puritan ministers. The Anglican-Royalist gentry wished to expel Puritan oligarchs from the corporate boroughs, which chose most Members of Parliament. Hence the Corporation Act was passed by the Cavalier Parliament in 1661. This act required all mayors and corporation officials to swear loyalty to the King, renounce the Solemn League and Covenant, and take Church of England communion. Failure to comply meant loss of office.[84] Ronald Hutton has described the Corporation Act as 'a partisan purge unprecedented in English municipal history'.[85] There is some truth in this as regards Suffolk. Dr Michael Reed has observed that 'For much of the period 1643–1662' Ipswich 'was dominated by a group of men of radical religious and political opinions', and that 'in 1662 all of this group were removed from the corporation'.[86] But the purge of Eye corporation in March 1661 was not on anything like so vast a scale. As Hutton reminds us, there was a 'geographical variation in the intensity of the purges',[87] and the so-called 'late great purges at Eye' involved 'the resignation of [only] ffower of thei principall members vizt Coll Harvey, Capt Blissett, Mr Holmes and Mr Harris'.[88]

The Corporation Act was aimed at the Puritan-Parliamentarian boroughs. The Act of Uniformity, 1662, targeted the Puritan clergy within the state church. This act required all Church of England clergymen to use the Book of Common Prayer, renounce the Covenant, and be episcopally ordained.[89] In Suffolk fifty Puritan ministers (mainly Presbyterians but also some non-separating Independents) could not accept this legislation and were deprived of their livings and forced to leave the Church of England by 24 August 1662 (St Bartholemew's Day). Another six were ejected at uncertain dates. Twelve lacked the courage of their convictions and later conformed. The statistics suggest that Suffolk was still a stronghold of advanced Protestantism. Indeed, Table 8.5 shows that, if we include the years 1660 and 1662, the number of ejections was higher in Suffolk than in all but three other English counties. Even the capital of England saw fewer ejections. Details of those particular counties are given in Table 8.5.

Table 8.5 Ejections of Puritan ministers from the Church of England after the Restoration in five English counties[90]

Counties	Total ejected	Ejected 1660	Ejected 1662	Ejected at uncertain date	Afterwards conformed
Suffolk	79	23	50	6	12
Devon	121	40	73	8	10
Essex	99	29	66	4	3
London and Westminster	76	22	50	4	3
Yorkshire	110	38	52	20	17

Thus there gradually came about in Suffolk and elsewhere the permanent cleavage between 'Church' and 'Chapel', with most Puritans worshipping very reluctantly as Dissenters outside the Church of England. At first the Dissenters were even forbidden to worship *outside* the Church. The Conventicle Act, 1664 (16 Chas. II, cap. 4), tried to prevent the ejected clergy from forming their own congregations. Under the act anyone aged sixteen or over who attended a nonconformist religious meeting of more than five individuals, in addition to a family, faced fines of £5 (or three months' imprisonment) for the first offence, £10 (or six months') for the second, and £100 (or transportation) for the third. A further blow to the Protestant Dissenters was the Five Mile Act, 1665 (17 Chas. II, cap. 5). This prohibited any ejected minister from residing within five miles of his old parish or any corporate town. Like the Corporation Act, 1661, it was partly an attack on urban Puritanism. On the face of it, then, 'the Clarendon Code ushered in a dark period for the nonconformists'.[91]

But in practice how severe was the religious persecution of the Protestant Dissenting clergy in Suffolk during the reign of Charles II? For most of our information we depend heavily on Dr Edmund Calamy's *An Account of Ministers, Lecturers etc. who were Ejected or Silenced after the Restoration* (1713), together with his *Continuation of the Account* (1727). These were edited in 1934 by A. G. Matthews, whose single volume is an essential reference work for the historian of Dissent.[92] As the grandson and name-sake of a leading Presbyterian minister ejected in 1662, Edmund Calamy generally knew what he was talking about. Calamy's biographies of ejected ministers make fascinating reading and enable us to assess the situation in Suffolk.[93]

A large place was given in Calamy's biographies to the sufferings of the ministers as the result of poverty or persecution or both. Obviously the loss of their means of livelihood presented a serious problem to all but a fortunate minority. A rather sad case is that of James King, who 'was thrown out of his Living' at Debenham, and 'knew not whither to go. His Enemies found a House for him, that is, a Jail: And when he was out of that he was for'd to take a Farm and mind secular Business very diligently, in order to a Subsistence'. He was also burdened with debts, yet discharged them.[94] King subsisted rather than prospered. But some ejected Dissenting ministers did well for themselves. Some became doctors. Henry Sampson, ex-Rector of Framlingham, went abroad and studied medicine at Padua University in 1666. Two years later he received the MD degree at Leyden University. In 1680 he became a Fellow of the College of Physicians. Nathaniel Fairfax, formerly Curate of Willisham, also became a MD of Leyden in 1670 and 'practis'd Physick, and had great Encouragement and Success in it'.[95] Thomas Taylor, previously a Congregational preacher at Bury St Edmunds, removed to London in about 1670 and became a tobacco merchant. A few ejected Dissenters, such as John Fenwick, Robert Franklin and Robert Mercer, became chaplains in Suffolk gentry households.[96] Richard Jennings, ex-Rector of Combs, eventually became chaplain to Madam Gould at Clapham, Surrey. Mention must also be made of the charitable relief bestowed by wealthy benefactors. In 1671 Lady Jane, widow of Sir Charles Crofts of Bardwell, named forty ejected ministers (not all Suffolk men) to whom she bequeathed £10 apiece.[97] Three ejected ministers – Bartholomew Adrian, John Fairfax and John Sanders – were actually helped by another ejected clergyman, John Meadows, who, as son of the lord of the manor of Witnesham, was 'a wealthy and benevolent man'.

Not all Dissenting ministers in Suffolk escaped hardship or were as fortunate as the above. John Salkeld, the ejected Rector of Worlington, was imprisoned at Bury St Edmunds in 1670 and again in 1683–86 for preaching 'seditious words'. Thus 'his Estate was much weaken'd, and his healthful Constitution was almost ruin'd by this Confinement'. A particularly serious case of religious persecution concerned Francis Crow, ex-Vicar of Hundon. He had a large congregation at Bury St Edmunds after 1672, but

> ... Towards the latter end of the Reign of King Charles, he was taken at Bury, put into Prison in the time of the Assizes, and had Tribulation ten Days ... After this he was so way-laid, and pursu'ed, that he could not get an Opportunity of Preaching without the utmost Difficulty, and thereupon went over to Jamaica [1686] and continu'd there.

As for John Manning, ex-Vicar of Sibton, it was said that 'There's scarce a Jail in Suffolk which he was not sent to at some time or other, of the latter part of his Life. He was at several times imprison'd at Bury, Ipswich, Bliburgh [Blythburgh] etc.'.

However, it is necessary to keep a sense of proportion and not exaggerate the amount of religious persecution in Suffolk. A careful study of *Calamy Revised* reveals only a small number of victims. Salkeld, Crow and John Manning were three of only ten Suffolk Dissenting ministers who suffered imprisonment.[98] One person, William Manning, ex-Rector of Middleton, was fined £20 in 1674 for attending a conventicle. Three Ministers were both fined and jailed.[99] Just five were prosecuted but not apparently convicted or sentenced.[100] In short, of the seventy-nine ejected ministers, only nineteen (24 per cent) apparently suffered persecution in Charles II's reign. Even if we concede that ejection itself was a form of persecution, it would have to be stressed that in Suffolk the number of Puritan ministers ejected after the Restoration was far less than the number of Anglican parsons ejected during the First Civil War: seventy-nine of the former but 136 of the latter.

Why did the vast majority of the ejected Puritan clergy escape persecution after 1662? It is hard to say. One reason may be that oppression of Dissenters under Charles II was intermittent. All the penal legislation was never enforced everywhere at one time, nor anywhere continuously throughout Charles II's reign. The worst years in Suffolk were apparently the early 1670s and early 1680s. Secondly, the authorities often turned a blind eye to the activities of the Dissenters. Thus Samuel Backler, ex-Rector of Whatfield, 'preach'd frequently in publick [parish] Churches after his Nonconformity, and was conniv'd at'. Likewise John Salkeld, before his second imprisonment, preached 'for some Years by connivance in a Publick Church'. But the main reason why the sufferings of Dissenters were limited in Suffolk was undoubtedly the sympathetic attitude of Dr Edward Reynolds, Bishop of Norwich from 1661 to 1676. Reynolds had been previously a Presbyterian and his earlier beliefs 'made his action towards

Edward Reynolds (1599–1676) by an
unknown artist.
When Bishop of Norwich (1661–76)
Reynolds, an ex-Presbyterian, adopted a
conciliatory attitude to the
Nonconformists of his diocese, hence
most escaped persecution.

the nonconformists conciliatory throughout. Hence the harshness of the Conventicle Act and the Five Mile Act was much mitigated in East Anglia'.[101]

But one nonconformist group in Suffolk still had to endure harsh treatment, the Quakers. The year 1660 is the commencement of what has been accurately termed the 'second period' of Quakerism. After the Restoration the majority of Friends gradually became pacifists.[102] Indeed, this more peaceful outlook was evident as early as 1661 when they strongly condemned Venner's uprising.[103] But although no longer a serious threat to government and society, they were, on balance, treated more harshly after than before the Restoration, at least in Suffolk. Of course, being more peaceful and sedate, they were no longer accused of interrupting min-

isters. Nor were they apparently indicted for vagrancy any more,[104] since, as Christopher Hill says, their 'itinerant preachers were restricted, not least by the Act of Settlement of 1662'.[105] But Quakers were still arrested and punished for non-payment of tithes. They were also frequently prosecuted for three other 'offences': refusal to swear the Oath of Allegiance to Charles II, non-attendance at the services of the Established Church, and holding their own religious meetings.

Let us begin with tithes. Quaker opposition to this payment is hardly surprising. The Friends were 'the first nationally organised sect which rejected compromise with the state church'[106] and tithes were the foundation of that church. According to Joseph Besse, forty-one Quakers in Suffolk refused to pay tithes in Charles II's reign.[107] Thirty-four of them suffered imprisonment, five distraint of goods and two both punishments. Prison sentences could be long. Robert Brightwell of Ufford 'lay in Melton gaol nine Years', Edward Plumstead of Old Newton was 'detained' in Ipswich gaol 'several years', Francis Leman was 'a Prisoner at Ipswich ... above four years', while Samuel Freeman, William Fidderman and George Deane ... were there confined ... about six years'.[108]

The Oath of Allegiance was imposed on all. But the Quakers refused to take it and were consequently suspected of disloyalty to the government.

Thus large numbers of Friends were imprisoned. In 1660 thirty-three were in gaol at Bury St Edmunds, nine at Blythburgh, thirteen at Melton, four at Aldeburgh and twenty-three at Ipswich.[109] From 1663 until 1684 nothing more is heard of the Oath of Allegiance. But Charles, determined that his brother, James, should not be excluded from the throne, imposed the oath again. Quakers once more refused to swear allegiance. In April 1684 a petition of eighteen Quakers in Bury gaol tried to explain that it was 'for Conscience-sake we cannot Swear, and not for any Disaffection to the King and Government'. But in vain. Quakers continued to be imprisoned for refusing to swear.[110]

What perhaps most grieved the Suffolk Quakers was their lack of religious liberty. Old Elizabethan and Jacobean statutes, intended originally for use against popish recusants, were revived to compel attendance at the services of the Anglican Church.[111] Besse names forty-four Suffolk Quakers who, in Charles II's reign, were penalised for absence from church, thirty-six of them suffering imprisonment.[112] Fines for non-attendance were also heavy. 'In May 1685, Exchequer processes against Quakers for failure to come to church amounted to £33,300 in Suffolk alone'.[113] Moreover, stiff penalties were provided by the Quaker Act, 1662, and the Conventicle Act, 1664, for those who attended separatist religious meetings. Under Charles II Suffolk Quakers were severely punished for disobeying these two laws. Besse records the names of 140 victims. Fifty-three of them suffered imprisonment, five both imprisonment and a fine, and eighty-two distraint of goods.[114] In today's climate of religious tolerance and indifference, it is hard to understand the harsh measures taken against those 'peaceably meeting together to worship God according to our Persuasions'.[115] But the Suffolk gentry of Charles II's reign were not so certain of the peaceful intentions of the Quakers. Indeed, they believed that their aim was sedition, not worship. In a letter of 18 December 1678 addressed to the Constables of Woodbridge, five local magistrates[116] expressed fears that

> certain seditious Persons ... under Colour or Pretence of the Exercise of Religion, in other Manner than according to the Liturgy and Practice of the Church of England ... meet ... at a spacious Meeting-house nigh the church of your Town [Woodbridge] ... where they may, at such Meetings or Conventicles and unlawful Assemblies, contrive Insurrections, or other evil and dangerous Practices against the Church and State.[117]

Professor Hugh Barbour argued that 'though Quakers were outnumbered by the puritans, they suffered disproportionately'.[118] Perhaps this was because Quakers were 'the bulwark of Dissent'.[119] But whatever the reason, Quakers, unlike other Dissenters, were persecuted in Suffolk almost continuously from May 1660 until April 1685. However, they enjoyed a respite in 1672 and again between 1680 and 1682. The latter period was the aftermath of the Popish Plot, when attention was focused on the Roman Catholics. But 1672 was a year of tolerance and 'the peaceable people called Quakers' were all released from the Suffolk gaols and elsewhere, under a special royal warrant.[120] On the other hand the Friends did not obtain licences to worship under the Declaration of Indulgence.[121]

Charles II's Declaration of Indulgence of 15 March 1672 suspended the penal laws against Protestant Dissenters and Roman Catholics. The former were allowed freedom of public worship if their ministers and meeting places were licensed, while the latter were allowed to worship in private. Meanwhile the Church of England was to 'be preserved'.[122] The licences granted under this short-lived indulgence enable us to trace the distribution of Dissent in different counties and localities. Map 15 shows that Dissent was strong in Suffolk and other eastern counties but even stronger in Middlesex (including London), the Midlands, Lancashire and the West Country (except Cornwall). Map 16 shows the distribution of Dissent *within* Suffolk.[123] Clive Paine has observed that '75 per cent of Independent meetings lay across the north of Suffolk, from the Blackbourne valley to the east coast' and that 'the main concentration of Presbyterian meetings lay, by contrast, in the south-west of the county, with a thin scattering in north Suffolk east of Hunston'.[124] Why the geographical differences between Presbyterians and Independents? It is tempting to suggest that the Independents – rather more radical than the Presbyterians – were strongest in north-east Suffolk because the region had a continuing tradition of heretical beliefs, which can probably be traced from the Lollards through the sixteenth-century Protestants to the Puritans of the Civil War period and beyond. So much for mainstream Dissenters. What about the radical sectaries, the Baptists and Quakers? Map 16 shows that the Baptists had only one licensed centre of worship, Bungay, near the Norfolk border.[125] However, during Charles II's reign there was a strong Baptist presence in both Framlingham and Sudbury.[126] Nevertheless, it was not until the nineteenth century that the Baptists achieved their greatest influence in Suffolk. As for the Quakers, Map 16 shows their forty-one places of worship. It will be seen that they were numerous and widely dispersed. Mendlesham and Woodbridge appear to have been the main strongholds of Quakerism.

Dissenters as a whole seem to have enjoyed much support in market towns, despite the Corporation and Five Mile Acts. In 1673 Richard Blome described twenty-nine market towns in Suffolk.[127] Twenty-one (72 per cent) of these were centres of Protestant Dissent in 1672.[128] A similar situation pertained in north-west England on the eve of the Civil War. In Lancashire twenty-one (68 per cent) of the thirty-one market towns showed 'signs of Puritanism'. In Cheshire eight (61 per cent) of the thirteen market towns were 'inclined to Puritanism'.[129] Of course not all Suffolk Dissenters lived in market towns. But Map 16 shows that most licensed *rural* centres of Dissent were in High Suffolk, a huge wood-pasture area. Dissenters were

Map 15: Distribution of Protestant Nonconformists in England and Wales, 1672

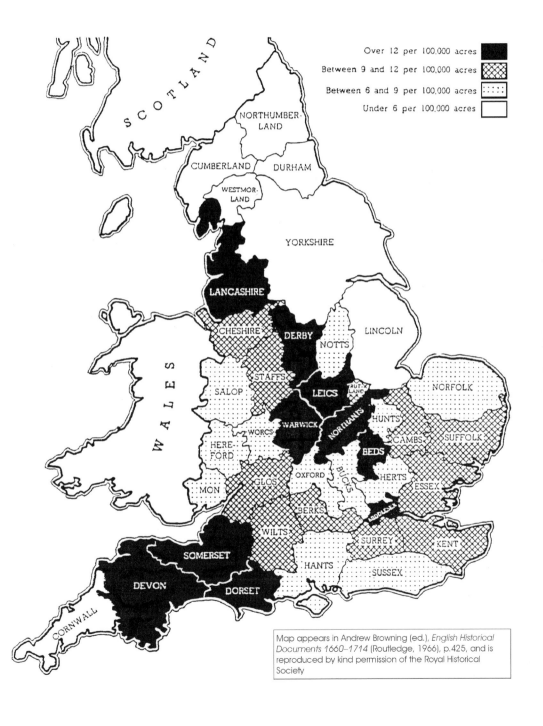

Over 12 per 100,000 acres

Between 9 and 12 per 100,000 acres

Between 6 and 9 per 100,000 acres

Under 6 per 100,000 acres

SCOTLAND

NORTHUMBER-LAND

CUMBERLAND

DURHAM

WESTMOR-LAND

YORKSHIRE

LANCASHIRE

CHESHIRE

DERBY

LINCOLN

NOTTS

WALES

STAFFS

SALOP

LEICS

RUT-LAND

NORFOLK

WARWICK

NORHANTS

HUNTS

WORCS

CAMBS

SUFFOLK

HERE-FORD

BEDS

MON

GLOS

OXFORD

BUCKS

HERTS

ESSEX

BERKS

MIDDLESEX

WILTS

SURREY

KENT

SOMERSET

HANTS

SUSSEX

DEVON

DORSET

CORNWALL

Map appears in Andrew Browning (ed.), *English Historical Documents 1660–1714* (Routledge, 1966), p.425, and is reproduced by kind permission of the Royal Historical Society

Map 16: Protestant Dissenters in Suffolk 1669–74

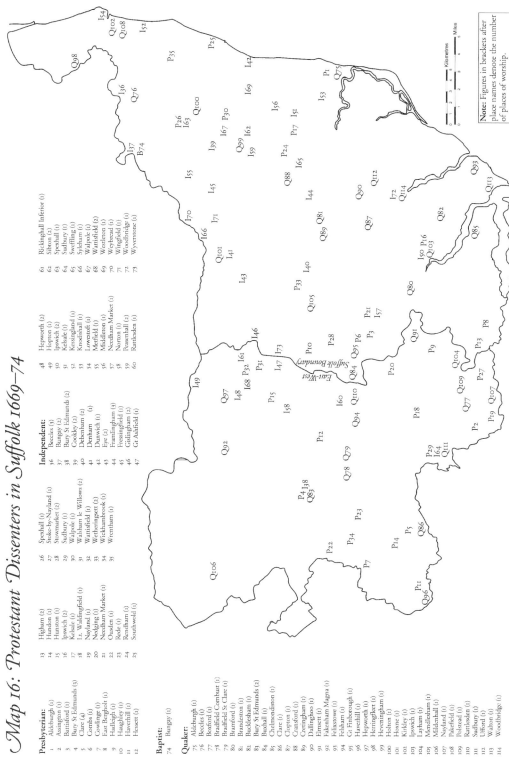

Presbyterian:

1 Aldeburgh (1)
2 Assington (1)
3 Battisford (1)
4 Bury St Edmunds (3)
5 Clare (4)
6 Combs (1)
7 Cowlinge (1)
8 East Bergholt (1)
9 Hadleigh (1)
10 Haughley (1)
11 Haverhill (1)
12 Hessett (1)
13 Higham (2)
14 Hundon (1)
15 Hunston (1)
16 Ipswich (2)
17 Kelsale (1)
18 Lt. Waldingfield (1)
19 Nayland (1)
20 Nedging (1)
21 Needham Market (1)
22 Ousden (1)
23 Rede (1)
24 Rendham (1)
25 Southwold (1)
26 Spexhall (1)
27 Stoke-by-Nayland (1)
28 Stowmarket (2)
29 Sudbury (1)
30 Walpole (1)
31 Walsham le Willows (2)
32 Wattisfield (1)
33 Wetheringsett (2)
34 Wickhambrook (1)
35 Wrentham (1)

Independent:

36 Beccles (3)
37 Bungay (2)
38 Bury St Edmunds (2)
39 Cookley (2)
40 Debenham (2)
41 Denham (1)
42 Dunwich (1)
43 Eye (2)
44 Framlingham (3)
45 Fressingfield (1)
46 Gislingham (2)
47 Gt Ashfield (1)
48 Hepworth (2)
49 Hopton (1)
50 Ipswich (2)
51 Kelsale (1)
52 Kessingland (1)
53 Knodishall (1)
54 Lowestoft (1)
55 Metfield (1)
56 Middleton (1)
57 Needham Market (1)
58 Norton (1)
59 Peasenhall (2)
60 Rattlesden (1)
61 Rickinghall Inferior (1)
62 Sibton (2)
63 Spexhall (1)
64 Sudbury (1)
65 Swefling (1)
66 Syleham (1)
67 Walpole (1)
68 Wattisfield (2)
69 Westleton (1)
70 Weybread (1)
71 Wingfield (1)
72 Woodbridge (1)
73 Wyverstone (1)

Baptist:

74 Bungay (1)

Quaker:

75 Aldeburgh (1)
76 Beccles (1)
77 Boxford (1)
78 Bradfield Combust (1)
79 Bradfield St Clare (1)
80 Bramford (1)
81 Brandeston (1)
82 Bucklesham (1)
83 Bury St Edmunds (2)
84 Buxhall (1)
85 Chelmondiston (1)
86 Clare (1)
87 Clopton (1)
88 Cransford (1)
89 Cretingham (1)
90 Dallinghoo (1)
91 Elmsett (1)
92 Fakenham Magna (1)
93 Felixstowe (1)
94 Felsham (1)
95 Gt Finborough (1)
96 Haverhill (1)
97 Hepworth (1)
98 Herringfleet (1)
99 Heveningham (1)
100 Holton (1)
101 Hoxne (1)
102 Kirkley (1)
103 Ipswich (1)
104 Layham (1)
105 Mendlesham (1)
106 Mildenhall (1)
107 Nayland (1)
108 Pakefield (1)
109 Polstead (1)
110 Rattlesden (1)
111 Sudbury (1)
112 Ufford (1)
113 Walton (1)
114 Woodbridge (1)

Note: Figures in brackets after place names denote the number of places of worship.

conspicuous by their absence in the more arable Fielding, though some nonconformist centres were in coastal areas like Chelmondiston, Felixstowe and Kessingland.

So much for the distribution of Disssenters. What about their numbers? Here we depend largely on the Compton Census of 1676. The census of the adult [130] religious population covers the province of Canterbury (South England, the Midlands and East Anglia). It was organised by Henry Compton, Bishop of London, at the request of Archbishop Gilbert Sheldon. Each parish is listed under diocese, archdeaconry and deanery, with totals of conformists (who accepted the Established Church), papists and non-conformists. Unfortunately figures for Suffolk are incomplete. None survive for the Archdeaconry of Suffolk, which covers most of East Suffolk. There are only details for the Archdeaconry of Sudbury, which covers West Suffolk, plus the deaneries of Hartismere and Stow and a few parishes in eastern Cambridgeshire. This means that it is not possible to compare Suffolk with other counties. However, the 'remarkably complete' returns for Sudbury archdeaconry are worth examining, since they reveal the composition of the religious population.

Details are given in Table 8.6.

Table 8.6 Religious groups in the Archdeaconry of Sudbury, 1676 [131]

Conformists	40,897 (96.0%)
Papists	247 (0.6%)
Nonconformists	1,463 (3.4%)
Total	42,607 (100.0%)

The immediate reaction to these bald statistics is one of incredulity. While the figures for Papists may have been quite accurate for much of the archdeaconry, those for Dissent are certainly a gross underestimate. There cannot have been just two nonconformist sympathisers in Bradfield St Claire, where the Quakers held a conventicle of '4 or 500' in 1669, nor just five in Rattlesden, where 100 Independents met 'att the house of Mr George Groome' in the same year.[132] So why were so few Dissenters recorded in the Compton Census? There are two possible explanations. One is that the purpose of the census was to show how few non-Anglicans there were. The second reason is that many people who were at heart Dissenters conformed by occasional attendance at the parish church, especially if they were Presbyterians or Independents. These occasional or partial conformists were labelled 'Conformists' in the census.[133] Thus the Non-conformists in the Compton Census only include the hardcore who, like the Popish recusants, never attended the Anglican Church.

The indubitable Dissenters varied in number from place to place, but, as previously stated, they seem to have been strongest in market towns.

Mildenhall had sixty-six Nonconformists, Sudbury about 100, Bury 167 and Clare an astonishing three hundred.[134] Only one rural parish had a *large* number of Dissenters:[135] Wattisfield with forty-nine. However, it is worth emphasising that in all those places, except Clare, the Nonconformists were overwhelmingly outnumbered by the conformists.[136] Nevertheless, the hardline Dissenters were important in Suffolk. As Professor Dickens has said, 'a heterodox congregation of forty people could have deeply influenced religious change in a typical market town with an adult population of only three or four hundred'.[137]

Finally, what was the social structure of Dissent in Suffolk? To attempt an answer we must first examine the survey or Return of Conventicles completed in 1669 on the instructions of Archbishop Sheldon. It covers more or less the whole country and includes a partial return for the diocese of Norwich. Parishes are listed under their respective deaneries: against each parish it records the names of those who hosted the conventicles, the sect or sects by whom they were held, the numbers and 'qualitie' of the Nonconformists meeting in them, and the names of their 'heads and teachers'. We are primarily concerned with the 'Qualitie' or status of the hosts and of those who attended the conventicles. Unfortunately the evidence for Suffolk is limited, but enough exists to warrant three very tentative conclusions. First, the Quakers belonged to the lower orders. The Friends who met at Felsham are described as 'very poore people'. The fifty attending a conventicle at the house of Thomas Tylott in St James parish, Bury, were called 'Inconsiderable'. The '4 or 500' who met 'att the house of one Thomas Rose' in Bradfield St Claire were of 'meane qualitie', while their 'Heads and Teachers' were 'Itinerants and Wanderers'. Second, the Presbyterians were more socially mixed. The conventicle in Rede, where the Presbyterian divine, Francis Crow, preached, consisted 'of the vulgar sort, but some of tolerable Quality'. The '3 or 400' meeting at four houses in Ipswich to hear sermons preached by two Presbyterian ministers[138] comprised 'meane persons, but some few pretty good estates'.[139] The Ipswich Presbyterian 'hearers' would perhaps have included people ranging from wealthy aldermen to 'water doggs' [sailors]. Third, as in Leicestershire, few gentry supported the Dissenters by hosting the conventicles.[140]

The best evidence of gentry support for the Dissenters is to be found among the licences obtained under the Declaration of Indulgence in 1672. In Suffolk at least eighty-four houses were licensed for Nonconformist worship, but only nine (11 per cent) of them were protected by the gentry. Six of these nine gentlemen had Presbyterian sympathies. John Gurdon, Esquire, a strong Puritan-Parliamentarian in the Civil Wars, allowed Rev. Thomas Walker to hold Presbyterian meetings at Assington Hall.[141] Giles Barnardiston, younger brother of Sir Nathaniel, the Suffolk Roundhead leader, had Quaker leanings for a time and in 1670 attended a meeting of Friends at Haverhill.[142] But two years later he apparently switched allegiance and permitted Presbyterian meetings at his house in Clare, which, as we have seen, was a Nonconformist stronghold. The other gentry whose dwellings were licensed for Presbyterian worship were John Clarke of Bury, Edmund Frost of Hunston Hall, Samuel Gibbs of Stoke-by-Nayland and Mistress Moslie of Ousden. Two gentlemen favoured the Congregationalists. George Groome of Rattlesden allowed '100 Independents' to meet at his house in 1669 and again in 1672. John Base of Saxmundham, a former Roundhead official, permitted the Independents to meet in both 1669 and 1672 at his house in Woodbridge, where the minister was Frederick Woodall, headmaster of Woodbridge School. He was described as 'a strict Independent, and zealous for the fifth monarchy'.[143] The last of our nine Dissenting gentry, Samuel Baker, Esquire, lord of the manor of Wattisfield, allowed both Presbyterian and Independent worship in his house in 1669 and again in 1672. In 1676 the Compton Census recorded as many as forty-nine Dissenters in Wattisfield, and their large numbers were almost certainly due to the protection they received from Squire Baker.[144]

However, the support given to the Dissenters by our nine gentry should be seen in perspective. Those Nonconformists formed a mere 1.5 per cent of the 577 Suffolk gentry families living around 1670. Even if we add three families of partial conformists – Barnardiston of Brightwell, Barnardiston

Cockfield Hall, Yoxford
(Drawn and engraved by T. Higham in *Excursions,* II, p. 96)
Cockfield Hall was the main residence of the Brooke family from 1597. Sir Robert rebuilt the central block of the Hall *c.* 1613. He and his son John were both passive Parliamentarians, but strong Puritans, during the Civil Wars. After the Restoration the Brookes were outwardly loyal to the Church of England, yet employed Nonconformist chaplains in their household.

of Kedington and Brooke of Cockfield Hall [145] – and call them Dissenters, the Protestant Nonconformist gentry would still form only a tiny minority of Suffolk families: twelve (2.0 per cent) out of 577.[146] Contrast this with the situation in the Civil War period when Puritan families numbered over 100 and formed nearly 15 per cent of the Suffolk gentry.[147] It would therefore appear that the post-Restoration period in Suffolk, as in Warwickshire, 'saw a dramatic defection of landed society from "Puritanism" or noncon- formity'.[148] Indeed, the loss of upper class support by radical Protestants seems to have been a European phenomenon during the seventeenth century.[149]

The Roman Catholics

Having dealt with the Protestant Dissenters, let us now consider the other imagined threat to government and society, the Roman Catholics. How many Catholics were there in Suffolk in Charles II's reign? As we have seen, the Compton Census of 1676 revealed only 247 Papists in the Archdeaconry of Sudbury, that is a mere 0.6 per cent of the religious population.[150] We have no figures for the Archdeaconry of Suffolk, but numbers are most unlikely to have been higher because of the strong Protestant tradition in the region. The numbers of recorded Papists varied not just from place to place but from year to year. Roman Catholics were ignored or persecuted at intervals as the public mood oscillated and this is reflected in the recusant rolls.[151] Between the death of Charles I in 1649 and of his son in 1685 there were three years in particular when persecution was severe and when the authorities made a determined effort to organise a full count of Catholic recusants: 1657, 1664 and 1679. At first sight it is surprising that the 1657 recusant roll records many Catholics because this was during Oliver Cromwell's rule, which is usually associated with *de facto* toleration of English (though not of Irish) Catholics. However, war with Spain caused great fear of England's 'Spaniolized' Catholic subjects and Parliament persuaded Cromwell to enforce the recusancy laws to the full. In 1664 harsh persecution in Suffolk, though not apparently elsewhere, was caused by the appointment of Sir Robert Hyde as the Assize judge. He was the first cousin of Edward Hyde, Earl of Clarendon, whose whole policy was opposed to the toleration of Papists. 1679 was of course the year after the Popish Plot when anti-Catholic feeling had seldom been fiercer. Consequently the numbers of indicted recusants increased. The numbers of Suffolk Catholic recusants indicted by the Exchequer were as follows: 187 in 1657, 115 in 1664 and 130 in 1679.

   Yet these numbers are not large. So why was anti-Popery so pronounced? There are several reasons. As Dr Seward says, 'seventeenth century English- men … were brought up on a diet of Foxe's *Acts and Monuments*, on stories of popish massacres of protestants in Paris in 1572 and in Ireland in 1641, of the Gunpowder Plot and deliverance from the Spanish Armada'.[152] Later in the 1670s there was intense fear of Catholic France – the leading power in Europe – and growing anxiety that Catholicism and absolutism might be imposed on England from overseas. Fear of Papists was strengthened when Charles II's brother, James, Duke of York, converted to Roman Catholicism in 1669. The Popish Plot of 1678 simply brought hatred of Catholics to a head. What also caused fear of Catholics was the fact that they were led and dominated by the gentry, who were arguably the most important social group in seventeenth-century England. A social analysis of recusants in 1657, 1664 and 1679 shows how important the gentry were to the Catholic cause. Details are in Table 8.7.

Table 8.7 Suffolk Catholic recusants in the later seventeenth century: A social analysis[153]

Status or Occupation	1657	1664	1679
Gentry	49 (26%)	21 (18%)	59 (45%)
Professionals	1 (0%)	–	–
Traders and Craftsmen	9 (5%)	–	2 (2%)
Yeomen	7 (4%)	70 (61%)	52 (40%)
Husbandmen	3 (2%)	–	–
Labourers and Servants	14 (7%)	1 (1%)	–
Others	29 (16%)	20 (17%)	2 (2%)
Unknown	75 (40%)	3 (2%)	15 (11%)
Total	187 (100%)	115 (100%)	130 (100%)
	(104 women,[154]	(67 women,	(37 women,
	i.e. 56%)	i.e. 58%)	i.e. 28%)

Table 8.7 shows that, except for the unknowns in 1657 and the yeomen in 1664, the gentry were the largest single group. Certainly the proportion of gentry in the Catholic recusant community was considerably larger than the proportion of gentry in the population at large. The gentry formed 2.5 per cent of the total population of Suffolk in 1657, and 2.0 per cent in both 1664 and 1679.[155] But the gentry comprised 26 per cent of the recusant population in 1657, 18 per cent in 1664 and 45 per cent in 1679. Moreover, the Catholic gentry had the advantage of wealth as well as numbers. Some of the better known Catholic gentry families were rich in lands or houses,[156] and this may have exacerbated the fear of Papists. Examples of rich Catholic gentry are given in Table 8.8.

So as in pre-Civil War days, Roman Catholicism in Suffolk was still essentially seigneurial. Another county where seigneurial Catholicism prevailed was Kent. In fact Suffolk and Kent contrasted sharply with the West Midlands and Lancashire where Catholicism was much more plebeian, as the statistics in Table 8.9 show.

Table 8.8 The wealth of some Catholic gentry in Charles II's reign

Family	Annual income from land[157] £	No. of hearths in main residence[158]
Gage of Hengrave	2,000	51
Mannock of Giffords Hall	1,500	27
Martin of Long Melford	1,500	?
Sulyard of Haughley	1,200	23
Tasburgh of Flixton	1,400	24
Warner of Parham	1,000	?

Table 8.9 Gentry and Plebeian Catholics, 1678–82[159]

Status	Suffolk (1679)	Kent (1678)	Staffs. (c. 1680)	Derbys. (1682)	Lancs. (1678–79)
Gentry	59 (45%)	45 (31%)	76 (11%)	14 (3%)	300 (5%)
Plebeians	71 (55%)	103 (69%)	621 (89%)	477 (97%)	5,482 (95%)
Total	130 (100%)	148 (100%)	697 (100%)	491 (100%)	5,782 (100%)

Especially in Lancashire, or at least western Lancashire, Catholicism was a religion of the people.[160] But in Suffolk it was the opposite, except perhaps in Wetherden.

Wetherden was the only Catholic community in Suffolk where popular Catholicism apparently prevailed. The Compton Census recorded eighteen Papists in 1676 but there was no Catholic gentleman in the parish to offer leadership or protection. In this respect Wetherden contrasted with Eye, Stanningfield, Long Melford and Bury St Edmunds. In Eye there were seventeen Catholics headed by the gentleman-surgeon, Thomas Hinchlow. There were sixteen in the parish of Stanningfield, home of the Rookwoods (of Gunpowder Plot fame) since the reign of Edward I.[161] There were thirty Papists in Long Melford, where three Catholic gentry families resided: the Harrisons, the Hinchlows and, above all, the Martins. The largest concentration of Catholics was at Bury, the Compton Census recording forty Papists in the town.[162]

Bury St Edmunds became the spiritual capital of Suffolk Catholicism during the reign of Charles II, despite the large number of Protestant Dissenters in the town. After the Restoration Bury seems to have become the headquarters of a Jesuit college. A Catholic chapel visited by large numbers of the townsfolk was established in the Abbey ruins, where the superior of the College also had his house. The Jesuits were also able to open a school in the town for both boarders and day boys.[163] As Bury was a town with 5,500 inhabitants in about 1670 [164] it might be thought that gentry influence would have been negligible, but not so. The leaders of the Bury Catholics were not just merchants and doctors but members of the landed gentry, like Ambrose Rookwood of Stanningfield, Esquire, and Sir

Edward Gage of Hengrave, Baronet, both of whom had town houses as well as country estates.[165] It would perhaps be true to say that Catholics in urban Bury were as much under gentry domination as Catholics in rural Suffolk.

So much for the Catholics of Bury. What about the other Suffolk Catholics? Joy Rowe is correct to say that they were 'scattered about the countryside around the houses of known Catholic gentry'. Map 17 shows the names and main residences of the thirty-one Catholic gentry families of Suffolk just after the Popish Plot.[166] They were, as Rowe observes, located 'especially in the villages of High Suffolk and along the Norfolk border'.[167] The map also shows that, as in pre-Civil War days, many parts of Suffolk were untouched, or barely touched, by Catholic recusancy. These included Risbridge hundred, most of Blackbourne and Lackford hundreds, and the Sandlings. Except for Risbridge, these were predominantly sheep-corn areas which some historians consider were religiously conservative.[168] But in Suffolk the opposite was the case. It was in the wood-pasture region of High Suffolk that Roman Catholicism found most of its support.

Mrs Rowe has commented on 'the perdurable character of Suffolk recusancy'.[169] This was undoubtedly due to the example set by the gentry. Families such as Bedingfield of Redlingfield, Daniel of Acton, Mannock of Gifford's Hall, Martin of Long Melford, Rookwood of Coldham Hall in Stanningfield, Rous of Badingham, Sulyard of Haughley Park, Timperley of Hintlesham and Yaxley of Yaxley crop up again and again in the records throughout the Elizabethan and Stuart periods, which suggests that they took their religion very seriously and refused to be reconciled to Protestantism. They were the most active of the activists. It is not surprising, then, that the Catholic gentry gave much spiritual support to their faith. It was thanks largely to the gentry that the Catholic Church in Suffolk was provided with mass centres, priests and nuns.

Mrs Rowe's map, in *An Historical Atlas of Suffolk*, shows the mass centres of the county, including those functioning in the later seventeenth century.[170] There were thirteen such centres and all but one – Wetherden – were provided by the gentry. Mass centres were, of course, extremely important because the mass was the touchstone of the Roman Catholic faith. Moreover, these mass centres 'kept many of the less well-to-do Catholics close to the faith'.[171]

Twenty Suffolk men were ordained Catholic priests, or took their professions as regular clergy, between 1643 and 1685. Of those twenty, at least twelve (60 per cent) were of gentry origins. All the twelve gentry priests joined religious orders, except John Sulyard of Haughley Park, ordained as a secular in 1658.[172] One gentleman – Sir Edward Golding, Baronet, – made his profession as a Capuchin friar in 1655.[173] Three gentlemen – Francis Rookwood of Coldham Hall, Richard Tasburgh of Flixton Hall and Henry Timperley of Hintlesham – made their professions as Benedictines in 1680,

Map 17: Roman Catholic Recusant Gentry Families of Suffolk in 1679–80

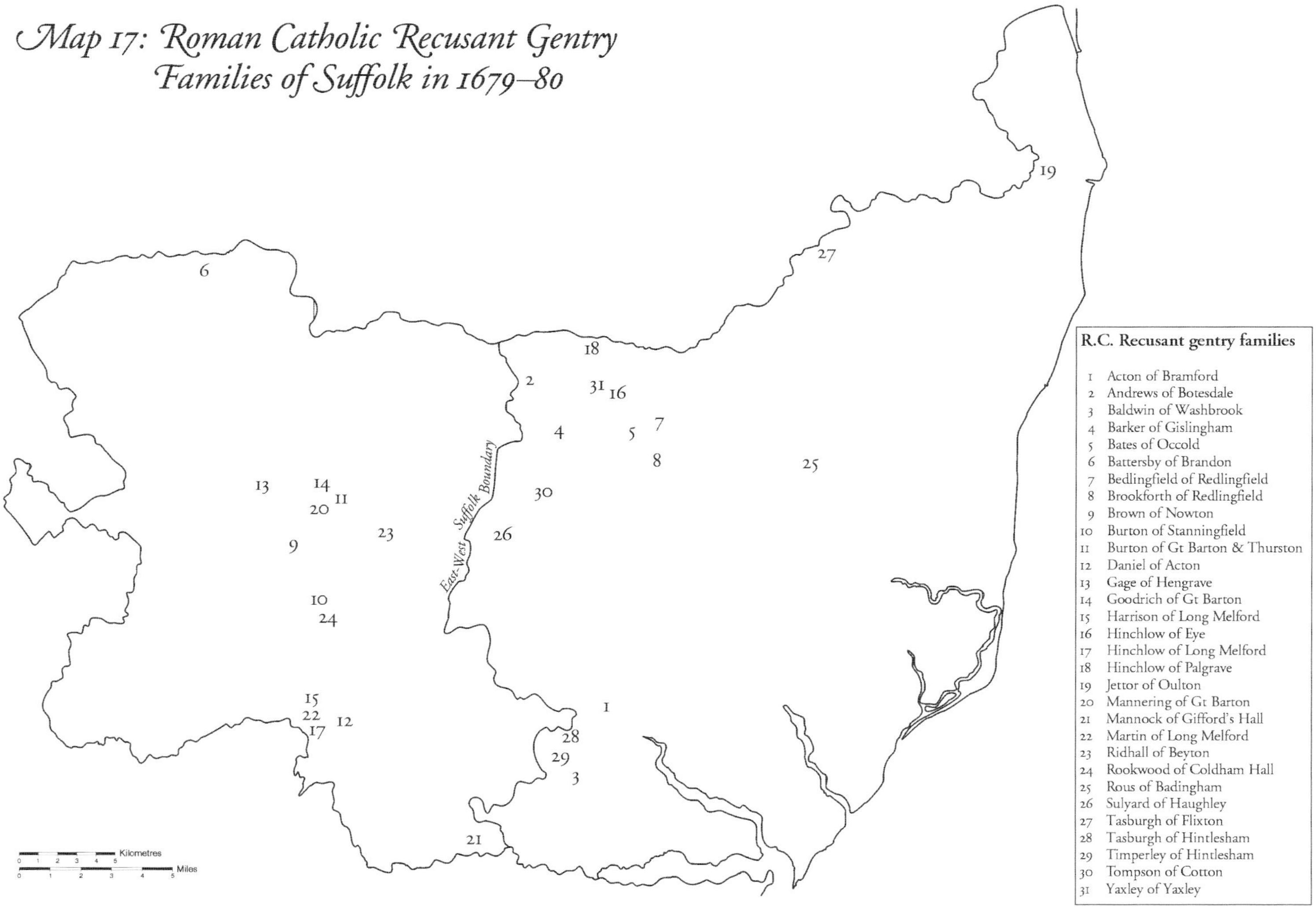
R.C. Recusant gentry families
1 Acton of Bramford
2 Andrews of Botesdale
3 Baldwin of Washbrook
4 Barker of Gislingham
5 Bates of Occold
6 Battersby of Brandon
7 Bedlingfield of Redlingfield
8 Brookforth of Redlingfield
9 Brown of Nowton
10 Burton of Stanningfield
11 Burton of Gt Barton & Thurston
12 Daniel of Acton
13 Gage of Hengrave
14 Goodrich of Gt Barton
15 Harrison of Long Melford
16 Hinchlow of Eye
17 Hinchlow of Long Melford
18 Hinchlow of Palgrave
19 Jettor of Oulton
20 Mannering of Gt Barton
21 Mannock of Gifford's Hall
22 Martin of Long Melford
23 Ridhall of Beyton
24 Rookwood of Coldham Hall
25 Rous of Badingham
26 Sulyard of Haughley
27 Tasburgh of Flixton
28 Tasburgh of Hintlesham
29 Timperley of Hintlesham
30 Tompson of Cotton
31 Yaxley of Yaxley
East-West Suffolk Boundary
Kilometres
Miles

1682 and 1677 respectively.[174] The other gentry priests became Jesuits. One – Henry Rookwood of Coldham Hall – was professed in 1681, while the rest were ordained: Michael Foster of Copdock (in 1667), John Gage of Hengrave (1679), Henry and John Martin of Long Melford (1672), Henry Tasburgh of Flixton (1671) and Sir John Warner of Parham, Baronet (1670).[175]

These priests came from well-known Suffolk Catholic families, except Sir John Warner. But he is the most interesting of all. Sir John's father, Captain Francis Warner of Framlingham, had been a Royalist in the First Civil War, but a strong Anglican. So it must have come as rather a shock to the Warner family when both Sir John and his wife, Lady Trevor, converted to Roman Catholicism in 1664 and mutually agreed to separate and enter religious orders. In 1665 Sir John made his profession as a Jesuit and was ordained priest in 1670. He seems to have had a successful religious career. In 1680 and 1683 he was in Paris acting as Procurator of the Province.[176] Meanwhile his former wife joined the English Poor Clares at Gravelines but died in 1670, three years after making her 'holy Profession'. Her obituary notice described her as 'a Lady of quality' with a 'husband and Children, whom she dearly loved, with other worldly advantages' who had 'left all to hear Gods call in a poor and humble Religious State of Life'.[177]

Lady Warner was just one of seventeen Suffolk women who became choir nuns in continental convents between 1643 and 1685. All but two of those women were from gentry families, that is 88 per cent. Four Suffolk gentlewomen joined the most famous religious order, the Benedictines. Three – Mary Bedingfield of Redlingfield (professed in 1646), Ann and Placida Foster of Copdock (1655) – became nuns in Brussels, and the fourth – Margaret Timperley of Hintlesham (1660) – was a nun in Pontoise.[178] Apart from the above named Trevor Warner of Parham, two ladies were attracted to the Poor Clares at Gravelines: Frances Rookwood of Coldham Hall (professed in 1646) and Sir John Warner's sister, Elizabeth (1667).[179] Four gentlewomen became 'English Canonesses of the Holy Sepulchre of Liège': Elizabeth and Dorothy Daniel of Acton (professed in 1649 and 1650 respectively), and Mary and Margaret Foster of Copdock (1652, 1653).[180] Only one Suffolk lady became a nun at St Ursula's convent in Louvain: Mary Tasburgh of Flixton, professed in 1684.[181] But three ladies became 'Blue Nuns' at Paris: Margery Mannock of Gifford's Hall (professed in 1671) and Frances (1661) and Elizabeth Timperley of Hintlesham.[182] The latter was the most successful of our seventeen nuns. She took her vows as a Franciscan nun at Nieuport in 1654, helped establish the 'Blue Nuns' at Paris in 1658 and just three years later was elected Abbess, a position she held for twenty years.[183]

The gentry nuns, like the gentry priests, with one or two exceptions, came from the most well-known Catholic families of Suffolk. Moreover, the number of women taking the veil had increased slightly since pre-Civil

Hintlesham Hall
(Engraved by J. Webb from a drawing by T. Higham in *Excursions*, I, p. 144).
The original Hintlesham Hall was built by the Catholic Timperleys in the 1570s. But the
family fell on hard times and in 1720 Hintlesham manor was sold to Richard Powys. He
rebuilt the Hall *c.* 1725 in the Georgian style, as the picture shows. But while the façade
is early Georgian, the house behind it is Elizabethan.

War days. On the other hand, far fewer gentlemen's sons were entering
the priesthood. Was this because of greater persecution? This was most
unlikely. For one reason persecution, whether official or unofficial, was
intermittent. Roman Catholics did not live in constant fear of ill-treatment.
There was very little unofficial persecution in the form of Protestant mob
violence. During the Stour Valley riots along the Suffolk-Essex border in
1642 a number of Catholic landlords had found themselves under physical
attack from anti-Papist mobs.[184] But under Charles II the Catholic gentry
in Suffolk do not seem to have been victims of serious or major anti-Popish
disturbances. Officially, Catholics could be fined or sequestered for their
religion and, if priests, could face the death penalty. In short, recusancy
was a criminal offence. But in practice few Suffolk Catholic gentlemen
suffered financial penalties in the later seventeenth century. A notable
exception was the Timperley family of Hintlesham. 'They were more than
once convicted as recusants, with the usual penalty of sequestration of
two-thirds of the family estate'.[185] The Hintlesham lands were encumbered
with many mortgages from 1668 to 1720 when the patrimonial estate had
to be sold. Yet it has been doubted whether this and other, earlier, sales
were caused solely by the financial penalties resulting from recusancy. Other
causes of the indebtedness of the Timperleys seem to have been generous

allowances to members of the family and to Catholic convents abroad, plus a predilection for building alterations.[186]

If Suffolk Catholics were not frightened by anti-Popish riots nor bankrupted by recusancy fines or sequestrations, surely they were persecuted at the time of the Popish Plot, when fear of Popery reached panic proportions? Once again they were apparently more leniently treated than their co-religionists in many other counties. This is suggested by the fact that only four Suffolk gentry families took refuge abroad temporarily for their own safety. On 12 December 1678 William Gage of Hengrave, his wife, three other persons and fifteen servants obtained a pass from the Secretary of State to go to 'parts beyond the seas'. Others obtaining similar passes in the winter of 1678–79 were Sir Roger Martin of Long Melford, his wife, Dame Tamworth, and three servants; Ambrose Rookwood of Coldham Hall, his wife, five children and two servants; and William Mannock of Gifford's Hall, his wife, two children and two servants.[187] The Popish Plot produced not only refugees but also a large prison population. But on 15 January 1685 a warrant of pardon was issued to about 730 named recusants.[188] Only two of the released prisoners were Suffolk men: Edward Rous of Horham (Gentleman?) and Henry Jermyn of Rushbrooke, Esquire.[189] Between 1678 and 1681 eighteen Catholic priests were executed,[190] but not one was from Suffolk. However, Suffolk did produce one martyr, Edward Coleman.

Coleman, a layman, was one of twenty Catholics martyred for their faith after the Popish Plot, and the first to be hanged, drawn and quartered.[191] He was the son of a Suffolk Anglican clergyman. He went to Trinity College, Cambridge, where he took his BA degree in 1656. He almost certainly spent some time abroad between then and 1670, when he reappears as Secretary to James, Duke of York, and a fanatical Roman Catholic. He was implicated as the main conspirator in the Popish Plot. He was tried and convicted on the evidence of Titus Oates and William Bedloe. Coleman was finally put to death at Tyburn and his dying speech is very revealing. He frankly and proudly admitted his Roman Catholicism. 'I thank God I am of it, and declare I die of it'. But he denied that he was politically seditious. He had never intended to subvert the government, and stir up the people to rebellion. 'But though I am ... a *Roman* Catholic ... yet I renounce that doctrine that Kings may be murdered and the like; I say I abominate it'. Speeches from the scaffold were often repentant, but there seems little reason to doubt the sincerity of Coleman when he declared that his Roman Catholic religion was not 'prejudicial to King or government'.[192] Coleman undoubtedly spoke for the overwhelming majority of Suffolk, and indeed of English, Catholics.

Finally, we must ask why persecution of Suffolk Roman Catholics was so limited. Four very tentative suggestions can perhaps be made. First, Catholics were so few in most parts of the county that the local justices did not consider them a serious threat. Hence in most years they were left undisturbed. In Devon, too, Catholics were very few (only 230 in 1676) and in that county 'the degree of persecution does not appear great', even though 'Catholics were generally so unpopular'.[193] Second, Suffolk Catholics were dominated but also protected by the gentry. We have seen that most plebeian Catholics were huddled round the houses of their social superiors. Third, the Catholic gentry, while protecting their plebeian co-religionists, did not constitute a serious threat to the state because their numbers were so small. The recusant rolls show that many Catholics were gentry. But few gentry were Catholics. Of the 577 Suffolk gentry families living around 1670, only thirty-one (5 per cent) were popish recusants. Contrast Lancashire where in 1642 29 per cent of gentry families were Roman Catholics.[194] Fourth, Suffolk Catholics were quiescent and did not invite persecution. As Dr Spurr has said, 'the Roman Catholic community was introspective, gentry dominated and politically loyal'.[195] Although Spurr is referring to *English* Catholics, his remarks aptly apply to Suffolk Papists.

Conclusion

Let us summarise the evidence concerning the gentry, the Dissenters and the Papists in Charles II's reign. Shortly after the Restoration Charles rewarded both the Parliamentarian and Royalist gentry of Suffolk. Both received titles. Neither obtained much bounty. Nine Royalists acquired paid offices, but only one Parliamentarian did. Yet the Parliamentarians had a greater share of unpaid local government positions. On balance ex-Royalists had limited rewards and limited power, while ex-Parliamentarians had reason to be satisfied. Between the outbreak of the Civil War and the Restoration unexpected social changes took place in Suffolk. Many new gentry families of plebeian or non-local origins emerged but most were not ex-Parliamentarians nor ex-Republicans but ex-Neutrals/Unknowns. About one-third of the Royalist gentry families disappeared into social oblivion. But so did the same proportion of the Parliamentarian gentry. Among the perdurable gentry, the Royalists were wealthier than the Parliamentarians. Yet the Cavaliers feared social and economic decline and felt threatened by the Dissenters.

The Protestant Dissenters in Suffolk were persecuted under the so-called Clarendon Code. More Puritan ministers were ejected from the Church of England in Suffolk than in most English counties. But once ejected, they did not suffer excessively, partly because of the sympathetic attitude of Bishop Reynolds of Norwich. Barely one-quarter of the ejected clergy were persecuted after deprivation, and such persecution was occasional rather than continuous. But if persecution of Presbyterian and Independent clergy was intermittent, harassment of Quakers was much more frequent and harsh, despite their increasingly pacifist outlook. As regards geographical distribution, Dissenters as a whole found much support in market towns and in wood-pasture regions. But numbers are difficult to establish partly because some Dissenters were partial conformists. Socially the Dissenters differed among themselves. Quakers were lower class, Presbyterians socially mixed. The Dissenters as a whole had very little gentry support, unlike the Puritans in the Civil War period.

The Roman Catholics in Suffolk are difficult to enumerate, but they were certainly infinitesimal compared with their brethren in Lancashire. Socially Suffolk Catholicism was essentially seigneurial; it depended heavily on the leadership and protection of the gentry, some of whom were wealthy. Unlike Lancashire, Suffolk had little popular Catholicism. Some Catholics lived in Bury St Edmunds but most were scattered about the countryside around the houses of known Catholic gentry. It is impossible to over-emphasize the part played by the gentry in the history of Suffolk Catholicism.

Indeed, the Catholic gentry ensured the very survival of the Catholic Church in Suffolk by providing it with mass centres, priests and nuns. There was little harsh persecution of Papists in the county, even at the time of the Popish Plot. Only one Suffolk Catholic, Edward Coleman, was martyred. The reasons for the limited persecution of Catholics seem to have been their small numbers, their upper class support and protection, and their essentially quiescent character.

CHAPTER NINE

Suffolk and 'the Glorious Revolution'

The Revolution of 1688–89, popularly known as 'The Glorious Revolution', is one of the most controversial subjects in British history. Scholars disagree as to its nature and importance. G. M. Trevelyan considered that the 1688 Revolution, and the decade that followed, saw the defeat of absolute monarchy, the balance between parliament and regal power decided in favour of Parliament, the granting of religious toleration to Protestant Dissenters, the ending of press censorship, and the establishment of an independent judiciary and the rule of law.[1] Eminent modern historians, such as J. R. Jones and W. A. Speck, broadly agree with Trevelyan's arguments.[2] But some scholars, such as Jonathan Clark, have denigrated the revolution, arguing that it brought few benefits, especially to the Roman Catholics, Scots and Irish, and that under the Hanoverians England remained essentially an *ancien régime.*[3]

So much for the nature of the so-called 'Glorious Revolution'. What about its importance? Here again modern scholars disagree. Blair Worden has remarked that 'in the history of the British Isles no event has been more decisive than the Revolution of 1688'.[4] This seems rather a sweeping statement. Other major events in British history were surely more decisive than the 'Glorious Revolution' (e.g. the Norman Conquest, the Reformation, the Industrial Revolution). But even if we confine ourselves to the seventeenth century not all historians would agree with Dr Worden. Professor Lawrence Stone has described the period from 1640 to 1660 as the years of 'England's only "Great Revolution".'[5] Dr Christopher Hill has emphasised that the 'Glorious Revolution' of 1688–89 was a mere *coup d'état,* and that the real revolution occurred during the 1640s and 1650s, which saw 'the execution of Charles I, the abolition of bishops and the House of Lords, the existence of an English Republic'. The world was never the same again. The restoration of the monarchy in 1660 was not a restoration of the old order, 'only its trappings'. The 1640s and 1650s 'marked the end of medieval and Tudor England'. Absolute monarchy 'had been abolished'.[6] Angus McInnes, however, profoundly disagrees. In an article entitled 'When was the English Revolution?', he answered emphatically – in 1688 and the following decade.[7] Despite all the legislation of the Long Parliament in 1640–42 and the subsequent establishment of a republic, the monarchy of Charles II was restored virtually unconditionally in 1660 and during the 1680s, especially under James II, 'England was fast approaching the condition of an absolute monarchy'.[8] Fortunately, the 'Glorious Revolution' of 1688 saved England from this fate. Here McInnes agrees with G. M. Trevelyan.

So which was the more important revolution? Christopher Hill's English Revolution of 1640–60, or Trevelyan's English Revolution of 1688–89? The answer is that *both* were important. Stuart Prall argues that 'the great divide between early and modern England is not 1640 or 1660 or even 1688. The divide is the first half-century from 1640 to 1689 ... The seventeenth century was indeed "a century of revolution".'[9] The roots of the 'Glorious Revolution' lay in the conflicts of the reign of Charles I which culminated in the Civil Wars, the execution of the King and the Interregnum, but which remained unresolved when the monarchy was restored in 1660. In constitutional terms the central issue was – where did ultimate power lie, with crown or Parliament? Or if sovereignty was to be shared between the two, what should be the balance of power?

Previous chapters have dealt with the conflicts of the 1640s, 1650s and Charles II's reign. So what happened under James II? What happened during and after the 'Glorious Revolution'? Let us deal with the causes, course and consequences of the Revolution of 1688–89 as they affected Suffolk.

The causes of the Revolution

Contrary to popular belief, James II had no conscious plan to impose 'Popery and arbitrary government'. His prime aim was religious toleration.[10] He desired to grant freedom of worship and civil rights to his Catholic co-religionists and, more arguably, to Protestant Dissenters.[11] James believed, naïvely no doubt, that once Papists were relieved of religious and civil disabilities, and appointed to public offices, there would be a mass return by his subjects to the Roman Catholic faith. Nothing was more unlikely. James 'failed totally to realise the strength and the depth of the English anti-Catholic tradition'.[12] Opposition to his policies – especially religious toleration for Roman Catholics – drove James to an unexpectedly fuller use of his prerogative powers than he had originally intended. He strengthened royal power in a number of respects. He increased the size of the standing army and systematically remodelled the institutions of local government, the commissions of the peace and the borough corporations, making them subservient to the royal will. The expansion of the royal army and the appointment of Catholic officers are of little importance in the history of Suffolk. But the policy of remodelling the commissions of the peace and the borough corporations had some effect on the county.

In 1660 the King's control over the appointment of county officials was restored. Charles II and, even more so, James II used their powers of dismissal to the full. Lionel Glassey has said that 'massive changes [were] made in the commissions of the peace in 1687 and especially in 1688'.[13] Many of the Anglican Justices of the Peace were dismissed and replaced by some Protestant Dissenters and by large numbers of Roman Catholics. Several of the latter were of lesser status than those they replaced.[14] Undoubtedly Catholics obtained a higher proportion of offices than their numbers in the population justified. Professor John Miller has demonstrated that by 1688, of 1,174 JPs and deputy lieutenants in all but five counties in England and Wales, at least 410 (24 per cent) were Catholics. Yet Papists comprised little over 1 per cent of the total population of England and only 7 per cent of the English gentry,[15] the class which provided the bulk of the commissioners of the peace. Unfortunately Miller found no lists of JPs and deputy Lieutenants for Suffolk during the years 1686–88.[16]

Miller and Glassey relied on lists of *nominated* JPs. If they had been able to use the Suffolk Quarter Sessions Order Books they would have discovered the names of the *acting* justices.[17] However, there are not many of these. Only fifty-three gentry served as magistrates at some time or other between 1686 and 1688. At most only seven were definitely or possibly removed from the commission of the peace : Sir Thomas Allin of Somerleyton, Sir Nicholas Bacon of Shrubland Hall, Edmund Bohun of Westhall, John Cornwallis of Wingfield, John Risby (of Bury St Edmunds?), Sir Thomas Smyth of Sutton and Edmund Tyrrell of Gipping.[18] It is difficult to know why these men were singled out. But Edmund Bohun could hardly have endeared himself to James II, since he was equally averse to Dissenters and Roman Catholics. 'As for Popery', he remarked, 'I have so great an aversion for it that I never willingly conversed with one of that religion: and if God permits me to choose my company, I never will'.[19] James II replaced the seven dismissed JPs with no Dissenters and only four Roman Catholics: Sir William Mannock of Gifford's Hall, Ambrose Rookwood of Stanningfield, Edward Sulyard of Haughley and Richard Tasburgh of Flixton.[20] These four gentlemen of ancient families formed only 8 per cent of the fifty men who made up the Suffolk Bench in 1688. Suffolk greatly differed from Lancashire where Catholics formed 55 per cent of the magistrates in 1688, and even more from Monmouthshire where they comprised 70 per cent. Suffolk was in fact one of those few English counties whose commission of the peace was hardly changed in the religious sense. Only Cambridgeshire, Cornwall, Devon, the Isle of Ely, Shropshire, Surrey and the West Riding of Yorkshire recorded smaller percentages of Catholic justices.[21] Perhaps these counties, plus Suffolk, had few Catholic JPs because they had small Catholic populations.

So much for the shires. What about the boroughs? These were dependent for their rights and privileges upon royal charters granted to them at some date in the past. After the overthrow of Shaftesbury and the Whigs in 1681 Charles II, and after him his brother James II, began systematically to call in these old charters. In their place they issued new charters which gave the King the power to nominate the governing bodies of the remodelled corporations and to remove members he found unacceptable. Under James II many Anglican-Tory corporation members were replaced by Catholics or Dissenters, several of the latter being of more obscure social origins than the officials they replaced. There was indeed a massive increase in royal influence in the boroughs. But as Angus McInnes reminds us, 'even more important were the political implications of the remodelling'. Around four-fifths of all English Members of Parliament sat for borough constituencies. 'Hence the crown's tightening hold on the municipalities meant that the King's chances of getting a compliant House of Commons were consider-ably enhanced'.[22] Obviously if the crown could change the political complexion of borough governments, it could increase its chances of packing Parliament with 'yes men'. James, of course, wanted to pack Parliament so that it would repeal the Test Acts and the penal laws by statute, thus establishing a clear legal basis for the civil and religious liberties of Catholics and Dissenters. One of the boroughs to be remodelled by James II was Bury St Edmunds, whose experiences have been so well documented by Dr Pat Murrell.[23]

Bury St Edmunds was a royally incorporated parliamentary borough and one of only nineteen towns whose franchise was vested solely in the mayor, twelve aldermen and twenty-four common councillors. Thus the clauses inserted in the town's charter by Charles II, making provision for the crown to displace corporation personnel, gave James II the opportunity to regulate directly the composition and character of its entire voting force. The local governing body was hostile to the King's religious and political aims in 1687 and the borough presented him with the model situation in which to operate his policy of 'regulation'. He succeeded in his attempt and purged the corporation three times in 1688 (16 March, 14 May, 18 Septem-ber) until eventually Bury had an entirely new governing body, that is, an entirely new electorate. James had made a clean sweep. The religious complexion of the 'Royal Substitutes', which Dr Murrell calls the new Corporation of Bury in 1688, was as shown in Table 9.1.

Table 9.1 Religious composition of the remodelled
Bury St Edmunds corporation in 1688[24]

Roman Catholics	5 (14%)
Presbyterians	2 (5%)
Independents/Congregationalists	5 (14%)
Quaker	1 (3%)
Others	23 (64%)
Total	36 (100%)

The five Catholics appointed were John Stafford, mayor and silk mer-chant; Ambrose Rookwood of Stanningfield, Esquire; Thomas and Richard Short, both doctors; and Henry Audley, an Essex gentleman with lands in Suffolk. Not one was of humble social origins. The eight Dissenters, however, were more socially obscure and no information can be recovered about them. It is worth noting that about two-thirds of the new councillors were neither Roman Catholics nor Dissenters. Whether the twenty-three 'Others' were practising Anglicans is hard to say; more likely they were opportunists or men who, through indifference or conviction, accepted James II's policy of religious toleration.

The political fortunes of Bury St Edmunds corporation are of more than local significance. Professor Jones has said that 'the campaign to pack Parliament itself was easily the most important is provoking the Revolution, more resented and feared even than the attack on the Church and its leaders'.[25] Yet one wonders whether it was more resented than James II's attack on the Church of England.

James aroused considerable resentment among Anglicans by his Declar-ations of Indulgence in 1687 and 1688. These declarations suspended the penal laws against Roman Catholics and Dissenters, allowing them freedom of worship and civil rights. Lawyers condemned the use of the suspending power as unconstitutional since it restricted the legislative power of Parliament. But it was perhaps mainly for religious reasons that the Declarations were opposed. James ordered the Second Declaration of April 1688 to be read from the pulpits. Many Anglican clergy refused, while the bishops openly denounced the Declaration. Eventually seven of them were arrested for 'seditious libel',[26] imprisoned in the Tower of London and tried before the Court of King's Bench. The accused said that the King had exceeded the bounds of his prerogative and that to read the Declaration would make them parties to an illegal act. On 29 June the jury acquitted the Seven Bishops to tumultuous applause, so strong was anti-Catholic feeling. The most famous of the seven recalcitrant bishops was William Sancroft, Archbishop of Canterbury, a native of Suffolk.[27] But more about him later.

Shortly before the acquittal of the Seven Bishops a son was born to the King's second wife, Mary of Modena. There was now fear of an unending Catholic dynasty, which would endanger Protestantism. This was not the least important reason for the famous Invitation of 30 June 1688. Seven leading Whigs and Tories invited William of Orange to come over and defend English liberty and the Protestant religion.[28]

The course of the Revolution
The national background

It is hardly necessary to give a full detailed account of the events of the Revolution of 1688–89. But a brief summary of the main constitutional and religious settlements seems in order.

The constitutional settlement

As Lionel Glassey reminds us, 'religion was not the all-important feature of the Revolution of 1688 ... Contemporaries bracketed together "Popery and arbitrary government".'[29] The Bill of Rights, 1689, was an attempt to prevent William III and Mary II from establishing arbitrary government. The Bill declared illegal the use of the suspending power and the dispensing power 'as it hath been exercised of late'. The levying of money and the maintenance of a standing army in peacetime without consent of Parliament were also declared illegal. Also Parliament was to be freely elected,[30] to have the right of free debate and to meet frequently. The emphasis on Parliament is obvious and it is clear that new constitutional arrangements shifted the balance away from the crown and towards Parliament. But fear of Popery was also evident in the Bill of Rights. To prevent the Establishment of a Catholic dynasty, the Bill declared that Roman Catholics, or those marrying the same, were to be excluded from the throne. Indeed, since 1689 every British monarch has been a Protestant.

The religious settlement

The most important piece of legislation was, of course, the Toleration Act, 1689. This guaranteed individual liberty in the spiritual sphere just as the Bill of Rights did in the temporal. The act allowed Protestant Nonconformists to worship in their own meeting houses, provided these had been licensed by a JP. The beneficiaries were the Presbyterians, Independents, Particular Baptists, General Baptists and Quakers. However, freedom of worship did not officially extend to Roman Catholics, deists, atheists, Jews and Unitarians.[31] The toleration allowed was indeed limited, even for Protestant Dissenters. The latter could not hold public office nor become MPs. This only became possible in 1828 when the Corporation and Test Acts were repealed. Moreover, it was not until 1871 that Dissenters could enter Oxford and Cambridge on the same terms as Anglicans. In short, Dissenters, though allowed to worship freely, had no civil rights and remained second class citizens until the nineteenth century. Indeed, the Declarations of Indulgence issued by James II in 1687 and 1688 were far more generous than the Toleration Act of 1689. They granted freedom of worship *and* civil rights to Dissenters and Roman Catholics alike. However, let us not play down the significance of the Toleration Act. The fact is that most, though not all, Dissenters preferred limited toleration by Act of Parliament to full toleration by royal prerogative.[32] Toleration based on the King's will could be reversed if he changed his mind, as Charles II had shown in 1673. But statute denoted security and legality, whereas royal proclamation spelt uncertainty and doubtful legality. Furthermore, it is wrong to judge the Toleration Act by twentieth-century standards. In 1689 it was ahead of its time. French Huguenots had been severely persecuted by Louis XIV's government in the early 1680s and later must have envied the religious liberty enjoyed by English Dissenters.

The situation in Suffolk

The 'Glorious Revolution' was undoubtedly a watershed in national politics and religion. But how much support did it enjoy in the provinces? Probably quite a lot. In eastern England there seems to have been genuine enthusiasm, judging by the joyous way in which William and Mary were acclaimed King and Queen throughout the region in late February 1689.[33]

The Association Oath Roll, 1696

The popularity of William III[34] was particularly evident in Suffolk in 1696, judging by the signatures to the Association Oath Roll. This roll was the result of a plot to assassinate William and restore James II to the throne. The plot was discovered and some of the conspirators were executed, including Ambrose Rookwood, a Catholic alderman of Bury St Edmunds and one of James II's 'Royal Substitutes' in 1688.[35] An Association was formed with the object of circulating an oath throughout the country. Subscribers to the oath vowed loyalty to William and pledged their lives and goods in the preservation of the constitution. 'There can be little doubt that the country went far beyond its Parliamentary representatives, and that a large majority of adult Englishmen, and, in some few cases, English women, signed the roll'.[36] The numbers of signatories, of course, varied between counties. In Suffolk approximately 70,000 signed the Association Oath Roll. This compares very favourably with the situation in Norfolk, where only about 48,000 took the Oath,[37] favourably because Norfolk had a far larger population than had Suffolk. It has been estimated that in 1701 Norfolk had a population of 210,200 while Suffolk had only 152,700 inhabitants.[38]

The Bury Riots[39]

The 'Glorious Revolution' had its inglorious side. The Revolution was the work of the peers and gentry, especially the former. Indeed, it has been termed an 'aristocratic' revolution.[40] But if the upper classes led, the people followed. Indeed, they sometimes took the law into their own hands. This is shown by the anti-Catholic riots during the crisis of the Revolution in 1688. Catholic chapels were attacked and many gutted in provincial towns such as Bristol, Gloucester, Newcastle-upon-Tyne, York, Norwich, and above all in London.[41]

Anti-Catholic riots also took place in Bury St Edmunds – the scene of a serious *anti-Puritan* riot forty years earlier[42] – perhaps in revenge for James II's manipulation of the borough council which had included the appointment of a Catholic mayor, John Stafford. In early December 1688 'the Rabble of Bury St Edmunds' joined forces with a Cambridge mob to attack the magnificent house of Henry Jermyn, 1st Baron Dover (1636–1708), at Cheveley, Cambridgeshire. The rioters also pulled down the Catholic chapel there. This done, the Bury mob returned home and a few days later (*c.* 20 December), re-aroused by 'the Rumour of some Irish soldiers approaching with Fire and Sword', went on the rampage again, this time at Bury St Edmunds itself.[43] Their main target was the Roman Catholic chapel – or 'the Mass House' as they disparagingly called it – in the grounds of Bury Abbey, which they pulled down stone by stone, not ceasing until they had levelled it to the very foundations. The Jesuits were forced to take refuge in a Catholic gentleman's house at nearby Great Barton.[44] Sheer mayhem now prevailed as the mob – consisting mostly of 'the Mobile' (i.e. paupers and vagrants) – roamed the streets of Bury at will and indiscriminately looted and plundered the homes of known Papists. But worse was to follow, for like the Gordon riots a century later, what began as an anti-Catholic demonstration quickly degenerated into 'a blind fury' whereby all men of property, whether Catholic or Protestant, found themselves the object of popular anger. In short, class war began to supersede religious conflict. A contemporary newspaper, *The London Mercury*,[45] gave a vivid description of the situation:

> ... the poor Mobile ... stiling themselves the Protestant reformers, rifled both Papists and Protestants, Test-Men and Anti-Test-Men,[46] without any Distinction ... rambling about Town and Country plundered a Lady's House ... as also the House of an Alderman[47] and another eminent Person, with two others that were Roman Catholicks.

Eventually the 'ravening' mob was 'suppressed by the Civil Magistrate' and 'many ... committed to the common Gaol' after 'being divested of their purloyn'd Goods'.[48] At least ten people were killed in the Bury riots. So the 'Glorious Revolution' was not entirely 'bloodless'.

The Ipswich Mutiny

On 13 March 1689 the Royal Scots Regiment of Foot, stationed at Ipswich *en route* for Holland, mutinied and declared for the exiled James II. There were two main reasons. First, the soldiers resented the fact that their newly appointed colonel, the Duke of Schomberg, was a Dutchman; hitherto they had always been commanded by fellow-Scots. Second, an inflammatory sermon preached by Rev. Thomas Alexander, a Jacobite, strengthened the anti-Williamite inclinations of the Scottish infantrymen crowded inside the Church of St Mary-le-Tower. To the horror of the respectable burghers, the soldiers ran amok in the streets of Ipswich. The Royal Scots then committed themselves irrevocably to the Jacobite cause by publicly declaring their allegiance to King James. Then the soldiers set off for Scotland, but were pursued by Anglo-Dutch cavalry and Dragoons under General Ginkel. A week later the mutineers surrendered at Sleaford in Lincolnshire. The ring leaders were tried for high treason at the next Bury assizes, but received the royal pardon.[49]

The impact of the Ipswich mutiny was more national than local, since it led to the passing of the Mutiny Act, 1689. This sanctioned the existence of a standing army by providing for the punishment of mutiny and desertion. But the temporary nature of the act guaranteed that Parliament would be regularly summoned in future. The mutiny at Ipswich thus had a lasting constitutional significance.

The Suffolk Jacobites and Nonjurors

The pro-Jacobite infantrymen who surrendered to General Ginkel's forces were Scots, not Suffolk men. So who were the *Suffolk* Jacobites? First we must define the term 'Jacobite'. It applied to those who remained loyal to the Stuart dynasty in exile after the Revolution of 1688–89 (from *Jacobus*, Latin for James). Compared with Lancashire and Norwich, Suffolk did not have many Jacobites. Lancashire was accurately described by Lord Macaulay as 'the most Jacobitical of all the counties of England', while 'of all the great towns of England Norwich was the most Jacobitical'. Indeed, 'the magistrates of that city were supposed to be in the interest of the exiled dynasty'.[50] But in Suffolk the Jacobites consisted almost entirely of a small number of clerical nonjurors.[51] These were High Church Anglicans who refused to take the oath of allegiance to William III and Mary II in 1689 and were deprived of their livings. The Nonjurors comprised Archbishop Sancroft, six other bishops[52] and just under 400 lesser clergy. Only twenty-three (6 per cent) of these clerics officiated in Suffolk.[53] They were scattered over the county and not concentrated in particular areas,[54] though Long Melford had three Nonjurors – Matthew Bisbie, rector; William Phillips, curate; Jonathan More, schoolmaster – and may have been something of a Jacobite centre.[55] The Nonjurors in Suffolk and elsewhere relinquished their livings to face poverty and want rather than conform to the Williamite régime. It is hard not to admire these clerical Jacobites who put their consciences before their material well-being.

The most famous of the Suffolk Nonjurors is, of course, William Sancroft.[56] He was born in 1617 at Fressingfield in north-east Suffolk, the second son of a yeoman. He was educated at Bury St Edmunds Grammar School and Emmanuel College, Cambridge. In 1642 he became a Fellow of his college. A Royalist sympathiser, he was deprived of his fellowship in 1651 for refusing to take the Engagement, the loyalty oath to the Commonwealth.[57] However, he was rewarded for his loyalty to the monarchy

William Sancroft (1617–93) by David Loggan in 1680.
As Archbishop of Canterbury (1678–90) Sancroft opposed the pro-Catholic policies of James II, yet refused to acknowledge the Protestants William and Mary as King and Queen.

at the Restoration, when he became Master of Emmanuel College, Rector of Houghton-le-Spring and a prebendary of Durham Cathedral. In 1664 he became Dean of St Paul's Cathedral. After the Great Fire of London in 1666 he raised large contributions for the cathedral restoration and worked actively with Sir Christopher Wren in deciding the architectural design of the new building. He reached the peak of his ecclesiastical career in January 1678 when he was consecrated Archbishop of Canterbury. As Archbishop he tried, but completely failed, to bring back the Duke of York (the future James II) to the Anglican Church. A Tory and a High Churchman, Sancroft refused to sit in James II's Ecclesiastical Commission and in 1688 was sent to the Tower of London as one of the Seven Bishops. But although Sancroft had led the Anglican resistance to James II's attempts to re-Catholicise England, he would have nothing to do with moves to de-throne him, declaring that 'As long as King James was alive, no other persons could be sovereigns of the country'. Having taken the oath of allegiance to James, Sancroft would not take it to William and Mary. Nor would he perform their coronation. Thus in 1689 he was suspended from office and ordered to leave Lambeth Palace, which he did in 1691. The deprived Archbishop then returned to his childhood home at Fressingfield where he lived like a hermit in a poor cottage close to the beautiful medieval church. He died two years later. Sancroft was arguably the most tragic victim of the 'Glorious Revolution'. Although successful in his career, no one charged him with personal ambition. He was a scholar and by nature a shy and retiring man. His closest friend remarked that 'He was the most pious, humble, good Christian I ever knew in all my life'. Certainly the religious devotion of the Anglican Sancroft was just as evident as that of the Catholic Roger Martin and of the Puritan Nathaniel Barnardiston.[58]

The consequences of the Revolution

The 'Glorious Revolution' established a plural or open society. England became, by the standards of the time, a fairly free country where people could choose their religion (within Protestant limits) and choose between two political parties, the Whigs and the Tories. Let us examine religion and politics in turn.

Religion

As we have seen, the Jacobites had little support in Suffolk, despite the leadership of Archbishop Sancroft. By contrast, the Dissenters went from strength to strength. A major consequence of the Toleration Act of 1689 was an expansion of Protestant Nonconformity. Several new chapels were built reflecting the new-found confidence of Dissenters after the 'Glorious Revolution'. Referring to Ipswich, Daniel Defoe commented that

> There is one Meeting House for the Presbyterians, one for the Inde-
> pendants, and one for the Quakers; the first [erected in 1699] is as
> large and as fine a Building of that kind as most of this side of England,
> and the inside best finished of any I have seen, London not excepted;
> that for the Independants is a handsome new-built Building, but not
> so gay or so large as the other.[59]

These new, sometimes large, meeting houses are not surprising. Now at last the Dissenters could assemble for worship in *public*, whereas under Charles II their meetings had normally been held in *secret* behind closed doors. When their faith was proscribed only the bravest attended Noncon-formist assemblies. In the freer atmosphere that followed the Revolution of 1688–89 there was a steady increase in the number of Nonconformist congregations. Excluding the Quakers, the number of Dissenting congregations in England increased between 1690 and 1716 from about 940 to around 1,200.[60]

What was the situation in Suffolk? Before answering this question, we must say a few words about the source material. There are in existence two major surveys of the distribution of Dissent in the late seventeenth and early eighteenth centuries: the so-called Compton Census of 1676, and the list of Dissenting congregations complied by Dr John Evans, in the main between 1715 and 1718. The Compton Census has already been discussed in the previous chapter, but some comments on the Evans list are necessary. The Evans MS. purports to list every Presbyterian, Independent and Baptist congregation in England and Wales, though no Baptist congregations appear in Suffolk. The list gives the locations of the congregations, the names of the ministers and an *estimate* of the number of 'hearers' who frequented their services. The results were mostly collected in by 1718, although further information continued to be added until 1729. The accuracy of the estimates has been questioned, but Dr Watts has convincingly argued that they are reliable, at least for England.[61]

What conclusions, then, can be drawn from the evidence? First, it would appear that the *size* of the congregations increased considerably between 1676 and 1715–18, at least in the Archdeaconry of Sudbury (mainly West Suffolk).[62] Indeed, Table 9.2 shows a fivefold increase.

Table 9.2 Protestant Dissenters[63] *in the Archdeaconry of Sudbury 1676–1718*

Location of congregations	Number of Worshippers	
	1676[64]	*1715–18*[65]
Bacton nr. Mendlesham	12	100
Bury St Edmunds	167	900
Clare	300	400
Combs	11	200
Eye	17	100
Haverhill	30	250
Lavenham	13	300
Long Melford	4	150
Mildenhall	66	150
Nayland	25	450
Palgrave	19	150
Sudbury	100	400
Walsham-le-Willows	3	400
Wattisfield	49	350
Total	816	4,300

Note: Locations *italicised* are towns with 1,000 or more inhabitants in the 1670s.

What about the distribution of the Dissenters in Suffolk? It would appear that they were far more urbanised than the population at large, both in Charles II's reign and in the early eighteenth century. Table 9.3 gives details.

Table 9.3 Protestant Dissenters in urban and rural areas of Suffolk 1676–1718

	Urban	Rural
General population of Suffolk (1670s) [66]	27%	73%
Dissenters in Sudbury Archdeaconry		
1676	43%	57%
1715–18	44%	56%
Dissenters in Suffolk Archdeaconry		
1715–18	49%	51%

Among the Suffolk Dissenters in 1715–18 47 per cent of Presbyterians and 51 per cent of Independents lived in towns of 1,000 or more inhabitants.[67] But in those years Nonconformity was less urbanised in Suffolk than it was nationwide. Referring to England in these same years Dr Watts has remarked that '63.2 per cent of Presbyterian, 69.5 per cent of Independents ... worshipped in cities, boroughs or market towns'.[68] It is hard to say why both in periods of toleration and times of persecution Dissenters contained a large proportion of town dwellers. One possible explanation is that rural Dissenters could be subjected to pressures to conform which did not exist in towns. In villages – and especially those in sheep-corn areas – the people were dependent on the (mainly) Anglican gentry for their livelihood. But in towns and industrialised areas, like Babergh hundred, the presence of trade and industry, by freeing men from the social and economic control of the parson or squire, created conditions which were favourable to the growth and survival of Dissent.[69]

The strength of Dissent varied between as well as within counties. Dr Watts has estimated the total number of Dissenters in the early eighteenth century in England as a whole and in every county, including Suffolk. The Dissenters of Suffolk differed from their brethren in the nation as a whole in four main respects. First, the percentage of Dissenters in Suffolk was below the national average. Watts shows that in 1715–18 Dissenters formed 6.2 per cent of the population of England, but just 5.3 per cent of the population of Suffolk. Second, the Dissenters of Suffolk, unlike those of most other counties, apparently included no Baptists of any kind. Third, the Presbyterians formed only 2.7 per cent of the population of Suffolk, and were below the national average of 3.3 per cent. By contrast Presbyterians constituted more than 8 per cent of the population of Lancashire and more than 7 per cent of Cheshire. Presbyterians also formed a larger proportion of the population of the West Country and of the north Midlands than they did of Suffolk. Fourth, the Independents of Suffolk were, in percentage terms, above the national average, though not as numerous as their brethren in other eastern counties, such as Essex, Hertfordshire and Northamptonshire.[70]

Although the Dissenters were clearly in a minority among both the English and Suffolk people during the early eighteenth century, their future looked promising, while the outlook for the Church of England seemed bleak. This is suggested by Daniel Defoe's account of the religious situation in Southwold in 1722:

> Southwold ... is a small Port-town upon the Coast ... There is but one Church in this Town, but it is a very large one and well-built, as most of the Churches in this County are ... I was surprized to see an extraordinarily large Church, capable of receiving five or six thousand People, but Twenty-Seven in it besides the Parson and the Clerk; but at the same time the Meeting House of the Dissenters was full to the very Doors, having, as I guess'd from 6 to 800 people in it.[71]

Defoe, a Dissenter himself, greatly exaggerated (the Evans list suggests

Church of St Edmund's, Southwold
(Engraved by E. Roberts from a drawing by T. Higham in *Excursions*, II, p. 127)
The parish church, built between 1430 and 1460, is generally thought to be one of the
finest Perpendicular churches in England. It includes a hammerbeam roof with a host of
angels. The church was funded by trade and fishing in the period 1350–1500. In 1722
Defoe found only 27 worshippers in the parish church, compared with *c.* 400 in the
Independent chapel.

there were 400 'hearers' in Southwold Independent chapel[72]), but Non-conformist chapels *were* gaining – and not just in Southwold – at the expense of Anglican churches after the 'Glorious Revolution'. Yet it was not just a matter of competition between rival denominations. As Professor Kishlansky reminds us, the Toleration Act of 1689 'enabled the irreligious to attend no church at all', so attendance at Anglican services declined.[73] The fall in numbers caused the cry 'Church in Danger'.

It was not just declining numbers that alarmed the Anglican clergy and laity. Even more perturbing was the way the less scrupulous Dissenting laymen found ways of evading the obstacles to civil office which the Corporation Act, 1661, and the Test Act, 1673, still legally imposed. Under the indulgent eye of William III and his Whig ministers there grew up a cynical practice called 'occasional conformity'. This practice was particularly rife in town corporations, where its origins went back to Charles II's reign. Dissenters found that provided they took communion in an Anglican Church *just once*, in the twelve months before they stood for local election, and provided they got a certificate to that effect from the local vicar or rector, they could then take their seats as town councillors, and even become aldermen and mayors, while cheerfully going week after week to their Nonconformist meeting-houses until the next Common Council election was in prospect. Occasional conformity became a political issue which divided the nation into two camps.

Politics

Most historians agree that the 'Glorious Revolution' was a Whig and Tory settlement. But from 1694 conflict between the two parties revived. Before discussing this conflict, it is necessary to explain the terms Whig and Tory. 'Whig' was applied – initially in the extended form 'whiggamore' – to extreme Scots Covenanters, and thence to those who opposed the Duke of York (the future James II) in the Exclusion Crisis of 1679–81. 'Tory', derived from *Toraidhe*, Irish for bandit, was applied to supporters of the Duke of York in the same crisis. Whig and Tory were both terms of abuse. Political divisions were fairly fluid, but broadly the Tories represented the landed interest, tended to be High Church Anglicans and believed in divine, hereditary right. The Whigs generally represented the monied interest, and favoured Low Church Anglicanism, toleration for Protestant Dissenters and constitutional kingship. There was both a conflict of interests and a conflict of ideologies.[74] Neither party had the rigid discipline or efficient, professional organisation of a modern political party. Nevertheless, Professor Kishlansky is right to say that 'party politics came of age at the beginning of the eighteenth century.[75] But before dealing with party strife, we need to say something about the electorate.

The electorate of Suffolk

Holmes and Speck have rightly said that the growth of the electorate in the seventeenth and early eighteenth centuries was 'a development utterly basic to the emergence of national political parties in England'.[76] Nationally the electorate greatly expanded between the accession of William III and Mary II in 1689 and the death of Queen Anne in 1714. The electorate grew from about 200,000 in 1689 to around 250,000 in 1714, a 20 per cent growth.[77] From 1691 to 1716 the population of England grew from 4,930,502 to 5,272,978, a mere 6 per cent growth.[78] Thus the electoral population grew much faster than the total population. In Suffolk the county electorate grew from about 4,500 in 1673 to probably 6,500 in 1715,[79] a 31 per cent growth. This was well above the national average of 20 per cent. The population of Suffolk was approximately 125,000 in 1673 but by 1715 it was around 155,000,[80] a 19 per cent growth. Thus in Suffolk as in the nation at large electoral growth outstripped population growth.

Not only did the county electorate grow in Suffolk, but so did the electorate in at least four of the seven Parliamentary boroughs, as Table 9.4 shows.

Table 9.4 Size of the Electorate in Suffolk 1673–1715

Constituency	Type	Estimated size of electorate	Approx. population 1679–1715
Aldeburgh	Freeman Borough	90 (1690)	Under 1,000
		95 (1715)	
Bury St Edmunds	Corporation Bor.	37 (1690)	c. 6,000
		37 (1715)	
Dunwich	Freeman Bor.	250 (1679)	Under 500
		Under 40 (1715)	
Eye	Ditto	120 (1679)	1,200
		200 (1715)	
Ipswich	Do.	271 (1698)	c. 8,000
		600 (1715)	
Orford	Do.	21 (1679)	Under 500
		150 (1715)	
Sudbury	Do.	730 (1702)	c. 2,500
		800 (1715)	
Suffolk	40/- Freehold	4,500 (1673)	125,000 (1673)
		6,500 (1715)	155,000 (1715)

Sources: Murrell, thesis, pp. 164–5, 168–71; Patten, *Pre-Industrial England*, p. 74.

The above table shows that the most representative borough was Sudbury. 'Here, after allowing for the fact that roughly 20% of its voters were non-resident, those enfranchised comprised 20–25% of a substantial sized town.' The least representative and narrowest Suffolk electorate was that of Bury St Edmunds 'where the rigid maximum of 37 voters at any given time constituted well below 1% of its 6,000 or so inhabitants'.[81] Yet, as the late Geoffrey Holmes pointed out, many of the rest of the inhabitants of Bury were not disfranchised because 282 of them voted in the General Election of 1710 for the *county* of Suffolk.[82] Only Ipswich had more *county* voters in this election, namely 372.[83] Indeed, poll books, minute books and deeds disprove the unrepresentative nature of Parliament. It was not only the gentry, clergy and urban oligarchs who voted. The 'middling sort' also did. Dr Murrell has given a sample of the trades practised by Suffolk electors in the period 1679–1715, and among those listed are Basket Maker, Clothier, Doctor of Physic, Husbandman, Joiner, Linen Weaver, Sailor, Silk Mercer, Stonemiller, Town Clerk, Worsted Weaver, Yeoman.[84] Murrell's evidence in fact justifies J. H. Plumb's remark that 'When men talked of the liberties of Englishmen, it was no empty rhetoric. It meant that tens of thousands of them had the right to choose their governors after 1688'.[85] Professor W. A. Speck has said that 'the electoral system was more representative in Queen Anne's reign than it had ever been before or was to be again until well into Victoria's reign'.[86] Speck was referring to England, but the situation in Suffolk was not quite identical. As we saw in Chapter 2, the county electorate in Suffolk was larger during the Interregnum than after the Glorious Revolution. Nevertheless, the growth of this electorate from 4,500 in 1673 to about 6,500 in 1715 is impressive. Moreover, Dr Murrell has rightly said that 'If the adult male population is taken to be 20–25% of the total population figure the number of enfranchised for the county of Suffolk as a whole represents something between 15–20% of this sector of the population'. 'All in all', says Murrell, 'Suffolk's constituencies do not, statistically, fare too badly on the representative front'.[87]

The 'rage of party' and voting behaviour
The Triennial Act, 1694, necessitated a general election every three years. This created a unique political situation and between 1694 and 1715 there were ten general elections. 'Never have English politicians been more in the thrall of a growing and volatile electorate'.[88] It has also been remarked that from 1701 to 1717 'religious animosities remained the most consistently divisive element in English politics'.[89] What above all divided the nation into two camps was the question of occasional conformity.

Occasional conformity was the key issue in Suffolk in the General Election of 1705.[90] Shortage of space forbids an account of the other nine general elections between 1694 and 1715, but the election of 1705 has been singled out because it was 'one of the fiercest elections the county [Suffolk] was ever to witness'.[91] It was also a fairly narrow victory for the Tories. Of the 5,323 voters, 2,327 supported only Whig candidates, 2,878 only Tories, while 118 split their votes between the rival candidates.[92] In Suffolk the gentry and Anglican clergy who voted were overwhelmingly Tory, as Table 9.5 shows.

Table 9.5 Voting behaviour of the gentry and Anglican clergy in the General Election, 1705, in the county constituency of Suffolk

	Gentry[93]	Clergy[94]
Tory voters only	71 (73%)	141 (82%)
Whig voters only	24 (25%)	28 (16%)
Those splitting their vote	2 (2%)	4 (2%)
Total polled	97 (100%)	173 (100%)

The Tories did better electorally in small villages and hamlets where there were fewer voters. There the gentry were well entrenched and influential. The Anglican clergy too were powerful and exercised great influence through the pulpit, which was more important than the free press at this time. As Dr Murrell reminds us, 'few places were without an Anglican establishment though scores were without dissenters' meeting houses which were the breeding ground of many a Whig supporter'.[95] This put the Tories at an advantage. But the Whigs were stronger in the larger, more urban communities, where Dissent was often strong. It is significant that in the General Election of 1705 for the county constituency of Suffolk, the Whigs obtained a majority in seventeen of the twenty-four parishes whose turnout exceeded thirty voters: 53.6 per cent voted for one or both of the Whig candidates only, while 46.4 per cent did the same for the two Tories.[96] Moreover, the Whigs also won a majority of those parishes where there were Dissenting congregations, as Table 9.6 shows.

Table 9.6 General Election 1705: Results in 24 Parishes where over 30 voted

Parish	Voters turning out	Winning Party
Beccles	131	Tory
Boxford	38	Whig
Bungay	64	T
Bury St Edmunds	241	W
Cavendish	35	W
Clare	45	T
Combs	33	W
Debenham	30	T
Eye	51	W
Framlingham	59	T
Hadleigh	43	T
Haverhill	38	W
Ipswich	391	W
Mildenhall	97	W
Nayland	40	W
Southwold	31	W
Stanton	41	W
Stoke-by-Nayland	56	W
Stowmarket	70	W
Stratford St Mary	39	W
Sudbury	153	W
Wattisfield	30	W
Waxtham	33	W
Woolpit	30	T

Note. Places italicised are those with Dissenting Congregations in 1715–18. See Evans list, Dr Williams's Library, London, MS. 38, 4, pp. 108–11.

It is worth noting that of the seventeen parishes with Dissenting congregations, eleven (65 per cent) returned Whigs. However, this is slightly below expectations, and it would appear that in Suffolk Dissent and Whiggery were probably not as closely connected as they were in some other parts of England slightly later in the eighteenth century.[97]

The Tories won four of the five general elections in Suffolk during Queen Anne's reign,[98] the exception being the 1708 election which the Whigs won as a result of an abortive Jacobite rising in Scotland. Suffolk was in fact a Tory stronghold. This is puzzling because during the First Civil War Suffolk – or at least East Suffolk – had been a Roundhead heartland, that is if we exclude the many neutrals and those of unknown allegiance. Suffolk had also been a Puritan county or, at any rate, an Anglican county with a strong Puritan presence. Indeed, it was the county's strong Puritan tendencies which had helped the Whigs to attain rapidly the ascendancy in Suffolk during the Exclusion Crisis of 1679.[99] In the second election of 1679 the Whigs had returned twelve of the sixteen Suffolk MPs. Yet in the 1705 General Election the Tories returned eleven of the sixteen members.[100] Moreover, Dr Murrell's map shows that in the 1705 election the Tories were stronger in East than in West Suffolk,[101] although during the First Civil War the former had been a Parliamentary stronghold and the latter – at least as regards the gentry – had been evenly divided.[102]

This discontinuity is particularly evident if we look at those Suffolk MPs elected to Parliament. In the Parliament of 1681 several of the Tory MPs – Sir Thomas Hervey, Thomas Jermyn, Sir Charles Gawdy, Sir John Barker and Thomas Glemham – were from ex-Royalist families, while the four Whigs – Sir Philip Skippon,[103] Sir Samuel Barnardiston, Sir William Spring, and John Bence – came from ex-Parliamentarian families. In the Parliament of 1705, however, the Suffolk Whigs still included Philip Skippon, but also Sir Thomas Felton from an ex-Royalist family. The Tories included Henry Pooley of an ex-Royalist family, but also Sir Charles Blois, John Bence and Sir Edmund Bacon, all from ex-Parliamentarian families.[104]

The voting behaviour of individuals from ex-Parliamentarian and ex-Royalist gentry families of Suffolk in the 1705 General Election is also revealing. Appendix VII records their votes in the county constituency of Suffolk. Of the fourteen voters from ex-Royalist families, twelve not surprisingly voted Tory and only two Whig. But of the eighteen voters from ex-Parliamentarian families, only six voted Whig while twice as many voted Tory. The five voters from former divided families in the Civil War were unanimously Tory. We can only speculate why Suffolk was a Roundhead dominated county during the Great Rebellion (1640–60) and became a Tory stronghold in the early eighteenth century. Yet Suffolk was not unique. In Glamorgan 'many of the high Tories under Queen Anne were descended from earlier Roundheads, even Regicides'.[105]

Conclusion

Suffolk experienced mixed fortunes under James II. Only a small number of JPs were apparently dismissed and just four Catholics – all gentry – replaced them. But if the commission of the peace was leniently treated, the corporation of Bury St Edmunds was not. Indeed, it was thoroughly purged and remodelled. The Catholic James also had seven Anglican bishops tried before the Court of King's Bench for refusing to read his second Declaration of Indulgence. Their leader, William Sancroft, Archbishop of Canterbury, was a Suffolk man. In view of the high handed treatment of Bury St Edmunds and Archbishop Sancroft, it is not surprising that there was considerable support for the 'Glorious Revolution' in Suffolk, shown particularly by the large number of signatures to the Association Oath Roll, and by the fierce anti-Catholic riots in Bury St Edmunds. There does not seem to have been much opposition to the Revolution. The soldiers who mutinied at Ipswich in 1685 were Scots, not Suffolk men, while the local Nonjuring clergy who refused to take the oath of allegiance to William III and Mary II were few in number, though their leader was the Suffolk born Archbishop Sancroft.

The 'Glorious Revolution' had important religious and political consequences for Suffolk. The Toleration Act, 1689, caused an expansion of Protestant Dissent. Membership of Nonconformist congregations increased fivefold in West Suffolk. As in Charles II's reign, the Dissenters were far more urbanised than the population at large. But the importance of the Dissenters in Suffolk should not be exaggerated. In percentage terms they were below the national average. However, the nonconformists were clearly flourishing compared with the Anglicans whose numbers were falling. Anglicans were also alarmed by the growing practice of occasional conformity, which enabled Dissenters to obtain local offices, especially in towns.

Politically, the post-Revolution years were important for Suffolk. The county electorate greatly increased and, more importantly, electoral growth outstripped general population growth. Though the Suffolk Parliamentary boroughs had small electorates, most of them increased in size. In short, the 'middling sort' as well as the gentry and clergy had strong political influence. Political conflict between Whigs and Tories was fierce during the reign of Queen Anne. 'The rage of party' was particularly evident during the General Election of 1705, mainly because the key issue was occasional conformity. In Suffolk, as elsewhere, the gentry and clergy who voted were overwhelmingly Tory in this election. The Whigs seem to have performed best in parishes with large turnouts and in those with Dissenting congregations. Surprisingly, the Tories seem to have had more electoral support in East than in West Suffolk in 1705. In fact there was a marked swing to the Tories throughout the county betwen 1679 and 1705. At the earlier date MPs representing Suffolk constituencies were mainly Whigs, whereas at the later date they were mostly Tories. But perhaps the most interesting and surprising fact of all is that in the General Election of 1705 there were large Tory majorities among persons belonging to *both* ex-Royalist and ex-Parliamentarian gentry families. Indeed, the political history of Suffolk during our period seems to be characterised as much by discontinuity as by continuity.

CHAPTER TEN

Conclusion

It is difficult to summarise the history of Suffolk during the Tudor and Stuart periods. But certain features stand out. First, the county was one of the most economically advanced parts of England, at least from the 1470s until the 1670s. Its wealth came from three main sources: the broadcloth industry in the south-west, coastal and overseas trade, and dairy farming. The broadcloth industry, however, had virtually collapsed by the end of our period and south-west Suffolk became one of the first rural manufacturing regions in England to *de*-industrialise. The coastal trade flourished until after the Restoration but by the end of the seventeenth century several east coast parts had declined, though others continued to prosper. There was a growing demand for Suffolk's dairy produce during the seventeenth century largely because of London's population explosion.

Administratively, Suffolk, with its parishes and hundreds, its JPs and Deputy-Lieutenants, was a microcosm of England, though the county included two ecclesiastical and four feudal liberties at the beginning of our period. However, by 1572 the Crown had annexed these liberties, thereby strengthening its power at the expense of the nobles and the Church. But the Tudors made no attempt to weaken Parliament and the parliamentary boroughs in Suffolk expanded in number during our period. The social structure of Suffolk was similar to that of most English counties during the Tudor and Stuart period. But it was not rigid for there seems to have been considerable upward and downward mobility. Suffolk witnessed the numerical rise of the gentry and yeomanry, at least until the First Civil War. It also saw the decline of the husbandmen, especially after 1650, and almost certainly an increase in the numbers of poor people.

The Reformation was surprisingly successful in Suffolk because the county was noted for its devout Catholicism during the later Middle Ages. The Reformation was imposed from above and appears to have had little popular support before the reign of Elizabeth I. Despite the strength of Catholicism, Henry VIII was able to dissolve the Suffolk monasteries without meeting any significant resistance. Most heads of religious houses, plus the monks of Bury Abbey, received adequate pensions and some had successful post-dissolution careers. But most unpensioned male ex-religious fared badly. Much monastic and convent land in Suffolk was sold between 1536 and

1547, the main beneficiaries being the gentry. The progress of Protestantism was slow in Suffolk between the 1520s and the death of Mary I. But this was not because of popular resistance. On the contrary, the churchwardens' accounts from 1547 to 1558 suggest that most Suffolk people meekly accepted religious change, whether imposed by the Protestant King Edward or by the Catholic Queen Mary. Genuine and committed Protestants were apparently a very small minority in Suffolk. Geographically, these Protestants were to be found mainly in Ipswich and in wood-pasture regions. Socially, the early Protestants received their strongest support from artisans. Suffolk produced thirty martyrs under Mary Tudor, and the bravery with which they died may well have strengthened their cause. Whatever the reason, Suffolk was almost certainly one of the most Protestant counties in England by the end of the sixteenth century.

Under Elizabeth I and the early Stuarts Popish recusants and Puritans suffered persecution, but in Suffolk it was not particularly severe. Catholic recusants formed a tiny and declining percentage of the local population, but they were feared by the Protestant authorities because their leaders came from the gentry. Moreover, in Suffolk it was mainly the gentry who provided the Catholic Church with mass centres, priests and nuns. Puritan clergy and laity both displayed opposition to the Established Church. Under Elizabeth clerics in particular hated the surplice and had qualms about the Prayer Book, while a minority during the 1580s hankered after a Presbyterian form of church government. All Puritan divines emphasised, or over-emphasised, the importance of preaching. Under Charles I Suffolk Puritan clerics clashed with Matthew Wren, Bishop of Norwich. His emphasis on ceremonial, his approval of Sunday sports, his opposition to lecturers, and, above all, his altar policy made him the most hated Anglican bishop after Laud. In Suffolk Puritan gentlemen worked closely with Puritan ministers. The Puritan gentry gave much help to their cause as patrons, as magistrates and, in 1585, as soldiers. Some Puritan families were noted for their godly household religion. The Puritan gentry increased in strength under Charles I and in the 1640s they outnumbered the Catholic gentry by three to one.

During the First Civil War (1642–46) the allegiances of most gentry and commoners are unknown. But Suffolk, though militarily quiet, was hardly a Roundhead heartland. Among the combatant gentry the Parliamentarians had a large majority over the Cavaliers only in East Suffolk; in West Suffolk, however, the two sides were almost evenly matched. A majority of both Parliamentarian and Royalist gentry actively supported the war effort of their own side, the former being more prominent as officials and the latter as soldiers. Among the commoners of Suffolk, and especially among the 'middle sort', there was much active support for Parliament. By contrast there was apparently very little popular Royalism in the county. It is hard to say what motivated the Suffolk gentry to support one side or the other. But social, local and political factors were apparently only of limited importance. The evidence suggests that religion was the key issue during the First Civil War.

It is hard to say what exactly caused the Second Civil War (1648). But it is likely that many people in Suffolk were alienated by the policies of the Puritans during the mid-1640s. Their strict Sabbatarianism, their suppression of Christmas celebrations, their attempt to set up a (strict) Presbyterian system, their persecution of 136 Anglican parsons, their iconoclasm and their witch-hunting must have been unpalatable to many Suffolk folk. Whatever the reasons, Suffolk people *did* participate in the Royalist risings of 1648, at Stowmarket, Newmarket and, especially, at Bury St Edmunds. Royalism in Suffolk in 1648 was essentially a plebeian phenomenon. But while most Royalist gentry were quiescent, many Parliamentarian gentlemen were not. At least fifty Parliamentarian gentry (mostly Puritan) helped their cause, a majority in a civil capacity. However, a small proportion of the Parliamentary gentry served as soldiers at the siege of Colchester (Essex) and the Suffolk militia which they commanded was highly regarded by the New Model Army, having greatly contributed to the victory of General Lord Fairfax.

The Interregnum in Suffolk was characterised by considerable political continuity. A majority who had served as JPs in the 1640s continued to do so in the 1650s. Large numbers of conservative Parliamentarians, including opponents of the Regicide, and even some ex-Royalists, supported the Republic in the interests of peace and stability. However, the radicals were the strongest supporters of the republican governments, but managed to work alongside the more conservative officials. There was less social than political continuity, however. During the late 1650s minor gentry and plebeians were far more conspicuous on the county assessment and militia commissions than they had been earlier. However, the greater gentry continued to dominate the Bench of acting magistrates during the Interregnum. Social and economic change was limited and extremely few Suffolk Parliamentary gentry and commoners acquired confiscated church, crown and delinquent land. A very small number of Suffolk Roundheads obtained Irish land, however. In Suffolk there was apparently no serious threat to the republican régime. Royalist conspiracy and armed rebellion were probably discouraged by sequestrations, compositions, confiscations and the decimation tax. Yet these penalties do not seem to have financially harmed most Suffolk Royalists. It was in fact not Royalists but Quakers who suffered the harshest persecution during the Interregnum.

During the Restoration period both the Parliamentarian and Royalist gentry of Suffolk were rewarded by Charles II with titles and offices, the former generously, the latter more modestly. Between 1642 and 1664 important social changes took place in Suffolk to the consternation of the Cavaliers. Many new families of plebeian or non-local origins entered the gentry, though most were not ex-Parliamentarians nor ex-Republicans but ex-Neutrals/Unknowns. An even greater number of families disappeared from the gentry, but not many were ex-Royalists; most were ex-Neutrals/Unknowns. About one third of both Royalist and Parliamentarian families disappeared into obscurity. Among the perdurable gentry, the Royalists were wealthier than the Parliamentarians. Yet ex-Cavaliers feared social and economic decline and felt threatened by the Protestant Dissenters. At the Restoration more Puritan ministers were ejected from the Anglican Church in Suffolk than in most English counties. But once ejected, most did not suffer excessive persecution. The Quakers were a notable exception among Suffolk Dissenters. They were harassed frequently and brutally, despite their increasingly pacifist outlook. The number of Dissenters is hard to establish since some were partial conformists. Many Dissenters resided in market towns and wood-pasture areas. Socially, Dissenters differed among themselves. Quakers were lower class, Presbyterians socially mixed. Unlike the Puritans in the Civil War period and earlier, the Dissenters had very little gentry support. By contrast, Suffolk Catholicism was still essentially seigneurial, and it was mainly the gentry who provided the Catholic Church with mass centres, priests and nuns. Yet there was apparently little persecution of Papists in Suffolk, even at the time of the Popish Plot.

Shortly before the 'Glorious Revolution' James II only dismissed a small number of JPs in Suffolk, replacing them by Catholics. But he thoroughly purged and remodelled the corporation of Bury St Edmunds. This, together with the trial of Archbishop Sancroft, a Suffolk man, because he refused to read the second Declaration of Indulgence, resulted in considerable support for the 'Glorious Revolution' in the county, shown particularly by the large number of signatures to the Association Roll and by fierce anti-Catholic riots in Bury. Moreover, there were only a handful of clerical Jacobites (Nonjurors) who refused to swear allegiance to William III and Mary II. The 'Glorious Revolution' had important consequences for Suffolk. The Toleration Act, 1689, caused a considerable expansion of Protestant Dissent. By contrast the number of Anglicans fell sharply. In post-Revolution Suffolk electoral growth exceeded population growth, thereby increasing the number of middle class voters. Political conflict between Whigs and Tories was fierce in Suffolk, especially during the General Election of 1705 when the key issue was occasional conformity. Most of the country gentry and Anglican clergy who voted were overwhelmingly Tory. The Whigs did best in parishes with large turnouts and Dissenting congregations. Between 1679 and 1705 there was a marked swing to the Tories throughout Suffolk, and in the General Election of 1705 there were large Tory majorities among persons belonging to both ex-Royalist and ex-Parliamentary gentry families.

Fundamental change in allegiance is an important characteristic of our period. In 1500 most Suffolk people were apparently devout Catholics. By 1700 they seem to have been overwhelmingly Protestant. When Elizabeth

I ascended the throne in 1558 Catholics were still a force to be reckoned with in Suffolk, but by the outbreak of the First Civil War in 1642, most had become real or nominal Protestants. On the other hand some Suffolk families which were staunchly Puritan under Elizabeth, such as the Jermyns, the Blagues and the Highams, were active Royalists during the First Civil War. We have seen, too, how appalled some Suffolk Parliamentarians were at the execution of Charles I in 1649 and how they nevertheless supported the Republic for pragmatic reasons. It should therefore come as no surprise that Suffolk changed from being a Roundhead dominated county during the Great Rebellion (1640–60) to a Tory stronghold during the reign of Queen Anne.

Notes

NOTES TO CHAPTER ONE

1. Reyce, *Breviary*, p. 25.
2. Ibid.
3. Kirby, *Suffolk Traveller*, p. 1.
4. Blome, *Britannia*, p. 208.
5. *Chorography*, p. 19.
6. Reyce, *Breviary*, pp. 13–14.
7. Ibid., p. 23.
8. Blome, *Britannia*, p. 208.
9. 'Woodland' did not imply dense tree coverage, although it may have been more thickly covered with trees in our period.
10. 'High Suffolk' was not high by national standards, but it was undoubtedly higher above sea level than the rest of the county.
11. *Chorography*, pp. 19–20.
12. The 'Fielding' is sometimes referred to as the 'Breckland', which takes its name from the natural area of the 'Brecks', that is areas of heathland periodically cultivated.
13. Kirby, *Suffolk Traveller*, pp. 1–2. For the location of these and other hundreds of Suffolk see Map 6.
14. Neither the Chorographer nor Kirby mentioned a fourth landscape, the Fens. But this hardly matters because these wetlands covered only a tiny part of Suffolk. The Fens were mostly in Lincolnshire, Cambridgeshire (including the Isle of Ely), Huntingdonshire and west Norfolk.
15. For Europe see Roger Mols, 'Population in Europe 1500–1700' in Carlo M. Cipolla (ed.), *The Fontana Economic History of Europe: The Sixteenth and Seventeenth Centuries* (Collins/Fontana Books, 1974), p. 38. For England see E. A. Wrigley and R. S. Schofield, *The Population History of England 1541–1871: A reconstruction* (Edward Arnold, 1981), pp. 208–9.
16. A. L. Beier and Roger Finlay, 'Introduction. The significance of the metropolis', in Beier & Finlay (eds), *London 1500–1700: The Making of the Metropolis.* (Longman, 1986) p. 3; E. Anthony Wrigley, 'Urban Growth and Agricultural Change: England and the Continent in the Early Modern Period', in Peter Borsay (ed.), *The Eighteenth Century Town 1688–1820* (Longman, 1990), p. 42.
17. Wrigley, 'Urban Growth', p. 42.
18. Ibid.; D. M. Palliser, *The Age of Elizabeth: England under the later Tudors 1547–1603* (2nd edn, Longman, 1992), p. 237.
19. Peter Clark and Paul Slack, 'Introduction', in Clark & Slack (eds), *Crisis and Order in English Towns 1500–1700* (Routledge & Kegan Paul, 1972) p. 6.
20. *Suffolk Facts 91* (Suffolk County Council, 1991), unpaginated.
21. John Patten, 'Population distribution in Norfolk and Suffolk during the sixteenth and seventeenth centuries', in J. Patten (ed.), *Pre-industrial England: Geographical Essays* (Dawson, Folkestone, 1979), p. 74. Patten's population estimates are based on the lay subsidy rolls for 1524/5, on the Communicant returns for 1603 and on the Compton Census and the Hearth Tax returns for the 1670s. These would seem to be the most reliable records, or rather – since no historical source is perfect – the least unreliable. For Patten's confidence in these sources, which I share, see ibid., pp. 74–85.
22. See above p. 4.
23. J. Patten, *English Towns 1500–1700* (Dawson, Folkestone, 1978), p. 28.
24. Ibid.
25. Ibid., p. 23.

265

26. Blome, *Britannia*, pp. 216–17. Other Suffolk market centres that had failed by the 1670s were Blythburgh, Burgh Castle, Exning, Offton, Rendlesham, Walberswick and Woolpit (ibid.).

27. Sybil M. Jack, *Towns in Tudor and Stuart Britain* (Macmillan, 1996), p. 160.

28. Peter Clark and Paul Slack, *English Towns in Transition 1500–1700* (OUP, 1976), p. 5.

29. Clark & Slack, *Crisis and Order*, p. 6; L. Stone, 'The Educational Revolution in England, 1560–1640', *P&P*, 28 (1964), p. 59.

30. Professor Gottfried gives the population of Bury in 1522 as 5,438 (Robert S. Gottfried, *Bury St Edmunds and the Urban Crisis 1290–1539* (Princeton UP, 1982), p. 54). This estimate seems much too high.

31. According to Angus McInnes Bury had approximately 5,500 inhabitants in the 1670s (A. McInnes, *The English Town 1660–1760* (Historical Association. Appreciations in History No. 7, 1980), p. 6).

32. Michael Reed gives the population of Ipswich in 1674 as 7,400 (M. Reed, 'Economic Structure and change in seventeenth-century Ipswich', in Peter Clark (ed.), *Country towns in pre-industrial England* (Leicester UP, 1981), p. 92).

33. See above p. 4.

34. Dr Patten has suggested that the proportion of Norfolk and Suffolk people living in towns was about 20 per cent in 1524, 25 per cent in 1603 and 32 per cent in the 1670s. But in his list of forty-nine towns Patten included eighteen (ten in Suffolk and eight in Norfolk) which had *under* 1,000 inhabitants at *all* the dates mentioned (Patten, *Pre-industrial England*, pp. 74–5, 84, 88).

35. Gottfried, op. cit., p. 186.

36. See Speed Map of Suffolk 1610 in SRO (I), MC 4/2.[b]

37. Wrigley, 'Urban Growth', p. 42.

38. The loan fell on all who possessed personal wealth of £5 and upwards or lands of equivalent value. Those below this level escaped the net until the great subsidy of 1524/5.

39. W. G. Hoskins, *The Age of Plunder: The England of Henry VIII 1500–1547* (Longman, 1976), pp. 22–3.

40. As the numbers of hearths can be used to measure the wealth of individuals, so they can be used to assess the wealth of counties and towns, provided we proceed with caution.

41. See Alan Everitt, *Change in the Provinces: The Seventeenth Century* (Leicester UP, 1969), pp. 54–5.

42. Alan Dyer, *Decline and Growth in English Towns 1400–1640* (Macmillan, 1991), pp. 68, 70; W. G. Hoskins, *Local History in England* (3rd edn, Longman, 1984), pp. 278–9.

43. David Dymond, 'The Woollen Cloth Industry', in Dymond & Martin, p. 140.

44. See chapter 2.

45. Speed, loc. cit.

46. Maurice Exwood and H. L. Lehmann (eds), *The Journal of William Schellinks' Travels in England 1661–1663* (Camden Fifth Series, vol. I, 1993), p. 162.

47. Frank Grace, 'A Historical Survey of Suffolk Towns', *Suffolk Review*, 5 (Winter, 1982), p. 110.

48. Mark Overton, *Agricultural Revolution in England: The transformation of the agrarian economy 1500–1850* (CUP, 1996), p. 22.

49. See above p. 4.

50. A. R. Bridbury, 'Sixteenth Century Farming', *Econ. HR*, 2nd series, xxvii (1974), p. 541.

51. Palliser, *Age of Elizabeth*, p. 231. The same author argued particularly strongly against the notion that early modern England ran into a 'Malthusian trap' as its population increased. See Palliser, 'Tawney's Century: Brave New World or Malthusian Trap?', *Econ. HR*, 2nd series, xxxv (1982), pp. 339–53.

52. Palliser, *Age of Elizabeth*, pp. 233–4.

53. This map is a simplified version of Dr Thirsk's map in Joan Thirsk, 'The Farming Regions of England', in J Thirsk (ed.), *The Agrarian History of England and Wales: vol. IV: 1500–1640* (CUP, 1967), p. 4.

54. This paragraph relies heavily on Joan Thirsk, 'The Farming regions of England', pp. 40–9.

55. B. A. Holderness, 'East Anglia and the Fens: Norfolk, Suffolk, Cambridgeshire, Ely, Huntingdonshire, Essex and the Lincolnshire Fens', in Joan Thirsk (ed.), *The Agrarian History of England and Wales: vol. V, Pt. I: 1640–1750* (CUP, 1984), p. 199. See also map on p. 198.

56. Quoted in Joan Thirsk, *The Rural Economy of England: Collected essays* (Hambledon Press, 1984), p. 222.

57. *Chorography*, pp. 19–20; Blome, *Britannia*, p. 207; Kirby, *Suffolk Traveller*, pp. 1–2.

58. See Joan Thirsk, 'Introduction', in J. Thirsk (ed.), *Agrarian Hist.*, vol. V, Pt. I, p. xxi; idem., *England's Agricultural Regions and Agrarian History, 1500–1750* (Macmillan, 1987), esp. pp. 37–8.

59. Overton, op. cit., p. 53.
60. For details see chapter 2.
61. Reyce, *Breviary*, p. 29.
62. Ibid.
63. Dymond & Northeast, p. 91.
64. Ibid.
65. Overton, op. cit., p. 199.
66. Holderness, 'East Anglia and the Fens', p. 221.
67. Thirsk 'Farming Regions of England', p. 44; Holderness, 'East Anglia and the Fens', p. 215; Overton, op. cit., p. 92.
68. Reyce, *Breviary*, p. 31. I owe this reference to Dr Joan Thirsk.
69. K. J. Allison, 'The Sheep-Corn Husbandry of Norfolk in the Sixteenth and Seventeenth Centuries', *Agricultural History Review*, 5 (1957), p. 12. Dr Allison excludes the Broads and Fens in his calculations.
70. *Chorography*, p. 19; Reyce, *Breviary*. p. 40; Defoe, *Tour*, vol. 1, p. 79.
71. Blome, *Britannia*, p. 207; Defoe, loc. cit.; Holderness, 'East Anglia and the Fens', p. 231.
72. N. Evans, 'Farming and Land-Holding in Wood-Pasture East Anglia 1550–1650', *PSIAH*, xxxv, pt. 4 (1984), p. 306.
73. *Chorography*, p. 19; Reyce, *Breviary*, p. 39; Defoe, *Tour*, vol. I, p. 90.
74. Thirsk, *Rural Economy*, pp. 213–14.
75. B. H. Slicher van Bath, *The Agrarian History of Western Europe AD 500–1850* (Edward Arnold, 1963), p. 213.
76. Palliser, *Age of Elizabeth*, pp. 277, 294, 307.
77. This section relies heavily upon Alec Betterton and David Dymond, *Lavenham, industrial town* (Terence Dalton Ltd., Lavenham, 1989); George Unwin, 'Industries', in *VCH Suffolk*, vol. II, pp. 247–73; Hoskins, *Age of Plunder*, esp. chapter 7; Thirsk, *Rural Economy*, pp. 217–33.
78. Tom Webster, 'The Changing Landscape', in John Morrill (ed.), *The Oxford Illustrated History of Tudor and Stuart Britain* (OUP, 1996), p. 21.
79. Palliser, *Age of Elizabeth*, p. 287.
80. That is, the hundreds of South Erpingham and Tunstead.
81. Especially Colchester, Braintree, Coggeshall and Dedham.
82. Worsted was a twisted thread or yarn spun out of long combed wool. The name is *not* derived from the Norfolk village of Worstead.
83. Broadcloth meant a fine kind of woollen fulled cloth used for men's garments. It was heavy and made of short fibred wool.
84. Kerseys were coarse woollen cloth. The name is *not* derived from the Suffolk village of Kersey but from the Arabic word meaning a ribbed heavy cloth.
85. Thirsk, 'Farming Regions of England', p. 48.
86. See above esp. pp. 17–19, 61–2, 64–6, 98, 172, 185, 252.
87. Dymond, 'Woollen Cloth Industry', p. 140
88. Betterton & Dymond, op. cit., p. 1.
89. S. H. A. Hervey (ed.), *Suffolk in 1524: Being the Return for a Subsidy granted in 1523*, Suffolk Green Books, No. X (Woodbridge, 1910), pp. 46, 114.
90. Hilary Todd & D. Dymond, 'Population Densities, 1327 and 1524', in Dymond & Martin, p. 203. Thingoe, including Bury St Edmunds, was the most populated hundred.
91. We must beware of exaggeration. North-east Norfolk, a sheep-corn region, supported a flourishing worsted cloth industry. See K. J. Allison, 'The Norfolk Worsted Industry in the Sixteenth and Seventeenth Centuries', *Yorkshire Bulletin of Economic and Social Research*, 12 (1960), pp. 73–83; ibid., 13 (1961), pp. 61–77.
92. John Pound (ed.) *The Military Survey of 1522 for Babergh Hundred* (Suffolk Records Society, vol. XXVIII, 1986), p. 4.
93. Betterton & Dymond, op. cit., p. 39.
94. Hoskins, *Age of Plunder*, p. 94.
95. Betterton & Dymond, p. 25.
96. Though they were also linked to, and dependent on, each other.
97. Gottfried, op. cit., p. 100.
98. *Chorography*, p. 43.
99. Blome, *Britannia*, pp. 208, 211–12.

100. Betterton & Dymond, p. 66.
101. Palliser, *Age of Elizabeth*, p. 300.
102. *VCH Suffolk*, Vol. II, p. 269.
103. Dymond & Northeast, p. 67.
104. Blome, *Britannia*, pp. 211–12. Blome does not make it clear whether Hadleigh manufactured the new fabrics.
105. Bays were lighter and finer than the modern baize and were made of worsted warp (combed fibres) and a woollen weft (carded). Says were a fine durable cloth, entirely of carded wool, with a texture resembling serge, a strong twilled fabric.
106. The New Draperies outside Suffolk were not entirely urban based. Some Essex villages, like 'Bocking and Cogggeshall, took to the making of "Dutch Bays" on a substantial scale' (D. C. Coleman, 'An Innovation and its Diffusion: The "New Draperies",' *Econ. HR*, 2nd series, xxii (1969), p. 427).
107. Ibid., p. 423.
108. *VCH Suffolk*, vol. II, p. 269.
109. Referring to England as a whole, D. C. Coleman says that the 'new draperies' reached 'a high point of prosperity around the end of the seventeenth century, only to decline slowly in the course of the eighteenth' (Coleman, 'Proto-Industrialization: A Concept Too Many', *Econ. HR*, 2nd series, xxxvi (1983), p. 443).
110. This section relies heavily upon Nesta Evans, *The East Anglian Linen Industry: Rural Industry and Local Economy 1500–1850* (Gower Publishing Co. Ltd., 1985).
111. Blome, *Britannia*, pp. 207–8.
112. Evans, op. cit., pp. ix–xiv.
113. Ibid., pp. 96–9, 106–7; Joan Thirsk, *Economic Policy and Projects: The Development of a Consumer Society in Early Modern England* (OUP, 1978), pp. 40–1, 143.
114. Evans, op. cit., pp. 97, 106.
115. Ibid., p. 43.
116. Ibid., p. 99.
117. Ibid., pp. 60, 100.
118. The exception was Palgrave, which was mostly an arable farming parish.
119. Evans, op. cit., pp. 75–6. The inventories cover the period 1600–1765 (ibid., p. 74).
120. Thirsk, *Economic Policy*, passim.
121. Evans, op. cit., p. 167 . Like Nesta Evans I shall use the term 'East Anglia' throughout this book to mean Norfolk and Suffolk only.
122. Evans, op. cit., p. 11.
123. R Davis, *English Overseas Trade 1500–1700* (Macmillan, 1973), p. 7.
124. Dymond & Northeast, pp. 68, 70; Reed, 'Economic Structure', p. 97.
125. Judith Middleton-Stewart, ' "Down to the sea in ships"; decline and fall on the Suffolk coast', in Carole Rawcliffe, Roger Virgoe and Richard Wilson (eds), *Counties and Communities: Essays on East Anglian History Presented to Hassell Smith* (Centre of East Anglian Studies, UEA, Norwich, 1996), pp. 74, 80. The herring industry of Lowestoft enjoyed better fortunes, however. See above p. 25.
126. Kirby, *Suffolk Traveller*, p. 7.
127. R. Gouldsmith, *Some Considerations of Trade and Manufacture addressed to the Inhabitants of the Town of Ipswich* (London, 1725), pp. 21–2. Frank Grace of University College, Suffolk, kindly drew my attention to this pamphlet, a copy of which is in SRO (I), S Ipswich 338.
128. In 1612 Ipswich provided ships for more cargoes of coal than did any of the other English east coast ports. For details see J. Binns, 'Sir Hugh Cholmley: Whitby's Benefactor or Beneficiary?', *NH*, xxx (1994), p. 103.
129. Reed, loc. cit.
130. Defoe, *Tour*, vol. I, pp. 57–8. Defoe attributed the decay of Ipswich to unfair competition from captured Dutch 'flyboats' put by the government into the coal-carrying trade (ibid., vol. I, p. 58).
131. So too did its main ancillary industry, the manufacture of sailcloth and canvas.
132. See Ralph Davis, *The Rise of the English Shipping Industry in the 17th and 18th centuries* (David & Charles, 1962), p. 55.
133. Defoe, *Tour*, vol. I, p. 61; Christopher Morris (ed.), *The Illustrated Journeys of Celia Fiennes c. 1682–1712* (Webb & Bower, 1988), p. 132.
134. Reed, loc. cit.

135. Blome, *Britannia*, p. 213.
136. Quoted in Davis, *Rise of English Shipping*, pp. 56–7.
137. Ibid.
138. Patten, *Pre-industrial England*, p. 75.
139. Blome, *Britannia*, p. 214.
140. *VCH Suffolk*, vol. II, p. 249.
141. Grace, 'Hist. Survey of Suffolk Towns', p. 109.
142. Blome, *Britannia*, p. 215; Defoe, *Tour*, vol. I, p. 80.
143. The first edition of Defoe's three-volume *Tour* was published in 1724–6.
144. Blome, *Britannia*, p. 215.
145. David Butcher, *The Ocean's Gift: Fishing in Lowestoft during the Pre-Industrial Era, 1550–1750* (Centre of East Anglian Studies, UEA, Norwich, 1995), pp. 43, 75–6.
146. Blome, *Britannia*, p. 216.
147. See Butcher, op. cit., pp. 104–5.
148. Michael Zell, *Industry in the countryside: Wealden Society in the sixteenth century* (CUP, 1994), esp. chapter 8.
149. *VCH Suffolk*, vol. I, p. 670.

NOTES TO CHAPTER TWO

1. Anthony Fletcher & Diarmaid MacCulloch, *Tudor Rebellions* (4th edn, Longman, 1997), pp. 18–20.
2. Pauline Croft, 'The Parliament of England', *TRHS*, 6th series, 7 (1997), p. 221.
3. Ken Powell & Chris Cook, *English Historical Facts 1484–1603* (Macmillan, 1977), p. 27; M. F. Keeler, *The Long Parliament, 1640–1641: A Biographical Study of its Members* (The American Philosophical Society, xxxvi, Philadelphia, 1954), p. 6.
4. Notable exceptions were perhaps the reign of Mary Tudor and the years 1587 and 1595. See MacCulloch, 'Consolidation', p. 41.
5. See chapter 9.
6. See William Hunt, *The Puritan Moment: The Coming of Revolution in an English County* (Harvard UP, 1983), esp. pp. 15, 104, 111, 160–1, 167; Blackwood, *Lancs. Gentry*, esp. pp. 4, 30n. 29, 47–8, 52, 58; Alan Everitt, 'The Local Community and the Great Rebellion', in R. C. Richardson (ed.), *The English Civil Wars: Local Aspects* (Sutton Publishing, 1997), p. 24.
7. The terms 'nobility' (or peers) and 'gentry' will be defined later in this chapter.
8. See J. S. Morrill, *Cheshire 1630–1660: County Government and Society during the 'English Revolution'* (OUP, 1974), p. 17; C. B. Phillips, 'The Gentry in Cumberland and Westmorland, 1600–1665' (unpublished PhD Thesis, University of Lancaster, 1974), p. 343; Mervyn James, *Family, Lineage and Civil Society: A Study of Society, Politics and Mentality in the Durham Region, 1500–1640* (OUP, 1974), pp. 51, 79, 147; A. M. Everitt, *The Community of Kent and the Great Rebellion 1640–60* (Leicester UP, 1966), p. 35; S. J. Watts, *From Border to Middle Shire: Northumberland 1586–1625* (Leicester UP, 1975), p. 55 seq.; David Underdown, *Somerset in the Civil War and Interregnum* (David & Charles, Newton Abbot, 1973), p. 19; Anthony Fletcher, *A County Community in Peace and War: Sussex 1600–1660* (Longman, 1975), pp. 22–4, 231; Ann Hughes, *Politics, Society and Civil War in Warwickshire, 1620–1660* (CUP, 1987), pp. 21, 26; J. T. Cliffe, *The Yorkshire Gentry from the Reformation to the Civil War* (Athlone Press, 1969), pp. 2–3.
9. John Guy, *Tudor England* (OUP, 1988), p. 176.
10. Alan G. R. Smith, *The Emergence of a Nation State: The commonwealth of England* (2nd edn, Longman, 1997), p. 135.
11. This section relies heavily upon MacCulloch, *Suffolk*; idem, 'Consolidation'; and Edward Martin, 'Hundreds and Liberties', in Dymond & Martin, pp. 26–7.
12. MacCulloch, *Suffolk*, p. 19.
13. See Angus Winchester, 'Parish, Township and Tithing: Landscapes of local administration in England before the nineteenth century', *The Local Historian*, 27 (1997), esp. pp. 5, 17.
14. In Wendy Goult, *A Survey of Suffolk Parish History*, 3 vols (Suffolk County Council, 1990), 326 parishes are listed for East Suffolk and 172 for West Suffolk. But she omits fourteen parishes in East Suffolk (Woodbridge, Lowestoft and the twelve parishes of Ipswich) and five in West Suffolk (Newmarket and two parishes each in Bury St Edmunds and Sudbury).
15. Twenty-one are given on Map 6 but the two small hundreds of Mutford and Lothingland were not united until 1763 (E. Martin, 'Hundred & Liberties', p. 26).

16. Ancient boroughs, like Ipswich and Bury St Edmunds, were largely outside the hundredal organisations. See ibid.
17. Smith, op. cit., p. 138; MacCulloch, 'Consolidation', p. 37.
18. Guy, op. cit., p. 169.
19. MacCulloch, 'Consolidation', p. 47.
20. Smith, op. cit., p. 136.
21. P. Williams, *The Tudor Regime* (OUP, 1979), p. 436.
22. Smith, loc. cit.
23. It could be argued that the forerunners of the JPs were the conservators of the peace, first appointed in the reign of Richard I (1189–99).
24. In the sixteenth century JPs and Quarter Sessions lost some of their previously extensive legal jurisdiction because the assize judges came to monopolise the trial of more serious breaches of the peace (MacCulloch, 'Consolidation', p. 41).
25. Modern JPs still have a few administrative tasks, such as licensing public houses.
26. Williams, op. cit., p. 408; MacCulloch, *Suffolk*, p. 34.
27. MacCulloch, op. cit., pp. 356, 390–1.
28. Smith, loc. cit.
29. MacCulloch, *Suffolk*, p. 34.
30. Ibid., p. 11.
31. J. H. Gleason, *The Justices of the Peace In England 1558–1640* (OUP, 1969), p. 148.
32. MacCulloch, *Suffolk*, p. 9.
33. Ibid., pp. 213, 233.
34. Ibid., p. 2. He seems to contradict this remark on pp. 124–5. See note 39 below.
35. Ibid., p. 19.
36. Since the monarch was now Head of the Church of England.
37. MacCulloch, *Suffolk*, pp. 23–4.
38. Dymond & Northeast, p. 18.
39. MacCulloch, in his *Suffolk*, pp. 124–5, has argued that particularism was still a strong force in the Suffolk of 1603, in the Liberties, in the Geldable, and in part of Lothingland. However, county unity was to be gradually strengthened.
40. MacCulloch, *Suffolk*, pp. 52.
41. Ibid., p. 24.
42. This was because the dukedom of Lancaster had been merged with the Crown since 1399.
43. MacCulloch, loc. cit.
44. Ibid., pp. 33–4.
45. Ibid., pp. 34, 98.
46. Ibid., pp. 26–7.
47. Gwyn Thomas, 'Parliamentary Constituencies' in Dymond & Martin, p. 30.
48. D. Hirst, *The Representative of the People? Voters and Voting in England under the Early Stuarts* (CUP, 1975), p. 105.
49. P. Pinckney, 'The Suffolk Elections to the Protectorate Parliaments', in Colin Jones, Malyn Newitt and Stephen Roberts (eds), *Politics and People in Revolutionary England* (Blackwell, 1986), pp. 207–12.
50. Pinckney, 'Suffolk Elections', pp. 207–8.
51. References are: (a) MacCulloch, *Suffolk*, p. 333; (b) Hirst, op. cit., p. 225; Pinckney, 'Suffolk Elections', p. 208; (c) Pinckney, loc. cit.; (d) Pinckney, p. 210; (e) P. E. Murrell, 'Suffolk: the Political Behaviour of the County and its Parliamentary Boroughs from the Exclusion Crisis to the Accession of the House of Hanover' (unpublished PhD Thesis, University of Newcastle-upon-Tyne, 1982), pp. 164, 169; (f) Ibid., pp. 165, 169.
52. I am extremely sceptical of this high estimate and even Pinckney seems to have doubts.
53. 'Scot and lot' was a contribution to municipal expenses, largely poor relief.
54. Hirst, op. cit., pp. 213–15. All the parliamentary boroughs mentioned, except Bury, are called freeman boroughs in the period 1673–1715. See Murrell, thesis, p. 169. Likewise Michael Brock describes them as freeman boroughs in 1830 (M. Brock, *The Great Reform Act* (Hutchinson Univ. Library, 1973), p. 21).
55. John Cannon, *Parliamentary Reform 1640–1832* (CUP, 1973), p. 14.
56. Pinckney, p. 208.
57. See chapter 9 Table 9.4.

58. Hirst, op. cit., p. 225.

59. MacCulloch, *Suffolk*, p. 47.

60. Ibid., pp. 94–5.

61. John Adamson, 'The Aristocracy and their Mental World', in John Morrill (ed.), *The Oxford Illustrated History of Tudor and Stuart Britain* (OUP, 1996), p. 174.

62. Lay peers, in descending order, were Dukes, Marquises, Earls, Viscounts and Barons.

63. T. Wilson, *The State of England Anno. Dom. 1600*, ed. F. J. Fisher (Camden Miscellany, XVI, Camden Third series, vol. 52, 1936), pp. 16–25.

64. Reyce, *Breviary*, pp. 56–82. Though Reyce does not devote a special paragraph to the esquire, he does give the title to several individual gentry (ibid., pp. 20, 88, 90, 95–7).

65. Wilson was a younger son of a country gentleman (Wilson, *State of England*, p.v). Robert Reyce of Preston Hall, Babergh hundred, was of the lesser gentry, with an income of only £200 p.a. in 1628 (PRO, Exchequer, Lay Subsidy Rolls, E 179/183/498).

66. W. Harrison, *Description of England*, ed. F. J. Furnivall, 4 vols (1877–1908), I, esp. pp. 105 seq., 130, 132–4; T. Smith, *De Republica Anglorum*, ed. L. Alston (CUP, 1906), pp. 31–47; E. Chamberlayne, *Angliae Notitia, or The Present State of England* (London, 1669), pp. 439–92.

67. David Cressy has criticised Wilson for including lawyers and clergy because 'gentility was a social condition, whereas the church or the law were careers' (D. Cressy, 'Describing the Social Order of Elizabethan and Stuart England', *Literature and History*, iii (1976), p. 37).

68. Yet on two occasions Reyce does use the word 'noble' to mean gentry. See Reyce, *Breviary*, pp. 58–9.

69. T. Wilson, *State of England*, pp. 20–1.

70. Knights and gentlemen will both come under the category of gentry.

71. Reyce, *Breviary*, pp. 72–3.

72. MacCulloch, *Suffolk*, p. 107.

73. Ibid., pp. 86–7.

74. Lawrence Stone, *The Crisis of the Aristocracy, 1558–1641* (OUP, 1965), p. 298.

75. Beckingsale, 'The Characteristics of the Tudor North', *NH*, iv (1969), p. 69; James, 'The Fourth Duke of Norfolk and the North', ibid., ii (1967), pp. 150–2.

76. MacCulloch, *Suffolk*, p. 109.

77. Smith, *De Republica*, p. 40.

78. I have been guided here by J. C. K. Cornwall, *Wealth and Society in early Sixteenth Century England* (Routledge & Kegan Paul, 1988), pp. 13, 29.

79. The knighthood composition papers suggest that £40 p.a. was the minimum landed income needed to sustain gentility in the 1630s. Gregory King apparently regarded five hearths and more as a qualification for gentry status in the later seventeenth century. See Philip Styles, 'The Heralds' Visitation of Warwickshire in 1682–3', *Birmingham Archaeological Society Transactions*, 71 (1953), pp. 100–1.

80. MacCulloch, *Suffolk*, p. 338.

81. See above p. 32.

82. For details see MacCulloch, *Suffolk*, pp. 422–3.

83. Ibid., pp 44, 47; S. T. Bindoff (ed.), *The House of Commons 1509–1558*, 3 vols (Secker & Warburg,1982), I, p. 191; P. V. Hasler (ed.), *The House of Commons 1558–1602*, 3 vols (HMSO, 1981), I, pp. 248–9.

84. MacCulloch, *Suffolk*, p. 44.

85. BL, Add. MS. 15,520 (Candler's notes on Suffolk 1655–7), f. 70.

86. Blome, *Britannia*, p. 210.

87. Christopher Morris (ed.), *The Illustrated Journeys of Celia Fiennes, c. 1682–1712* (Webb & Bower, 1988), p. 140.

88. Defoe, *Tour*, vol. I, pp. 66, 71–2, 74.

89. The dukedom of Norfolk was restored in 1660.

90. Robert Halliday, 'Bury Fair', *Suffolk/Norfolk Life*, viii, no. 54 (September, 1996), pp. 6–7; *Borough of St Edmundsbury: Official Guide* (St Edmundsbury Borough Council, 1976), pp. 18–19.

91. MacCulloch, *Suffolk*, pp. 286–7.

92. Of the 571 Suffolk communities, 384 had resident gentry while 187 had none. See John Adams, *Index Villaris* (London, 1680), in which pages 265–8 are missing.

93. Julian Cornwall's excellent *Wealth and Society* covers the early Tudor period, mainly the years 1522–25. I have given a very brief account of the social and economic state of the Parliamentarian

and Royalist gentry on the eve of the Civil War. See Gordon Blackwood, 'The Cavalier and Roundhead Gentry of Suffolk updated', *Suffolk Review*, New series 22 (Spring, 1994), pp. 18–30.

94. Nikolaus Pevsner, *The Buildings of England, Suffolk* (2nd edn, Penguin Books, 1974); Norman Scarfe, *The Suffolk Guide* (4th edn, Alistair Press, Bury St Edmunds, 1988); Maurice Howard, *The Early Tudor Country House: Architecture and Politics 1490–1550* (George Philip, 1987).

95. Professor Colin Platt, in his *The Great Rebuilding of Tudor and Stuart England* (UCL Press, 1994), considers that there was a second Great Rebuilding from the 1650s to the early eighteenth century. But in Suffolk only twenty-four 'Halls' seem to have been constructed during this period.

96. It could also testify to extravagance, but few of the 'building' gentry appear to have been in serious financial difficulties before the First Civil War (1642–46).

97. Howard, op. cit., pp. 38, 215.

98. Pevsner, op. cit., p. 298.

99. Howard, pp. 37, 215.

100. Pevsner, pp. 126, 173, 228, 251, 259, 386; Scarfe, op. cit., pp. 59, 97, 142.

101. Reyce, *Breviary*, pp. 49–50.

102. Ibid., p. 60.

103. Alan Simpson, *The Wealth of the Gentry 1540–1660: East Anglian Studies* (CUP, 1961), pp. 152, 207–8).

104. Everitt, *Suffolk*, pp. 17–18.

105. Reyce, loc. cit.

106. Felicity Heal and Clive Holmes, *The Gentry of England and Wales 1500–1700* (Macmillan, 1994), p. 12.

107. For the 1520s, 1603 and the 1670s see J. Patten, *Pre-industrial England*, p. 74. My figure for 1642 is a real 'guestimate', but its use is justified by the fact that the population of England (and probably Suffolk) was almost exactly the same in 1641 as in the 1670s. See Wrigley and Schofield, *Population History of England*, p. 209.

108. For statistical purposes the family unit includes the head of the family, his wife and children, his younger brothers and unmarried sisters, and the widow of any previous head of the family. However, where the head and younger brother both had adult sons, these have been counted as two separate families.

109. Main sources for identifying the gentry are John Pound (ed.), *The Military Survey of 1522 for Babergh Hundred* (Suffolk Records Society, vol. XXVIII, 1986); S. H. A. Hervey (ed.), *Suffolk in 1524: Being the Return for a Subsidy granted in 1523*, Suffolk Green Books, No. X (Woodbridge, 1910); PRO, *List of Sheriffs*, vol. IX, p. 88 for sheriffs in the 1520s; MacCulloch, *Suffolk*, pp. 358, 361, 364, 366–7, 370, 372–3 for names of JPs in the same decade.

110. MacCulloch makes an estimate of the number of gentry families by conflating three contemporary heraldic visitations (1561, 1577, 1612) with the one extant summary of the county's gentry made in 1578. For details see MacCulloch, thesis, p. 12 n. 8.

111. Main sources are V. B. Redstone (ed.), *The Ship Money Returns for Suffolk, 1639–40* (*PSIA*, 1904); C. B. Banks (ed.), *The Able Men of Suffolk* (Boston, USA, 1931); PRO, Exchequer, knighthood composition lists 1631–32, E 178/7356; PRO, Exchequer, Lay Subsidy Rolls 1628 and 1641, E 179/183/495; 183/498; 183/501; 183/510–21; 183/529–34; 183/549; Wards 5/40; 41.

112. The number of Suffolk gentry families in about 1670 can be estimated by conflating the following sources: PRO, Voluntary Gift 1661, E 179/257/7; PRO, Lay Subsidy Rolls 1663, E 179/183/508; 183/563; 183/564; 183/602; 257/11; *Statutes of the Realm*, vol. 5, 15 Car. II, cap. 9 for Suffolk Lay Subsidy Commissioners 1663; W. H. Rylands (ed.), *Visitation of Suffolk, 1664–68* (Harleian Society, lxi, 1910); Blome, *Britannia* (1673), pp. 427–31; S. H. A. Hervey (ed.), *Suffolk in 1674: The Hearth Tax Returns*, Suffolk Green Books, No. XI, vol. 13 (Woodbridge, 1905).

113. For calculations in this table and subsequently the generally accepted 4.5 multiplier has been used.

114. Reyce, *Breviary*, p. 59. But at the same time Reyce lamented that Suffolk had 'scarce twenty [knights] at most', compared with 'Sixty Knights … in the dayes of King Henry the third' (ibid., pp. 60–1).

115. Blackwood, *Lancs. Gentry*, p. 5.

116. A. Hassell Smith, *County and Court: Government and Politics in Norfolk, 1558–1603* (OUP, 1974), p. 53.

117. Yet in 1603 Norfolk had approximately 143,000 inhabitants, while Suffolk had just 108,000 (Patten, loc. cit.). So *in proportion* to the general population the gentry were more conspicuous in the latter than in the former county.

118. This family total roughly tallies with that of Professor Everitt who reckoned that Suffolk had

about 700 gentry families in Charles I's reign (A. M. Everitt, 'Social Mobility in Early Modern England', P&P, 33 (1966), p. 60).

119. See Heal & Holmes, op. cit., pp. 11, 388 n. 14.

120. Ibid., pp. 117, 158.

121. Reyce, *Breviary*, p. 58.

122. T. Fuller, *The Holy State and the Profane State* (Cambridge, 1642), p. 106.

123. Reyce, loc. cit.

124. N. Evans, 'Farming and Land-Holding in Wood-Pasture East Anglia 1550–1650', *PSIAH*, xxxv, pt. 4 (1984), pp. 303–15, esp. 312–13.

125. Nesta Evans has argued that the detailed evidence of wills shows that during the first half of the seventeenth century the yeomen increased, and the husbandmen decreased, in number in 'a number of wood-pasture parishes' of Suffolk (ibid., p. 303). Unfortunately she does not specify the number of wills studied, nor does she indicate the parishes concerned.

126. These parishes are all located in High Suffolk, except Barningham, Coney Weston, Culford, Dalham, Gazeley, Mildenhall and Westley, which are in the Fielding, and Rushmere and Shotley, which are in the Sandlings.

127. These parishes are located in the Fielding or Sandlings regions, except East Bergholt, Layham, Palgrave, Redgrave, Rougham, Shelley, Stuston and Woolpit, which are all in High Suffolk.

128. Blome, *Britannia*, p. 208.

129. *Chorography*, p. 19. The italics are mine.

130. Evans, 'Farming and Land-Holding', pp. 304, 309, 312–13; idem., *The East Anglian Linen Industry*, esp. pp. 8, 66, 74–6, 116, 151.

131. In fact Suffolk had been conspicuous since Domesday Book (1086) for its large number of freeholders, who at that time formed 42 per cent of the population. See *VCH Suffolk*, vol. I, p. 633.

132. See R. H. Tawney, *The Agrarian Problem in the Sixteenth Century*, with introduction by Lawrence Stone (Torchbook edn, New York, 1967), p. 25, Table I.

133. BL, Lansdowne MS. 5/7, ff. 16–26. Suffolk had a considerably higher number of non-gentry freeholders in 1561 than the following six counties: Bedford, Berkshire, Essex, Hertford, Nottingham and Oxford. For details see J. P. Cooper, 'The Social Distribution of Land and Men in England, 1436–1700', *Econ. HR*, 2nd series, xx (1967), p. 426 & n. 4.

134. Cornwall, *Wealth and Society*, pp. 24, 147.

135. Eric Kerridge, *Agrarian Problems in the Sixteenth Century and After* (Allen and Unwin, 1969), pp. 37–40.

136. Evans, 'Farming and Land-Holding', p. 312.

137. Reyce, *Breviary*, pp. 29, 57.

138. Evans, 'Farming and Land-Holding', p. 303. But Mrs Evans rightly adds: 'it seems improbable that the increase in the number of yeomen is due solely to the sons of husbandmen giving themselves a superior title' (ibid.).

139. Cornwall, loc. cit.

140. Reyce, *Breviary*, p. 58.

141. Palliser, *Age of Elizabeth*, p. 180.

142. See chapter I.

143. Palliser, op. cit., pp. 144–5, 184.

144. K. Wrightson, *English Society 1580–1680* (Hutchinson, 1982), pp. 35, 138.

145. Wilson, *State of England*, pp. 19–20.

146. This was about the national average. Professor Alan Everitt has said that 'in the Tudor and early Stuart period the labouring population probably formed about one-quarter to one-third of the entire population of the countryside' (Everitt, 'Farm Labourers', in Joan Thirsk (ed.), *Agrarian History of England and Wales 1500–1640*, p. 398).

147. Pound (ed.), *Military Survey*, pp. 8, 15.

148. Ibid., pp. 8, 15–16.

149. Dr Pound has recently revised his estimates, suggesting that poor people in Babergh numbered at least 20 per cent. I would go further and suggest that even this figure should perhaps be doubled. See J. F. Pound, 'Rebellion and Poverty in Sixteenth-Century Suffolk: The 1525 Uprising against the Amicable Grant', *PSIAH*, xxxix, pt. 3 (1999), p. 323.

150. Catharina Lis and Hugo Soly, *Poverty and Capitalism: Pre-Industrial Europe* (Revised edn, Harvester Press, 1982), p. 71.

151. Reyce, *Breviary*, p. 57.
152. N. Evans, 'People and Poor in 1674', in Dymond & Martin, pp. 96–7.
153. Blome, *Britannia*, p. 208. The italics are mine.
154. Ibid., pp. 208, 214.
155. Evans, 'People and Poor', p. 96

NOTES TO CHAPTER THREE

1. By 'Catholic' I mean *Roman* Catholic only.
2. The doctrine of predestination, present in a modified form in medieval Catholicism and restated with more one-sided emphasis by Luther, was taken to its fully rigorous extreme by Calvin: 'By predestination we mean the eternal decree of God, by which He has decided in His own mind what He wishes to happen in the case of each individual. For all men are not created on an equal footing, but for some eternal life is pre-ordained, for others eternal damnation' (*Christianae Religionis Institutio* (1559 edn), Book III, cap. xxi, quoted in H. Bettenson (ed.), *Documents of the Christian Church* (OUP, 1943, repr. 1956), p. 300).
3. See pp. 89–90.
4. See A. G. Dickens, *The English Reformation* (2nd edn, Batsford, 1989).
5. See J. J. Scarisbrick, *The Reformation and the English People* (Blackwell, 1984); Eamon Duffy, *The Stripping of the Altars: Traditional Religion in England 1400–1580* (Yale UP, 1992); Christopher Haigh, *English Reformations. Religion, Politics and Society under the Tudors* (OUP, 1993).
6. Scarisbrick, op. cit., p. 12.
7. Patrick Collinson, review of Haigh, *English Reformations*, in *Times Literary Supplement*, 22 October 1993, p. 15.
8. MacCulloch, *Suffolk Review*, p. 1.
9. Duffy, op. cit., p. 132.
10. For further details see Nikolaus Pevsner, *The Buildings of England, Suffolk* (2nd edn, Penguin Books, 1974), pp. 71, 102, 177, 316, 353, 430, 472; Norman Scarfe, *The Suffolk Guide* (4th edn, Alastair Press, Bury St Edmunds, 1988), pp. 39, 51, 121, 155, 169; H. Munro Cautley, *Suffolk Churches and their Treasures* (5th edn, the Boydell Press, 1982), pp. 225–6, 257, 305, 327, 348, 360; Jean Corke, John Blatchly, John Fitch and Norman Scarfe (eds), *Suffolk Churches: Pocket Guide* (Suffolk Historic Churches Trust 1980), pp. 16–19.
11. Pevsner, op. cit., pp. 438–9.
12. Cautley, op. cit., p. 326.
13. See Preface by Rev. A Bird to the *Guide to Lavenham church* (ND, NP).
14. Cautley, p. 308; Pevsner, pp. 322–3.
15. Cautley, loc. cit.
16. Duffy, op. cit., p. 302.
17. MacCulloch, *Suffolk*, p. 139.
18. Pevsner, p. 33.
19. J. R. Lander, *Government and Community: England 1450–1509* (Edward Arnold, 1980), p. 148.
20. On his recusancy see chapter 4.
21. This refers to the Martin Chapel on the south side of the chancel; it was completed in 1484, endowed as a chantry and contained an altar dedicated to Jesus (David Dymond & Clive Paine, *The Spoil of Melford Church: The Reformation in a Suffolk Parish* (Salient Press, 1989), p. 2 n. 5).
22. The Easter Sepulchre represented the tomb in which Christ's body was laid after the Crucifixion.
23. A tabernacle was a carved frame and canopy of stone or timber, to contain and show off an image.
24. For full details of Martin's account of the furnishings of Long Melford church see Dymond & Paine, op. cit., pp. 1–4.
25. The Sunday before Easter which began the dramatic ceremonies of Holy Week.
26. The consecrated bread or 'Host', believed to be the body of Christ.
27. Dymond & Paine, pp. 5–7.
28. Ibid., pp. 10, 15–16, 19.
29. William Holland, *Cratfield: A Transcript of the Accounts of the Parish AD 1490 to AD 1642 with Notes*, ed. J. J. Raven (Jarrold & Sons, London, 1895), pp. 41–5. For an explanation of the various kinds of church goods in Melford and Cratfield see glossary in Dymond & Paine, pp. 77–84.
30. The population of Cratfield in the 1520s is unknown, but in 1603 it had only 200 adults (Wendy

Goult, *A Survey of Suffolk Parish History, East Suffolk* (Suffolk County Council, 1990), vol. I (unpaginated). For the population of Long Melford see chapter 1, p. 5.

31. This paragraph owes much to discussions with Peter Northeast.

32. Scarisbrick, op. cit., pp. 19–20. The guilds described by Scarisbrick are to be distinguished from trade or craft guilds whose interests were essentially mundane. However, rural Suffolk had no trade or craft guilds, while even in large towns, like Bury St Edmunds and Ipswich, they were the exception rather than the rule.

33. Too much should not be made of the distinctions between membership of the parish and membership of a guild. As Duffy says, 'the majority of guilds worked within and for the structure of the parish, not against it'. Indeed, 'many gilds were expressly founded to maintain the fabric or ornaments of the parish churches' (Duffy, p. 145).

34. P. Northeast, 'Parish Gilds', in Dymond & Martin, p. 74.

35. In addition, the guild of Our Lady is mentioned in these accounts in 1537 (Peter Northeast (ed.), *Boxford Churchwardens Accounts 1530–1561* (Suffolk Records Society, XXIII, 1982), pp. 26, 98).

36. Information kindly supplied by David Dymond.

37. V. B. Redstone, Extracts from Wills and other Material showing the history of Suffolk Churches, Chantries and Guilds, *PSIA*, xxiii (1937), p. 66.

38. Robert S. Gottfried, *Bury St Edmunds and the Urban Crisis, 1290–1539* (Princeton UP, 1982), pp. 188–9.

39. Some were of course built earlier, like the originally enormous fifteenth-century guildhall of Hadleigh. See Scarfe, op. cit., p. 95.

40. Pevsner, pp. 186–7, 207, 274, 313, 326–7; *The Guild of St Mary and its Guildhall in Laxfield, Suffolk* (Laxfield & District Museum, 1977), passim.

41. F. E. Warren (ed.), 'The Gild of St Peter in Bardwell', *PSIA*, xi (1903), p. 136.

42. Scarisbrick, p. 39.

43. Haigh, *English Reformations*, p. 9.

44. Ibid., p. 41.

45. MacCulloch, *Suffolk*, p. 346; also p. 139.

46. In 1518 Wolsey was given the bishopric of Bath and Wells, to hold with York- the first time sees had been held in plurality since the mid-eleventh century.

47. Haigh, op. cit., pp. 84–5.

48. For details see David Knowles, *The Religious Orders in England*: Vol. III, *The Tudor Age* (CUP pbk, 1979), p. 470.

49. Peter Gwyn, *The King's Cardinal: The Rise and Fall of Thomas Wolsey* (Barrie & Jenkins, 1990), opposite p. 442. For a full discussion of Wolsey as a churchman, see ibid., pp. 265–355, 464–80.

50. The word Lollard or *Lollaerd* is from middle Dutch, meaning a mumbler.

51. See J. A. F. Thomson, *The Later Lollards 1414–1520* (OUP, 1965), passim; Anne Hudson, *The Premature Reformation: Wycliffite Texts and Lollard History* (OUP, 1988), esp. pp. 120–4.

52. See N. P. Tanner (ed.), *Heresy Trials in the Diocese of Norwich, 1428–31* (Camden Fourth Series, 20, 1977).

53. See map in ibid., p. 27.

54. Ibid., pp. 57–8, 81, 86, 111–12, 134–5.

55. Conrad Russell, 'The Reformation and the Creation of the Church of England, 1500–1640', in John Morrill (ed.), *The Oxford Illustrated History of Tudor and Stuart Britain* (OUP, 1996), p. 265.

56. In the Norwich heresy trials John Reve, Richard Knobbyng, Richard Grace, Baldwin Cowper and Matilda Fletcher, all from Beccles, condemned as many as five sacraments: Baptism, Confession, the Eucharist, Confirmation and Matrimony (Tanner, op. cit., pp. 111, 115, 121, 126, 131).

57. MacCulloch, *Suffolk*, p. 148.

58. Anne Eljenholm Nichols, *Seeable Signs: The Iconography of the Seven Sacraments, 1350–1544* (The Boydell Press, 1994), pp. xix–xx.

59. See ibid., pp. xix–xx, 90–128.

60. See especially J. F Davis, *Heresy and Reformation in South-East England 1520–1559* (RHS Studies in History Series, 34, 1983), passim; Dickens, *English Reformation*, chapter 3.

61. For Protestants see Fines *Register*, passim. For fuller details of this important work see p. 96.

62. Dickens, op. cit., pp. 14, 59.

63. Bury St Edmunds and Stoke-by-Nayland are possible exceptions. But even here there are doubts. Dr Davis says that Stoke-by-Nayland – Protestant at the Reformation – had 'Lollard traditions' (Davis, op. cit., p. 39). But Dr Tanner seems uncertain whether the two accused of Lollardy in

1429 – John Kynget and Thomas Chatrys – came from Nayland or Needham Market (Tanner, op. cit., p. iv). As for Bury St Edmunds, a chaplain of the town was accused of Lollardy in 1530. But Bury became truly Protestant, indeed Puritan, only in the 1580s (J. S. Craig, 'Reformation, Politics and Polemic in Sixteenth Century East Anglian Market towns' (unpublished PhD thesis, University of Cambridge, 1992), Chapter 3).

64. For the main Nonconformist places see chapter 7 pp. 200–3, chapter 8 Map 16, chapter 9 Table 9.6, and Appendix VI.

65. K. B. McFarlane, *Wycliffe and English Nonconformity* (Pelican edn, 1972), p. 170.

66. Christopher Haigh, 'The Recent Historiography of the English Reformation', in C. Haigh (ed.), *The English Reformation Revised* (CUP, 1987), p. 19.

67. F. M. Powicke, *The Reformation in England* (OUP, 1941), p. 1.

68. D. MacCulloch, 'England', in Andrew Pettegree (ed.), *The early Reformation in Europe* (CUP, 1992), p. 166.

69. Annates were the first year's revenue of bishops and certain other preferments.

70. My italics.

71. J. J. Scarisbrick, *Henry VIII* (New edn, Yale UP, 1997), p. 324.

72. Ibid.

73. Haigh, *English Reformations*, p. 121.

74. See *The Martyrs of England and Wales, 1535–1680* (Catholic Truth Society pamphlet, 1979), pp. 10, 18.

75. G. W. Bernard, 'The Church of England *c.* 1529–*c.* 1642', *History*, 75 (1990), p. 184.

76. J. R. H. Moorman, *The Franciscans in England* (Mowbray, 1974), p. 91.

77. Not to be confused with secular canons of cathedrals, etc.

78. Well before the end of the Middle Ages manual work was generally performed by lay brothers, especially in the larger monasteries. Those taught were mainly novices (trainee monks) and the sick, cared for in the infirmary, were usually monks. The amount of hospitality and poor relief provided varied between monasteries.

79. Although Benedictine monks and Augustinian canons had a substantial urban presence.

80. Peter Northeast, 'Religious Houses', in Dymond & Martin, p. 70.

81. MacCulloch, *Suffolk*, p. 139. Friaries were less favoured than parish churches, however (ibid.).

82. Roberta Gilchrist, 'Religious Women in Medieval East Anglia', *The Annual: Bulletin of the Norfolk Archaeological and Historical Research Group*, 3 (1994), p. 40.

83. See Claire Cross & Noreen Vickers (eds), *Monks, Friars and Nuns in Sixteenth Century Yorkshire* (Yorkshire Archaeological Society Record Series, CL, 1995).

84. These houses are listed in Appendix I(a) and located in Map 9.

85. For convenience the abbeys and priories for monks, the houses of canons regular and the preceptories of Knights Hospitallers are collectively called monasteries.

86. Cross & Vickers, op. cit., p. 4.

87. Quoted in M. R. James, *On the Abbey of St Edmund of Bury* (CUP 1895), p. 126. I owe this reference to David Dymond.

88. *VCH Suffolk*, vol. II, p. 69.

89. Ideally, monasteries were meant to be at least thirteen strong, the same number as Christ and the Apostles.

90. J. E. Oxley, *The Reformation in Essex to the death of Mary* (Manchester UP, 1965), Appendix IV, p. 285.

91. See Knowles & Hadcock, p. 241; Chambers, *Register*, pp. 162, 180. The best known source – J. Hunter, *A Catalogue of the Deeds of Surrender of Certain Abbeys, etc., 8th Report of the Deputy Keeper of the Public Records* (London, 1847), Appendix II, pp. 1–51 – does not mention a single friar resident in Suffolk.

92. A. Savine, *English Monasteries on the Eve of the Dissolution* (Oxford Studies in Social and Legal History, Vol. I, OUP, 1909), p. 83.

93. See chapter 2 above.

94. *Valor*, vol. III, p. 465. The *Valor Ecclesiasticus* – completed by royal commissioners in 1535 – provides a detailed list of the annual income of each ecclesiastical benefice and of most monastic houses in England, and is considered fairly reliable by historians. In Appendix I(a) incomes of religious houses suppressed in the 1530s are mostly derived from this source.

95. Gottfried, op. cit., pp. 73–4.

96. Ibid., p. 74: *LP*, XIV, pt. ii, no. 462.

97. John Pound (ed.), *The Military Survey of 1522 for Babergh Hundred* (Suffolk Records Society, XXVII, 1986), pp. 13, 15.

98. This may be a slight underestimate. See A. G. Dickens (ed.), 'The Register or Chronicle of Butley Priory, Suffolk', in A. G. Dickens, *Late Monasticism and the Reformation* (Hambledon Press, 1994), p. 13.

99. Ibid., pp. 13, 71–3.

100. Suffolk with only three rich monasteries – worth over £200 per annum – compares unfavourably with Essex, where six out of twenty-four monasteries were wealthy. See Oxley, loc. cit.

101. We are ignorant of the income of the Knights Hospitallers at Dunwich.

102. G. W. O. Woodward, *Dissolution of the Monasteries* (Blandford Press, 1966), p. 17.

103. Dickens, 'Register ... Butley Priory', p. 11.

104. Ibid., p. 12.

105. The reports of the commissioners were not always critical and occasionally they spoke well of houses or of some of the religious, but their main object was to provide material for an unfavourable report.

106. *LP* IX, no. 772. Quoted in Knowles, *Religious Orders*, vol. III, p. 288.

107. Ibid.

108. MacCulloch, *Suffolk*, p. 133.

109. For examples of scandal see Knowles, op. cit., pp. 73–5.

110. Roberta Gilchrist and Marilyn Oliva, *Religious Women in Medieval East Anglia* (Centre of East Anglian Studies, UEA, 1993), esp. chapters 3 and 4.

111. Scarisbrick, *English Reformation*, p. 68.

112. Ibid.

113. Knowles, op. cit., p. 470.

114. For details see ibid.

115. The scandal-ridden Norfolk monasteries mentioned above were not typical.

116. G. R. Elton, *England under the Tudors* (3rd edn, Routledge, 1991), p. 141.

117. Susan Doran and Christopher Durston, *Princes, Pastors and People: The Church and Religion in England 1529–1689* (Routledge, 1991), p. 164.

118. See Anthony Fletcher & Diarmaid MacCulloch, *Tudor Rebellions* (4th edn, Longman, 1997), pp. 18–10.

119. *VCH Suffolk*, vol. II, p. 132.

120. Ibid., pp. 67, 90, 98. The early surrender of Sibton is at first sight surprising. The value of this house being well over £200 a year, it would not have fallen for another two years; but the recently-appointed abbot, William Flatbury, had apparently been put in through the influence of the Duke of Norfolk, and with the connivance of Thomas Cromwell, on purpose to bring about a speedy surrender.

121. F. A. Gasquet, *Henry VIII and the English Monasteries* (Geo. Bell & sons, 1906); Geoffrey Baskerville, *English Monks and the Suppression of the Monasteries* (Jonathan Cape, 1937); G. A. J. Hodgett (ed.), *The State of the Ex-Religious and Former Chantry Priests in the diocese of Lincoln 1547–1574* (Lincoln Record Society, 53, 1959); idem, 'The Unpensioned Ex-Religious in Tudor England', *Journal of Ecclesiastical History*, XIII (1962), pp. 195–202.

122. Many pensions were not paid in 1552, a year of acute inflation (A. G. Dickens, 'Edwardian Arrears in Augmentations Payments and the Problem of the Ex-Religious', *English Historical Review*, LV (1940), p. 385). But, as Hodgett says, 'there seems no evidence to suggest that, from 1554 onwards, pensions were not regularly paid. Moreover, payments were being made to ex-religious as late as 1569 and 1575' (Hodgett, *The State of the Ex-Religious*, p. xix).

123. Christopher Haigh, *The Last Days of the Lancashire Monasteries and the Pilgrimage of Grace* (Chetham Society, 3rd series, XVII, 1969), p. 112.

124. For examples see Appendix I(b).

125. Some monks and nuns received small one-off payments when their religious houses were suppressed, but these hardly count.

126. *VCH Suffolk*, vol. II, p. 98.

127. Chambers, *Register*, p. 73; Geoffrey Baskerville, 'Married Clergy and the Pensioned Religious in the Diocese of Norwich 1555', *English Historical Review*, XLVIII (1933), pp. 61, 202, & n. 3.

128. Ibid., p. 202, & n. 4.

129. David Knowles, op. cit., pp. 57–8.

130. Baskerville, 'Married Clergy, etc.', p. 215; idem, *English Monks*, pp. 138, 240.

131. *VCH Suffolk*, vol. II, p. 124.
132. Hodgett, 'The Unpensioned Ex-Religious', p. 202.
133. Marilyn Oliva, *The Convent and the community in Late Medieval England: Female Monasteries in the Diocese of Norwich, 1350–1540* (The Boydell Press, 1998), pp. 198, 202.
134. This, like the fate of the ex-religious, is a vast subject and space permits us to do no more than scratch the surface and concentrate on the reign of Henry VIII.
135. An Act of 1536 set up the Court of Augmentations to control and administer the former monastic lands on behalf of the Crown, and to arrange and supervise sales and leases.
136. For Dr Savine's calculations see H. A. L. Fisher, *The Political History of England*, 12 vols (London, 1905–20), V, pp. 499–500.
137. Ibid., p. 499. The sales were always expressed as being 'grants' because the king was the vendor. The purchasers were called 'grantees', though some were actually agents rather than genuine buyers.
138. Ibid.
139. Ibid., p. 500.
140. Ibid., p. 499.
141. Copinger, *Manors*, vol. I, p. 336 and Appendix I(c).
142. *LP*, XIV (2), no. 780/36.
143. Joyce Youings, *The Dissolution of the Monasteries* (Allen & Unwin, 1971), p. 121.
144. An analysis based on annual value rather than on counting manors would perhaps slightly modify the following figures but would not alter the situation substantially.
145. The 3rd Duke of Norfolk, though powerful throughout East Anglia, has been assigned to Norfolk for statistical purposes.
146. Knowles, op. cit., pp. 397–8.
147. S. B. Liljegren, *The Fall of the Monasteries and the Social Changes in England leading up to the Great Revolution* (Lund, 1924), pp. 109–10.
148. Oxley, op. cit., p. 251.
149. MacCulloch, *Suffolk*, pp. 68–9.
150. Copinger, *Manors*, vol. II, p. 150, vol. IV, p. 227; *DKR*, IX, App. ii, p. 209; *LP*, XIX(1), no. 812/17.
151. See Appendix I(c); *DKR*, X, App. ii, p. 249; *LP*, XX (2), no. 496/66.
152. *LP*, XV, no. 436/63.
153. *DKR*, X, App. ii, p. 305; *LP*, XIX (1), no. 80/55.
154. Pevsner, op. cit., p. 298.
155. See Appendix I(c); Maurice Howard, *The Early Tudor Gentry House: Architecture and Politics 1490–1550* (George Philip, 1987), pp. 38, 215; Copinger, *Manors*, vol. VII, p. 50; *LP*, XV, no. 436/74.
156. See W. C. Metcalfe (ed.), *Visitations of Suffolk, 1561, 1577, 1612* (Exeter, 1882), pp. 48, 59, 82, 176; S. H. A. Hervey (ed.), *Suffolk in 1568: Being the Return for a Subsidy granted 1566*, Suffolk Green Books, No. XII (Bury St Edmunds, 1909), pp. xvii, 9, 166, 252.
157. Lawrence Stone & Jeanne C. Fawtier Stone, *An Open Elite? England 1540–1880* (OUP, 1984), p. 197.
158. Liljegren, op. cit., p. 117.
159. T. H. Swales, 'The redistribution of the monastic lands in Norfolk at the Dissolution', *Norfolk Archaeology*, XXXIV, pt. i (1966), p. 32.
160. See chapter 2, p. 48.
161. Alan Simpson, *The Wealth of the Gentry 1540–1660: East Anglian Studies* (CUP, 1961), p. 52.
162. For details of manorial acquisitions see Appendix I (c). For information on posts held by royal officials see MacCulloch, *Suffolk* pp. 71, 74, 76, 229, 231; *The Concise DNB*, vol. II, p. 1234, vol. III, p. 2801; Swales, op. cit., p. 33.
163. E. A. Wasson, 'The penetration of new wealth into the English governing class from the middle ages to the First World War', *Econ. HR*, li (1998), p. 36.
164. *DKR*, X, App. ii, pp. 262–3; *LP*, XV, no. 436/88, XX (2), no. 496/43.
165. See Appendix I(c); MacCulloch, op. cit., pp. 59 n. 15, 70.
166. Henry Payne of Bury and Sir Humphrey Wingfield of Brantham.
167. These included two Suffolk officials of the peerage – Sir Arthur Hopton of Blythburgh and Sir Anthony Rous of Dennington – and five royal officials: Sir Edmund Bedingfield of Oxburgh, Norfolk, and John Gosnold of Otley, Sir Nicholas Hare of Homersfield, Sir Robert Southwell of Barham, Sir Anthony Wingfield of Letheringham, all Suffolk men.
168. Youings, 'The Terms of the Disposal of Devon Monastic Lands, 1536–58', *English Historical Review*, LXIX (1954), p. 31; idem. (ed.), *Devon Monastic Lands: Calendar of Particulars for Grants, 1536–1558*,

Devon and Cornwall Record Society, New Series, I (1953), pp. xxv–xxvii; C. Haigh, *Last Days of Lancs. Monasteries*, chapter 10 and appendix B; Swales, op. cit., p. 43; Oxley, op. cit., pp. 251–4.

169. The mere gentry were those depending for their income solely or mainly upon land and not upon trade, the law or office-holding.

170. For details and documentation see Appendix I(c).

171. The thirty-one families include the twenty-three named in Appendix I(c), plus the two lawyers and six office-holders of Suffolk gentry stock. See above n. 166, 167.

172. Two grantees – the Dean and Chapter of Ely and the Dean and Chapter of Norwich – are excluded. We are ignorant of the religion of the following grantees: Thomas Bacon, Richard Codington, Christopher Coote, Sir John Crofts, William Edgar, Richard Goodrich, Sir Richard Gresham, Sir Thomas Gresham, Reginald Guybon, Sir Percival Hart, Sir John Jenny, John Kene, Sir Francis Lovell, George Smith, Nicholas Smith, John Southwell, Paul Withipoll.

173. Protestants or ancestors thereof: Anne of Cleves, Nicholas Bacon, Charles Brandon, 1st Duke of Suffolk, Richard Cavendish, William Clopton, Thomas Cromwell, Earl of Essex, Thomas Darcy, Lord Darcy of Chiche, Sir Anthony Denny, John de Vere, 16th Earl of Oxford, William Forth, Francis Framlingham, Sir Arthur Hopton, Sir Thomas Jermyn, Thomas Poley, Sir John Spring, Robert Spring, Sir William Willoughby, Sir Anthony Wingfield, Sir John Wingfield, Adam Winthrop. Catholics or ancestors thereof: Sir Edmund Bedingfield, Sir William Cordell, Sir John Cornwallis, Sir Thomas Cornwallis, Thomas Daniel, Sir William Drury, Sir Richard Freston, John Gosnold, Sir Nicholas Hare, John Harvey, Sir Clement Higham, Thomas Howard, 3rd Duke of Norfolk, Sir Ambrose Jermyn, Henry Jerningham, Sir Thomas Kitson, Henry Payne, William Rede, Nicholas Rookwood, Sir Anthony Rous, Sir Robert Southwell, John Tasburgh, William Tyrrell, Sir Humphrey Wingfield. For evidence of the religious faith of these individuals or their descendants see MacCulloch, *Suffolk*; idem., 'Catholic and Puritan', pp. 232–89.

174. Woodward, op. cit., p. 133.

175. BL, Cotton MS. Cleopatra E.V., f. 389.

176. J. F. Davis calls Bilney an Evangelical Reformer. See Davis, 'The Trials of Thomas Bilney and the English Reformation', *HJ*, 24 (1981), pp. 775–90.

177. Craig, thesis, pp. 141–2.

178. For a good brief account of Bale's early career see Knowles, op. cit., pp. 57–8. We are not concerned with his later career.

179. Scarisbrick, *Henry VIII*, p. 337.

180. A. G. Dickens and Dorothy Carr (eds), *The Reformation in England to the Accession of Elizabeth I* (Edward Arnold, 1967), p. 82.

181. R. A Houlbrooke, 'Persecution of Heresy and Protestantism in the Diocese of Norwich under Henry VIII', *Norfolk Archaeology*, 35, Pt. III (1972), p. 316.

182. Northeast, *Boxford Churchwardens' Accounts 1530–1561*, pp. xiv, 37; G. B. Baker (ed.), 'Extracts from Churchwardens' Books, Bungay St Mary', in *East Anglian Notes & Queries*, Old Series, 3 vols (1864–9), II, p. 148; Dymond & Paine, *The Spoil of Melford Church*, pp. 26–35, esp. 29–30. These seem to be the only Suffolk churchwardens' accounts which cover the whole Reformation period from the 1530s to the 1560s. *The Cratfield ... Accounts ... 1490 to 1642*, promising at first sight, are unfortunately incomplete for the Reformation period.

183. Haigh, *English Reformations*, pp. 131–2.

184. See Dickens & Carr, op. cit., pp. 115–18.

185. Haigh, op. cit., p. 161.

186. The other five in trouble were Alan Gifford and William Grey, both of East Bergholt, Richard Mannock of Stoke-by-Nayland, and two pastors, Nicholas Shaxton and Rowland Taylor. See Houlbrooke, op. cit., pp. 324–5. On Kirby and his wife see Fines *Register* (unpaginated).

187. For more details see the next section of this chapter.

188. J. J. Scarisbrick, 'Henry VIII and the dissolution of the secular colleges', in Claire Cross, David Loades & J. J. Scarisbrick (eds), *Law and Government under the Tudors* (CUP, 1988), pp. 52, 58.

189. *VCH Suffolk*, vol. II, pp. 142, 145, 149, 151–2.

190. See above p. 65.

191. Northeast, 'Parish Gilds', in Dymond & Martin, p. 74.

192. Oxley, op. cit., p. 262.

193. Christopher Haigh, *Reformation and Resistance in Tudor Lancashire* (CUP, 1975), p. 72; Oxley, p. 63; Judith Middleton-Stewart, 'Singing for Souls in Suffolk 1300–1548', *Suffolk Review*, New series 16 (spring 1991), p. 10.

194. On the other hand the suppression of the chantries apparently did little harm to education in Suffolk. The only chantry priests who served also as schoolmasters were at Clare, Melford, Orford and Eye, and the stipendiary priest of St Peter's guild at Lavenham (Middleton-Stewart, op. cit., p. 16).

195. Gerard Culkin, *The English Reformation* (2nd edn, Sands & Co. (Publishers) Ltd., 1955), p. 46.

196. D. M. Palliser, 'Popular reactions to the Reformation', in Christopher Haigh (ed.), *The English Reformation Revised* (CUP, 1987) , p. 100; Houlbrooke, op. cit., pp. 317, 322.

197. Ronald Hutton, 'The local impact of the Tudor Reformation', in Peter Marshall (ed.), *The Impact of the English Reformation 1500–1640* (Arnold, 1997), pp. 147, 151.

198. Dickens & Carr, op. cit., pp. 146–7.

199. Main sources for this and the next three paragraphs are Northeast, *Boxford*, pp. 49, 51, 54–5, 58, 64–5, 68, 82 n. 55; Baker, *East Anglian Notes etc.*, OS, II, pp. 227–30, 275–7; Dymond & Payne, op. cit., pp. 37 & n. 91, 40 & n. 96, 49 & n. 119, 53 & n. 125, 58 & n. 136, 59–62.

200. It was not mindless vandalism, however. Protestants associated images and the rood lofts with the worship of saints who, far from interceding on behalf of sinners, were a barrier between God and man. Altars and tabernacles were, rightly, linked with the sacrifice of the Latin mass.

201. In 1547–48 the walls of Melford Church were whitened by John Kendall; biblical texts were then added by one Stayworth. In Mary's reign the texts or 'vayne scrybylyng' were erased, and in the chancel probably replaced by new paintings (Dymond & Paine, p. 40 n. 98).

202. In the later Middle Ages parish churches often had more than one organ.

203. Banner clothes were embroidered or painted banners supported by staffs and carried in pre-Reformation religious processions.

204. A censer was a metal container for burning incense, suspended by chains and swung from the hand.

205. A pix was a vessel for holding the reserved Sacrament. It was often suspended over the high altar, surrounded by a canopy cloth.

206. The Blessed Sacrament was reserved by the Church before the Reformation in the altar, or in a hanging tabernacle over the altar, above which a canopy was placed.

207. A processionary or processional is a book containing the order of service for the different processions.

208. A pax is a plate used in giving the kiss of peace at the celebration of Mass.

209. For examples of the destruction of altars, images and rood lofts in Suffolk in 1559–62, see Baker in *East Anglian Notes* etc., OS, II, p. 278; III, p. 19; Northeast, *Boxford*, pp. 70, 82 n. 63; Dymond & Paine, *Spoil of Melford Church*, pp. 40 n. 98, 72–3.

210. Hutton, op. cit., p. 161.

211. These dates were selected because 1525 was the time when Tyndale's New Testament was printed, while 1558 saw the death of Mary Tudor.

212. A provisional first volume (A–C) was published by the Sutton Courtenay Press, 1981. Part 2 (D–Z) was published by the West Sussex Institute of Higher Education, 1985.

213. J. Foxe *Actes and Monuments*, ed. S. R. Cattley, & G. Townsend, 8 vols (Seeley & W. Burnside, London 1837–41), hereafter Foxe, *A&M*. Foxe was in a good position to be accurately informed about East Anglian events; he had been the 4th Duke of Norfolk's boyhood tutor, and was on corresponding terms with Bishop Parkhurst.

214. Christina H. Garrett, *The Marian Exiles: A Study of the Origins of Elizabethan Puritanism* (CUP, 1938, repr. 1966).

215. A. G. Dickens, 'The early expansion of Protestantism in England, 1520–1558' in *Impact of English Reformation, 1500–1640*, p. 89.

216. Map 10 and Tables 3.2, 3.3 are based on the Fines *Register*.

217. So was the peculiar of Isleham, which was in Cambridgeshire.

218. See Appendix II.

219. MacCulloch, *Suffolk*, p. 174.

220. Idem, *Suffolk Review*, pp. 6–8.

221. Idem, *Suffolk*, p. 179. The Mannocks of Gifford Hall, devout Catholics, were not yet *prominent* gentry.

222. Haigh, *English Reformations*, p. 229.

223. Foxe, *A&M*, VIII, pp. 556–7. The two communicants were John Foxe (not the martyrologist) and John Steyre.

224. MacCulloch, 'Catholic and Puritan', p. 263.

225. During the sixteenth century the term 'spinster' denoted a woman employed in the domestic textile industry.

226. See MacCulloch, *Suffolk*, pp. 291–8, 305, 311–12.

227. See chapter 5.

228. See chapter 9 and Appendix VI.

229. Foxe, *A&M, VI, pp. 676–7.*

230. Craig, thesis, p. 140.

231. Ibid., pp. 144, 152, 154, 156–8.

232. MacCulloch, *Suffolk*, p. 178.

233. Davis, *Heresy and Reformation*, p. 117.

234. Ibid.

235. Fines *Register.*

236. Susan Brigden, *London and the Reformation* (OUP, 1991), p. 2.

237. MacCulloch, *Suffolk*, p. 157.

238. BL, Cotton MS. Cleopatra E.V., f. 389.

239. Dickens, 'Early expansion of Protestantism', p. 94.

240. For full details see Foxe, *A&M*, VIII, pp. 598–600.

241. MacCulloch, *Suffolk*, p. 175.

242. Ibid., p. 180.

243. This section relies mainly on the Fines *Register.*

244. This table, together with Tables 3.3, 4.1, 7.6 and 8.7 below, is based on the status and occupational terms adopted by Professors Houston and Cressy in their studies of literacy in early modern England. See R. A. Houston, 'The Development of literacy: Northern England 1640–1750', *Econ. HR*, 2nd series xxv (1982), pp. 205–6 & fn. 33, 211; D. Cressy, *Literacy and the Social Order* (CUP, 1980), pp. 104–41; and especially idem, 'Describing the Social Order of Elizabethan and Stuart England', *Literature and History*, III (1976), pp. 29–44.

245. The Suffolk nobleman was Thomas, 2nd Lord Wentworth of Nettlestead (d. 1551).

246. These were Mother Beriff of Ipswich, a midwife, and William Frobisher of Stowmarket, a 'singingman'.

247. In this table, and in Tables 3.3, 4.1, 4.2, 8.7 and 8.9, women have been assigned the same status as their husbands, ex-husbands, fathers or brothers.

248. Haigh, *English Reformations*, p. 196.

249. William Cliftlands, 'The "Well-Affected" and the "County": Politics and Religion in English Provincial Society, *c.* 1640–*c.* 1654' (unpublished PhD thesis, University of Essex, 1989), p. 246.

250. See MacCulloch, *Suffolk*, pp. 178–9.

251. Haigh, op. cit., p. 195.

252. In Norfolk twenty-nine of the thirty professionals were ex-priests, the exception being William Harrison of Aylsham, schoolmaster. In Lancashire all but two of the professionals were former clergymen, the exceptions being William Hesketh, lawyer, and John Henshaw, schoolmaster. In Suffolk twenty-five of the twenty-nine professionals were ex-priests, the exceptions being John Hopkins, schoolmaster, one Playsto, a physician, Thomas Spurdance, a royal official, and Anthony Yaxley, a lawyer.

253. In Suffolk the Protestants received gentry support from Sir Nicholas Bacon of Redgrave and his wife, Alice Thwaites of Winston, gentlewoman, and Mr Lyons and Mrs Frenkel, both of Ipswich. The last two were of borderline gentility. In Norfolk the Protestants obtained gentry support from John Ashley and his wife Katherine, Lady Anne Knyvet and Sir William Butts, the King's doctor.

254. These included six ex-priests – Alexander and Lawrence Nowell of Read, James and Leonard Pilkington of Rivington Hall, Edwin Sandys of Esthwaite Hall, Thomas Lever of Little Lever – and two theology students: Ralph and John Lever. For details see Garrett, op. cit., pp. 218–21, 237–9, 250–2, 283–4.

255. Ibid., pp. 181–3.

256. Seven weavers, three wives of weavers, five shearmen, one wife of a shearman, five tailors, one wife of a tailor, one coverlet maker and his wife, one fuller, one mercer and two spinsters.

257. Nine shoemakers, two wives of shoemakers, two tanners, one cobbler, one saddler.

258. Three carpenters, one sawyer.

259. One locksmith and his wife.

260. One butcher, one printer, one bricklayer, one wheelwright, one [unspecified] artisan, one [unspecified] apprentice, wife of a beer brewer, wife of a miller, and the widow of a mariner.

261. Among the Protestant lower orders in Suffolk were ten husbandmen, four labourers, one wife of a labourer, five menservants and four maidservants.

262. See David Cressy, *Literacy & the Social Order*, esp. chapter 6.
263. The main source is the Fines *Register*.
264. My italics
265. Foxe, *A&M*, VII, p. 383.
266. These were Thomas Hitten of Martham, ex-priest, Richard Crashfield of Wymondham, tailor, Thomas Myles of Norwich, capper, and Cecily Ormes, wife to Edmund, a worsted weaver, and the daughter of a tailor. The occupations of the remaining two – Thomas or William Carman of Hingham and Simon Miller of Middleton near Lynn – are unknown.
267. Brigden, op. cit., Table 6, pp. 608–12.
268. Foxe said: 'Many other, yea a great multitude were persecuted in Suffolk also, which for that I lack their names, I omyt at this time'. See Dickens, 'Early expansion of Protestantism', p. 111 n. 9.
269. They would not, however, have been impressed by Lancashire which produced only two martyrs, John Bradford of Manchester, priest, and George Marsh of Dean, priest.
270. This is actually a rather generous estimate because the sole gentleman among the Suffolk exiles – Henry Cornwallis of Brome – seems to have been a political rather than a religious refugee. See Garrett, op. cit., pp. 128–9. The other Suffolk exiles were indubitable Protestants, however, and included John Bale, ex-Carmelite and former Bishop of Ossory; John Peddar, possibly an ex-priest; one Playsto, physician; Thomas Sampson, ex-religious (?), and his wife; William Cheston, weaver and spinner; John Day, printer; Richard Cook, weaver, and his wife; Edmund Laurence, yeoman and preacher; John Agar, artisan; William Betts of Hadleigh, weaver, and his wife (ibid., pp. 69, 77–8, 89, 118, 127–9, 142–3, 216–17, 246, 252, 279–81).
271. S. Brigden, 'Youth and the Reformation', in *Impact of English Reformation*, pp. 74, 84 n. 176.
272. Ibid., p. 66.
273. Of the other five, four refused to attend Mass, while one was generally hostile to it. None gave specific reasons for their hostility. See Appendix I (d).
274. Brigden, *London and Reformation*, pp. 608–12.
275. My italics.
276. Davis, *Heresy and Reformation*, pp. 110, 115, 143; Foxe, *A&M*, VIII, pp. 424, 431; BL, Harleian MS. 421, f. 192.
277. Davis, op. cit., pp. 114, 119; Foxe, *A&M*, VIII, p. 157.
278. Foxe, *A&M*, IV, p. 638, VIII, pp. 488–9.
279. Davis, pp. 114, 118, 121–2; Foxe, *A&M*, VIII, pp. 146, 432.
280. MacCulloch, *Suffolk*, p. 346.
281. Ibid.
282. For more information on these clergy see Houlbrooke, 'Persecution of Heresy and Protestantism', pp. 313–19, 321–2.
283. BL, Cotton MS. Cleopatra E.V., f. 389.
284. MacCulloch, op. cit., p. 158.
285. Ibid., pp. 159–61.
286. Ibid., p. 158.
287. W. J. Sheils, *The English Reformation 1530–1570* (Longman, 1989), p. 72.
288. MacCulloch, op. cit., p. 181.
289. R. J. Knecht, *The French Wars of Religion 1559–1598* (2nd edn, Longman, 1996), p. 11.
290. C. Haigh, *English Reformations*, p. 28
291. But about twenty-three hospitals did not survive the main dissolution. See Peter Northeast, 'Religious Houses', in Dymond & Martin, p. 70. *VCH Suffolk*, vol. II, gives an inadequate account of the hospitals.

NOTES TO CHAPTER FOUR

1. Norman Scarfe, *The Suffolk Guide* (4th edn, Alastair Press, 1988), p. 144.
2. S. Doran, *Elizabeth I and Religion 1558–1603* (Routledge, 1994), p. 18.
3. The late Professor Patrick McGrath suggested that 'The Elizabethan settlement was a *via media*, not between Catholicism and Protestantism, but between different forms of Protestantism, a half-way house between the Prayer Book of 1549 and the Genevan order of service' (P. McGrath, *Papists and Puritans under Elizabeth I* (Blandford Press, 1967), p. 13). This interpretation has not, however, attracted the support of most historians.

4. C. Hill, *Reformation to Industrial Revolution: A Social and Economic History of Britain 1530–1780* (Weidenfeld & Nicolson, 1967), p. 88.
5. Conrad Russell, 'The Reformation and the Creation of the Church of England, 1500–1640', in John Morrill (ed.), *The Oxford Illustrated History of Tudor & Stuart Britain* (OUP, 1996), p. 280.
6. During the reigns of Elizabeth I and James I 'recusants' included Protestant Separatists (sectary recusants) as well as Roman Catholics (popish recusants). But until the 1660s the former constituted only a small fraction of the total number.
7. Professor Morrill has convincingly shown that it is not anachronistic to use the word 'Anglican' during our period. See John Morrill, 'The Church in England 1642–1649', in his *The Nature of the English Revolution* (Longman, 1993), p. 148 n. 2.
8. A. Walsham, *Church Papists: Catholicism, Conformity and Confessional Polemic in Early Modern England* (The Boydell Press for RHS, 1993), p. 118.
9. Quoted in Hugh Bowler (ed.), *Recusant Roll No. 2 1593–1594*, CRS, 57 (1965), p. viii & n. 6. See also MacCulloch, *Suffolk*, p. 192.
10. Quoted in Walsham, op. cit., p. 10.
11. MacCulloch, 'Catholic and Puritan', p. 258.
12. *The Martyrs of England and Wales, 1535–1680* (Catholic Truth Society pamphlets, 1979), p. 38. The only Suffolk priests to suffer capital punishment under the early Stuarts were Bartholemew (Alban) Roe, a Benedictine, and Henry Morse, a Jesuit. They were hanged, drawn and quartered at Tyburn in 1642 and 1645 respectively (ibid., p. 16).
13. For details see Patrick McGrath and Joy Rowe, 'The Recusancy of Sir Thomas Cornwallis', *PSIA*, xxviii, Pt. 3 (1961), pp. 226–71, esp. 233–52, 258–9; MacCulloch, op. cit., p. 257 n. 112.
14. Zillah Dovey, *An Elizabethan Progress: The Queen's Journey into East Anglia, 1578* (Alan Sutton, 1996), p. 107.
15. MacCulloch, op. cit., p. 260.
16. Ibid.
17. See Patrick McGrath and Joy Rowe, 'The Imprisonment of Catholics for Religion under Elizabeth I', *RH*, 20 (1991), pp. 415–35.
18. By the Common Law a month contained twenty-eight days, thirteen such lunar months constituting a year. A recusant's yearly fine therefore amounted to £260.
19. MacCulloch, *Suffolk*, p. 342. For details see Timothy J. McCann (ed.), *Recusants in the Exchequer Pipe Rolls 1581–1592*, CRS, 71 (1986), pp. 76, 145, 164.
20. Ibid., p. 164.
21. Ibid., p. 76
22. MacCulloch, 'Catholic and Puritan', p. 259.
23. McCann, op. cit., p. 145.
24. Wm. R. Trimble, *The Catholic Laity in Elizabethan England 1558–1603* (Harvard UP, 1964), p. 227.
25. BL, Add. MS. 15,520, f. 72.
26. Dymond & Paine, *Spoil of Melford Church*, pp. vi–vii; McCann, op. cit., p. 118.
27. MacCulloch, op. cit., p. 256. There is, for example, little reason to doubt the sincerity of William Cornwallis, a priest and brother of Sir Thomas Cornwallis, who said that 'if the pope should send an army into the realm to establish the Catholic Romish religion, he would in that case fight against such an army to the uttermost of his power on Her Majesty's side' (Quoted in Patrick McGrath, 'The Bloody Questions Reconsidered', *RH*, 20 (1991), p. 318 n. 36).
28. *DNB*, vol. XVII, pp. 211–12, vol. XIX, p. 879.
29. Michael A. Mullett, *Catholics in Britain and Ireland, 1558–1829* (Macmillan, 1998), p. 26.
30. K. J. Lindley, 'The Lay Catholics in the reign of Charles I', *Journal of Ecclesiastical History*, xxii (1971), p. 214.
31. See chapter 5, Table 5.5.
32. Martin J. Havran, *The Catholics in Caroline England* (OUP, 1962), p. 83.
33. The Communicant returns of the archdeaconries of Suffolk and Sudbury in 1603 have been printed in *PSIA*, vi (1888), pp. 361–400; ibid., xi (1903), pp. 1–46.
34. John Bossy, *The English Catholic Community 1570–1850* (Darton, Longman and Todd, 1975), pp. 188, 191–3, 422; E. A. Wrigley and R. S. Schofield, *The Population History of England 1541–1871: A reconstruction* (Edward Arnold, 1981), pp. 208–9.
35. For sources concerning Suffolk recusants see below note 38. For the population of Suffolk in 1603 and 1642 see Chapter 2, notes 107–8, 110–11, 113, and Table 2.3.

36. Anne C. Parkinson, *A History of Catholicism in the Furness Peninsula 1127–1997* (Centre for North-West Regional Studies, University of Lancaster, 1998), p. 30.

37. These years have been chosen because they were times of severe persecution when the government made a determined effort to organise a full count of recusants.

38. The statistics refer to individuals, not families. Main sources are M. M. C. Calthrop (ed.), *Recusants Exchequer Roll No. 1 1592–93*, CRS, 18 (1916), pp. 309–25; PRO, Exchequer, Recusant Roll 1606, E 377/15, ff. 48–50; /49, ff. 146–7. For other sources concerning the year 1641, see below note 42.

39. Not just the recusant rolls but the Bishops' Visitation Books also record a fall in recusant numbers. The visitation of 1606 revealed 195 recusants, while that of 1627 mentioned only 130. See SRO (I), VIS/4 & 5.

40. They settled on their estate in Costessey.

41. Joy Rowe, ' "The lopped tree": the re-formation of the Suffolk Catholic community', in Nicholas Tyacke (ed.), *England's Long Reformation 1500–1800* (University College, London, Press, 1998), pp. 178–9.

42. Main sources are PRO, Exchequer Recusant Roll 1641, E 377/49, ff. 146–7; Exchequer, Lay Subsidy Rolls 1628 & 1641, E 179/183/495; 183/498; 183/501; 183/510–21; 183/529–34; 183/549; Chancery, Petty Bag Office, C 203/4, ff. 49–50; *CCC*, vols I–V, supplemented where necessary by original records in PRO (SP 23).

43. This is worth emphasising because it is now becoming fashionable among some historians of East Anglia to play down the importance of the gentry in the history of Catholicism prior to 1700. See particularly Joy Rowe's article in *England's Long Reformation*, esp. pp. 167, 172, 174, 178–80, 184–5, and Andrew Sulston, 'Catholic Recusancy in Elizabethan Norfolk', *Norfolk Archaeology*, XLIII, Pt. 1 (1998), pp. 98–110.

44. See chapter 2, Table 2.3.

45. The Bishops' Visitation Books also reveal large percentages of gentry-recusants. They show that in 1606 sixty-three (32 per cent) of the 195 recusants were gentry and that in 1627 twenty-eight (21 per cent) of the 130 recusants were also gentry. For sources see note 39 above.

46. For sources see B. G. Blackwood, 'Plebeian Catholics in the 1640s and 1650s', *RH*, 18 (1986), p. 51.

47. P. Caraman (ed.), *John Gerard: The Autobiography of an Elizabethan* (2nd edn, Longmans, 1956), pp. 32–3.

48. Rowe in *England's Long Reformation*, pp. 169–70, 178.

49. See Sulston, op. cit., p. 109.

50. By Professor Patrick Collinson in a lecture delivered to the Long Melford History Society on 18 March 1993.

51. MacCulloch, *Suffolk*, pp. 212–13.

52. Idem, 'Catholic and Puritan', pp. 241–3.

53. Idem, *Suffolk*, pp. 214, 417.

54. Ibid., pp. 214–15.

55. J. J. Scarisbrick, *The Reformation and the English People* (Blackwell, 1984), p. 149.

56. Rowe, op. cit., pp. 174–5.

57. Joy Rowe, 'Roman Catholic Recusancy', in Dymond & Martin, p. 113.

58. These dates have been deliberately chosen. 1588 saw the sailing of the Spanish Armada, while 1642 was the start of the First Civil War.

59. The Suffolk residence of Thomas Bedingfield is uncertain, but his gentility is not in doubt.

60. See above note 12 concerning the fates of Bartholomew Roe and Henry Morse.

61. Aidan Bellenger (ed.), *English and Welsh Priests 1558–1800: a working list* (Downside, 1984), pp. 183–4; Thomas M. McCoog (ed.), *English and Welsh Jesuits 1555–1650*, 2 vols, CRS, 74–5 (1994–5), I, pp. 139, 154–5, 163, II, pp. 228, 241, 284, 294, 306; H. Foley (ed.), *Records of the English Province of the Society of Jesus*, 7 vols (Burns & Oates, 1875–83), VII, Part I, pp. 45–6, 234, 272–3, 275–6, 436, Part II, p. 749; H. N. Birt, *Obit. Book of the English Benedictines 1600–1912* (2nd edn, Gregg International Publishers Ltd., 1970), pp. 24, 31, 38; Godfrey Anstruther, *The Seminary Priests: A Dictionary of the Secular Clergy of England and Wales 1558–1850*, 4 vols (St Edmund's College, Ware, 1968, Mayhew – McCrimmon, Gt. Wakering, 1975, 1976, 1977), I, pp. 295–6, II, pp. 96–7, 210–11, 271–2, 295; Michael Sharratt (ed.), *Lisbon College Register 1628–1813*, CRS, 72 (1991), p. 181; Martin Murphy (ed.), *St Gregory's College, Seville 1592–1767*, CRS, 73 (1992), p. 65; Anthony Kenny (ed.), *The Responsa Scholarum of the English College, Rome, Part I: 1598–1621*, CRS, 54 (1962), pp. 19,178, 185, 277, 338.

62. For Benedictines see Birt, op. cit., pp. 214, 215, 217; J. Gillow (ed.), English Benedictine nuns, Cambrai, 1620–1793, in *Miscellanea* VIII, CRS, 13 (1913), pp. 40–2; Lady Abbess Ward and community (ed.), English Benedictine Nuns of Ghent: Obituaries, 1627–1811, in *Miscellanea* XI, CRS, 19 (1917), pp. 21–2; J. S. Hanson (ed.), English Benedictine nuns, Brussels, 1598–1856, in *Miscellanea* IX, CRS, 14 (1914), p. 183. For Poor Clares see J. Gillow (ed.), English Poor Clares, Gravelines, 1608–1837, in ibid., pp. 49, 59, 72–3. For information on Suffolk nuns at St Ursula's convent, I am grateful to Mrs Audrey Butler of Pickering, N. Yorks.

63. My italics.

64. Quoted in A. Hassell Smith, *County and Court: Government and Politics in Norfolk, 1558–1603* (OUP, 1974), p. 201.

65. Quoted in J. T. Cliffe, *The Puritan Gentry: The Great Puritan Families of Early Stuart England* (Routledge &Kegan Paul, 1984), p. 172.

66. MacCulloch, 'Catholic and Puritan', p. 283.

67. Cliffe, op. cit., pp. 11–12.

68. Quoted in Patrick Collinson, *The Elizabethan Puritan Movement* (Jonathan Cape, 1967), p. 27.

69. Ibid., pp. 26–7.

70. Barry Coward, *The Stuart Age: England 1603–1714* (2nd edn, Longman, 1994), pp. 81–2.

71. John F. H. New, *Anglican and Puritan: The Basis of their Opposition 1558–1640* (A&C. Black, 1964), p. 2.

72. Paul Hentzner, *A Journey into England in the year 1598* (Strawberry Hill, 1757, edn & trans. Horace Walpole), pp. 58–9. I owe this reference to Peter Northeast.

73. Ibid., p. 59.

74. Some readers might object that the Family of Love was also Separatist. So it was at first. But in its second and third generation the Family succumbed to the attractions of conformity, and, as Christopher Marsh says, 'faded back into the Church' [of England]. See C. Marsh, 'Piety and Persuasion in Elizabethan England: the Church of England meets the Family of Love' in *England's Long Reformation*, p. 162. See also p. 76. It is impossible to say how many Familists there were in Suffolk in the reigns of Elizabeth I and James I.

75. N. C. P. Tyack, 'Migration from East Anglia to New England before 1660' (unpublished PhD thesis, University of London, 1951), pp. 240–1; J. S. Craig, 'The Bury Stirs Revisited: An analysis of the Townsmen', *PSIAH*, xxxvii, Pt. 3 (1991), pp. 214–15.

76. *DNB*, vol. III, pp. 57–61.

77. See chapters 7, 8 and 9.

78. See end of this chapter, and chapters 5 and 6.

79. Quoted in MacCulloch, *Suffolk*, p. 347.

80. Reyce, *Breviary*, p. 21.

81. Lilian J. Redstone, *Ipswich through the Ages* (East Anglian Magazine Ltd., 1969), p. 89.

82. Information of Peter Northeast.

83. J. F. Williams (ed.), *The Diocese of Norwich: Bishop Redman's Visitation 1597* (Norfolk Record Society, XVIII, 1946), pp. 114–59. The Court book of 1597, containing presentments for the Archdeaconry of Sudbury, is missing.

84. The number of Suffolk parishes during our period was 517, but not all would have had a resident incumbent.

85. Collinson, *Elizabethan Puritan Movement*, pp. 218–19.

86. Ibid., pp. 244–5.

87. The Puritan clergy are listed in Patrick Collinson, 'The Puritan Classical Movement in the Reign of Elizabeth I' (unpublished PhD thesis, University of London, 1957), pp. 1259–62.

88. Another nine Suffolk Puritan ministers, including John Knewstub, were associated with the Classical Movement but were not members of the Dedham Classis. Main source for these fifteen ministers is Roland G. Usher (ed.), *The Presbyterian Movement in the Reign of Elizabeth as illustrated by the Minute Book of the Dedham Classis 1582–1589* (Camden Third series, viii, 1905), pp. xxxv–xlviii, 43.

89. Williams, *Bishop Redman's Visitation*, p. 156.

90. Information of Peter Northeast.

91. Patrick Collinson, *The Religion of Protestants: The Church in English Society 1559–1625* (OUP, 1982), p. 82.

92. Nikolaus Pevsner, *The Buildings of England, Suffolk* (2nd edn, Penguin Books, 1974), passim; N. Scarfe, *Suffolk Guide*, passim.

93. H. Munro Cautley, *Suffolk Churches and their Treasures* (5th edn, Boydell Press, 1982), p. 181.
94. J. Goring, *Godly exercises or the devil's dance? Puritanism and Popular Culture in pre-Civil War England* (Friends of Dr Williams's Library, 1983), p. 21.
95. Christopher Hill, *Society and Puritanism in pre-revolutionary England* (Secker & Warburg, 1964), pp. 24–6; H. R. Trevor-Roper, *Religion, the Reformation and social change* (Macmillan, 1967), pp. 70–1; Kevin Sharpe, 'Archbishop Laud and the University of Oxford' in his *Politics and Ideas in Early Stuart England: Essays and Studies* (Pinter Publishers, London & New York, 1989), pp. 127–8.
96. For details see H. Parker, *A Discourse Concerning Puritans* (London, 1641), pp. 11–14, 45, 53, 58, 61. I owe these references to Dr Jeremy Goring.
97. Lucy Hutchinson, *Memoirs of the Life of Colonel Hutchinson*, ed. Rev. Julius Hutchinson (J. M. Dent & Sons, Ltd., 1968), pp. 64–5; R. Baxter, *Reliquiae Baxterianae*, ed. Matthew Sylvester (1696), p. 3.
98. Not to be confused with Samuel Ward (1572–1643), the Puritan Master of Sidney Sussex College, Cambridge.
99. BL, 4466. e. 25, Samuel Ward, *Woe to Drunkards* (London, 1627), pp. 14–15, 36, 47–50, 53.
100. This paragraph relies heavily on *DNB*, vol. XX, pp. 790–1; and especially on Frank Grace, ' "Schismaticall and Factious Humours": opposition in Ipswich to Laudian Church Government in the 1630s', in David Chadd (ed.), *Religious Dissent in East Anglia III* (Centre of East Anglian Studies, UEA, 1996), pp. 97–103, 109.
101. Clarendon, *Rebellion*, vol. I, p. 137.
102. Nicholas Tyacke, *Anti-Calvinists: The Rise of English Arminianism c. 1590–1640* (OUP, 1987), pp. 48, 205; Andrew Foster, *The Church of England 1570–1640* (Longman, 1994), pp. 66, 77, 125.
103. See chapter 3 note 2.
104. Nicholas Tyacke, 'Puritanism, Arminianism and Counter-Revolution', in Conrad Russell (ed.), *The Origins of the English Civil War* (Macmillan, 1973), p. 128.
105. D. W. Boorman, 'The Administrative and Disciplinary Problems of the Church on the Eve of the Civil War in the light of the extant records of the Dioceses of Norwich and Ely under Bishop Wren' (unpublished BLitt thesis, University of Oxford, 1959), pp. 69–70.
106. Ibid., pp. 79–80.
107. Paul S. Seaver, *The Puritan Lectureships: The Politics of Religious Dissent 1560–1662* (Stanford UP, 1970), p. 19.
108. Lawful recreations included archery and morris-dancing, but excluded cruel sports like bear- and bull-baiting (S. R. Gardiner, *Constitutional Documents of the Puritan Revolution 1625–1660* (3rd edn, OUP, 1906), pp. 101–2).
109. Ibid., p. 103.
110. Boorman, thesis, p. 77.
111. As a staunch Arminian Wren suspended John Allot, minister of Little Thurlow and future Presbyterian, because he had preached a sermon favourable to predestination (ibid., p. 65).
112. Ibid., pp. 62–4.
113. Hill, *Society and Puritanism*, p. 80.
114. *CSPD*, 1636–7, p. 223.
115. Seaver, op. cit., p. 22.
116. Hill, op. cit., pp. 114–15.
117. R. W. Ketton-Cremer, *Norfolk in the Civil War: A Portrait of a Society in Conflict* (repr. Gliddon Books, Norwich, 1985), p. 67.
118. Tyacke, *Anti-Calvinists*, p. 246.
119. Ketton-Cremer, op. cit., p. 64.
120. Ibid.
121. Boorman, thesis, pp. 70–1.
122. Ibid., pp. 82–4. See also note 84 above.
123. Ketton-Cremer, op. cit., p. 86. They are likely to have been conformists through choice rather than through fear because, as Boorman says, 'although the church courts could suspend or deprive ministers, the Church could not force them to conform' (Boorman, thesis, p. 78).
124. Roger Thompson, *Mobility & Migration: East Anglian Founders of New England 1629–1640* (University of Massachusetts Press, 1994), p. 22.
125. Kevin Sharpe, *The Personal Rule of Charles I* (Yale UP, 1992), p. 755.
126. Tyack, thesis, p. 347.

127. *Articles of Impeachment*, art. 16. Printed in C. Wren, *Parentalia, or Memoirs of the Family of the Wrens.* (London, 1750), p. 101.

128. See Sharpe, op. cit., pp. 751–5; Thompson, op. cit., pp. 20–23, 143; D. Cressy, *Coming Over: Migration and Communication between England and New England in the Seventeenth Century* (CUP, 1987).

129. Reyce, *Breviary*, p. 59.

130. See especially Collinson, *The Elizabethan Puritan Movement;* idem, *The Religion of Protestants;* Cliffe, *The Puritan Gentry.*

131. Collinson, *Religion of Protestants*, p. 157.

132. An advowson gave the right to nominate a clergyman for a living.

133. Bradfield Clare, Bradfield St George, Rushbrooke, Horringer Magna, Horringer Parva, Depden, Wattisfield, Stanton All Saints, Stanton St John, Great Welnetham (Collinson, thesis, p. 656 n. 2).

134. Barrow, Walsham-le-Willows, Nedging, Semer (ibid., p. 656 n. 3).

135. For the names of the livings of these patrons see ibid., p. 657 n. 1.

136. Ibid. p. 868.

137. J. S. Craig, 'Reformation, Politics and Polemic in Sixteenth Century East Anglian Market Towns' (unpublished PhD thesis, University of Cambridge, 1992), pp. 79–80; Collinson, *Religion of Protestants*, pp. 158–9.

138. MacCulloch, 'Catholic and Puritan', pp. 284–5; Collinson, *Religion of Protestants*, p. 186.

139. See above pp. 147, 194.

140. See above p. 120.

141. Cliffe, *Puritan Gentry*, pp. 174–6, 177–8; *Concise DNB*, vol. I, p. 961, vol. III, p. 2571.

142. For a good account of household religion in a Catholic setting see John Bossy, 'The Character of Elizabethan Catholicism', in Trevor Aston (ed.), *Crisis in Europe 1560–1660* (Routledge & Kegan Paul, 1965), pp. 223–7.

143. Hill, op. cit., p. 501.

144. Ibid., p. 454.

145. Samuel Fairclough, *The Saints' Worthinesse* (1653), pp. 17–18. Quoted in Everitt, *Suffolk*, p. 19.

146. Cliffe, op. cit., p. 145.

147. Ibid., pp. 53, 83, 140–1.

148. Quoted in Anthony Fletcher, *The Outbreak of the English Civil War* (Edward Arnold, 1981), p. 105.

149. Quoted in Cliffe, op. cit., p. 157.

150. Quoted in Fletcher, op. cit., p. 109.

151. C. Hill. 'Archbishop Laud's place in English History', in his *A Nation of Change and Novelty* (Routledge, 1990), p. 79.

152. Cliffe, op. cit., pp. 228–33.

153. Ibid., p. 223; M. F. Keeler, *The Long Parliament, 1640–1641: A Biographical Study of its Members* (American Philosophical Society, xxxvi, Philadelphia, 1954), p. 295.

154. L. Stone, *The causes of the English Revolution 1519–1642* (Routledge & Kegan Paul, 1972), p. 128.

155. F. Grace, op. cit., p. 113.

156. Quoted in John Walter, 'Anti-Popery and the Stour Valley Riots of 1642', in David Chadd (ed.), *Religious Dissent in East Anglia III*, p. 135. Historians are divided as to whether Laud himself was an Arminian. Compare Tyacke, *Anti-Calvinists*, esp. Appendix II, with Peter White, *Predestination, Policy and Polemic* (CUP, 1992).

157. *Calendar of State Papers, Venetian, 1636–9*, pp. 240, 479.

158. The evidence of presentations generally needs to be corroborated by other information.

159. That the Presbyterian lay elders for Suffolk were simply nominated and may not have actively served does not necessarily mean that they were all lukewarm. As Professor Hexter has argued, 'those who allowed their names to appear on the eldership lists must have done so with full knowledge that the national Church was to be Presbyterian in form' (J. H. Hexter, 'The Problem of the Presbyterian-Independents', in his *Re-appraisals in History* (Longman, 1961), p. 166).

160. Wills must, of course, be used extremely cautiously because they sometimes reflect the views of the scribe rather than of the testator.

161. Main sources for names of Puritans are Cliffe, *Puritan Gentry;* idem., *Puritans in Conflict: The Puritan Gentry during and after the Civil Wars* (Routledge, 1988); Boorman, thesis; K. W. Shipps, 'Lay Patronage of East Anglian Puritan clerics in Pre-Revolutionary England' (unpublished PhD thesis, University of Yale, 1971); Clive Holmes (ed.), *The Suffolk Committee for Scandalous Ministers 1644–1646* (Suffolk Records Society XIII, 1970); *CJ*, vol. II, pp. 437–8, 589; W. A. Shaw, *A History*

of the English Church during the Civil Wars and under the Commonwealth, 2 vols (Longmans, Green & Co., 1900), II, pp. 423–31. For location of the Puritan gentry see Appendix II.

162. It might be larger if we knew the religious sympathies of many of the smaller gentry.

163. Sharpe says that 'The puritans, even in their strongholds in Essex and Northamptonshire, were never more than a well organised, minority sect which failed to win over the commonalty and had only limited success in recruiting the better sort' (Sharpe, op. cit., p. 750).

NOTES TO CHAPTER FIVE

1. S. R. Gardiner, *History of the Great Civil War, 1642–1649*, 4 vols (Longmans, Green & Co., 1886–91); G. M. Trevelyan, *England under the Stuarts* (19th edn, Methuen, 1947). The religious factor has been stressed by some eminent modern historians. See p. 159.

2. C. Hill, *The English Revolution 1640* (3rd edn, Lawrence & Wisheart, 1955); idem, *The Century of Revolution, 1603–1714* (Nelson, 1961); B. Manning, *The English People and the English Revolution 1640–1649* (Heinemann, 1976).

3. A. M. Everitt, *The Local Community and the Great Rebellion* (Historical Association pamphlet, G. 70, 1969); idem, *The Community of Kent and the Great Rebellion 1640–60* (Leicester UP, 1966); J. S. Morrill, *Cheshire, 1630–1660* (OUP, 1974); idem *The Revolt of the Provinces* (Allen & Unwin, 1976). For brilliant critiques of the local interpretation of the Civil War see esp. C. Holmes 'The "County Community" in Stuart Historiography', *JBS*, 19 (1980), pp. 54–73; A. Hughes, 'Local history and the Origins of the Civil War' in R. Cust & A. Hughes (eds), *Conflict in Early Stuart England* (Longman, 1989), pp. 224–49.

4. J. Morrill, *The Nature of the English Revolution* (Longman, 1993); J. S. A. Adamson, 'The Baronial Context of the English Civil War', *TRHS*, 5th series, 40 (1990), pp. 93–120; C. Russell, *The Causes of the English Civil War* (OUP, 1990); idem, *The Fall of the British Monarchies, 1637–1642* (OUP, 1991).

5. R. Sherwood, *The Civil War in the Midlands 1642–1651* (repr. Alan Sutton, Stroud, 1992), p. 2.

6. Kingston, passim; Everitt, *Suffolk* pp. 11, 21 n. 1; P. Fincham, *The Suffolk we live in* (George Nobbs, Norwich, 1976), p. 47; Dymond & Northeast, p. 74.

7. Main sources for names of Parliamentarians are Everitt, *Suffolk*; N. Evans, *Beccles Rediscovered* (The Beccles Society, 1984); Firth & Rait, vol. I; *The Great Champions of England* (1646), BL, 669, f. 10 (69); *An Account of Receipts and Payments of the county of Suffolk* (1648), BL, E. 448 (13); BL, Add. MS. 5508 (Accounts and papers concerning sequestered estates 1642–8); PRO, SP28, vols 23–7; 32; 39; 131; 176; 190; 216; 243; 251–3; 255–6; 332; 334; E113/11; SRO (I), EE1/o1/1; FB 19/I/1 & 2; 130/I1/8, 9 & 10; HD 36/2672 & 2781; HD 224/1. For both Parliamentarians and Royalists see Kingston; Peter Young, *Edgehill 1642* (Roundwood Press, Kineton, 1967); idem, *Naseby 1645* (Century Publishing, London 1985); Northants. Rec. Off., Finch-Hatton MS. 133; BL, Add. MS. 15,520 and the following Suffolk collections of David Elisha Davy: Add. MSS. 19,077; 19,080; 19,081; 19,103; 19,116. For names of Royalists only see P. R. Newman, *Royalist Officers in England and Wales 1642–1660: A Biographical Dictionary* (Garland, New York, 1981); T. Dring, *Catalogue of the Lords, Knights and Gentlemen who have compounded for their Estates* (1655); *A List of Officers claiming to the Sixty Thousand Pounds etc.* (1663); *The Royal Martyrs* (1663); J. Prestwich, *Respublica* (1787); *CCAM*, vols I–III; *CCC*, vols I–V, supplemented where necessary by original records in PRO (SP 23); PRO, W. H. Black (ed.), *Docquets of Letters Patent 1642–6* (1837); A List of Severall Colonells, SP 29/'159/45. Uncited information in this chapter comes from sources listed in this note.

8. Like the Castletons of Bury St Edmunds. In 1642 Sir William, head of the family and high sheriff of Suffolk, was nominated a commissioner of array by the King and a deputy lieutenant by Parliament, but whether he served either side is unknown.

9. Clarendon, *Rebellion*, vol. II, p. 469.

10. Henry Jermyn was one of the more intransigent Royalists excluded by Parliament from pardon as early as 1644. See S. R. Gardiner (ed.), *Constitutional Documents of the Puritan Revolution 1625–1660* (3rd edn, OUP, 1906), p. 278.

11. BL, Add. MS. 19,080, f. 12. Glover may have lent under duress but had he been a more committed Royalist, he would have refused to contribute.

12. See memorial tablet on north wall of chancel in Frostenden Parish Church.

13. D. Underdown, *Pride's Purge* (OUP, 1971), pp. 371, 375.

14. BL, Add. MS. 19,103, f. 266.

15. My statistics of gentry allegiances during the Civil War differ from those of Everitt, who stated that there were '99 leading families of the Suffolk [Parliamentary] County Committee' and '75 Royalist families, or 98 individuals' (*Suffolk*, pp. 11, 20). But Everitt did not specifically confine his attention to the gentry. Moreover, his figures concerned the period 1642–60, whereas mine deal only with the years 1642–46.

16. T. May, *The History of the Parliament of England* (1647), Book 2, p. 108, Book 3, p. 78.

17. My italics.

18. R. Baxter, *Reliquiae Baxteriana*, ed. M. Sylvester, vol. 1 (1696), p. 30.

19. BL, Add. MS. 15,520, f. 63.

20. See Barker monuments in Sibton Parish Church.

21. Another eleven were nominated, of whom nine became Parliamentarians and two remained neutral.

22. Agents included high collectors, assessors, treasurers, clerks, solicitors, etc. Most were industrious.

23. This figure is extrapolated from Everitt, *Suffolk*, p. 23.

24. Ibid., p. 27.

25. C. Holmes, *The Eastern Association* (CUP, 1974), p. 50.

26. Committeemen signing ten or more documents are deemed activists.

27. Nathaniel Bacon, *The Annalls of Ipswiche*, ed. W. H. Richardson (1884), pp. iv–v. Bacon took his BA at Christ's College, Cambridge, in 1611, when he was admitted to Gray's Inn. After the First Civil War he became a Presbyterian elder. See *Al. Cant.*, vol. I, p. 65; *GI Adm. Reg.*, p. 128; W. A. Shaw, *A History of the English Church during the Civil Wars and under the Commonwealth*, 2 vols (Longmans, Green & Co., 1900), II, p. 424.

28. Sixty-five Parliamentarians and fifty-three Royalists.

29. Main sources for ages include *Al. Cant.; Al. Oxon.*; D. Brunton and D. H. Pennington, *Members of the Long Parliament* (Allen & Unwin, 1954); Copinger, *Manors;* M. F. Keeler, *The Long Parliament 1640–1641* (American Philosophical Society, xxxvi, Philadelphia, 1954); J. J. Muskett, *Suffolk Manorial Families*, 3 vols (privately printed, Exeter 1900–10); Newman, op. cit.; Underdown, op. cit.; PRO, Wards 9/207–9. I am indebted to the late Gwenyth Dyke for the ages of some Royalists.

30. Information kindly supplied by Clive Holmes, Lady Margaret Hall, Oxford.

31. Information kindly supplied by Professor Ian Gentles, York University, Ontario.

32. CUL, Additional MS. 6967 (Pedigrees and Arms of Suffolk Families), f. 10.

33. M. Toynbee & P. Young, *Strangers in Oxford* (Phillimore, 1973), p. 199.

34. D. Lloyd, *Memoirs of the Lives* (1668), pp. 662–3.

35. Newman, op. cit., p. 294; *CCC*, vol. II, p. 1290.

36. R. Ollard (ed.), *Clarendon's Four Portraits* (Hamish Hamilton, 1989), pp. 5, 7, 48, 125; Clarendon, *Rebellion*, vol. V, p. 233.

37. Newman, op. cit., p. 211.

38. Clarendon, *Rebellion*, vol. II, p. 286.

39. G. R. Smith & M. Toynbee, *Leaders of the Civil Wars 1642–1648* (Roundwood Press, 1977), pp. 72–3; Lloyd, op. cit., p. 552, n(a).

40. K. Shipps, 'Lay patronage of East Anglian Puritan clerics in Pre-Revolutionary England' (unpublished PhD thesis, University of Yale, 1971), p. 145.

41. However, this does not necessarily mean that they were neutrally inclined, like Newcastle-upon-Tyne and other, mostly West Country, towns. See Roger Howell, Jr., 'The Structure of Urban Politics in the English Civil War', *Albion*, xi (1979), pp. 112–21, 126–7; idem, 'Neutralism, Conservatism and Political Alignment in the English Revolution : The Case of the Towns, 1642–9', in John Morrill (ed.), *Reactions to the English Civil War 1642–1649* (Macmillan, 1982), pp. 67–88.

42. P. Styles, 'The Royalist government of Worcestershire during the Civil War, 1642–6', *Transactions of the Worcestershire Archaeological Society*, 3rd series, v (1976), p. 24.

43. R. W. Ketton-Cremer, *Norfolk in the Civil War* (repr. Gliddon Books, Norwich, 1985), p. 179. For details of the siege of Lowestoft see ibid., pp. 179–86.

44. Russell, *Causes*, pp. 21–2, 226.

45. Everitt, *Suffolk*, pp. 13–14.

46. M. Reed, 'Ipswich in the seventeenth century' (unpublished PhD thesis, University of Leicester, 1973), p. 256.

47. Kingston, op. cit., pp. 81–3.

48. Ive, thesis, p. 243.

49. H. P. Clodd, *Aldeburgh : the History of an Ancient Borough* (Norman Adlard, Ipswich, 1959), p. 119. Everitt says that 'there was a powerful group in favour of the King' in Aldeburgh 'throughout the years 1642–60' (Everitt, *Suffolk*, p. 14). But there is little sign of Royalism during the First Civil War.

50. May, op. cit., Book 2, p. 108; J. Rushworth, *Historical Collections*, 8 vols (1721–72), IV, p. 680.

51. SRO (I), HD 224/1, f. 8r.

52. Bod. Lib., Tanner MS. 284, ff. 42, 45–7.

53. For details of Margery's military career see J. & R. Lock, 'Captain Raphe Margery, A Suffolk Ironside', *PSIAH*, xxxvi, pt. 3 (1987), pp. 207–18. For various reasons I cannot agree with the Locks that Margery was a gentleman before the Civil War.

54. For William Dowsing's iconoclasm see next chapter.

55. D. Underdown, *Revel, Riot and Rebellion* (OUP, 1985), pp. 192, 295–6.

56. Unfortunately the Quarter Sessions rolls for Suffolk do not begin until 1682.

57. SRO (I), B105/2/5; 2/7; 2/10.

58. I have found another eighty-three plebeian Parliamentarians whose habitations are unknown.

59. Underdown, op. cit., chapter 7. Underdown's field/pasture model is also applicable to Somerset, Derbyshire and Warwickshire, but not in three of the four regions of Civil War Devon. See Underdown, *Somerset in the Civil War and Interregnum* (David & Charles, Newton Abbot, 1973), pp. 31–40, 116–17; Jill R. Dias, 'Lead, Society and Politics in Derbyshire before the Civil War', *Midland History*, 6 (1981), p. 52; Ann Hughes, *Politics, Society and Civil War in Warwickshire, 1620–1660* (CUP, 1987), esp. pp. 4–5, 151, 157; Mark Stoyle, *Loyalty and Locality: Popular Allegiance in Devon during the English Civil War* (Exeter UP, 1994), pp. 152–6.

60. *Chorography*, p. 19.

61. This was also the view of the Royalist Earl of Clarendon (Clarendon, *Rebellion*, vol. II, p. 318).

62. B. Manning, 'The outbreak of the English Civil War', in R. H. Parry (ed.), *The English Civil War and After* (Macmillan, 1970), p. 18.

63. B. Manning, *The English People and the English Revolution* (2nd edn, Bookmarks, 1991), pp. 244, 252–9.

64. J. Walter, *Understanding Popular Violence in the English Revolution* (CUP, 1999). This work appeared too late to be addressed by the present author.

65. R. Ashton, *The English Civil War* (2nd edn, Weidenfeld & Nicolson, 1989), p. 152.

66. Holmes, *Eastern Association*, p. 52; J. T. Cliffe, *Puritans in Conflict* (Routledge, 1988), p. 38.

67. I. Roots, 'The central government and the local community', in E. W. Ives (ed.), *The English Revolution 1600–1660* (Arnold, 1968), p. 37; Everitt, *Suffolk*, p. 7.

68. Anthony Fletcher, *The Outbreak of the English Civil War* (Arnold, 1981), pp. 327, 380–81; Trevelyan, *England under the Stuarts*, p. 209.

69. D. Wilson, *A Short History of Suffolk* (Batsford, 1977), p. 104.

70. P. Young, *Marston Moor 1644* (Roundwood Press, 1970), pp. 104–5.

71. The known marriages contracted before the First Civil War totalled 178, of which 113 were contracted by eighty-seven Parliamentarians and sixty-five by fifty-one Royalists. For gentry marriages see printed sources in note 29 above; also W. H. Rylands (ed.), *The Visitation of Suffolk 1664–1668* (Harleian Society, lxi, 1910).

72. This section relies heavily on Dymond & Northeast, p. 72.

73. Richard Cust., *The forced Loan and English Politics 1626–28* (OUP, 1987), pp. 144–5, 226.

74. Quoted in J. T. Cliffe, *The Puritan Gentry* (Routledge and Kegan Paul, 1984), p. 156.

75. Ibid., p. 195.

76. Fletcher, op. cit., pp. 92–3.

77. Morrill, *Nature of English Revolution*, esp. p. 68; Fletcher, op. cit., p. 346; Russell, *Causes*, p. 62.

78. Two of these families – Fiske of Rattlesden and Winthrop of Groton – had members who were Parliamentarian in the Second Civil War of 1648. At least another five – Atherold of Burgh, Bloomfield of Wattisham, Plumstead of Felsham, Vesey of Hintlesham and Wall of Stratford – were to support the Republic for a time.

79. For the names of those six Catholic royalist families see Appendix III(a).

80. Of the eighty-nine individual Suffolk Cavaliers, only seven (barely 8 per cent) were Catholic. Professor Derek Hirst wildly states that about half the Royalist gentry in Suffolk were Catholic in his, otherwise excellent, *England in conflict, 1603–1660: Kingdom, Community, Commonwealth* (Arnold, 1999), p. 195. But Keith Lindley's too low estimate – that three out of forty-four Suffolk Royalist gentry were Catholic – is at least considerably nearer the truth. See K. Lindley, 'The part played by the Catholics', in B. Manning (ed.), *Politics, Religion and the English Civil War* (Arnold, 1973), p. 148.

81. J. T. Cliffe, *The Yorkshire Gentry from the Reformation to the Civil War* (Athlone Press, 1969), p. 345; B. G. Blackwood, 'Parties and Issues in the Civil War in Lancashire and East Anglia', *NH*, xxix (1993), p. 123.

82. For the names of Puritan Parliamentarian families see Appendix III(a).

83. Blackwood, loc. cit.

84. This statement is qualified but not contradicted by the fact that only a small number of Parliamentary gentry soldiers fought outside Suffolk in the First Civil War.

NOTES TO CHAPTER SIX

1. Barry Coward, *The Stuart Age: England 1603–1714* (2nd edn, Longman, 1995), p. 234.

2. John Morrill, 'The Northern Gentry and the Great Rebellion', in his *Nature of English Revolution*, p. 207; idem, *The Revolt of the Provinces* (2nd edn, Longman, 1980), p. 126.

3. Bryan Lyndon 'Essex and the King's Cause in 1648', *HJ*, 29 (1986), pp. 17–39, esp. p. 19. See also idem, 'The South and The Start of the Second Civil War, 1648', *History*, 71 (1986), pp. 393–407.

4. R. Ashton, *Counter-Revolution : The Second Civil War and its Origins, 1646–8* (Yale UP, 1994).

5. Ibid., p. 478

6. Everitt, *Suffolk*, pp. 109–10. I owe this reference to Frank Grace of University College, Suffolk.

7. Firth & Rait, vol. I, p. 580.

8. *A Perfect Relation of the Horrid Plot and Bloudy Conspiracie of the Malignant Party at St Edmundsbury in Suffolk* (4 January 1648), BL, E 370(8), p. 1.

9. BL, E 422(1), p. 1. Quoted in Ashton, op. cit., p. 241.

10. Firth & Rait, op. cit., vol. I, pp. 749–54.

11. W. A. Shaw, *Hist. of the English Church during Civil Wars*, vol. II, pp. 423–31.

12. George Yule, *Puritans in Politics : The Religious Legislation of the Long Parliament 1640–1647* (The Sutton Courtenay Press , 1981), p. 266.

13. See chapter 7, p. 185–6.

14. *LJ*, vol. IX, pp. 18–19.

15. Yule, op. cit., p. 271.

16. Morrill, 'The Church of England 1642–1649', in his *Nature of English Revolution*, p. 156.

17. See Ashton, op. cit., p. 270.

18. See chapter 4.

19. Of the remaining 860 clerics, 400 obtained new livings, 200 were pluralists allowed to keep one of their livings, while at least 260 managed to cling onto, or succeeded in returning to, their original livings. See I. M. Green, 'The persecution of "scandalous" and "malignant" parish clergy during the English Civil War', *English Historical Review, XCIV* (1979), pp. 522, 525; Morrill, op. cit., p. 160.

20. Green, op. cit., p. 522; Morrill, op. cit., p. 161.

21. This was the number of parishes in the county. But the total number of ministers (including rectors, vicars, curates and lecturers) is difficult to estimate, especially as some were pluralists.

22. These seven include Thomas Honekin, Rector of Palgrave, who was 'Hurried and Frighted into a Resignation' and John Lowes, Vicar of Brandeston, who was hounded as a witch. See *Walker Revised*, pp. 337, 339. For the names of all 136 Suffolk clergy see ibid., pp. 87, 151, 156–7, 167, 265–9, 271–2, 325–48. Thirty-four other Suffolk clergy appear in this work, but are excluded from consideration. They comprise five whom Matthews thought were not ejected or molested, four accused before 1643 of religious offences, four ejected during the Interregnum, two sequestered at unknown dates, two wrongly accused and seventeen (including two Puritans and one Antinomian) who have little known reason for being listed among the sufferers.

23. See Appendix IV for a detailed account of those clergy.

24. There is no doubt about the actual sequestration or harassment of those fifty-six clerics, but no reasons are given, although Richard Atkinson, Matthew Brook and William Whitby were said to be guilty of 'sevall gt misdemeanours', a meaningless phrase. See *Walker Revised*, p. 347; BL, Add. MS. 15,669, ff. 45,252.

25. For a detailed account of these committees see Holmes, pp. 9–18.

26. This was sometimes paid irregularly or even withheld altogether by the new Puritan incumbent.

27. The social and economic consequences for the dispossessed Anglican priests lie outside the scope of this work.

28. Main sources for the cases that follow are *Walker Revised*; Walker, *Sufferings*; John White, *The*

First Century of Scandalous, Malignant Priests (London, 1643); Holmes; BL, Add. MS. 15,669–71 (Plundered Ministers, 1644–47). Uncited information in the next seven paragraphs comes from sources listed in this note.

29. See Nicholas Tyacke, *Anti-Calvinists: The Rise of English Arminianism, c. 1590–1640* (OUP, 1987), p. 196.
30. Ibid.
31. Blower seems to have died before he could be ejected, but his superior, Richard Watts, was held responsible for his utterances. See Holmes, pp. 34–5. For the other seven see ibid., p. 78; Walker, *Sufferings*, p. 186; White, *First Century*, pp. 8, 18, 29, 43; John Twigg, *The University of Cambridge and the English Revolution 1625–1688* (The Boydell Press, 1990), p. 33.
32. Holmes, p. 37; White, *First Century*, p. 26.
33. Ibid., p. 42; Holmes, pp. 56, 80.
34. See Appendix IV.
35. Holmes, p. 71.
36. Ibid., p. 79.
37. See Appendix IV.
38. See Appendix IV.
39. Walker, *Sufferings*, p. 208.
40. Apart from Barton, Mayor and Pratt, these were Nicholas Bloxham, John Brown, Seth Chapman, Matthew Clay, Robert Cotesford, William Evans, Thomas Geary, Miles Goltey, Williams Jones, John Ranew, Thomas Sayer, Richard Topcliffe and Daniel Wicherley.
41. See Appendix IV. All graduates were Cambridge men, except John Crofts, John Gregson, Edmund Hinde and William Proctor, who had all attended Oxford. Three of our sample – Edmund Boldero, Anthony Sparrow and Daniel Wicherley – were Fellows of Cambridge colleges as well as Suffolk parsons.
42. See Appendix IV.
43. Holmes, p. 62; Walker, *Sufferings*, p. 256; White, *First Century*, p. 28.
44. See Appendix IV.
45. Walker, *Sufferings*, p. 256.
46. See Appendix IV.
47. Walker, *Sufferings*, p. 289; Holmes, p. 71; White, *First Century*, p. 50.
48. *Walker Revised*, p. 341.
49. Ibid.
50. To give three examples. Nicholas Coleman, Edward Key and William Raymond were all accused of swearing, merely for having said 'by my faith and troth'. See Walker, *Sufferings*, pp. 226, 289, 347.
51. Jim Sharpe, 'Scandalous and Malignant Priests in Essex: the Impact of Grassroots Puritanism', in Colin Jones, Malyn Newitt and Stephen Roberts (eds), *Politics and People in Revolutionary England* (Blackwell, 1986), p. 271.
52. *Walker Revised*, pp. 328, 332, 334, 336–7, 340.
53. Ibid., p. 337; White, *First Century*, pp. 28, 34, 42.
54. Walker, *Sufferings*, p. 247.
55. Holmes, p. 84; *Walker Revised*, p. 338.
56. This political outlook was no more negative than that of most British voters today, who are more aware of what they are against than of what they are for.
57. See Appendix IV.
58. For a lucid explanation of the two covenants see Holmes, pp. 21–2.
59. See Appendix IV.
60. Green, op. cit., p. 516.
61. Holmes, pp. 32, 41, 57.
62. These were William Alcock, John Brown, John Crofts, William Evans, Paul Gosnal, Lionel Playters, William Walker and Richard Watts.
63. Holmes, p. 80.
64. Even if we subtract the six clerics whose Royalism is in doubt, the percentage of loyalists among our eighty clergy is still high: 65 per cent.
65. Ashton, *Counter-Revolution*, p. 230.
66. My italics.
67. Holmes, pp. 38n. 2, 60n. 2, 68.

68. BL, Add. MS. 15,671, ff. 100,147.

69. Walker, *Sufferings*, p. 348.

70. Dowsing is more famous than Richard Culmer of Kent whose iconoclastic activities were much more restricted. See J. Morrill, 'William Dowsing, the Bureaucratic Puritan', in J. Morrill, Paul Slack and Daniel Woolf (eds), *Public Duty and Private Conscience in Seventeenth-Century England* (OUP, 1993), p. 189 and n. 97. The latest work on Dowsing – Trevor Cooper (ed.), *The Journal of William Dowsing* (Boydell Press, 2001) – appeared too late to be addressed by the present author.

71. As such he was in charge of discipline and provisions in the Association.

72. PRO, SP 28/13, pt. II, f 210r.

73. Morrill, 'William Dowsing', p. 197. The Cambridgeshire figures exclude Cambridge college chapels.

74. Firth & Rait, vol. I, p. 265.

75. The commission is printed in E. H. Evelyn White (ed.), *The Journal of William Dowsing* (Ipswich, 1885), pp. 6–7.

76. According to F. J. Varley, 'pictures' refer not to stained glass windows but to 'pictures ... painted on panels ... canvas or paper or on the walls and fabric of churches'. In Suffolk only fifteen churches had their glass damaged by Dowsing. See Varley, *Cambridge during the Civil War 1642–1646* (CUP, 1935), pp. 39–41.

77. White, *Journal of William Dowsing*, pp. 15, 23, 27.

78. E.g., the heraldic glass of 1617 containing the names of benefactors in the east window at Clare parish church.

79. E.g., the eighteen feet high canopied font-cover at Ufford church.

80. For 'soldierly iconoclasm' see Ian Gentles, *The New Model Army* (Blackwell, 1992), pp. 109–10.

81. This paragraph relies heavily on Morrill, 'William Dowsing', esp. pp. 176, 178–83, 191, 200–2.

82. M. Aston, *England's Iconoclasts* (OUP, 1988), p. 82.

83. Morrill, op. cit., p. 191.

84. White, *Journal of William Dowsing*, pp. 22, 26, 29.

85. See map in Morrill, op. cit., p. 194.

86. Morrill, op. cit., p. 190.

87. Richard Deacon, *Matthew Hopkins, Witch Finder General* (Frederick Muller, 1976), pp. 12–13, 19, 58.

88. Ibid., pp. 58–9.

89. Dymond & Northeast, p. 77.

90. Deacon, op. cit., pp. 142–52.

91. Dymond & Northeast, loc. cit.

92. The figures in the table are somewhat conservative estimates. Main sources are Alan MacFarlane, *Witchcraft in Tudor and Stuart England* (2nd edn, Routledge, 1999), p. 135; Ketton-Cremer, *Norfolk in the Civil War*, pp. 307–8; Deacon, op. cit., pp. 127–8, 133–6, 160, 166, 172–3.

93. Deacon, p. 170.

94. John Gaule, *Select Cases of Conscience touching witches* (London, 1646), pp. 4–5. This tract was widely read and no doubt influential.

95. This was not the end of persecution, however. Two widows from Lowestoft were accused of witchcraft and hanged at Bury St Edmunds in 1664 (Dymond & Northeast, loc. cit.). Still, the worst was over when Hopkins died.

96. Deacon, pp. 194–5.

97. Brian P. Levack, *The Witch-Hunt in Early Modern Europe* (2nd edn, Longman, 1995), p. 145.

98. Hans Guggisberg, 'Men and ideas on the margin of history', in Pierre Chaunu (ed.), *The Reformation* (2nd edn, Alan Sutton, 1989), p. 254.

99. My italics.

100. K. Thomas, *Religion and the Decline of Magic* (Penguin University Books, 1973), p. 537.

101. Ibid., p. 597; MacFarlane, op. cit., p. 186.

102. He charged at least £2 a time to investigate witches. See David Ryan's introduction to *The Discovery of Witches* by Matthew Hopkins (Partizan Press, 1988), p. vi.

103. Deacon, p. 74.

104. A. L. Rowse, *Reflections on the Puritan Revolution* (Methuen, 1986), p. 245.

105. Ryan, op. cit., pp. iii, v.

106. Rowse, op. cit., p. 247.

107. Lyndon 'The South and ... Second Civil War', pp. 394, 397–8; Ashton, *Counter-Revolution*, pp. 425–9.

108. Ibid., pp. 368, 425–7, 429; Everitt, *Suffolk*, p. 14.
109. Kingston, p. 257.
110. None of these colonels was a Suffolk man.
111. Quoted in Peter May, *The Changing Face of Newmarket*, 2 vols (Peter May publications, Newmarket, 1984), II, p. 15.
112. On the equation of Royalism with the culture of Merry England, see Underdown, *Revel, Riot and Rebellion*, passim.
113. Ashton, op. cit., pp. 376–7; Kingston, pp. 255–7; Gentles, op. cit., p. 241. For an original account of the Bury 'great combustion', to which John Sutton drew my attention, see *An exact relation of the late rising at Bury* (17 May 1648), BL, E 443 (9), unpaginated.
114. Stoyle, *Loyalty and Locality*, p. 252.
115. It is not impossible that the popular uprising in Bury in 1648 may have been a delayed reaction to the witch trials held in the town in 1645.
116. Stuart Reid, *Officers and Regiments of the Royalist Army*, 5 vols (Partizan Press, ND), III, p. 119; Kingston, p. 267 n. 1; *CCAM*, Vol. II, p. 1115.
117. See chapter 5 above.
118. Ketton-Cremer, op. cit., p. 353.
119. See chapter 7 below.
120. These were Thomas Bedingfield of Darsham, Thomas Edgar of Ipswich, Samuel Fairweather of Halesworth, John Fiske of Rattlesden, Henry Fulcher of Eye, Robert Manning of Walton, Robert Sparrow of Wickhambrook and Stephen Winthrop of Groton.
121. But one Suffolk peer – Lord Willoughby of Parham – changed sides. An active Parliamentarian in the First Civil War, he was an equally active Royalist in the Second. See Ashton, op. cit., pp. 410–11; Clive Holmes, *Seventeenth-century Lincolnshire* (Lincoln, 1980), pp. 146–50, 155–9, 161, 164, 168–9, 171–2, 182–5, 187, 203, 217.
122. Everitt, *Community of Kent and Great Rebellion* (Leicester UP, 1966), pp. 244, 246; C. B. Phillips, 'County Committees and Local Government in Cumberland and Westmorland, 1642–1660', *NH*, v (1970), p. 55.
123. See Appendix V.
124. For sources see chapter 5 above, p. 288, n. 7.
125. These were Sir Thomas Barnardiston of Kedington, William Blois of Grundisburgh, John Deynes of Coddenham, John Fiske of Rattlesden, Henry Fulcher of Eye, Brampton Gurdon of Assington junior, James Harvey of Wickham Skeith, John Hodges of Woodbridge, Richard Le Hunt of Little Bradley, Robert Sparrow of Wickhambrook and Stephen Winthrop of Groton. Barnardiston, Blois and Gurdon were also active as officials.
126. In about 1670 Colchester ranked as the seventh largest provincial town in England. See Angus McInnes, *The English Town, 1660–1760* (Historical Association, Appreciations in History No. 7, 1980), p. 6.
127. Ashton, op. cit., p. 466; Kingston, pp. 260–1; Lyndon, 'Essex and the King's Cause', p. 29.
128. This and the next three paragraphs on the siege rely heavily on Kingston, pp. 260–3., 268–73, 277–83; Lyndon, 'Essex', pp. 17–39; idem, 'The Parliament's Army in Essex, 1648', *JSAHR*, lix (autumn and winter, 1981), pp. 140–60, 229–42; Gentles, op. cit., pp. 251–7; Ashton, op. cit., pp. 438, 464, 466–8, 472–5; Charles Carlton, *Going to the Wars* (Routledge, 1992), pp. 321–4, 327–8; D. Woodward and C. Cockerill, *The Siege of Colchester 1648*. (2nd edn, Essex County Library, 1979).
129. Gentles, op. cit., p. 256.
130. A contemporary reckoned that the 'slaine on both sides' amounted to 'no lesse than 1500 dead bodies' (Woodward and Cockerill, op. cit., p. 10).
131. As many as '186 householders were burned out' (Stephen Porter, *Destruction in the English Civil Wars* (Alan Sutton, 1994), p. 68).
132. Hence 800 horses were apparently eaten during the siege (Kingston, p. 282 n. 2).
133. Gentles, op. cit., pp. 256, 513 n. 82.
134. Lyndon, 'Essex', p. 29.
135. Unlike the other four Suffolk colonels, Fothergill was not of gentry stock, but probably the son of a medical doctor of Sudbury (Information of Clive Holmes).
136. Lyndon, 'Parliament's Army', pp. 145–6; Philip Morant, *The Hist. and Antiquities of Colchester* (London, 1748), pp. 57–8.
137. The fourth fort – Rainsborough – was not built by Suffolk soldiers.

138. Lyndon, op. cit., pp. 155, 158, 239.
139. As well as Barnardiston, Blois, Gurdon and Harvey, three other Suffolk gentlemen fought at Colchester on the Parliamentary side: Lieut. Colonel John Fiske of Rattlesden, Major John Deynes of Coddenham and Capt. John Hodges of Woodbridge. For Deynes see CUL, Additional MS. 6967, f. 10. For information on Fiske and Hodges I am indebted to the late Gwyneth Dyke.
140. Younger brother of Sir Nathaniel Barnardiston of Kedington and a civilian supporter of Parliament, it is not certain whether he was a soldier at Colchester.
141. For these and other commissioners see Matthew Carter, *A True Relation of that Honourable, Though Unfortunate Expedition of Kent, Essex and Colchester in 1648* (2nd edn, Colchester, 1789), pp. 173–6; *LJ*, vol. X, p. 478.
142. R. L. Greaves & R. Zaller (eds), *Biographical Dictionary of British Radicals in the Seventeenth Century*, 3 vols (The Harvester Press, 1982–4), II, p. 33.
143. Lyndon, op. cit., pp. 234–5.
144. This was a view apparently shared by Oliver Cromwell, judging by his letter of 20 November 1648 to Robert Jenner and John Ashe. See W. C. Abbot (ed.), *The Writings and Speeches of Oliver Cromwell*, 4 vols (Harvard UP, 1937–47), I, pp. 686–7, 690–2.

NOTES TO CHAPTER SEVEN

1. See chapter 6 above.
2. Nathaniel Bacon, *Annalls of Ipswiche*, p. 550.
3. *DNB*, vol. II, pp. 115–16: Firth & Rait, vol. I, pp. 975, 1093.
4. D. Underdown, *Pride's Purge* (OUP, 1971).
5. He was not, however, a regicide. His refusal to sign the King's death warrant saved him from execution at the Restoration (Greaves & Zaller, *British Radicals*, vol. II, p. 69).
6. Francis Bacon, Nathaniel Bacon, Sir Thomas Barnardiston, Brampton Gurdon, junior, and Sir Philip Parker served as justices of the peace and were also nominated to the Suffolk assessment commission between 1649 and January 1660. Sir Nathaniel Barnardiston, Maurice Barrow, Alexander Bence, Sir Roger North and Sir William Spring were also nominated to county assessment commissions. They may or may not have served. For the *acting* JPs between 1649 and 1659 see SRO (I), B 105/2/1; /2/2; 2/3; 2/4. For nominated members of the county assessment commission from 1649 to 1660 see Firth & Rait, op. cit., vol. II, pp. 43, 309, 478, 675–6, 1080–1, 1248, 1379. Uncited information in this chapter comes from sources listed in this note.
7. See pp. 186, 188.
8. See Thomas Birch (ed.), *A Collection of the State Papers of John Thurloe, Esq.*, 7 vols (London 1742), IV, p. 225. These new commissioners were quite distinct from the traditional justices of the peace.
9. On the political activities of Sir Thomas Barnardiston see Paul Pinckney, 'The Suffolk Elections to the Protectorate Parliaments', in Jones, Newitt & Roberts (eds), *Politics and People in Revolutionary England*, pp. 205–24, esp. pp. 214, 221–2.
10. This figure excludes Sir Robert Crane of Chilton who died in 1643.
11. Justices of the Peace exclude peers, 'foreigners' and *ex-officio* members of the Bench. Moreover, we are concerned only with serving magistrates in this chapter. Nominated JPs who cannot be shown to have served at any time are ignored. A majority of the serving JPs were active men, activity being defined in terms of attending at least one quarter session per annum. For the names of serving magistrates between 1642 and 1659 see SRO (I), B 105/2/1; 2/2; 2/3; 2/4.
12. It is not possible to compare *active* committeemen before and after 1649 because the County Committee was virtually abolished in 1650.
13. This figure excludes four who died before 1649.
14. Firth & Rait, vol. I, pp. 94, 115, 150, 168, 234–5, 242–3, 293, 537–8, 624, 639, 745, 975, 1093, 1113, 1243–4, vol. II, pp. 43, 309, 478, 675–6, 1080–1, 1248, 1333, 1379.
15. PRO, *List of Sheriffs*, vol. IX, p. 132.
16. Ronald Hutton, *The British Republic 1649–1660* (Macmillan, 1990), p. 38.
17. See, for example, Andrew M. Coleby, *Central Government and Localities: Hampshire 1649–1689* (CUP, 1987), p. 19; Ann Hughes, *Politics, Society and Civil War in Warwickshire, 1620–1660* (CUP, 1987), pp. 273, 359.
18. Ibid., p. 289.
19. These were Sir Henry Felton of Playford, John Garnish of Mickfield, William Greenwood of Burgh, Thomas Scrivener of Sibton and Thomas Waldegrave of Smallbridge.

20. *DNB*, vol. XV, p. 998.

21. He attended eighty-two quarter sessions from 1649 to 1659.

22. Quoted by Barry Coward, 'The Experience of the Gentry 1640–1660', in R. C. Richardson (ed.), *Town and Countryside in the English Revolution* (Manchester UP, 1992), p. 216.

23. See Quentin Skinner, 'Conquest and Consent: Thomas Hobbes and the Engagement Controversy', in G. E. Aylmer (ed.), *The Interregnum: The Quest for Settlement 1646–1660* (Macmillan, 1972), pp. 79–98.

24. PRO, SP 25/76A/30 (Draft Order Books); Firth & Rait, vol. II, p. 1333.

25. In April and December 1649, 1650, 1652 and 1657.

26. Austin Woolrych, *Commonwealth to Protectorate* (OUP, 1982), pp. 412–13, 416–17; B. S. Capp, *The Fifth Monarchy Men* (Faber & Faber, 1972), esp. pp. 228–32.

27. Clarendon, *Rebellion*, vol. IV, p. 287.

28. See especially Blackwood, *Lancs. Gentry*, pp. 77–88; Everitt, *Community of Kent and Great Rebellion*, pp. 16, 296, 329; Anthony Fletcher, *A Community in Peace and War: Sussex 1600–1660* (Longman, 1975), pp. 133, 295, 316, 355; idem, *Reform in the Provinces* (Yale UP, 1986), pp. 31–3; C. Holmes, *Seventeenth-century Lincolnshire* (Lincoln, 1980), p. 207; Ann Hughes, op. cit., pp. 271–7, 353–6; Morrill, *Cheshire, 1630–1660*, pp. 223–5, 233–4, 256–8; David Underdown, 'Settlement in the Counties 1653–1658', in Aylmer (ed.), *The Interregnum*, pp. 178–80; idem, *Somerset in the Civil War and Interregnum* (David & Charles, 1973), pp. 158, 168–9.

29. See chapter 2 above.

30. Underdown, 'Settlement', p. 177.

31. Coleby, op. cit., p. 20; Fletcher, *Sussex*, pp. 133, 355.

32. In this table and also in Tables 7.3 – 7.5 social rank is that held in 1642. For names of the JPs see references in note 11 above.

33. For names of serving JPs see references in note 11, also PRO, SP 16/60; SRO (I), B 105/2/5.

34. Sources for status of JPs in the Restoration period are given above p. 272, n. 112.

35. Woolrych, op. cit., pp. 269, 412.

36. For names of assessment commissioners see Firth & Rait, vol. I, pp. 975, 1093, vol. II, pp. 43, 309, 478, 675–6, 1080, 1248, 1379; *Statutes of the Realm*, vol. 5, 13 Car. II, stat. ii, cap. 3. The few non-Suffolk nominees are ignored.

37. For status of commissioners in 1661 see *Stat. Realm* vol. 5, 13 Car. II, stat., ii, cap. 3.

38. Stephen K. Roberts, *Recovery and Restoration in an English County: Devon Local Administration 1646–1670* (Exeter UP, 1985), p. 28.

39. As suggested in Underdown, 'Settlement', p. 177.

40. G. E. Aylmer, *Rebellion or Revolution? England 1640–1660* (OUP, 1986), p. 205.

41. In a very brief paragraph on the Interregnum, Everitt argued on similar lines. See his *Suffolk*, p. 36; also pp. 16, 18, 27.

42. For names of militia commissioners in 1648, 1659 and 1660 see Firth & Rait, vol. I, pp. 1243–4, vol. II, pp. 1333, 1443. For those in 1655 see PRO, SP 25/76 A/30. The few non-Suffolk nominees are again ignored.

43. W. Haller & G. Davies (eds), *The Leveller Tracts* (Peter Smith, Gloucester, Mass., 1964), p. 79.

44. Thomas Fuller, *The History of the Worthies of England*, ed. P. Austin Nuttall, 3 vols (London, 1840), I, p. 70.

45. G. Lewis in *The French Revolution: The Story so far* (Channel Four Television Publication, 1989), p. 35.

46. For details of the Acts of Sale see Firth & Rait, vol. I, pp. 887–905, vol. II, pp. 81–104, 168–91, 358–62, 520–45, 591–8, 623–52.

47. *CJ*, vol. VI, p. 476.

48. Five of these deeds refer to episcopal land and the rest to capitular (cathedral) property.

49. PRO, C54/3381/1; 3418/16; 3484/34; 3502/28; 3522/30; 3557/31; 3558/16; 3561/2; 3565/2; 3566/13, 19; 3570/4; 3589/24; 3596/23, 24; 3598/43; 3602/43; 3654/25; 3659/22; 3664/4; 3691/21; 3703/35; 3876/47.

50. According to David Underdown, Brampton Gurdon of Assington, junior, also bought church land, but where and when is not stated. See *Pride's Purge*, p. 375.

51. Firth & Rait, vol. I, pp. 94, 115, 150, 168, 235.

52. PRO, C54/3502/28.

53. This was formerly the property of the Dean and Chapter of Ely. See PRO, C54/3570/4.

54. PRO, C54/3515/34; Copinger, *Manors*, vol. II, p. 212.

55. *DNB*, vol. IX, p. 81; Greaves & Zaller, loc. cit.

56. PRO, C54/3445/25.

57. I. G. Gentles, 'The Debentures Market and Military Purchases of Crown Land 1649–1660' (unpublished PhD thesis, University of London, 1969), pp. 246, 272, 274, 276, 282, 291, 310, 313, 317, 335. See also PRO, SP 28/176 Part I, f. 20; 243, ff. 37, 58.

58. Jean and Ray Lock say that Margery 'increased his property substantially', buying the hundreds of Clifton and Biggleswade in Bedfordshire and land in Poynton, Lincolnshire, about 1652. 'No longer could he be called a man of little estate'. See 'Captain Raphe Margery', *PSIAH, xxxvi*, Pt. 3 (1987), p. 217.

59. Gentles mistakenly describes all four, plus Thomas Ogle, as esquires. He also errs in regarding Charles Fleetwood and Capt. Thomas Ireton as Suffolk men. See Gentles, thesis, pp. 281–2, 301.

60. Moreover, only two Parliamentarians seem to have bought Royalist land sold privately, these being Thomas Edgar, Esquire, Recorder of Ipswich, and John Base, Yeoman of Saxmundham. See p. 198.

61. See p. 198.

62. Those 150 persons helped the Parliamentary cause in one or more of the two Civil Wars (1642–46, 1648).

63. Karl S. Bottigheimer, *English Money and Irish Land* (OUP 1971), pp. 176, 181, 190, 199, 203, 210.

64. This phrase denotes committed Puritan-Parliamentarians. See Keith Lindley, 'Irish adventurers and godly militants in the 1640s', *Irish Historical Studies, xxix* (1994), pp. 1–12.

65. Bottigheimer, op. cit., pp. 187, 207. Not surprisingly, four other Suffolk plebeians – John Grocer, Hugh Grove, John Hall and John Sparrow – acquired far smaller amounts of Irish land (ibid., pp. 182–3, 191, 203, 210). Whether they were godly militants is unknown.

66. D. E. Underdown, *Royalist Conspiracy in England 1649–1660* (Yale UP, 1960, reprint 1971), p. viii.

67. Ibid., p. 1.

68. Ibid.

69. See ibid., pp. 97–103

70. Suffolk men fighting on the other side at Worcester included two militia foot regiments under Colonels John Fothergill and James Harvey, plus a horse regiment under Brampton Gurdon, junior (Ive, thesis, pp. 213–14, 231–2).

71. Newman, *Royalist Officers*, p. 31; Peter Young, *Edgehill 1642*, pp. 85, 89.

72. For details see Underdown, *Royalist Conspiracy*, pp. 40–5.

73. Ibid., p. 191.

74. Ibid., pp. 269–70; Ive, op. cit., p. 19.

75. Underdown, pp. 75, 322; Ive, op. cit., p. 14.

76. Information of the late Gwenyth Dyke.

77. P. R. Newman, *Atlas of the English Civil War* (Croom Helm, 1985), pp. 110–11; A. H. Woolrych, *Penruddock's Rising 1655* (Historical Association Pamphlet G. 29, 1955), esp. pp. 3–4, 17–22.

78. Ive, op. cit., p. 16.

79. See Underdown, p. 325.

80. Major-General Hezekiah Haynes, writing to Secretary John Thurloe from Bury St Edmunds on 21 November 1655, remarked that there were 'not many delinquents [Royalists] in this county' [Suffolk]. See *Thurloe State Papers*, vol. IV, p. 227.

81. BL, Add. MS. 34,013 (Major-Generals' returns), ff. 1, 8, 10, 14, 16, 19, 22, 29, 32, 35, 37, 40, 43, 51, 55.

82. For details see B. G. Blackwood, 'Parties and Issues in the Civil War in Lancashire and East Anglia', *NH, xxix* (1993), pp. 114–16; David Underdown, *Revel, Riot and Rebellion* (OUP, 1985), pp. 200–1, 296.

83. Bod. Lib., MS. Eng. hist c. 309 (Roger Whitley's notebook), f. 42.

84. Francis Bacon became a Master of Requests in 1657 and favoured a Cromwellian monarchy (Pinckney, op. cit., pp. 212, 223). But following Oliver Cromwell's death in 1658, he became a Royalist.

85. Underdown, *Royalist Conspiracy*, p. 317.

86. Firth & Rait, vol. I, pp. 106–10.

87. Everitt, *Suffolk*, pp. 11, 13. The high yield was partly because of efficient administration and partly because almost half those sequestrated were recusants who were not allowed to compound in order to regain their estates (ibid., p. 14 & n. 5).

88. Neither Catholic Royalists nor Catholic Neutrals were allowed to compound for their estates before October 1653, although most Protestant Royalists were permitted to do so (Paul H. Hardacre, *The Royalists during the Puritan Revolution* (Martinus Nijhoff, The Hague, 1956), pp. 55–6,

60, 116–17). In practice, some papist delinquents, like Edward Rookwood of Euston Hall, did pay composition fines. See p. 198.

89. *CCC*, vol. II, pp. 845, 864, 891, 1237, 1290, 1389, 1413, 1415, 1425, 1475, vol. III, pp. 1810, 1816, 1867, 1869–70, 1962, vol. IV, pp. 2811, 2978.

90. Ibid., vol. II, pp. 1236–7.

91. H. J. Habakkuk, 'Landowners and the Civil War', *Econ. HR*, 2nd series, xviii (1965), p. 134.

92. *CCC*, vol. III, p. 1810.

93. PRO, E 179/183/518. The use of the lay subsidy rolls to assess annual landed income is vindicated in B. G. Blackwood, 'The Economic State of the Lancashire Gentry on the Eve of the Civil War', *NH*, xii (1976), pp. 55–7; Cliffe, *Yorkshire Gentry*, p. 139; M. D. G. Wanklyn, 'Landed Society and Allegiance in Cheshire and Shropshire in the First Civil War' (unpublished PhD thesis, University of Manchester, 1976), chapter 4.

94. *CCC*, vol. II, p. 1415; *CCAM*, vol. II, p. 1126; PRO, E 179/183/513.

95. Unlike the public sales of confiscated church, crown and delinquent property.

96. Clarendon, *Rebellion*, vol. V, p. 129.

97. C. Hill, *The Century of Revolution 1603–1714* (2nd edn, Thomas Nelson, 1980), p. 126; idem, *Puritanism and Revolution* (Secker & Warburg, 1958), p. 164.

98. H. E. Chesney, 'The Transference of Lands in England, 1640–1660', *TRHS*, 4th series, 15 (1932), pp. 183, 189, 204–5, 207.

99. F. Walker, *Historical Geography of Southwest Lancashire before the Industrial Revolution* (Chetham Society, NS ciii, 1939), p. 132. Unfortunately Walker made little attempt to elaborate or substantiate his argument.

100. This is of course a conservative estimate because for many Suffolk families few records survive of private sales, particularly for the smaller landowners, who were probably the most likely to sell.

101. *CCC*, vol. III, p. 1867; PRO, SP 23/207/480.

102. *CCC*, vol. II, p. 1467; Copinger, *Manors*, vol. III, p. 121; BL, Add. MS. 15,520, f. 110.

103. *CCC*, vol. II, p. 1128; Copinger, *Manors*, vol. V, p. 162; BL, Add. MS. 15,520, ff. 39,124.

104. *CCAM*, vol. II, p. 679.

105. *CCC*, vol. II, p. 1425; Copinger, *Manors*, vol. I, p. 293; BL, Add. MS. 15,520, f. 72.

106. PRO, E 379/138, ff. 8–9, 16.

107. *CCC*, vol. II, p. 1394; *CCAM*, vol. II, p. 811.

108. Firth & Rait, vol. II, pp. 631–2, 634.

109. PRO, C54/3731/2; 3734/1.

110. PRO, INDEX 1/17349, f. 78.

111. S. H. A. Hervey (ed.), *Suffolk in 1674: The Hearth Tax Returns* (Suffolk Green Books, No. XI, vol. 13, Woodbridge, 1905), p. 84.

112. Dymond & Northeast, p. 81. In 1674 Allin possessed four hearths in Blundeston, eleven in Lowestoft and eighteen in Somerleyton (Hervey, op. cit., pp. 30, 198, 251).

113. See Blackwood, *Lancs. Gentry*, chapter 4; P. G. Holiday, 'Land Sales and Repurchases in Yorkshire after the Civil Wars, 1650–1670', *NH*, v (1970), pp. 67–92; Joan Thirsk, 'The Sale of Royalist Lands during the Interregnum', *Econ. HR* 2nd series, v (1952), pp. 188–207; idem, 'The Restoration Land Settlement', *Journal of Modern History*, xxvi (1954), pp. 315–28.

114. These fifty-six are named in J. T. Cliffe (ed.), 'The Cromwellian Decimation Tax of 1655: the Assessment Lists', in *Seventeenth Century Political and Financial Papers. Camden Miscellany* XXXlll. (Camden Fifth series, vol. 7, 1996), pp. 447–8.

115. 'Generally, the county commissioners preferred to tax real estate rather than personal estate' (ibid., p. 423).

116. Dr Cliffe gives the true incomes of nine of the delinquents assessed for the decimation tax. See ibid., pp. 482–5. I have discovered the annual incomes of another nine from *CCAM*, vol. II, pp. 679, 965; *CCC*, vol. II, pp. 891, 984–5, vol. IV, p. 2978; BL, Add. MS. 15,520, f. 26; Add. MS. 19,082, f. 359; PRO, E 179/183/602; Wards 5/41 (unfoliated).

117. Cliffe, op. cit., pp. 447, 482.

118. Ibid., p. 447; PRO, E 179/183/602.

119. Two other gentry overassessed – Sir William Hervey of Ickworth and Edward Warner of Mildenhall – were not adversely affected.

120. Cliffe, op. cit., p. 447; *CCC*, vol. IV, p. 2978.

121. See above p. 198.

122. Cliffe, op. cit., pp. 447, 482.

123. Francis J. Bremer, *Congregational Communion* (Northeastern UP, Boston, Mass., 1994), p. 174.
124. Ibid., p. 197.
125. Barry Coward, *The Stuart Age*, p. 267. Catholics were, however, persecuted in 1657. See Chapter 8.
126. Claire Cross, 'The Church in England 1646–1660', in Aylmer (ed.), *The Interregnum*, p. 113.
127. For literary convenience I shall use both terms.
128. Walpole claimed to be the oldest surviving nonconformist meeting-place in England and was probably in use from the early 1640s. See Dymond & Northeast, p. 78.
129. Virtually Congregational from 1642. See Bremer, op. cit., p. 181. The Congregational church at Wrentham was greatly encouraged by the Brewsters, lords of the manor (S. Wilton Rix (ed.), *Diary and Autobiography of Edmund Bohun* (Beccles, 1853), pp. 28–9).
130. Founded in 1646. See J. Browne, *History of Congregationalism and Memorials of the Churches in Norfolk and Suffolk* (Jarrold & Sons, London, 1877), p. 164.
131. See Chapter 4 p. 123.
132. Geoffrey Nuttall, *Visible Saints: The Congregational Way 1640–1660* (Blackwell, 1957), pp. 27–8.
133. My italics. Quoted in Browne, op. cit., p. 394.
134. These Suffolk churches with their ministers are listed in Nuttall, op. cit., p. 22 n. 2; idem, 'Congregational Commonwealth Incumbents', *Transactions of the Congregational Historical Society*, xiv (1943), pp. 155–67.
135. Nuttall, *Visible Saints*, p. 22.
136. Nuttall, loc. cit.; Bremer, op. cit., p. 171.
137. The term was applied by the Quaker leader, George Fox, to his followers.
138. There were certainly Quakers in Aldeburgh, Bredfield, Burgh, Knodishall and Little Bealings before 1660 (Information kindly supplied by Mrs Valerie Norrington). Clive Paine has discovered Quakers at Botesdale, Bury and Woodbridge in 1655 (C. Paine, 'Protestant Nonconformity', in Dymond & Martin, p. 208).
139. Only Essex, Berkshire and Norfolk made higher contributions. See W. C. Braithwaite, *The Beginnings of Quakerism* (2nd edn, CUP, 1955), p. 324.
140. Barry Reay, *The Quakers and the English Revolution* (Temple Smith, 1985), p. 53.
141. Besse, vol. I, pp. 659, 664.
142. My italics.
143. Reay, op. cit., pp. 66–8.
144. Ibid., p. 43.
145. Quakers referred to a minister of any kind, even if Presbyterian, Independent or Baptist, as a 'priest'.
146. Not to be confused with George Fox, the founder of Quakerism.
147. Quakers called any church a 'steeple-house'.
148. Beese, vol. I, pp. 658–61, 668.
149. Barry Reay, 'Quaker Opposition to Tithes 1652–1660', *P&P*, 86 (1980), p. 99.
150. Ibid., p. 103.
151. Besse, vol. I, pp. 662, 666.
152. Cumberland, Essex, Kent, Lancashire, Somerset and Yorkshire. See Reay, 'Quaker Opposition', pp. 100–4.
153. Besse, vol. I, pp. 662, 666–7.
154. Quoted in Margaret James, 'The Political Importance of the Tithes Controversy in the English Revolution, 1640–60', *History*, 26 (1941), p. 6.
155. Everitt, *Suffolk*, pp. 35–6.
156. See Chapter 8.

NOTES TO CHAPTER EIGHT

1. This phrase is from Stephen K. Roberts, *Recovery and Restoration ... Devon*, p. 153.
2. On the two settlements see Ronald Hutton, *The Restoration* (OUP, 1985), pp. 125–84.
3. On constitutional Royalism at the Restoration see David L. Smith, *Constitutional Royalism and the Search for Settlement, c. 1640–1649* (CUP, 1994), pp. 290–305.
4. A total of fifty-nine regicides and twenty-nine others were originally exempted from the general pardon. See A. L. Rowse, *The Regicides* (Duckworth, 1994), p. 69; Nicholas Fellows, *Charles II and James II* (Hodder & Stoughton, 1995), p. 16.

5. Bishop Gilbert Burnet, *History of His Own Time* (Everyman's Library, Dent, 1979), p. 39.

6. Blackwood, *Lancs. Gentry*, p. 142; P. G. Holiday, 'Royalist Composition Fines and Land Sales in Yorkshire after the Civil Wars, 1645–65' (unpublished PhD thesis, University of Leeds, 1966), pp. 309–10.

7. Hutton, op. cit., pp. 127, 138.

8. Morrill, 'A Glorious Resolution?', in his *Nature of English Revolution* p. 403.

9. For details see Richard L. Greaves, *Deliver Us from Evil: The Radical Underground in Britain, 1660–1663* (OUP, 1986), pp. 49–57.

10. The name derives from that of Edward Hyde, 1st Earl of Clarendon, the chief minister, though he was not the prime instigator.

11. *Calamy Revised*, p. xiii.

12. Some Puritans remained to form the Low Church party, while others were to be partial conformists. See pp. 225, 227–8, 303 n.133.

13. C. Hill, *Some Intellectual Consequences of the English Revolution* (Weidenfeld & Nicholson, 1980), p. 73. I am more convinced by Christopher Hill than by Dr Goldie, who rather plays down the divisions between Anglicans and Dissenters in the period 1660–89 (Mark Goldie, 'The Search for Religious Liberty, 1640–1690', in John Morrill (ed.), *The Oxford Illustrated History of Tudor and Stuart Britain* (OUP, 1996), pp. 293–309).

14. G. Holmes, *Religion and Party in Late Stuart England* (Historical Association Pamphlet G 86, 1975), p. 9.

15. On the Whig and Tory parties in Suffolk see chapter 9.

16. G. E. Cokayne, *The Complete Peerage*, 13 vols (The St Catherine Press, 1910–59), III, pp. 453, 544, IV, pp. 85–6.

17. So was John Rous of Henham, a Royalist from a politically divided family.

18. G. E. Cokayne, *The Complete Baronetage*, 5 vols (Wm. Pollard, Exeter, 1900–6), III, pp. 41, 44, 51–2, 88, 114, 186, 202, 220, 251, 271–4.

19. W. A. Shaw, *The Knights of England*, 2 vols (Sherratt & Hughes, 1906), II, pp. 226–38.

20. W. A. Shaw (ed.), *Calendar of Treasury Books, 1660–1667* (HMSO, 1904), vol. I, p. 547.

21. Charles II and Parliament did of course make feeble attempts to assist the poorer Royalists. In 1662 an Act was passed reserving £60,000 to be distributed among loyal and Indigent officers (*Statutes of the* Realm, vol. 5, 14 Car. II, cap. 8; 15 Car. II, cap. 3). But since there were 5,353 such officers in England and Wales (*A List of Officers claiming to the Sixty Thousand Pounds etc.* (1663), cols. 1–160), the sum was totally inadequate. How much, if anything, the twenty Suffolk Indigent Officers obtained, it is impossible to say.

22. Andrew Browning (ed.), *English Historical Documents 1660–1714* (Routledge, 1966), p. 245.

23. Ibid.; PRO, LR 2/56 (unfoliated); BL, Add MS. 30,208, ff. 124–5.

24. Newman, *Royalist Officers in England and Wales 1642–1660*, p. 31

25. *DNB*, vol. II, pp. 115–16.

26. Newman, loc. cit.; Copinger, *Manors*, vol. VII, p. 68.

27. Cokayne, *Complete Peerage*, vol. III, p. 453; Copinger, *Manors*, vol. III, p. 243; BL, Add. MS. 36,781, ff. 2,5,19.

28. Newman, op. cit., p. 93; Cokayne, vol. III, p. 544; *Concise DNB*, vol. I, p. 690; E. S. De Beer (ed.), A List of the Department of the Lord Chamberlain of the Household, autumn 1663, *BIHR*, xix (1942–43), p. 14.

29. Andrew Hervey, 'The family of Hervey', *PSIA*, ii (1859), pp. 383, 396.

30. de Beer, op. cit., p. 15.

31. *CSPD*, 1660–1661, p. 142; BL, Egerton MS. 2,551, f. 40.

32. Charles Dalton (ed.), *English Army Lists and Commission Registers, 1661–1714*, 2 vols (London, 1892), I, p. 31.

33. Newman, op. cit., p. 318.

34. Cokayne, op. cit., vol. VII, pp. 85–6; Dalton, op. cit., pp. 10–11; Newman, p. 211; *DNB*, vol. X, p. 780.

35. This excludes those who might have received rewards as Indigent Officers. The following gentry are also excluded from our calculations: divided families, like Le Hunt of Little Bradley and Rous of Henham; new Royalists emerging in the 1650s, like Tollemache of Helmingham; and Royalist families living outside the county until the Restoration, like Elwes of Stoke-by-Clare and Gage of Hengrave.

36. Sons are classed with the same party as the father. Where the family was divided the allegiance

of the appointee has been counted. The abbreviations are mostly self-explanatory, but 'SC' denotes a side-changer and 'Rep' applies to an individual who served the Republic but apparently not Parliament during the Civil Wars. Among MPs 'carpetbaggers' are excluded. Among JPs, peers, 'foreigners' and *ex-officio* members of the Bench are ignored.

37. References are: (a) *Return of Members of Parliament. Part I: The Parliaments of England 1213–1703* (House of Commons 1878), pp. 516, 528–9; B. D. Henning (ed.), *The House of Commons 1660–1690*, 3 vols (Secker & Warburg, 1983), I, pp. 539, 579–81, 614, 669, 713, 726–7, II, pp. 101, 134–5, 171–2, 306, 452–3, III, pp. 152–4, 256–7, 319–21, 352–3, 433, 649; (b) SRO (I), B 105/2/5; (c) PRO, SP 29/60/66; (d) PRO, *List of Sheriffs*, vol. IX, p. 112; (e) *Statutes of the Realm*, vol. 5, 13 Car. II, stat. ii, cap. 3; (f) PRO, E 179/257/7; (g) *Stat. Realm*, vol. 5, 15 Car. II, cap. 9.

38. Felicity Heal and Clive Holmes, *The Gentry in England and Wales 1500–1700* (Macmillan, 1994), p. 189.

39. See ibid. pp. 216–17.

40. Of those twenty-four, fourteen, including three ex-Royalists, had served the Republic only, while ten were acting JPs during both the 1640s and 1650s.

41. Coleby, *Central Government and the Localities: Hampshire*, p. 90. The survival rate seems to have been lower in several other counties, but higher in Devon where 57 per cent continued as JPs at the Restoration. See Fletcher, *A Community … Sussex*, p. 134; G. C. F. Forster, 'Government in Provincial England under the Later Stuarts', *TRHS*, 5th series, xxxiii (1983), p. 31; Clive Holmes, *Seventeenth-century Lincolnshire*, p. 219; P. Jenkins, ' "The old Leaven": the Welsh Roundheads after 1660', *HJ*, xxiv (1981), pp. 815–16; Roberts, *Recovery and Restoration … Devon*, p. 148.

42. These were Allington of Lavenham, Barnardiston of Brightwell, Barnardiston of Clare, Base of Saxmundham, Battell of Elmham St James, Beaumont of Hadleigh, Brown of Lavenham, Byett of Bures, Canham of Milden, Chaplin, Chapman and Clark, all of Bury St Edmunds, Cole of Little Fakenham, Cook of Pakenham, Cordell of Long Melford, Cullum of Hawstead, Darcy of Long Melford, Dunston of Hopton, Fox of Syleham, Gooding of Wherstead, Groome of Rattlesden, Haward of Carlton Colville, Keble of Gipping, Kerrington of Newton, Lurkin of Hunston, Maltwood of Rougham, Man of Edwardstone, Morse of Wrentham, Phillips of Ipswich, Scot of Theberton, Smith of Parkfield, Smyth of Sutton, Sorrell of Ipswich, Sothebie of Bury, Wells of Lavenham, Westrupp of Hundon and Whiting of Ipswich.

43. See above p. 207.

44. Cliffe, *The Puritan Gentry*, pp. 57–8.

45. Dymond & Northeast, p. 81.

46. Henning, *The House of Commons*, vol. II, pp. 129–30.

47. Alan Simpson, *The Wealth of the Gentry, 1540–1660: East Anglian Studies* (CUP, 1961), pp. 127–8, 131; Paul Pinckney, 'The Suffolk Elections to the Protectorate Parliaments', in Jones, Newitt & Roberts, *Politics and People in Revolutionary England*, p. 219.

48. For Chaplin and Base see above p. 212. For Groome see BL, Add. MS. 15,520, f. 56.

49. Thomas Fuller, *The History of the Worthies of England*, ed. P. Austin Nuttall, 3 vols (London, 1840), I, p. 70.

50. Holmes, p. 112; Copinger, *Manors*, vol. V, p. 162; BL, Add. MS. 15,520, f. 124; W. H. Rylands (ed.), *The Visitation of Suffolk 1664–1668*, Harleian Society, 61 (1910), p. 83.

51. *CCC*, vol. II, p. 1128.

52. Copinger, *Manors*, vol. IV, p. 233. See also memorial tablet on north wall of chancel in Frostenden Parish Church.

53. Paul Seward, *The Restoration, 1660–1688* (Macmillan, 1991), p. 5; also pp. 4, 6–7, 27–9.

54. This total figure includes those families participating in one or more of the two Civil Wars (1642–46, 1648).

55. Two families – Bacon of Culford and Coke of Huntingfield – failed in the male line.

56. Blackwood, *Lancs Gentry*, pp. 100–1.

57. Clive Holmes, *The Eastern Association* (CUP, 1974), p. 137. See also Heal & Holmes, op. cit., pp. 117, 158.

58. See note 54 above.

59. Three families – Baker of Whittingham Hall, Cage of Ipswich and Crane of Chilton – failed in the male line.

60. Disappearing families are absent from, and new (and perdurable) families are present in, the sources listed in Chapter 2 n. 112 above.

61. No Republican disappeared from the Suffolk gentry.

62. Copinger, *Manors*, vol. V, p. 65.

63. Sir Gervase Elwes came from Woodford, Essex (Newman, op. cit., p. 122). Sir Edward Gage was from Firle, Sussex (Rylands, op. cit., p. 202). Sir Henry Wood was previously a courtier from Hackney (Cliffe, 'The Cromwellian Decimation Tax of 1655', p. 482). The other new Royalist gentry family – Aylmer of Claydon – was of local clerical origins (Rylands, op. cit., p. 3).

64. Blackwood, loc. cit.

65. It is hard to explain the disappearance of so many gentry families. But one reason, apart from high taxation, must have been the mid-seventeenth century agricultural depression, with its 'decay of rents' and falling prices. These must have been particularly harmful to the small gentry.

66. According to Professor Fletcher, the half-century after 1660 'witnessed the triumph of the Stuart gentry' (Fletcher, *Reform in the Provinces*, pp. 351–73).

67. In the late seventeenth century some gentlemen and others could be found, like their counterparts today, living in houses they could not afford to keep up, but, as a rough standard of living index, the tax is adequate. The main problem with the hearth tax returns is that of regional variations.

68. Several gentry had more than one house, but this table concentrates on their main residence, as does Table 8.8.

69. Main source is S. H. A. Hervey (ed.), *Suffolk in 1674: The Hearth Tax Returns*, Suffolk Green Books, No. XI, vol. 13 (Woodbridge, 1905). For Blackbourne hundred I have relied on Sylvia Colman (ed.), 'The Hearth Tax Returns for the Hundred of Blackbourne, 1662', *PSIA*, xxxii (1973), pp. 168–92. The Hearth Tax return for Suffolk in 1664 (PRO, E 179/257/12) is too badly defaced and incomplete to be useful.

70. In this and the next table Royalists include three gentry families ennobled *after* the outbreak of the First Civil War: Cornwallis, Crofts and Jermyn.

71. One Royalist newcomer to the county, Sir Edward Gage, had an even larger house, Hengrave Hall with fifty-one hearths.

72. Two Parliamentarian newcomers, Sir Robert Cordell and Sir Thomas Cullum, had forty-nine and thirty-five hearths respectively.

73. For evidence used to assess annual landed incomes in 1642 see Gordon Blackwood, 'The Cavalier and Roundhead Gentry of Suffolk Updated', *Suffolk Review*, NS 22 (Spring 1994), p. 27 n. 5.

74. PRO, E 179/183/508; 183/563; 183/564; 183/602; 257/11.

75. Thomas Wootton, *The English Baronetage*, 4 vols (London, 1741), IV, p. 373.

76. BL, Add. MS. 15,520.

77. I am very grateful to Dr J. T. Cliffe for supplying me with this information in his communication of 25 April 1994.

78. Cliffe, *Puritan Gentry*, p. 118.

79. 'Phanatick' was a contemporary, abusive term for Dissenter.

80. Bod. Lib., Tanner MS. 239, f. 53. Holland was a very moderate Parliamentarian during the First Civil War, but, like most moderates, he strongly supported the Restoration in 1660.

81. S. Wilton Rix (ed.) *Diary ... of Edmund Bohun*, p. 42. See also p. xvii.

82. Barry Coward, *Oliver Cromwell* (Longman, 1991), p. 111.

83. *Calamy Revised*, p. xiii.

84. For details see J. P. Kenyon (ed.), *The Stuart Constitution 1603–1688: Documents and Commentary* (2nd edn, CUP, 1986), pp. 351–3.

85. Hutton, op. cit., p. 161.

86. For details see M. Reed, 'Ipswich in the seventeenth century' (unpublished PhD thesis, University of Leicester, 1973), pp. 257–64.

87. Hutton, loc. cit.

88. SRO (I), HD 36/A/262 (Purge of Eye Corporation 23 March 1661). 'Harvey' is easily recognised. He had served Parliament as a Colonel of Foot at the siege of Colchester in 1648. But virtually nothing is known about the other three corporation officials.

89. Kenyon, op. cit., pp. 353–6.

90. *Calamy Revised*, pp. xii–xiii. See also ibid. for details of ejections in the other thirty-six English counties, including the Channel Islands.

91. Francis J. Bremer, *Congregational Communion*, p. 208.

92. See *Calamy Revised*.

93. Since the biographies are in alphabetical order in *Calamy Revised*, it has seemed unnecessary, except in a few cases, to give page references.

94. *Calamy Revised*, pp. xxxiii–iv.

95. Ibid., pp. xxxiv, 189, 425.
96. J. T. Cliffe, *The Puritan Gentry Besieged 1650–1700* (Routledge, 1993), pp. 124, 207, 209.
97. *Calamy Revised*, p. lvi.
98. The other seven were John Fairfax, James King, Samuel Manning, Zephaniah Smith, Henry Stephens, Benjamin Stoneham, Thomas Taylor.
99. Robert Franklin, Stephen Scandrett, Edmund Whincop.
100. Edward Barker, John Meadows, John Page, Samuel Slater, John Storer.
101. *VCH Suffolk*, vol. II, p. 47. As against the leniency of Bishop Reynolds must be set the harshness of Edmund Bohun, a zealous Anglican JP who hounded the Dissenters in Suffolk. But a single magistrate had far less power than a Bishop of Norwich. On Bohun's activities see Anthony Fletcher, 'The Enforcement of the Conventicle Acts 1664–1679', in W. J. Sheils (ed.), *Persecution and Toleration* (Blackwell, 1984), pp. 242–3.
102. Reay, *The Quakers and the English Revolution*, pp. 110, 121.
103. See *CSPD*, 1660–1661, p. 481.
104. However, in the 1669 Return of Nonconformist Conventicles, the Quaker preachers at Bradfield St Claire were described as 'Itinerants and Wanderers'. See C. B Jewson, 'Return of Conventicles in Norwich Diocese 1669 – Lambeth MS. No. 639', *Norfolk Archaeology*, xxxiii (1965), p. 31.
105. C. Hill, 'Quakers and the English Revolution', *JFHS*, lvi (1992), p. 176.
106. C. Hill, *Some Intellectual Consequences*, p. 73.
107. Besse, vol. I, pp. 671–4, 677–9, 681, 683, 685.
108. Ibid., vol. I, pp. 677, 683.
109. Ibid., vol. I, pp. 671–2. The majority were indicted for refusing to take the oath of allegiance.
110. Ibid., vol. I, pp. 685–7.
111. 23 Eliz., cap. 1, sect. 5; 29 Eliz., cap. 6, sections 3, 4; and 3 Jac. I, cap. 4.
112. Besse, vol. I, pp. 673, 678, 681, 683–4.
113. Tim Harris, *Politics under the later Stuarts* (Longman, 1993), p. 179.
114. Besse, vol. I, pp. 671–2 674–82, 686.
115. Ibid., vol. I, p. 683.
116. John Barker of Trimley, Robert Brooke of Yoxford, Nicholas Bacon of Shrubland, Thomas Bacon of Friston and John Brame of Ash.
117. Besse, vol. I, pp. 679–80.
118. H. Barbour, *The Quakers in Puritan England* (Yale UP, 1964), p. 225.
119. W. C. Braithwaite, *The Second Period of Quakerism* (2nd edn, CUP, 1961), p. 108.
120. *VCH Suffolk*, vol. II, p. 47.
121. 'Quakers claimed liberty of worship as a natural, or supernatural, right, and therefore ignored the proferred indulgence' (*Calamy Revised*, p. xv).
122. For details see Kenyon, op. cit., pp. 382–3.
123. The information given in this map is derived from Clive Paine, 'Protestant Nonconformity', in Dymond & Martin, pp. 114–15; *VCH Suffolk*, vol. II, p. 48 n. 2; G. Lyon Turner, *Original Records of Nonconformity under Persecution and Indulgence*, 3 vols. (T. Fisher Unwin, London, 1911–14), I, pp. 613–15, II, pp. 903–22.
124. Paine, op. cit., p. 114.
125. But Bungay Baptists were able to share one meeting place with Independents.
126. See A. J. Klaiber, *The Story of Suffolk Baptists* (Kingsgate Press, London, 1931), pp. 23, 35–6.38–9.
127. Aldeburgh, Beccles, Bildeston, Botesdale, Bungay, Bury St Edmunds, Clare, Debenham, Dunwich, Eye, Framlingham, Hadleigh, Halesworth, Haverhill, Ipswich, Ixworth, Lavenham, Lowestoft, Mendlesham, Mildenhall, Nayland, Needham Market, Newmarket, Orford, Saxmundham, Southwold, Stowmarket, Sudbury, Woodbridge (Blome, *Britannia*, pp. 209–16).
128. Aldeburgh, Beccles, Bungay, Bury St Edmunds, Clare, Debenham, Dunwich, Eye, Framlingham, Hadleigh, Haverhill, Ipswich, Lowestoft, Mendlesham, Mildenhall, Nayland, Needham Market, Southwold, Stowmarket, Sudbury, Woodbridge.
129. R. C. Richardson, *Puritanism in north-west England: A regional study of the diocese of Chester to 1642* (Manchester UP, 1972), p. 13.
130. An adult in seventeenth century England was a person aged sixteen or over.
131. Figures in this table are from Anne Whiteman & Mary Clapinson (eds), *The Compton Census of 1676: A Critical Edition* (OUP, 1986), pp. 192, 231–41; hereafter *Compton Census*.
132. Ibid., pp. 235, 238; Jewson, op. cit., pp. 30–1.
133. There is insufficient space to describe in detail those partial conformists. But the best Suffolk

examples are the Barnardistons of Brightwell, the Barnardistons of Kedington and the Brookes of Cockfield Hall. These families were outwardly in communion with the Church of England, but had Nonconformist chaplains in their households (Cliffe, *Puritan Gentry Besieged*, pp. 207–10).

134. I am suspicious of the large round number given for Clare.

135. By 'large' I mean forty or more Dissenters in one parish.

136. *Compton Census*, pp. 232, 235, 237, 241.

137. A. G. Dickens, 'The Early Expansion of Protestantism in England 1520–1558', in Peter Marshall (ed.), *The Impact of the English Reformation 1500–1640* (Arnold, 1997), p. 93.

138. Samuel Backler and Owen Stockton. A third preacher, William Hayter, cannot be identified.

139. Phrases such as 'meane psons' or 'Considerable Quality' are vague. But more precise or detailed information about the status of the conventiclers in general cannot be obtained from the 1669 Return.

140. For the Suffolk evidence for this paragraph see Jewson, op. cit., pp. 27, 30–32; Lyon Turner, op. cit., vol. I, pp. 102–5. For Leicestershire see R. H. Evans, 'Nonconformists in Leicestershire in 1669', *Transactions of Leicestershire Archaeological Society*, xxv (1949), pp. 111–14.

141. Cliffe, op. cit., pp. 116, 215.

142. Besse. vol. I, p. 675.

143. *Calamy Revised*, pp. 542–3.

144. This paragraph is based on Lyon Turner, op. cit., vol. I, pp. 104–5, 613–15, vol. II, pp. 903–21; Jewson, op. cit., pp. 30–1, 33.

145. See above, n. 133.

146. For a full explanation of these statistics see chapter 2.

147. See chapter 5 Table 5.5.

148. Ann Hughes, *Politics, Society and Civil War in Warwickshire, 1620–1660* (CUP, 1987), p. 329.

149. For noble defections from Calvinism in Scotland and France see David Stevenson, *The Covenanters*, Saltire Pamphlets, NS 11 (1980), chapter 7; David Parker, *La Rochelle and the French Monarchy*, RHS Studies in History Series, no. 19 (1980), chapter 4.

150. Those Papists were Catholics who stayed away from the Anglican church and did not include the few 'Church Papists', who were included among the Conformists.

151. I have discussed the strengths and weaknesses of the recusant rolls of the later seventeenth century in B. G. Blackwood, 'Plebeian Catholics in the 1640s and 1650s', *RH*, 18 (1986) , pp. 43–4; idem., 'Plebeian Catholics in Later Stuart Lancashire', *NH*, xxv (1989), pp. 155–6.

152. Seward, op. cit., pp. 61–2.

153. Main sources are PRO, E. 377/63, ff. 65–72; /74 (unfoliated); *Miscellanea* 5, CRS, 6 (1909) , pp. 298–302. The statistics refer to individuals, not families.

154. In this table women have been assigned the same status as their husbands, ex-husbands, fathers or brothers.

155. For a full explanation of these statistics see chapter 2.

156. By rich I mean having an annual landed income of £1,000 upwards or a house with twenty or more hearths.

157. Dr J. T. Cliffe kindly supplied the data on incomes in a communication of 25 April 1994.

158. See Hervey, *Suffolk 1674: Hearth Tax Returns*, pp. 335–6.

159. For details and documentation see Blackwood, *NH*, xxv (1989), pp. 153–73.

160. See ibid.

161. *DNB*, vol. XVII, p. 211.

162. *Compton Census*, pp. 235, 237–8, 240; also PRO, E 377/74 (unfoliated).

163. Joy Rowe, *The Story of Catholic Bury St Edmunds, Coldham and the Surrounding District* (privately printed, 1980), p. 10.

164. Angus McInnes, *The English Town 1660–1760* (Hist Assoc., Appreciations in History No. 7, 1980), p. 6.

165. Rookwood had seven hearths and Gage seventeen in Bury (Hervey, op. cit., pp. 52–3). For further gentrification of Bury in the early eighteenth century see chapter 2.

166. For evidence see PRO, E 377/74 (unfoliated); HLRO, Main Papers, Papist Returns, Suffolk, 3 December 1680, ff. 123–4.

167. Joy Rowe, 'Roman Catholic Recusancy', in Dymond & Martin, p. 112.

168. See especially David Underdown, *Revel, Riot and Rebellion* (OUP, 1985), passim.

169. Rowe in Dymond & Martin, loc. cit.

170. Ibid.

171. Rowe, *Catholic Bury St Edmunds*, p. 11.

172. Aidan Bellenger (ed.), *English and Welsh Priests 1558–1800: a working list* (Downside, 1984), p. 184.

173. Ibid.

174. H. N. Birt, *Obit. Book of the English Benedictines 1600–1912* (2nd edn, Gregg International Publishers Ltd., 1970), pp. 71, 86, 98.

175. Geoffrey Holt, *The English Jesuits 1650–1829: A Biographical Dictionary*, CRS, 70 (1984), pp. 95, 97, 159–60, 214, 241, 259; H. Foley (ed.), *Records of the English Province of the Society of Jesus*, 7 vols (Burns & Oates, 1875–83), VII, Part I, pp. 274, 282, Part II, pp. 670, 762, 817–18.

176. Holt, op. cit., p. 259; Foley, op. cit., vol. VII, Pt. II, pp. 817–18.

177. J Gillow (ed.), English Poor Clares, Gravelines, 1608–1837, in *Miscellanea* IX, CRS, 14 (1914), p. 90.

178. J. S. Hansom (ed.), English Benedictine nuns, Brussels, 1598–1836, in ibid., pp. 186, 188; The Lady Abbess (ed.), English Benedictine nuns at Pontoise, 1680–1713, in *Misc.* IX, CRS, 17 (1915), p. 286. See also Gerald H. Ryan & Lilian J. Redstone, *Timperley of Hintlesham* (Methuen, 1931), pedigree opposite p. 50.

179. English Poor Clares, in *Misc.* IX, CRS, 14 (1914), pp. 77, 90–1.

180. R. Trappes-Lomax (ed.), English canonesses at Liège, 1652–1793, in *Misc.* X, CRS, 17 (1915), pp. 3–5, 8. The two plebeian nuns – Mary and Judith Cocks from Long Melford – also became English canonesses.

181. Information kindly supplied by Mrs. Audrey Butler of Pickering, N. Yorks.

182. J. Gillow & R. Trappes-Lomax (eds), *The Blue Nuns of Paris, 1658–1810*, CRS, 8 (1910), pp. 236, 238, 423–4; J. Gillow (ed.), English Benedictine nuns, Cambrai, 1620–1793, in *Misc.* VIII, CRS, 13 (1913), p. 48; Ryan & Redstone, loc. cit.

183. R. Trappes-Lomax (ed.), Records of English Franciscan nuns, 1619–1821, in *Franciscana*, CRS, 24 (1923), pp. 32, 142; Gillow & Trappes-Lomax, *Blue Nuns*, p. 236; Ryan & Redstone, loc. cit.

184. Brian Manning, *The English People and the English Revolution* (2nd edn, Bookmarks, 1991), pp. 244, 252–59; W. Hunt, *The Puritan Moment* (Harvard UP, 1983), pp. 302–6, 308–9.

185. Ryan and Redstone, op. cit., p. 88.

186. Ibid., pp. vii–viii, 61–2, 68, 85–6, 89–91, 90 n. 1, 106, 108; Gillow & Trappes-Lomax, op. cit., pp. 423–4.

187. *CSPD*, 1678, pp. 618–19; *CSPD*, 1679–80, pp. 333, 340. Other Suffolk gentry families may have gone abroad without applying for passes, but they are difficult to trace.

188. John Kenyon, *The Popish Plot* (Penguin Books, 1974), p. 271.

189. PRO, SP 44/335, f. 439. Henry Jermyn was nephew and namesake of the famous Royalist. But unlike the Cavalier, he was a strong Roman Catholic (*DNB*, vol. X, p. 781).

190. John Miller, *Popery & Politics in England 1660–1688* (CUP, 1973), p. 168.

191. See *The Martyrs of England and Wales, 1535–1680* (Catholic Truth Society pamphlet, 1979),pp. 16–17, 31–2, 43.

192. Richard Challoner, *Memoirs of Missionary Priests*, ed. J. H. Pollen (New edn, Burns, Oates & Washbourne Ltd., 1924), p. 518.

193. Robert Hole, 'Devonshire Catholics 1670–1688', *Southern History*, 16 (1994), pp. 86, 93.

194. B. G. Blackwood, 'Parties and Issues in the Civil War in Lancashire and East Anglia', *NH*, xxix (1993), p. 123.

195. John Spurr, *The Restoration Church of England 1646–1689* (Yale UP, 1991), p. 65.

NOTES TO CHAPTER NINE

1. G. M. Trevelyan, *The English Revolution, 1688–1689* (OUP, 1938), passim.

2. J. R. Jones, *The Revolution of 1688 in England* (Weidenfield & Nicolson, 1972); W. A. Speck, *Reluctant Revolutionaries : Englishmen and the Revolution of 1688* (OUP, 1988).

3. See J. C. D. Clark, *Revolution and Rebellion* (CUP, 1986); idem, *English Society, 1688–1832* (CUP, 1985); idem, 'The Glorious Revolution debunked', *The Sunday Telegraph*, 24 July 1988.

4. B. Worden, 'Lawful Resistance', *London Review of Books*, 24 November 1988, p. 5.

5. L. Stone, 'The Results of the English Revolutions of the Seventeenth Century', in J. G. A. Pocock (ed.), *Three British Revolutions, 1641, 1688, 1776* (Princeton UP, 1980), p. 24.

6. C. Hill, 'A Bourgeois Revolution?' in Pocock (ed.), *Three British Revolutions*, p. 135; idem, *Reformation to Industrial Revolution* (Weidenfeld & Nicolson, 1967), p. 106; idem & E. Dell (eds), *The Good Old Cause: The English Revolution of 1640–60* (Lawrence & Wishart, 1949), p. 472.

7. A. McInnes, 'When was the English Revolution?', *History*, 67 (1982), pp. 377–92.

8. Ibid., p. 387.

9. S. E. Prall, *The Bloodless Revolution: England, 1688* (Wisconsin UP, 1985), pp. viii–ix.

10. See especially Maurice Ashley, *James II* (Dent, 1977).

11. Professor John Miller has said that James II's 'concessions to Dissent were dictated by expediency'. Michael Mullett argues on similar lines. See J. Miller, *Popery and Politics in England 1660–1688* (CUP, 1973), p. 228; M. Mullett, *James II and English Politics 1678–1688* (Routledge, 1994), esp. p. 58.

12. Miller, loc. cit.

13. Lionel K. J. Glassey, *Politics and the Appointment of Justices of the Peace 1675–1720* (OUP, 1979), p. 91.

14. Ibid., chapter 3.

15. Miller, *Popery*, pp. 11–12, 219, 272.

16. Ibid., pp. 269–71.

17. SRO (I), B 105/2/11, ff. 39–87. The names are of JPs only, although some of them were probably deputy lieutenants as well.

18. The fact that these gentlemen were acting JPs in 1686 but not after April 1687 and definitely not in 1688 suggests that they may have been dismissed. Some reappear on the Bench soon after the 'Glorious Revolution'. See SRO (I), B 105/2/11, ff 88–91.

19. Quoted in Copinger, *Manors*, vol. II, pp. 187–8.

20. SRO (I), B 105/2/11, ff. 59, 61–2, 64, 68, 70, 72, 75, 79, 81, 84–5, 87.

21. Miller, *Popery*, pp. 270–1. Unlike Miller, I have calculated the percentages of Catholic *justices only*.

22. McInnes, op. cit., p. 386.

23. Pat E. Murrell, 'Bury St Edmunds and the Campaign to pack Parliament, 1687–8', *BIHR*, liv (1981), pp. 188–206.

24. Ibid., pp. 205–6.

25. J. R. Jones, op. cit., pp. 129–30.

26. So James designated the petition which these bishops had presented to him begging that the clergy should not be forced to read the Declaration.

27. The other six prelates were William Lloyd, Bishop of St Asaph; Francis Turner, Bishop of Ely; John Lake, Bishop of Chichester; Thomas Ken, Bishop of Bath and Wells; Thomas White, Bishop of Peterborough; and Sir Jonathan Trelawney, Bishop of Bristol.

28. The Whigs were William Cavendish, Earl of Devonshire; Charles Talbot, Earl of Shrewsbury; Admiral Edward Russell; and Henry Sidney. The Tories were Thomas Osborne, Earl of Danby; Richard Lord Lumley; and Henry Compton, Bishop of London.

29. Lionel K. J. Glassey, 'Introduction' in Glassey (ed.), *The Reigns of Charles II and James VII & II* (Macmillan, 1997), p. 8.

30. This was to prevent packed Parliaments.

31. Unitarians were non-Trinitarian Protestants.

32. The Quakers, however, had welcomed James II's Declarations of Indulgence.

33. Information of John Sutton, Senior Lecturer, Anglia Polytechnic University.

34. His wife, Mary II, had died in 1694.

35. After 1688 Rookwood served as a brigadier under James II. He was executed at Tyburn. For details see *DNB*, vol. XVII, p. 212.

36. Wallace Gandy (ed.), *Lancashire Association Oath Rolls 1696* (Society of Genealogists, 1985), p. X.

37. Thomas Babington Macaulay, *History of England*, 4 vols (repr. Everyman's Library, 1980), IV, p. 231. I owe this reference to John Sutton.

38. P. E. Murrell, 'Suffolk: The Political Behaviour of the County and its Parliamentary Boroughs from the Exclusion Crisis to the Accession of the House of Hanover' (unpublished PhD thesis, University of Newcastle-upon-Tyne, 1982), p. 168. Dr Murrell also gives higher population figures for both counties, but I have relied on her more conservative estimates.

39. This section relies heavily upon information and comments supplied by John Sutton.

40. See particularly J. P. Kenyon, *The Nobility in the Revolution of 1688* (Univ. of Hull Publications, 1963), esp. p. 19; Mullett, *James II*, esp. pp. 81–2.

41. W. L. Sachse, 'The Mob and the Revolution of 1688', *JBS*, 4 (1964), pp. 23–40, esp. 28, 31.

42. See chapter 6, p. 178.

43. Pat Murrell, 'Bury St Edmunds', p. 202.

44. The gentleman was Thomas Burton (Information of Mrs Joy Rowe).

45. See CUL, *The London Mercury*, Monday December 31st to Thursday January 3rd 1688 (unpaginated). John Sutton drew my attention to this work.

46. 'Test-Men and Anti-Test-Men' were supporters and opponents of the Test Acts of 1673 and 1678. The first act excluded Roman Catholics and Dissenters from public office, and the second from Parliament. The acts were repealed in 1828.

47. The Alderman was probably John Stafford (Information of John Sutton).

48. See *The London Mercury*.

49. Macaulay, op. cit., vol. II, pp. 409–12. For information on Thomas Alexander, I am indebted to John Sutton.

50. Macaulay, op. cit., vol. IV, p. 231.

51. Nonjurors, of course, included Catholic and Protestant laymen as well as Anglican clergy. See B. Gordon Blackwood, 'Lancashire Catholics, Protestants and Jacobites during the 1715 Rebellion', *RH*, 22 (1994), pp. 41–59.

52. Like Sancroft, four of these prelates had been among the Seven Bishops tried and acquitted in 1688 : Ken of Bath and Wells; Lake of Chichester; Turner of Ely; and White of Peterborough. The other two bishops – Robert Frampton of Gloucester and William Lloyd of Norwich – had not been put on trial in 1688.

53. For the names of the Suffolk Nonjurors see *VCH Suffolk*, vol. II, p. 49 n. 1.

54. Nine were located in East and fourteen in West Suffolk (ibid.).

55. The three Catholic gentry families in Long Melford – the Harrisons, the Hinchlows and especially the Martins – were almost certainly Jacobite sympathisers.

56. The following account of Sancroft relies heavily on *DNB*, Vol. XVII, pp. 733–9, and has benefited from discussions with John Sutton.

57. John Twigg, *The University of Cambridge and the English Revolution, 1625–1688* (The Boydell Press, 1990), pp. 152–3, 302.

58. See chapters 3 and 4 for Martin and chapters 4 and 5 for Barnardiston.

59. Defoe, *Tour*, vol. I. p. 66.

60. Geoffrey Holmes, *Politics, Religion and Society in England, 1679–1742* (Hambledon Press, 1986), p. 193.

61. M. R. Watts, *The Dissenters from the Reformation to the French Revolution* (OUP, 1978), pp 268–9, 491–508.

62. It is impossible to compare the numbers of Dissenters in East Suffolk in 1676 with those in 1715–18 because the Compton Census does not cover the Archdeaconry of Suffolk.

63. Since the Compton Census, unlike the Evans List, does not distinguish between Presbyterians and Independents, these groups have been lumped together in both columns and called Protestant Dissenters.

64. See Whiteman & Clapinson (eds), *The Compton Census*, pp. 232–3, 235–7, 240–1.

65. See John Evans List of Dissenting Congregations and Ministers in England and Wales (1715–29), Dr Williams's Library, London, MS. 38.4, pp. 108–11.

66. For the population of Suffolk in the 1670s, including towns with 1,000 or more people, see chapter 1 p. 4–5.

67. For a list of the Presbyterian and Independent congregations and their numbers of worshippers see Appendix VI.

68. Watts, op. cit., p. 285.

69. See ibid., pp. 286–7, 353–4.

70. Ibid., pp. 270, 281, 509. As regards the Quakers, Suffolk was below the national average, though in fact there were few Friends in any English county according to Dr Watts. See ibid., p. 509.

71. Defoe, *Tour*, vol. I, pp. 82–3.

72. See Appendix VI.

73. Mark Kishlansky, *A Monarchy Transformed: Britain 1603–1714* (Allen Lane: The Penguin Press, 1996), p. 313.

74. Geoffrey Holmes & W. A. Speck, *The Divided Society: Party Conflict in England 1694–1716* (Edward Arnold, 1967), pp. 4–5.

75. Kishlansky, op. cit., p. 317.

76. Holmes and Speck, op. cit., p. 1, n. 1.

77. G. Holmes, *Politics, Religion and Society*, pp. 14–15; J. H. Plumb, 'The Growth of the Electorate in England from 1600 to 1715', *P&P*, 45 (1969), p. 111.

78. E. A. Wrigley & R. S. Schofield, *The Population of England 1541–1871 : a reconstruction* (Edward Arnold, 1981), pp. 208–9.

79. Murrell, thesis, pp. 164–5, 169.
80. J. Patten, 'Population distribution in Norfolk and Suffolk during the sixteenth and seventeenth centuries', in J. Patten (ed.), *Pre-industrial England: Geographical Essays* (Dawson, Folkestone, 1979), p. 74; Murrell, op. cit., p. 168.
81. Murrell, p. 170.
82. Holmes, *Politics, Religion and Society*, pp. 28–9.
83. See Murrell, thesis, p. 523.
84. Ibid., pp. 474–5.
85. Plumb, *P&P*, 45 (1969), p. 116.
86. Quoted in Murrell, thesis, p. 172.
87. Murrell, loc. cit.
88. Holmes & Speck, op. cit., p. 1.
89. Ibid., p. 3.
90. Pat Murrell, 'The County Voters of 1705', in Dymond & Martin, p. 102.
91. Murrell, thesis, p. 165.
92. Ibid., p. 527.
93. For gentry voters see SRO (B), Suffolk Poll Book, 1705, 0.55.7.
94. For clergy voters see Murrell, thesis, Table 33, p. 424.
95. Murrell, thesis, pp. 423–4.
96. Murrell in Dymond & Martin, loc. cit. For details of voter turnout in 1705 see Murrell, thesis, pp. 519–27.
97. See James E. Bradley, 'Nonconformity and the Electorate in Eighteenth-Century England', *Parliamentary History*, 6 (1987), pp. 236–61, esp. 243–51.
98. Murrell, thesis, pp. 461–3.
99. Ibid., p. 451.
100. Ibid., pp. 456, 461.
101. See Murrell in Dymond & Martin, p. 103.
102. For details of the First Civil War in Suffolk, see chapter 5.
103. Although mainly a Norfolk gentleman, he also had land in Suffolk.
104. For a full list of Suffolk MPs in the Parliaments of 1681 and 1705 see Murrell, thesis, pp. 457, 461.
105. Philip Jenkins, *The making of a ruling class: The Glamorgan gentry 1640–1790* (CUP, 1983), p. 143.

APPENDIX I

The Reformation in Suffolk

(a) Religious Houses in Suffolk in 1536

Key to symbols
See Map 9

Religious House	Order	Number of Religious at Dissolution	Net Income p.a. in 1535 £[1]	Date of Dissolution	Superior's Pension £
Babwell	FF	?	?	1538	None
Battisford	KH	3?	53	1540	None
Blythburgh	AC	4	48	1537	6
Bruisyard	FN	15	56	1539	?
Bungay	BN	9	61	1536	?
Bury St Edmunds	BM	44	1,659	1539	333
Butley	AC	13	318	1538	?
Campsey Ash	AN	20	182	1537	23
Clare	AF	8	?	1538	None
Dunwich	DF	?	?	1538	None
Dunwich	FF	?	?	1538	None
Dunwich	KH	?	?	1540	None
Eye	BM	8	160	1537	18
Flixton	AN	11	23	1537	6
Gorleston	AF	?	?	1538	None
Hoxne	BM	8	18	1538	?
Ipswich	CF	?	?	1538	None
Ipswich	DF	7	?	1538	None
Ipswich	FF	?	?	1538	None
Ipswich, Holy Trinity	AC	6	82	1537	15
Ixworth	AC	18	168	1537	20
Leiston	PC	15	181	1537	20
Letheringham	AC	3	26	1537	5
Mendham	CM	11	19	1537	?
Orford	AF	?	?	1538	None
Redlingfield	BN	13	67	1537	[20 marks [2]]
St Olave	AC	7	49	1537	[10 marks [3]]
Sibton	CTM	8	250	1536	?
Sudbury	BM	2	9	*c.* 1538	?
Sudbury	DF	11	?	1538	None
Thetford, Holy Sepulchre [4]	AC	7	39	1536	[10 marks [3]]
Thetford, St George [4]	BN	10	40	1537	5

Religious House	Order	Number of Religious at Dissolution	Net Income p.a. in 1535 £[1]	Date of Dissolution	Superior's Pension £
Wangford	CM	5?	30	1540	?
Whelnetham	XF	?	?	1538	None
Woodbridge	AC	7	50	1537	6

1. Values are rounded off to the nearest £.
2. Equivalent to £13 6s. 8d.
3. Equivalent to £6 13s. 4d.
4. This house was in Thetford St Mary, a *Suffolk* parish.

Notes: (1) Main sources are *Valor* III, pp. 403–83; Dugdale, III–VI pt. iii; *LP*, XIII (1), no. 1520; Knowles & Hadcock; Chambers, *Register*, pp. 70, 73, 80, 87–9, 93, 128, 162, 180; Gilchrist & Oliva, p. 93; Sybil M. Jack, 'Dissolution Dates for the Monasteries Dissolved under the Act of 1536', *BIHR*, xliii (1970), pp. 161–81; *VCH Suffolk*, vol. II, pp. 53–132. (2) Hospitals and secular colleges have been omitted from the above list.

(b) The fate of the dispossessed monks of Bury St Edmunds Abbey

Key to symbols

C   Curate   R   Rector   V   Vicar

Name (including alias)	Pension p.a. £	s	d	Career post–1540	Date of death/burial
John Melford alias Reve, abbot	[500 marks[1]]			'Retired'	1540
Thos. Ringstead al. Denysse, STD, prior	30	0	0	Ditto	1545
Edw. Rougham al. Maltward, DD, sacrist	20	0	0	R. West Stow 1547–53	1556
Wm. Thaxted al. Gardiner	10	0	0	?	?
Thos. Gnatsall al. Eldred	13	6	8	'Retired'	1546
Thos. Stonham al. Cooke	10	0	0	Ditto	1542
Simon Bardwell al. Saffere, sub-prior	13	6	8	Do	1545
Ralph Norwich al. Glanfeld	8	0	0	?	?
Thos. Denston al. Stoke	13	6	8	'Retired'	1543
John Westgate al. Bower	6	13	4	Chantry priest?	1557
John Claydon al. Helperby	6	13	4	Unemployed in 1555	?
Edm. Bury al. Fennyng	6	13	4	'Retired'	1548
Robt. Hinderclay al. Fenne	6	13	4	'Retired'	1545
John Woolpit al. Bucknam	6	13	4	?	?
Thos. Sudbury al. Hall	6	13	4	R. Tuddenham St Mary 1540–50	1550
Edm. Wetherden al. Halley, BTh	10	0	0	?	?
John Cambridge al. Langham	6	13	4	R. Barnham St Martin 1543–54	1554
John Osmond	6	13	4	R. Chedburgh 1552–58	1558
Gregory Eleigh al. Moptide	8	0	0	V. Foulden, Norfolk, 1541–66; R. Lt. Cressingham, Norfolk, 1560–83	1583

Name (including alias)	Pension p.a. £ s d	Career post–1540	Date of death/burial
Wm. Elsmwell al. Bockhill	6 13 4	R. Elmswell 1550–68; R. Gt. Livermere 1559–71	1571
Robt. Hessett al. Potkyn	8 0 0	R. Tostock 1556–75	1575
Humph. Attleborough al. Younger	6 13 4	R. Foxley, Norfolk, 1551–76; R. Brinton, Norfolk, 1557–59	1576
John Bury al. Howes	6 13 4	V. Swilland 1540–41	1541
John Lavenham al. Hunt	8 0 0	?	?
Thos. Mildenhall al. Cole	6 13 4	R. Flempton 1541–57	1557
Oliver Melford al. Marche	6 13 4	?	?
Thos. Diss al. Fenne	6 13 4	R. Lt. Thornham 1554–57; R. Burgate 1558–63	1563
John Bradfield al. Wright	6 13 4	R. Lt. Whelnetham 1556–87	1587
Thos. Ipswich al. Dawes	6 13 4	C. Garboldisham, Norfolk, 1548, 1553	?
Aylott Hawstead al. Holt	6 13 4	Chantry priest; R. Norton 1556–59	1570
John Foulden al. Page	6 13 4	R. Drinkstone 1547–82	1582
Robt. Honington al. Howes	8 0 0	R. Yelverton, Norfolk, 1560–83	1583?
John Hadley al. King	6 13 4	High Master, King Edward's School, Bury St Ed. 1550–52	1552
Robt. Needham al. Brunning	6 13 4	Schoolmaster in Lavenham	1577
John Hicklingham al. Rede	6 13 4	?	?
John Woolpit al. Starre	6 13 4	?	?
John Barton al. Harrison	6 13 4	R. Rushbrooke 1555–72; R. Horringer 1558–81	1581
Thos. Hessett al. Rowght	6 13 4	Notary in Bury c. 1552	?
Thos. Harlow al. Bird	6 13 4	R. St George, Southwark, 1561–64	1564
John Lopham al. Sanderson	6 13 4	Weaver in 1555	?
Roger Maldon	6 13 4	V. Moulton 1547–64	1564
Peter Dunwich al. Kilburn	6 13 4	R. Thwaite 1555–57; R. Hepworth 1559–79	1579
Ralph Warkton al. Marshall	6 13 4	V. Wood Ditton, Cambs., 1554–77	?
John Walsingham al. Beckham	6 13 4	Chantry priest; R. Little Dunham, Norfolk?	?

1. *LP, XV*, no. 1032 gives the sum of £333 6s. 8d.

Notes: (1) Main sources are Dugdale III, pp. 116, 170–1; *LP*, XIV (2), no. 462; Geoffrey Baskerville, 'Married Clergy and the Pensioned Religious in the Diocese of Norwich 1555', *English Historical Review*, XLVIII (1933), pp. 43–64, 199–228; PRO, E 101/76/21 (unfoliated); E 164/31, ff. 16–17; E 178/3251 (unfoliated and partially faded); BL, Add. MS. 8102 (Cardinal Pole's Pension List), ff. 14–15; and Michael Tupling, who supplied considerable information on the Bury monks in his communication of 11 May, 1995.

(2) In the above list the Bury monks are named in the order in which they appear in Dugdale and *LP*, XIV (2), no. 462.

(3) Benefices named in the list are in Suffolk, unless otherwise stated.

(c) Persons granted monastic and convent land in Suffolk 1536–47

Key to symbols

C	Church	NS	Nobility of Suffolk
GN	Gentry of Norfolk	OG	Other gentry
GS	Gentry of Suffolk	ON	Other nobles
L	Lawyer	OP	Officials of peers
LM	London merchant	RO	Royal officials
NM	Norwich merchant	Unc.	Uncertain status
NN	Nobility of Norfolk		

Grantees	Social category	Manors obtained	Religious House	Price paid £[1]	Date
ANNE of CLEVES	Queen in 1540	Occold Hall	Eye	(Lifegrant)	1540
BACON, Nicholas	RO	Hinderclay	Bury	488	1545
		Ingham	Bury		1540
		Rickinghall Inferior	Bury	785	1544
		Lawford, Gislingham	Battisford		1544
		Wortham Abbots	Bury		1545
		Mildenhall	Bury		?
		Redgrave	Bury		1544
BACON, Thos of Hessett, Suffolk	GS	Troston	Bury		1547
		Hessett	Bury	249	1540
		Netherhall, Pakenham	Bury	599	1544
BEDINGFIELD, Sir Edmund	RO	Redlingfield	Redlingfield	562	1537
		Stoke Ash	Eye		1537
		Fressingfield	Eye		1537
		Laxfield Rectory	Eye		1537
BRANDON, Charles, 1st Duke of Suffolk	NS	Darsham Abbots	Leiston		?
		Culpho Abbots	Leiston		1537
		Eye Priory	Eye		1537
		Occold Hall	Eye		1537
		Bilston Hall, Hazlewood	Leiston		1537
		Abbots Hall, Pettaugh	Leiston		1537
		Mendham Priory	Mendham		1537
		Mendham Hall	Mendham		1539
		Mendham Kingshall	Mendham		1540
		Thornham Magna	Eye		1537
		Stratford St Andrews	Butley		1538
		Harlston	Bury		1540
		Laxfield	Leiston		1537
		Leiston	Leiston		1537
CAVENDISH, Richard of Trimley, Suffolk	GS	Grapton Hall, Belton	Leigh's Priory, Essex		1536

Grantees	Social category	Manors obtained	Religious House	Price paid £[1]	Date
CLOPTON, Wm. of Long Melford, Suffolk	GS	Demford Hall, Swefling	Bury		1536
		Monks Melford	Bury		1545
CODINGTON, Richard of Codington, Surrey	OG	Badwell Ash	Ixworth		1538
		Shakerland Hall	Ixworth		1538
		Brookshill	Ixworth		1538
		Tiptofts	Ixworth		?
		Hunston	Ixworth		1538
		Ixworth	Ixworth		1538
		Sapiston Grange	Ixworth		1538
		Ixworth Thorpe	Ixworth		1546
		Santon Downham	Ixworth		1538
COOTE, Chris. of Bloodmoor, Norfolk	GN	Culford	Bury		1541
CORDELL, Sir Wm. of Long Melford, Suffolk	GS	Long Melford	Bury		1545
CORNWALLIS, Sir John of Brome, Suffolk	GS	Monks Brome	Thetford Priory		Before 1544
CORNWALLIS, Sir Thos. of Brome, Suffolk	GS	Fenhouse, Palgrave	Bury		?
		Faucons, Stuston	Flixton		1544
CROFTS, Sir John of West Stow, Suffolk	GS	West Stow	Bury	497	1540
CROMWELL, Thomas, Earl of Essex	ON & Vicegerent	Abbot's Hall, Stowmarket	St Osyth, Essex		?
DANIEL, Thos. of Sudbury, Suffolk	GS	Abbas Hall, Gt. Cornard	Malling, Kent		1540
DARCY, Thos., Lord Darcy of Chiche	ON	Hardwick	Bury		1546
		Horringer Magna	Bury		1546
		Horringer Parva	Bury		1540
DEAN & CHAPTER of Ely	C	Lakenheath	Ely		1541
DEAN & CHAPTER of Norwich	C	Hopton	Norwich		1540
DENNY, Sir Anthony	RO	Rendham	Sibton		1547
		Rendham Barnes	Sibton		1547
de VERE, John, 16th Earl of Oxford	NS	St John's, East Bergholt	Battisford		1544
DRURY, Sir Wm. of Hawstead, Suffolk	GS	Lawshall	Ramsey, Kent		1547
		Barnham	Thetford Abbey		1540
		Whepstead	Bury	820	1540
		Whepstead Cage's	Bury		?

Grantees	Social category	Manors obtained	Religious House	Price paid £[1]	Date
EDGAR, Wm. of Gt. Glemham, Suffolk	GS	Lowdham Hall	Butley		1545
FORTH, Wm. of Hadleigh, Suffolk	GS	Boyton Hall, Butley	Butley	488	1545
		Butley	Butley	910	1544
FRAMLINGHAM, Francis of Debenham, Suffolk	GS	Ashfield-with-Thorpe	Butley		1542
		Debenham Priory	Butley		1542
FRESTON, Sir Richard	OP	Wickham Skeith	St John's, Colchester	400	1542
GOODRICH, Richard	Unc.	Chillesford	Butley	146	1545
GOSNOLD, John	RO	Coddenham Priory	Royston, Herts		1547
GRESHAM, Sir Richard	RO	Yaxley Priory	Hoxne		1546
		Hoxne Priory	Hoxne		1538
GRESHAM, Sir Thos.	LM	St John's, Battisford	Battisford		1543
GUYBON, Reginald of Thursford, Norfolk	GN	Abbots, Darsham	Leiston		1544
HARE, Sir Nicholas	RO	Bruisyard	Bruisyard		1539
		Bocking Hall, Winston	Bruisyard		1539
HART, Sir Percival of Lullingstone, Kent	OG	Brandeston, Harkstead	Dartford, Kent		1539
		Amor Hall, Washbrook	Dartford, Kent		1538
HARVEY, John of Oulton, Suffolk	GS	Carlton Colville Priory	Broomholm, Norfolk		1541
HIGHAM, Sir Clement of Barrow, Suffolk	GS	Semer	Bury	427	1542
HOPTON, Sir Arthur	OP	Blythburgh Priory	Blythburgh		1538
		Blythburgh Hinton	Blythburgh		1538
HOWARD, Thos., 3rd Duke of Norfolk	NN	Darsham-cum-Yoxford	Thetford Priory		1540
		Linstead Parva	Sibton		1536
		Surdis, Peasenhall	Sibton		?
		Sibton	Sibton		1536
		Wangford	Wangford	1,000	1540
		Wenhaston Grange	Sibton		1536
		Westleton Grange	Sibton		1536
		Offton Monks	Thetford Priory		1540
		Monks Brome	Thetford Priory		?
		Bungay Priory	Bungay		1537
		Thorney Campsey, Stowmarket	Campsey		1545

Grantees	Social category	Manors obtained	Religious House	Price paid £[1]	Date
		Rougham Hall	Bury	1,651	1545
		Butley	Butley		1538
		Monks Hall, Elveden	Bury	1,329	1540
		Limburn, Homersfield	Bungay		1537
		Monks Hall, Syleham	Thetford Priory		1540
JENNY, Sir John of Brightwell, Suffolk	GS	St John, Coddenham	Holy Trinity, Ipswich	392	1545
		Creeting All Saints	Holy Trinity, Ipswich		1544
		Foxhall	Holy Trinity, Ipswich		1545
JERMYN, Sir Ambrose of Rushbrooke, Suffolk	GS	Wattisfield	Bury	248	1544
JERMYN, Sir Thos. of Rushbrooke, Suffolk	GS	Stanton All Saints	Bury		1540
		Bradfield St George	Bury	1,036	1540
		Rougham Eldo	Bury		1545
JERNINGHAM, Henry of Somerleyton, Suffolk	GS	Herringfleet	St Olave	992	1547
KENE, John	Unc.	Occold Benningham	St John's, Colchester	239	1545
KITSON, Sir Thos.	LM	Monks Hall, Santon Downham	Bury	3,710	1540
		Fornham St Genevieve	Bury		1540
		Fornham St Martin	Bury		1540
		Fornham All Saints	Bury		1540
		Chevington	Bury		1540
		Hargrave	Bury		1540
		Risby	Bury		1540
		Westley Sextons	Bury		1540
LOVELL, Sir Francis of East Harling, Norfolk	GN	Coney Weston	Bury		1545
PAYNE, Henry of Bury, Suffolk	L	Nowton	Bury	648	1545
POLEY, Thos.	Unc.	Hitcham Mantons	Bury		1544
REDE, Wm.	NM	Beccles	Bury	120 (at least)	1540–42
ROOKWOOD, Nicholas of Lawshall, Suffolk	GS	Livermere Grange	Warden, Beds.		1546

Grantees	Social category	Manors obtained	Religious House	Price paid £[1]	Date
ROUS, Sir Anthony	OP	Monk Soham	Bury	2,198	1545
		Southolt	St John's, Colchester		1545
		Worlingworth	Bury	1,678	1540
		St James Icklingham	Bury		1540
SMITH, George	Unc.	Clopton Hall, Rattlesden	Bury		1540
		Coldhall, Woolpit	Bury		1541
SMITH, Nicholas	Unc.	Cockley Grange	Sibton		1537
SOUTHWELL, John of Ipswich, Suffolk	GS	Barham	Ely		1545
SOUTHWELL, Sir Robert	RO	Blaxhall Valence	Campsey		1544
		Hoxne Priory	Hoxne	1,513	1543
SPRING, Sir John of Bures, Suffolk	GS	Abbot's Hall, Brent Eleigh	St Osyth, Essex		1543
		Cockfield	Bury	1,154	1545
SPRING, Robert of Lavenham, Suffolk	GS	Preston Maister's	Battisford		1543
		Preston Priory	Holy Trinity, Ipswich		1543
		Pakenham	Bury	1,432	1545
TASBURGH, John of Elmham St Peter, Suffolk	GS	Flixton	Flixton	988	1544
TYRRELL, Wm. of Gipping, Suffolk	GS	Rishangles	Redlingfield		1540
WILLOUGHBY, Sir Wm. of Parham, Suffolk	GS	Campsey Priory	Campsey		1543
WINGFIELD, Sir Anthony	RO	Haberdon	Bury		1542
		Bring Hall, Pettistree	Campsey		1538
		Harpole, Wickham Mkt.	Campsey		1539
		Gelham Hall, Wickham Mkt.	Campsey		1538
		Letheringham	Letheringham		1539
WINGFIELD, Sir Humphrey of Brantham, Suffolk	L	Creping Hall, Stutton	Earl's Colne, Essex		1537
WINGFIELD, Sir John of Woodbridge, Suffolk	GS	Haspley-with-Newbourne	Woodbridge		1541
		Woodbridge Priory	Woodbridge		1541
WINTHROP, Adam	LM	Groton	Bury	409	1544
WITHIPOLL, Paul	LM	Holy Trinity	Holy Trinity, Ipswich		1546

1. Values are rounded off to the nearest £.

Notes: (1) Main sources are *DKR*, IX, App. ii, pp. 161–2, 195, 199, 202, 209–10, 212–13, 221; X, App. ii, pp. 242, 249, 262–3, 276, 305; *LP*, XI no. 385/17, XII(1), nos. 795/39, 1311/24, XIII(1), no. 1519/70, XIII(2), nos. 734/26, 967/20, 1182/18, XIV(1), no. 651/22, XV, nos. 282/116, 436/31, 57–8, 63, 74–5, 88, 942/44, XVI, no. 580/62, XVII(1), nos. 137/11, 220/15, XVIII(1), nos. 474/5, 802/11, XVIII(2), no. 107/34, XIX(1), nos. 80/55, 278/31, 610/114, 812/17, 1035/49, XIX(2), nos. 166/16, 690/26, XX(1), no. 846/90, XX(2) nos. 266/12, 28, 496/18, 43, 50, 61, 66, XXI(1), nos. 302/56, 504/3, XXI(2), no. 771/30; and Peter Northeast, who supplied me with a multitude of relevant references in Copinger, *Manors*, vols I-VII.

(2) I have ignored the dispersal of lands which belonged to hospitals, secular colleges, chantries and monasteries dissolved by Cardinal Wolsey.

(d) Suffolk's Marian Martyrs

Name	Status or Occupation	Place of birth/activity	Age at death	Place and date of execution	Heresy
ABBES, James	shoemaker	Stoke-by-Nayland		Bury St Edmunds, 1 Aug. 1555	denial of transubstantiation; calling the Mass an idol
ALLEN, Wm.	labourer	Somerton		Walsingham, Sept. 1555	denial of transub.; refused to confess; despising ceremonies
ASHLEY, James		Stoke-by-Nayland?		Bury St Ed., Aug. 1558	denial of transub. and humanity of Christ; calling the Mass an idol; refusal to confess
BARNARD, Roger	labourer	Framsden		Bury St Ed., 30 June 1557	refusal to go to Mass and confession
COBBE, Thos.	butcher	Haverhill		Thetford, Sept. 1555	denial of transub.; saying that baptism was not a sacrament
COO, Roger	shearman	Long Melford 'old man'		Yoxford, Sept. 1555	denial of transub.; refusal to confess
COOKE, John	sawyer	Stoke-by-Nayland		Bury St Ed., Aug. 1558	denial of transub. and humanity of Christ; calling the Mass an idol; condemning confession
DAVYE, Henry	carpenter	Stradishall		Bury St Ed., 1558	denial of transub.
DAVYE, John	shearman	Stradishall		Bury St Ed., 1558	denial of transub.
DENNYE, John	tailor	Earl Soham		Beccles 21 May 1556	denial of transub. and papal supremacy; refusal to confess; despising ceremonies

Name	Status or Occupation	Place of birth/activity	Age at death	Place and date of execution	Heresy
DRYVER, Margaret	wife of a husbandman	Grundisburgh	30	Norwich, 4 or 7 Nov. 1558	denial of transub.
FOLKES, Eliz.	maidservant	Stoke-by-Nayland	20	Colchester, 2 Aug. 1557	denial of transub. and papal supremacy; refusal to confess and hear Mass
FOSTER, Adam	tailor	Mendlesham	26	Bury St Ed., 30 June 1557	refusal to hear Mass
GOOCH, Alex.	weaver	Woodbridge	36	Norwich, 4 or 7 Nov. 1558	denial of transub. and papal supremacy
LANE, Alex.	wheelwright	Stoke-by-Nayland		Bury St Ed., Aug. 1558	denial of transub. and humanity of Christ; calling the Mass an idol; condemning confession
LAWSON, Eliz.		Bedfield	60	Ipswich, Nov. 1558	denial of transub.; despising ceremonies
LAWSON, Robt.	linen weaver	Bedfield	30	Bury St Ed., 30 June 1557	refusal to hear Mass
MILES, Robt.	shearman	Stoke-by-Nayland		Bury St Ed., Aug. 1558	denial of transub. and humanity of Christ; calling the Mass an idol; condemning confession
NOYES, John	shoemaker	Laxfield		Laxfield, 22 Sept. 1557	denial of transub.
PIKES, Wm.	tanner	Ipswich		Brentford, 14 July 1558	not attending Mass for five years
POOLE, Edm.	tailor	Needham Mkt.		Beccles, 21 May 1556	denial of transub. and papal supremacy; refusal to confess; despising ceremonies
POTTON, Anne	wife of a beer brewer	Ipswich		Ipswich, 19 Feb. 1556	denial of transub.; calling Mass idolatry
SAMUELL, Robt.	curate of East Bergholt	East Bergholt		Ipswich, 31 Aug. 1555	denial of transub.; calling Mass idolatry
SEMAN, Wm.	husbandman	Mendlesham	26	Norwich, 19 May 1558	Calling the Mass an idol

Name	Status or Occupation	Place of birth/activity	Age at death	Place and date of execution	Heresy
SPICER, Thos.	labourer	Winston	19	Beccles, 21 May 1556	denial of transub. and papal supremacy; refusal to confess; despising ceremonies
SPURDANCE, Thos.	royal servant	Crowfield		Bury St Ed., Nov. 1557	denial of transub. and paper supremacy; refusal to confess and go in procession; despising ceremonies
TAYLOR, Rowland	domestic chaplain to Cranmer, 1540; rector of Hadleigh, 1544–54	Hadleigh	c. 46	Aldham Common, nr. Hadleigh, 9 Feb. 1555	denial of transub. and papal supremacy; accepting only two sacraments; emphasising justification by faith; defending marriage of priests
TRUNCHFELD, Joan	wife of a shoemaker	Ipswich		Ipswich, 19 Feb. 1556	denial of transub.; saying Mass was idolatry
UMFREYE, Phil.	tailor	Onehouse		Bury St Ed., Nov. 1558	denial of transub.; calling church ceremonies abominable
YEOMAN, Rich.	curate of Hadleigh, 1544–54	Hadleigh	70	Norwich, 10 July 1558	showing hostility to Mass; denying papal supremacy; defending marriage of priests

Sources: Fines *Register*; Craig, thesis, pp. 147–51; Davis, *Heresy and Reformation*, pp. 113–23, 143–4, 146–7; Foxe, *A&M*, IV, pp. 683–4, VI, p. 681, VII, pp. 374, 382–3, VIII, pp. 101–2, 145–7, 157–60, 387–90, 424–6, 430–2, 462, 479–81, 487–9, 492–6, 548; BL, Harleian MS. 421, esp. ff. 186–7, 191–3.

Appendix II Map i: Puritan Noble and Gentry Families of Suffolk during the Civil War Period

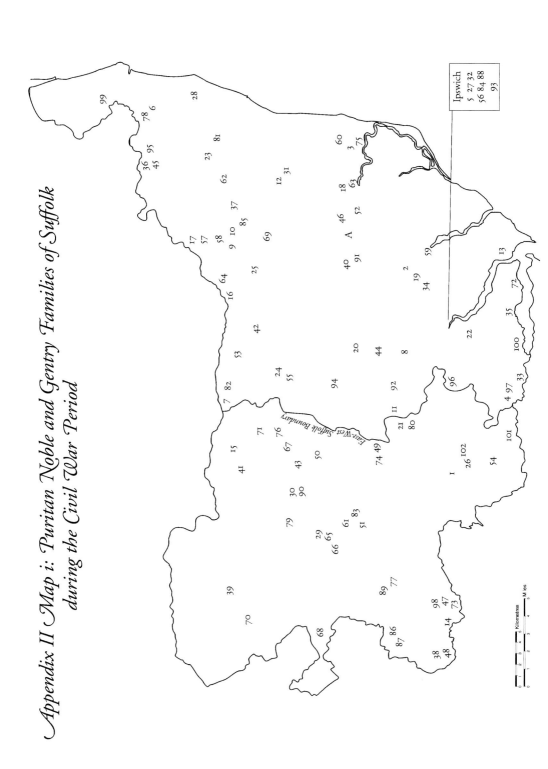

Ipswich
5 27 32
56 84 88
93

East-West Suffolk Boundary

Kilometres
Miles

APPENDIX II

Puritan Noble and Gentry Families of Suffolk during the Civil War Period

Nobility

A Francis Willoughby, 5th Baron Willoughby, of Parham

Gentry families

1	Appleton of Gt. Waldingfield	31	Brooke of Cockfield Hall
2	Atherold of Burgh	32	Cage of Ipswich
3	Bacon of Friston	33	Cardynall of Old Hall
4	Bacon of Higham	34	Clench of Culpho
5	Bacon of Ipswich	35	Clench of Holbrook
6	Bacon of Mutford	36	Cocke of Barsham
7	Bacon of Redgrave	37	Coke of Huntingfield
8	Bacon of Shrubland	38	Cole of Haverhill
9	Baker of Whittingham Hall	39	Cook of Eriswell
10	Bancroft of Fressingfield	40	Cotton of Earl Soham
11	Barker of Ringshall	41	Dandy of Sapiston
12	Barker of Sibton	42	Dey of Eye & Hoxne
13	Barker of Trimley St Martin	43	D'Ewes of Stowlangtoft
14	Barnardiston of Kedington	44	Dove of Coddenham
15	Barrow of Barningham	45	Echard of Barsham
16	Barry of Syleham	46	Edgar of Gt. Glemham
17	Baxter of Mendham	47	Edwards of Stoke-by-Clare
18	Bence of Benhall	48	Farrant of Haverhill
19	Blois of Grundisburgh	49	Fiske of Clopton Hall
20	Bloomfield of Stonham Aspall	50	Frost of Norton
21	Bloomfield of Wattisham	51	Gippes of Gt. Whelnetham
22	Blosse of Belstead	52	Glemham of Glemham Hall
23	Bohun of Westhall	53	Gray of Gassolds Hall
24	Bokenham of Thornham Magna	54	Gurdon of Assington
25	Borrett of Stradbroke	55	Harvey of Wickham Skeith
26	Brand of Edwardstone	56	Hawys of Ipswich
27	Brandling of Ipswich	57	Herring of Mendham
28	Brewster of Wrentham	58	Hobart of Walsham Hall
29	Bright of Bury St Edmunds	59	Hodges of Woodbridge
30	Bright of Netherhall	60	Jenny of Knodishall

61 Jermyn of Rushbrooke
62 Keble of Halesworth
63 King of Farnham
64 Lawrence of Syleham
65 Lelam of Bury St Edmunds
66 Lucas of Horringer
67 Marleton of Langham
68 Moody of Moulton
69 North of Laxfield
70 North of Mildenhall
71 Osborne of Wattisfield
72 Parker of Erwarton
73 Peppys of Stoke-by-Clare
74 Plumstead of Felsham
75 Pratt of Friston
76 Rampley of Walsham-le-Willows
77 Raye of Denston
78 Rede of North Cove
79 Reynolds of Ampton
80 Rivett of Bildeston
81 Rous of Henham

82 Rust of Wortham
83 Sage of Lt. Whelnetham
84 Sicklemore of Ipswich
85 Smith of Cratfield
86 Soame of Lt. Bradley
87 Soame of Lt. Thurlow
88 Sparrow of Ipswich
89 Sparrow of Wickhambrook
90 Spring of Pakenham
91 Stebbing of Brandeston
92 Theobald of Barking
93 Tyler of Ipswich
94 Tyrrell of Gipping
95 Vaughan of Beccles
96 Vesey of Hintlesham
97 Wall of Stratford St Mary
98 Ward of Hundon
99 Wentworth of Somerleyton
100 Wingfield of Brantham
101 Winterfloud of Stoke-by-Nayland
102 Winthrop of Groton

Sources. See above p. 287, n. 161.

Parliamentarian and Royalist Noble and Gentry Families of Suffolk during the First Civil War (1642–46)

(a) Parliamentarian Noble and Gentry Families of Suffolk during The First Civil War (1642–46)

Key to symbol
P   Puritan family

Nobility

A   Francis Willoughby, 5th Baron Willoughby, of Parham P

Gentry families

1	Appleton of Gt Waldingfield P	25	Brewster of Wrentham P
2	Artis of Chediston	26	Bright of Bury St Edmunds P
3	Bacon of Friston P	27	Bright of Netherhall P
4	Bacon of Higham P	28	Brock of Southolt
5	Bacon of Ipswich P	29	Brooke of Cockfield Hall P
6	Bacon of Mutford P	30	Bryan of Stradbroke
7	Bacon of Redgrave P	31	Cage of Ipswich P
8	Bacon of Shrubland Hall P	32	Cardynall of Old Hall P
9	Baker of Whittingham Hall P	33	Chaplin of Ipswich
10	Bales of Wilby	34	Clayton of Bedfield
11	Barnardiston of Kedington P	35	Cleere of Ipswich
12	Barrow of Barningham P	36	Clench of Culpho P
13	Barry of Syleham P	37	Cole of Haverhill P
14	Bateman of Homersfield	38	Cook of Bramfield
15	Baxter of Mendham P	39	Copland of Stradbroke
16	Bence of Benhall P	40	Crane of Chilton
17	Blois of Grundisburgh P	41	Dade of Beccles
18	Bloomfield of Stonham Aspall P	42	Dade of Tannington
19	Blosse of Belstead P	43	Dandy of Sapiston P
20	Bohun of Westhall P	44	Day of Eye & Hoxne P
21	Bokenham of Thornham Magna P	45	Deynes of Coddenham
22	Borrett of Stradbroke P	46	Dove of East Bergholt
23	Brand of Edwardstone P	47	Edwards of Stoke-by-Clare P
24	Brandling of Ipswich P	48	Ellis of Stradbroke

Appendix III Map i: Parliamentarian Noble and Gentry Families of Suffolk during the First Civil War

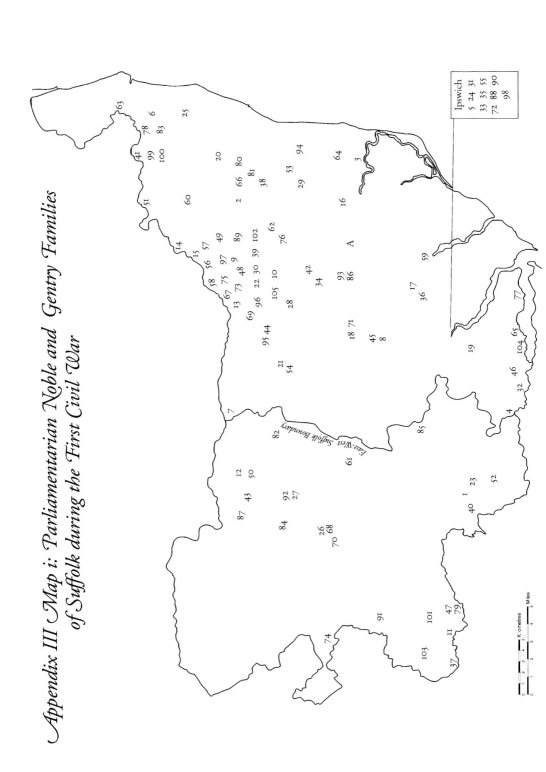

Ipswich

5 24 31
33 35 55
72 88 90
98

49	Franklin of Metfield	78	Peck of North Cove
50	Futter of Stanton	79	Peppys of Stoke-by-Clare P
51	Gooch of Mettingham	80	Porter of Halesworth
52	Gurdon of Assington P	81	Rabbit of Bramfield
53	Hart of Darsham	82	Rampley of Walsham-le-Willows P
54	Harvey of Wickham Skeith P	83	Rede of North Cove P
55	Hawys of Ipswich P	84	Reynolds of Ampton P
56	Herring of Mendham P	85	Rivett of Bildeston P
57	Hobart of Walsham Hall P	86	Rivett of Brandeston
58	Hobart of Weybread	87	Rushbrooke of Gt. Fakenham
59	Hodges of Woodbridge P	88	Sicklemore of Ipswich P
60	Hunne of Ilketshall St Margaret	89	Smith of Cratfield P
61	Isaac of Drinkstone	90	Sparrow of Ipswich P
62	Jacob of Ubbeston	91	Sparrow of Wickhambrook P
63	Jenkinson of Oulton	92	Spring of Pakenham P
64	Jenny of Knodishall P	93	Stebbing of Brandeston P
65	Jermy of Stutton	94	Thompson of Westleton
66	Keble of Halesworth P	95	Thrower of Eye
67	Lawrence of Syleham P	96	Thurston of Hoxne
68	Lelam of Bury St Edmunds P	97	Tyrrell of Mendham
69	Lovell of Hoxne	98	Tyler of Ipswich P
70	Lucas of Horringer P	99	Vaughan of Beccles P
71	Malby of Stonham Aspall	100	Ward of Beccles
72	Man of Ipswich	101	Ward of Hundon P
73	Millicent of Wingfield	102	Warren of Cratfield
74	Moody of Moulton P	103	Warren of Gt. Thurlow
75	Moon of Weybread	104	Wingfield of Brantham P
76	North of Laxfield P	105	Wythe of Athelington
77	Parker of Erwarton P		

Sources. See above p. 288, n. 7.

(b) Royalist Noble and Gentry Families of Suffolk during the First Civil War (1642–46)

Key to symbols

P   Puritan family
RC   Roman Catholic family

Nobility

A Thomas Wentworth, 1st Earl of Cleveland, of Nettlestead
B Thomas Windsor-Hickman, 7th Lord Windsor, of Stoke-by-Nayland

Gentry families

1	Bacon of Culford	6	Blague of Horringer
2	Barber of Bury St Edmunds	7	Bowle of Kersey Priory
3	Barker of Sibton P	8	Broke of Nacton
4	Barker of Trimley St Martin P	9	Chapman of Livermere
5	Bing of Hitcham	10	Chesney of Eye

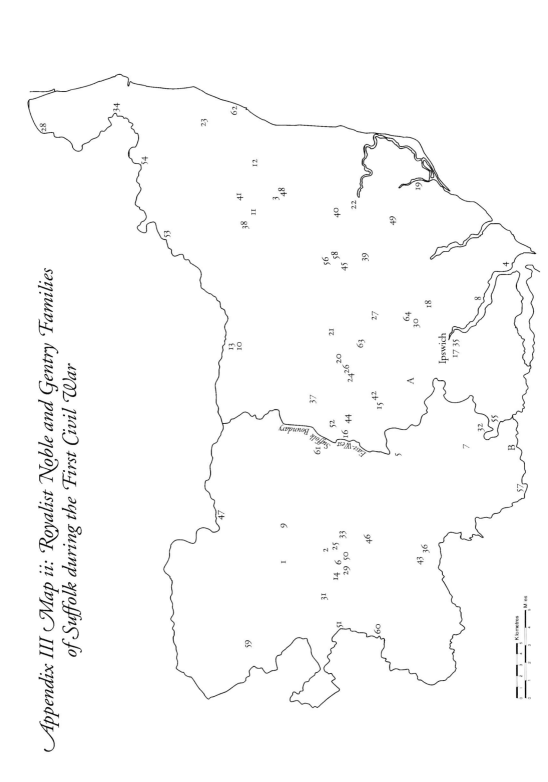

Appendix III Map ii: Royalist Noble and Gentry Families of Suffolk during the First Civil War

11	Coke of Huntingfield Hall P		38	Mynne of Cratfield
12	Coke of Thorington		39	Naunton of Letheringham
13	Cornwallis of Brome Hall		40	Penning of Gt. Glemham
14	Crofts of Little Saxham		41	Pettus of Cheston Hall
15	Crompton of Badley		42	Pooley of Badley
16	Cropley of Haughley & Shelland		43	Pooley of Boxted
17	Cutler of Ipswich		44	Pooley of Columbine Hall
18	Felton of Playford		45	Rolleston of Kettleburgh
19	Forth of Butley		46	Rookwood of Coldham Hall RC
20	Garnish of Mickfield		47	Rookwood of Euston RC
21	Gawdy of Crows Hall		48	Scrivener of Sibton
22	Glemham of Glemham Hall P		49	Spencer of Rendlesham
23	Glover of Frostenden		50	Staunton of Horringer
24	Goodall of Earl Stonham		51	Stuteville of Dalham
25	Gooding of Bury St Edmunds		52	Sulyard of Haughley Park RC
26	Goodwin of Little Stonham		53	Tasburgh of Flixton RC
27	Gosnold of Otley		54	Trott of Beccles
28	Greenwood of Burgh Castle		55	Tylney of Shelley
29	Hervey of Ickworth		56	Waldegrave of Framlingham
30	Havers of Tuddenham		57	Waldegrave of Smallbridge
31	Higham of Barrow Hall		58	Warner of Framlingham
32	James of Layham		59	Warner of Mildenhall
33	Jermyn of Rushbrooke P		60	Webb of Cowlinge
34	Jettor of Oulton RC		61	Webb of Elmswell
35	Lany of Ipswich		62	Whiting of Southwold
36	Lumley of Stanstead		63	Wingfield of Crowfield
37	Mounsey of Cotton RC		64	Wolverston of Tuddenham

Sources. See above p. 288, n. 7.

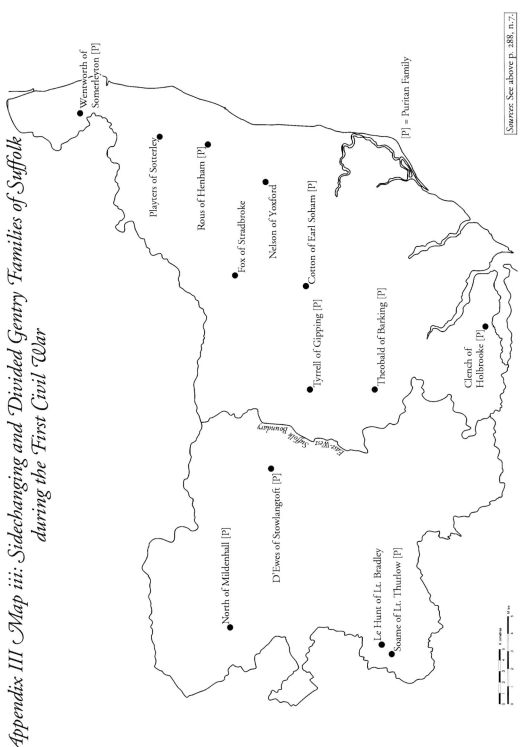

Appendix III Map iii: Sidechanging and Divided Gentry Families of Suffolk during the First Civil War

Wentworth of Somerleyton [P]

Playters of Sotterley

Rous of Henham [P]

Fox of Stradbroke

Nelson of Yoxford

Cotton of Earl Soham [P]

Tyrrell of Gipping [P]

Theobald of Barking [P]

Clench of Holbrooke [P]

North of Mildenhall [P]

D'Ewes of Stowlangtoft [P]

Le Hunt of Lt. Bradley

Soame of Lt. Thurlow [P]

Suffolk Boundary

East-West

[P] = Puritan Family

Sources: See above p. 288, n.7.

Miles

APPENDIX IV

Accusations against scandalous and malignant priests in Suffolk 1643–46

Key to Symbols

C   Curate
F   Fellow
R   Rector
V   Vicar

Clergyman	RELIGION				IMMORALITY			MALIGNANCY			
	Unsound doctrine	Ritualism	Reading Book of Sports	General negligence & Unfitness	Drunkenness	Swearing	Sexual offences	With King's Army	Anti. Parl. remarks	Anti. Parl. actions	No enthusiasm for Parl.
[1] ALCOCK, Wm., MA, R. Brettenham		X	X						X	X	
[2] ALDUS, Wm., MA, R. Copdock	X	X			X						
[3] ALSOP, Sam., MA, V. Acton		X		X			X				X
[4] AMBLER, Thos., MA, V. Wenhaston		X	X		X	X			X	X	
[5] BARTON, Edw., MA, R. Grundisburgh				X							
[6] BEADLE, John, MA, R. Trimley St Martin		X		X	X					X	
[7] BEALE, Theo., MA, V. Ashbocking	X	X			X				X		
[8] BIRD, John, MA, R. Baylham				X							
[9] BLOXHAM, Nich., MA, R. Gt. Waldingfield				X	X	X	X		X		
[10] BOLDERO, Edm., F. Pembroke, Camb., R. Westerfield		X			X			X			
[11] BOND, Thos., MA, V. Debenham		X	X						X		
[12] BRANDERETH, Hugh, MA, R. Swefling				X							
[13] BREWSTER, Edw., MA, R. Lawshall		X			X				X		
[14] BRIDGMAN -, C. Mildenhall				X	X					X	

Clergyman	RELIGION				IMMORALITY			MALIGNANCY			
	Unsound doctrine	Ritualism	Reading Book of Sports	General negligence & Unfitness	Drunkenness	Swearing	Sexual offences	With King's Army	Anti Parl. remarks	Anti Parl. actions	No enthusiasm for Parl.
[15] BROUGHTON Thos., MA, R. Chillesford				X							
[16] BROWN, John, MA, R. Moulton		X	X	X					X		
[17] BUCK, Jas., MA, V. Stradbroke	X	X									X
[18] CARTER, Geo. MA, R. Elmsett, R. Whatfield				X							
[19] CARTWRIGHT, Edm., DD, R. Norton	X										
[20] CHAPMAN, Seth, MA, R. Hasketon	X	X		X					X		
[21] CLARKE, Alex., MA, R. Iken, R. Bredfield	X	X	X						X		
[22] CLAY, Matt., MA, R. Chelsworth				X	X	X				X	
[23] COLEMAN, Nich., MA, R. Preston		X			X	X			X	X	
[24] COTESFORD, Robt., DD, R. Hadleigh, R. Monks Eleigh	X	X		X	X		X			X	
[25] CROFTS, John, DD, R. West Stow, R. Barnham		X						X	X		
[26] DALE, Cuth., MA, R. Kettleburgh	X	X	X	X	X	X			X		
[27] DUNCON, John MA, R. Stoke-by-Ipswich		X									
[28] EVANS, Wm., MA, R. St George, South Elmham				X	X				X		
[29] FENN, Wm., BA, R. Theberton				X							
[30] FERROR, John, MA, R. Trimley St Mary		X							X	X	
[31] FLICK, Nathan, MA, R. Creeting St Peter		X			X				X		
[32] FRANKLIN, Wm., MA, R. Flowton		X		X	X		X				X
[33] GATFORD, Lionel, MA, R. Dennington								X			

Clergyman	RELIGION				IMMORALITY			MALIGNANCY			
	Unsound doctrine	Ritualism	Reading Book of Sports	General negligence & Unfitness	Drunkenness	Swearing	Sexual offences	With King's Army	Anti. Parl. remarks	Anti. Parl. actions	No enthusiasm for Parl.
[34] GEARY, Thos., MA, V. Bedingfield	X	X		X	X	X				X	
[35] GIBB, Fred, MA, R. Hartest-with-Boxted									X		
[36] GIBBONS, Wm BA, R. Gt. & Lt. Bealings					X		X				
[37] GOLTEY, Miles, MA, V. Walton-with-Felixstowe		X		X	X				X	X	
[38] GOODWYN, Nathan, MA, V. Cransford				X							
[39] GORDON, John, R. Oakley					X			X	X		
[40] GOSNAL, Paul, MA, R. Bradfield St Clare					X				X		
[41] GREGSON, John, BA, V. Lakenheath											X
[42] GRIGGE, Stephen, MA, R. Whitton-with- Thurlston										X	
[43] HART, Rich., MA, R. Hargrave					X		X		X		
[44] HINDE, Edm., BD, R. Whepstead								X			
[45] JONES, Wm., MA, R. East Bergholt, R. Brantham			X	X						X	
[46] KENDAL, Rich. MA, V. Santon Downham		X			X	X				X	
[47] KEY, Edw., R. Sotherton, R. Tunstall-with-Dunningworth		X				X					
[48] KING, Nich., MA, V. Friston & Snape				X	X		X				X
[49] LARGE, Robt., MA, C. Charsfield, C. Hoo & Letheringham		X			X						X
[50] LINDSELL, Sam, MA, R. Stratford St Mary		X							X	X	
[51] LOWES, John, MA, V. Brandeston				X							
[52] MAYOR, Edm., MA, R. Finningham		X		X	X	X				X	

Clergyman	RELIGION				IMMORALITY			MALIGNANCY			
	Unsound doctrine	Ritualism	Reading Book of Sports	General negligence & Unfitness	Drunkenness	Swearing	Sexual offences	With King's Army	Anti. Parl. remarks	Anti. Parl. actions	No enthusiasm for Parl.
[53] NASH, Gawen, MA, R. St Mary-le-Tower, Ipswich		X									
[54] NEWMAN, Thos., MA, R. Lt. Cornard		X	X		X				X		
[55] PARSONS, Phil., MA, V. Gt. Finborough		X						X		X	
[56] PEARSON, John, MA, R. Thorington		X						X			
[57] PLAYTERS, Lionel, MA, R. Uggeshall	X	X	X						X	X	
[58] PRATT, Wm., MA, R. Melton		X		X						X	
[59] PROCTOR, Wm., MA, R. Stradishall		X	X	X	X	X					
[60] RANEW, John, MA, R. Kettlebaston		X	X	X	X					X	
[61] RAVEN, Nathan, MA, R. Otley							X			X	
[62] RAVENS, Jeremiah, MA, V. Chattisham, R. Gt. Blakenham	X	X		X	X		X			X	
[63] RAYMOND, Wm., MA, R. Blyford				X	X	X					
[64] REYNOLDS, Mark, MA, R. Wixoe		X			X				X	X	
[65] ROLINSON, Henry, MA, V. Bawdsey, R. Hollesley		X	X		X				X	X	
[66] SAYER, Thos., MA, V. Hoxne		X		X					X		
[67] SCRIVENER, Sam, MA, R. Westhorpe		X			X		X		X		
[68] SHEPARD, Robt., MA, R. Hepworth		X		X	X		X		X		
[69] SPARROW, Ant., F. Queen's, Camb., R. Hawkedon	X	X									
[70] STONEHAM, Nich., BA, R. Eyke		X				X			X		
[71] SUGDEN, Robt., MA, V. Benhall		X	X	X	X		X		X	X	
[72] SUMPTER, Simon, MA, R. Badingham, V. Ubbeston				X							

Clergyman	RELIGION				IMMORALITY			MALIGNANCY			
	Unsound doctrine	Ritualism	Reading Book of Sports	General negligence & Unfitness	Drunkenness	Swearing	Sexual offences	With King's Army	Anti. Parl. remarks	Anti. Parl. actions	No enthusiasm for Parl.
[73] TAYLOR, Sam, MA, R. Lt. Wenham							X				
[74] TOPCLIFFE, Rich., MA, V. Aldeburgh		X		X							
[75] TYLLOT, Thos., MA, R. Depden	X	X	X								
[76] UTTING, John, BA, V. Corton					X		X				
[77] WALKER, Wm., MA, V. Winston	X	X			X				X	X	
[78] WATTS, Rich., MA, V. Mildenhall	X	X	X	X					X		
[79] WELLS, John, MA, R. Shimpling					X	X	X		X		
[80] WICHERLY, Daniel, F. Queen's, Camb., R. Hemingstone		X		X					X	X	

Sources. See above p. 291, n. 28.

Parliamentarian gentry and Royalist nobility and gentry of Suffolk during the Second Civil War (1648)

(a) Parliamentarian gentry of Suffolk during the Second Civil War (1648)

Key to Symbol

P Puritan

Note Gentry of the same family are listed in order of seniority.

1. Nathaniel Bacon of Ipswich P
2. Francis Bacon of Ipswich P
3. Sir Butte Bacon of Mutford P
4. Sir Edmund Bacon of Redgrave P
5. Nicholas Bacon of Shrubland P
6. Thomas Baker of Fressingfield P
7. Sir Nathaniel Barnardiston of Kedington P
8. Gyles Barnardiston of Clare P
9. Sir Thomas Barnardiston of Kedington P
10. Maurice Barrow of Barningham P
11. Sir Thomas Bedingfield of Darsham
12. Alexander Bence of Benhall & Aldeburgh P
13. William Blois of Grundisburgh P
14. Thomas Blosse of Belstead P
15. Joseph Brand of Edwardstone P
16. John Brandling of Ipswich P
17. Robert Brewster of Wrentham P
18. Francis Brewster of Wrentham P
19. Humphrey Brewster of North Cove P
20. John Brooke of Yoxford P
21. Thomas Cole of Haverhill P
22. Thomas Dandy of Sapiston P
23. John Deynes of Coddenham
24. Thomas Edgar of Ipswich
25. Samuel Fairweather of Halesworth
26. John Fiske of Rattlesden P
27. Henry Fulcher of Eye
28. Brampton Gurdon of Assington, snr. P

29   John Gurdon of Great Wenham P
30   Brampton Gurdon of Assington, jnr. P
31   Edmund Harvey of Wickham Skeith P
32   James Harvey of Wickham Skeith P
33   James Hobart of Mendham P
34   John Hodges of Woodbridge P
35   Richard Le Hunt of Little Bradley
36   Gibson Lucas of Horringer P
37   Robert Manning of Walton
38   Henry North of Laxfield, senior P
39   Henry North of Laxfield, junior P
40   Sir Roger North of Mildenhall P
41   Sir Philip Parker of Erwarton P
42   Henry Parker of Erwarton
43   Richard Peppys of Stoke-by-Clare P
44   Sir William Soame of Little Thurlow P
45   Robert Sparrow of Wickhambrook
46   Sir William Spring of Pakenham P
47   Francis Theobald of Barking P
48   Thomas Tyrrell of Gipping P
49   Theophilus Vaughan of Beccles P
50   Stephen Winthrop of Groton P

Sources: See above p. 288, n. 7.

(b) Royalist Nobility and Gentry of Suffolk during the Second Civil War (1648)

Key to Symbol
P Puritan

Nobility

Francis Willoughby, 5th Baron Willoughby, of Parham P

Gentry

1   Roger D'Ewes of Stowlangtoft
2   Sir Thomas Glemham of Glemham Hall P
3   John Morden of Great Bradley

Sources: See above p. 288, n. 7.

Estimates of Dissenting numbers in early eighteenth-century Suffolk

Location of congregations	PRESBYTERIAN Hearers	INDEPENDENT Hearers
Bacton nr. Mendlesham	100	–
Beccles	–	350
Bungay	–	150
Bury St Edmunds	700	200
Clare	400	–
Combs	–	200
Debenham	250	–
East Bergholt	200	–
Eye	–	100
Framlingham	300	–
Hadleigh	250	–
Haverhill	250	–
Ipswich	800	500
Lavenham	–	300
Long Melford	150	–
Lowestoft	300	–
Mildenhall	150	–
Nayland	450	–
Needham Market	300	–
Palgrave	–	150
Southwold	–	400
Sudbury	400	–
Sweffling	–	100
Walpole	–	350
Walsham-le-Willows	400	–
Wattisfield	–	350
Wickhambrook	–	150
Wrentham	400	–
Woodbridge	–	350
Total	5,800	3,650

Notes: (1) The source is John Evans list of Dissenting Congregations and Ministers in England and Wales (1715–29), Dr Williams's Library, London, MS. 38.4, pp. 108–11. David Dymond drew my attention to this list.

(2) Locations italicised are towns with 1,000 or more inhabitants in the 1670s.

(3) Centres of Dissent without estimates of numbers of hearers or attenders (e.g. Stowmarket) are excluded.

Voting behaviour of some gentry in the 1705 general election in the county constituency of Suffolk

Note: Only persons whose families were Suffolk gentry both in the Civil Wars and in 1705 are named below.

(a) Voters from ex-Parliamentarian families

Name	Parish	Party allegiance
Sir Edmund Bacon, Bt.	Herringfleet	Tory
Sir Robert Barnardiston, Bt.	Kedington	Whig
Sir Samuel Barnardiston, Bt.	Brightwell	W
Robert Bedingfield, Esq.	Bedingfield	T
John Bence, Esq.	Heveningham	T
Sir Charles Blois, Bt.	Yoxford	T
Steven Bloomfield, Gent.	Stonham Aspall	T
Richard Bokenham, Esq.	Weston	T
John Brandling, Esq.	Ipswich	W
John Brewster, Esq.	Wrentham	W
Thomas Bright, Esq.	Pakenham	T
Nathaniel Day, Esq.	Eye	W
Devereux Edgar, Esq.	Ipswich	T
John Gurdon, Esq.	Assington	T
James Harvey, Gent.	Eye	W
Edward Hobart, Esq.	Mendham	T
Robert Jenney, Esq.	Leiston	T
William Rivett, Gent.	Rishangles	T

Source: SRO (B), Suffolk Poll Book, 1705, 0.55.7.

(b) Voters from ex-Royalist families

Name	Parish	Party allegiance
Francis Barker, Esq.	Sibton	Tory
Robert Broke, Esq.	Nacton	T
William Cropley, Gent.	Shelland	T
Sir Thomas Felton, Bt.	Playford	Whig

Name	Parish	Party allegiance
John Garnish, Gent.	Mickfield	W
Robert Glover, Gent.	Frostenden	T
Thomas Glover, Gent.	Frostenden	T
William Glover, Gent.	Frostenden	T
Lionel Gosnold, Gent.	Otley	T
Robert Naunton, Esq.	Letheringham	T
Henry Pooley, Esq.	Stowmarket	T
John Pooley, Esq.	Boxted	T
John Scrivener, Esq.	Sibton	T
John Spencer, Esq.	Rendlesham	T

Source. As above.

(c) Voters from ex-Divided families

Name	Parish	Party allegiance
Sir Edmund D'Ewes, Bt.	Stowlangtoft	Tory
John Fox, Esq.	Stradbroke	T
Sir John Playters, Bt.	Sotterley	T
Sir John Rous, Bt.	Henham	T
Thomas Tyrrell, Esq.	Gipping	T

Source. As above.

Index

Notes: (1) This index is confined mainly to Suffolk persons and places, but contains a fairly comprehensive list of subjects.

(2) Family seats are named after gentry, but not after plebeians.

(3) Date of death is given wherever possible to aid identification.

(4) Figures in **bold** refer to pages with illustrations and captions.

Key to symbols

App.	Appendix
DM	Dissenting minister
EP	Early Protestant
L	Lollard

PM	Puritan minister
Q	Quaker
SJ	Society of Jesus
SP	'Scandalous priest'